Pharmacy Business Management

Pharmacy Business Management

Edited by

Steven B Kayne

PhD, MBA, LLM, MSc (Sp Med), DAgVetPharm,
FRPharmS, FCPP, FIPharmM, MPS (NZ), FNZCP

Independent Consultant Pharmacist

Visiting Lecturer, School of Pharmacy
University of Strathclyde, Glasgow

London • Chicago **Pharmaceutical Press**

Published by the Pharmaceutical Press
1 Lambeth High Street, London SE1 7JN, UK
1559 St. Paul Avenue, Gurnee, IL 60031, USA

(**PP**) is a trade mark of Pharmaceutical Press

Pharmaceutical Press is the publishing division of the Royal
Pharmaceutical Society of Great Britain

Reprinted 2010

Typeset by Type Study, Scarborough, North Yorkshire
Printed in Great Britain by Antony Rowe, Chippenham

ISBN 978 0 85369 563 9

Contents

Foreword   xi
Preface   xiii
About the editor   xv
Contributors   xvii

Part One – The foundation of pharmacy management   1

1   Professionalism and business practice   3
Introduction   3
The development of the pharmacy profession   3
The nature of a profession   4
Professions and business   7
Client views   8
Consumer-led expectations   9
Professional dilemmas   18
Concluding remarks   19
References   20
Further reading   20

2   The economics of business   21
Introduction   21
Microeconomics   23
Macroeconomics   40
References   53
Further reading   54

3   Overview of the pharmacy sector   55
Introduction   55
Structural change   55
Distribution   56
Pricing of pharmaceuticals   59
References   63
Further reading   64

4 The essentials of pharmacy business 65

Introduction 65
Pharmacy premises 65
What does a retail pharmacy sell? 66
Margins and product mix 68
Product mix 70
NHS remuneration 71
Buying from wholesalers 74
How should the business be structured? 76
Value added tax 79
Pay as you earn taxation 81
Income tax and corporation tax 83
Accountants 83
Obtaining tax relief 84
Further reading 84

5 Acquiring and financing a pharmacy 85

Introduction 85
Competitive risks in the whole (macro) market environment 85
Assessing the micro-environmental risks associated with acquiring
   a pharmacy 87
Factors relating to the acquisition 88
Transferring the NHS Contract 96
Purchase of a limited company 96
Calculating the cost of a business 98
Sources of finance 101
Cost of financing 103
Structural alterations 104
Further reading 104

6 Legal aspects of pharmacy business 105

Introduction 105
Individual ownership 105
Partnerships 105
Companies 106
Registration of pharmacy premises 109
Employment legislation 110
Working conditions 111
National Health Service Contracts 112
Sale or supply of medicines 112
Poisons 113
Code of conduct 114
Summary 114
Further reading 114

7 **Consumer law** 115

Introduction 115
Consumers and contracts generally 116
Contract terms 116
Terms implied in consumer transactions 117
Further reading 122
Websites 122
Useful addresses 122

8 **Practical risk management** 123

Introduction 123
What went wrong? 123
Doing it right first time 125
Risk management – making a difference 128
Health and safety – risk and benefit 131
Insurance – a tool of financial risk management 141
Clinical risk management 142
Dispensing with risk 147
Concluding remarks – risk management and quality 151
References 152
Further reading 153

9 **Insurance** 155

Introduction 155
The insurance process 158
The structure of the policy 160
Types of policies 163
Risk management 169
How to make a claim 171
Complaints – concerns and procedures 173
Other policies 174
Further information 175
Further reading 175

Part Two – Putting management into practice 177

10 **Financial management** 179

Introduction 179
Accounting – an introduction 180
Recording and reporting financial data 183
Analysis of accounts 190
Planning and control 193
Further reading 196

11 **Managing service delivery** 197
Introduction 197
The service organisation 197
Customer expectations 198
Staff roles in service delivery 200
Analysing services 203
Capacity considerations 209
Converting demand to output 214
Quality counts 216
Waste 219
Controlling performance 220
Points to remember 221
References 222
Further reading 222

12 **Managing profit** 225
Introduction 225
The analytical stage – answering the question 'Where are we now?' 225
SWOT analysis 226
PEST analysis 231
The planning stage – answering the question 'What are we going to do?' 232
The managing stage – answering the question 'How do we do it?' 233
Improving profit margins 236
Enhancing counter sales 237
Reducing expenses 238
Further reading 240

13 **Marketing within the pharmacy environment** 243
Introduction 243
What exactly *is* marketing? 244
Marketing strategy as part of a business plan 247
Understanding your customer 247
Factors affecting customer purchasing decisions 253
References 266
Further reading 266

14 **Pharmacy design, merchandising and stock control** 269
Introduction 269
Design problems 269
Refitting a pharmacy 271
Suggested pharmacy design 272
Stock management 276
Merchandising 281
Further reading 283

15 **ePharmacy – Information Technology and the Internet as a business resource** 285
Introduction 285
Healthcare and the Internet 285
Establishing a web presence 292
Online pharmacies 294
Legal and ethical issues 296
References 307
Websites for further information 308

16 **Human resource management in community pharmacy** 311
Introduction 311
Managing human resources 311
Training and development 318
Performance management 322
Further reading 325

17 **Pharmacy management in secondary care** 327
Introduction 327
The hospital environment 327
Demand management 330
Marketing management 331
Resource management 336
References 347
Further reading 348

18 **Medicines management** 349
Introduction 349
What is medicines management? 349
The need for medicines management 350
Medicines management and the pharmacist 351
Getting started in medicines management 352
Medicines management in practice 354
Medicines management involving other professionals 356
Summary 356
References 357
Further reading 358

Appendix 1 Pharmaceutical organisations involved in business practice 359
The Royal Pharmaceutical Society of Great Britain 359
The Royal Pharmaceutical Society Scottish Department 360
The Pharmaceutical Society of Northern Ireland 360
The Pharmaceutical Services Negotiating Committee 360

The Scottish Pharmaceutical General Council   361
Community Pharmacy Wales   361
The National Pharmaceutical Association   362
The Scottish Pharmaceutical Federation   363
Company Chemist Association Ltd   363
The Association of Independent Multiple Pharmacies   363
The NHS Confederation   364
Bodies providing CPE and CPD   364

Index   367

Foreword

Some would argue that professionals cannot trade. A trader is concerned with profitability, whereas a professional must judge what is best for their clients or customers irrespective of profit. However, perhaps uniquely, the Dickson case established pharmacy as a trading profession (Pharmaceutical Society of Great Britain v. Dickson, [1970] AC 403 (HL)).

Pharmacists and their staff now control a wide and growing range of resources, with at least 10% of NHS expenditure passing through pharmacies. There are some 45 000 people on the Royal Pharmaceutical Society of Great Britain register and many more technical and support staff involved in controlling these resources. There are of course many products sold commercially over the counter and an increasing number of new services now being locally negotiated or provided nationally by multiples that are commercially funded.

It is fundamental to the future of the profession and to patient safety that these resources are used wisely and safely and that staff understand methods of safe and effective management, yet little is taught about management at undergraduate level in most UK Schools of Pharmacy or in technician training programmes and postgraduate courses. There are many new NHS organisations that require pharmacy management skills if they are to get the best service and patient care from the pharmacy team. Government policies talk of governance and medicines management; whilst we know much about the medicines, we know much less about how to manage them. Further, our knowledge about how to persuade the policy-makers and planners to involve pharmacy is also limited. We should remember that pharmacy is about people as much as it is about medicines!

The Institute of Pharmacy Management (IPM) was established in 1964 to help highlight the importance of management training for pharmacists and those working in pharmacy business and practice. Many of the well-qualified contributors to this wide-ranging and excellent book are members of the IPM, including the editor, Dr Steven Kayne, who is an IPM Council member. This long overdue publication highlights many of the areas that pharmacists and those working within the pharmacy business need to understand and apply. The book will certainly provide a focus for continuing professional development. I hope that it will also stimulate Schools of Pharmacy to implement aspects of management in their undergraduate and postgraduate teaching programmes.

Ian Jones
President IPM
Emeritus Professor of Pharmacy Practice
University of Portsmouth School of Pharmacy

Preface

Over 70% of new graduates in pharmacy enter the profession at community level – that is, they are employed in pharmacies as assistant pharmacists or pharmacy managers; some eventually own their own shops. Around half the balance become hospital pharmacists, a few more enter the pharmaceutical industry and the balance fall into the all-encompassing group known universally as 'others'. Despite this well-known bias in favour of business, few of the Schools of Pharmacy offer any exposure to business studies. Most young pharmacists find themselves struggling during the first few years of their career, picking up bits of important information by trial and error.

The situation is particularly visible at the present time because some multiple pharmacies are offering two distinct career paths for their recruits – one down the business road and one more towards clinical practice. In both the hospital service and industry, there is a need for budgeting and internal marketing skills. It seemed to be an appropriate time to produce a book on the subject and I am obliged to the Pharmaceutical Press for their support.

This book aims to provide a background knowledge for pharmacists and a resource for Schools of Pharmacy and postgraduate training bodies. It is not meant to be an 'all you ever wanted to know text' – more an introduction to be used to complement the many excellent financial, marketing and management books that exist. I hope that it will reach parts that other books cannot, being written for, and largely by, pharmacists and providing material not easily accessible elsewhere.

I would hope that readers could dip into the book as circumstances demand, picking up salient facts to point them in the right direction. There is some repetition of material in chapters. This is for the benefit of busy community pharmacists, to reduce the need to flick back and forth. It should also help to revise previously read material.

None of these resources can replace expert professional advice from accountants and lawyers, particularly those who deal with pharmacists on a regular basis.

I offer my thanks to my friends for giving their valuable time to contribute to this book. All are experts in their own fields and bring a blend of theoretical and practical knowledge to the material presented.

Steven Kayne
May 2004

About the editor

Steven Kayne has been a Community Pharmacist in Glasgow for almost 30 years, combining his pharmacy practice with several years as a part-time lecturer in Marketing and Finance at Paisley University. He writes and lectures in the UK and overseas on subjects related to pharmacy, is currently a visiting lecturer in the School of Pharmacy at the University of Strathclyde, Glasgow and holds a number of advisory positions. Steven is a member of the Scottish Executive of the Royal Pharmaceutical Society of Great Britain and Chairman of the College of Pharmacy Practice in Scotland. He was the first pharmacist to be awarded a Fellowship by portfolio of the Institute of Pharmacy Management and is currently its Vice Chair.

Contributors

Gordon Appelbe LLB, PhD, MSc, BSc (Pharm), FRPharmS, Hon MPS (Australia), FCPP
Independent pharmaceutical and legal consultant, London

Charles P Butler BPharm, MSc, MIPharmM, FCPP, FRPharmS
Director, Fourways Professional Services, Reading

Ian Caldwell PhC, MPhil, FRPharmS
Retired Community Pharmacist; Past President RPSGB, Larkhall, Lanarkshire

Gerry Gracias BSc, MRPharmS
Human Resources Committee, Day-Lewis Group, Thornton Heath, Surrey

Ian Harrison BSc, MBA, MPhil, FRPharmS, MCPP, MIPharmM
Regional Pharmaceutical Adviser, Oxford

Lee Kayne PhD, MRPharmS, MFHom(Pharm)
Community Pharmacist, Glasgow

Rebecca Kayne BA
IT Specialist, Glasgow

Steven B Kayne PhD, MBA, LLM, MSc (Sp Med), DAgVetPharm, FRPharmS, FCPP, FIPharmM, MPS(NZ), FNZCP
Independent Consultant Pharmacist and Visiting Lecturer, School of Pharmacy, University of Strathclyde, Glasgow

Anne Loh BPharm, MRPharmS
Human Resources and Training Manager, Day-Lewis Group, Thornton Heath, Surrey

Martin McBeth BAcc, CA
Partner, Bannerman Johnstone Maclay Chartered Accountants, Glasgow

John Paul Marney BA (Hons), PhD
Senior Lecturer in Economics, University of East London, London

Kirit Patel FRPharmS, MBA, Dip Phil, FIMgt
Chief Executive, Day-Lewis Group, Thornton Heath, Surrey

Andrew Radley BPharm (Hons), MPhil, FRPharmS, MCPP
Lead Principal Pharmacist, NHS Tayside, Perth Royal Infirmary, Perth

Alan Reeves BA, BPhil, PhD
Senior Lecturer, University of Paisley Business School, Paisley

Richard Seal MSc, MRPharmS, MCPP
National Programme Director for the Collaborative Medicines
Management Services Programme, National Prescribing Centre, Liverpool

Mel Smith BPharm, MRPharmS, MIPharmM, ACCP
Professional Relations, Reckitt and Colman, Hull

Adrian Spooner BSc(Pharm) (Hons), MRPharmS
Consultant Pharmacist and Solicitor, London

Alan B Watson, PhD, FCII, MIRM, ILTM
Senior Lecturer, Division of Risk, Glasgow Caledonian University,
Glasgow

Part One

The foundation of pharmacy management

1

Professionalism and business practice

Ian Caldwell

Introduction

This chapter addresses three fundamental questions relating to professionalism in pharmacy and discusses how they relate to business practice:

- Are professionalism and business compatible?
- Does professionalism make a profit for anyone?
- Is it possible to capitalise on professional characteristics?

To answer these questions we need to understand the origins of modern pharmacy and consider briefly why it was inevitable that professionalism would emerge as the guiding principle of knowledge-based service provision. Dictionaries have long sought to define 'profession', whilst sociologists and others have erected various explanatory structures around the concept. In the process they have sometimes clouded the issue by wrapping professionalism in political theory rather than considering it in terms of what is fundamental – the relationship between responsible expert providers and their clients. It is this latter aspect that, by looking at the requirements of governments and professional bodies, the expectations of consumer interests and, most importantly, the perceptions of individual members of the public, we use to demonstrate that professionalism pays dividends.

However, there can be times when the advantages of being a professional person have to be balanced against the problems arising from the underlying responsibilities, and so we take a brief look at some areas of possible conflict.

The development of the pharmacy profession

There is some evidence that even in Babylonian times, there was a formal structure to health provision. The Egyptian Empire had physician-priests and the Ancient Greeks had both schools of medicine and schools of philosophy, some of which considered the origins, nature and treatment of disease. Many of the physicians and compounders (pharmacists) in the Roman era were Greek and formal training was standard. Physicians, surgeons and pharmacists all charged fees for their services.

The collapse of the Roman Empire and the advent of the Dark Ages meant that the expanding Saracen influence became the repository of the advanced knowledge of medicine, architecture, chemistry and mathematics at the time, while northern Europe struggled with myth, superstition and a fragmented knowledge base. The north became more prominent after the final expulsion of Islam from Spain in 1492 but had, since the 12th century, been creating a system of quality assurance for the provision of services to the public in the form of guilds. These were groups of experts in various crafts that were important at the time, and their origins are still evident today in a range of surnames – millers, coopers, a variety of wrights, clerks and a plethora of smiths, later joined by spicers, apothecaries, physicians, barbers and surgeons.

Admission to a guild demanded a lengthy apprenticeship followed by a period as a journeyman (an itinerant craftsman), with the aim of proving to clients that the guild member was competent – an early form of quality assurance. The system generally served society fairly well until the 18th century, but the explosion of proven knowledge as opposed to manual or doctrinal skills made the rigid guild framework outdated and inadequate to deal with emerging specialisations such as chemistry, anatomy, physics and pharmacy. By the early 19th century these new providers were beginning to combine apprenticeship or practical training with university or college education, and more uniform standards of qualification were emerging rather than the localised city- or burgh-based craft training. Learned societies began to appear, which further improved standards and in many cases became the core of specialist professional bodies that operated at national level. Initially these organisations were completely voluntary and had no statutory obligations or privilege, but that was about to change.

The nature of a profession

The 1986 edition of Webster's Collegiate Dictionary[1] gave a comprehensive definition of a profession:

> A calling requiring specialised knowledge and often long and intensive preparation including instruction in skills and methods, as well as in scientific, historical or scholarly principles underlying such skills and methods, maintaining by force of organisation or concerted opinion high standards of achievement and conduct, and committing its members to continued study and to a kind of work which has for its prime purpose the rendering of a public service.

This is very different from the definition of over a hundred years before, when the 1883 edition of the Imperial Dictionary[2] claimed a profession was:

> The business which one professes to understand and to follow for subsistence.

Thus, in a century, the emphasis seems to have moved from using knowledge to turn a profit to demanding knowledge to provide an assured level of service. Is this the case and if so, is it the whole story?

While contemporary professions are striving to ensure uniformity of professional service by mechanisms such as renewable practice certificates and continuing professional development (CPD), it is not true to say that the Victorians were solely focused on using knowledge and skills to generate profit. The history of pharmacy is well documented elsewhere,[3] but it is worth considering the opening phrase of the very first Pharmacy Act of June 1852[4] because it contains the key to the reason for the existence of professions in general and pharmacy in particular:

> Whereas it is expedient for the safety of the public that persons exercising the business or calling of Pharmaceutical Chemists in Great Britain should possess a competent knowledge of Pharmaceutical and General Chemistry and other branches of useful knowledge.

This was a business deal, an expedient, just like any other negotiation. A government wanted one thing, in this case public safety with respect to drugs, and an interested group wanted another, in this case a monopoly tied to a restricted title. Of course the whole thing is hedged with terms and conditions about who does what for whom, when and where they do it and what the penalties are for failure to comply, but these are to be expected with any contract. This was a new type of contract – a social contract in the public interest. Pharmacy was one of the first expert groups to negotiate such a deal, even though it resulted in a voluntary Pharmaceutical Society, a situation that lasted until the Pharmacy and Poisons Act 1933[3] made registration compulsory. The framework was essentially the same for other succeeding groups that sought statutory recognition. Who got what from this state recognition of pharmacy can be summed up as follows:

PHARMACY		STATE
Monopoly	*Trade off*	Safety
Status	*for*	Expertise
Reward		Honesty

The main obligations undertaken by pharmacy were the creation of a register of people who had satisfied the examiners or were exempt from the examination process, the appointment of Boards of Examiners, the holding of examinations and the setting up of an administrative structure to control the whole thing. This may seem like a lot of work, but other organisations obviously considered it to be a good deal because the next 50 years saw a rush to attain the same goals by, for example, the Institute of Chartered Accountants of Scotland in 1854 and the General Council of the Bar of England and Wales in 1894. Other bodies sought the same recognition through the Royal Charter route, but the basis was always the same – an exchange of benefits for responsibilities; an exchange that the fledgling professions thought very worthwhile.

A mid-20th century view of a profession can be summed up in the following terms:[5]

- Provides skill based on theoretical knowledge.
- Ensures training and learning.
- Tests the competence of members.
- Possesses an organisational structure.
- Requires adherence to a code of conduct.
- Encourages altruistic service.

These are the attributes of any group that has been given recognition by the state as forming the expert, dependable and accountable practitioners in any given speciality. Anyone who wants to join such a group has to sign up not just to the regulatory requirements but also to the principles underlying them. The public are not forced to use the services of a professional in cases such as accountancy or finance, but if they choose not to use professionals they lose the benefit of assured competence and accountability. The general public are probably not aware of the changes in philosophy within professions over the past century and a half.[6] The Victorians enjoyed professional competence based on knowledge, the early 20th century saw the advent of accountability through knowledge and codes of conduct, while today we have professions offering quality assurance through knowledge, codes of conduct and career-long competence.

To some extent this change is the result of self-protection from an increasingly litigious client base, where knowing what to do is on a par with proving that you did everything that could be expected of a professional. It is also the result of increasing public expectations, which are actively fostered by consumer interests, government and the media.

Professions and business

Pharmacy is a profession. It exhibits all of the six characteristics listed above.[5] Some people view this as a millstone that is oppressive and inhibits their freedom to operate successfully in a commercial environment. This attitude probably had its roots in the class-consciousness of the 19th century, when trade of any description was not quite 'the done thing'. This was probably exacerbated by the fact that pharmacy operates to a large extent in the public eye, in the high street, and not in an enclosed office, laboratory or surgery.

Pharmacy today is noted for providing many other services than the dispensing and sale of medicines. The reasons for diversification in community pharmacy are many, but they can be traced back to the profession's earliest days. Whilst the early Pharmacy Acts granted monopoly on the sale of poisons they did not provide a monopoly in the sale and dispensing of medicines. To make up for the shortfall in their potential income, pharmacists used their knowledge of chemistry to:

- supply photographic chemicals and develop plates and films
- produce aerated waters, manufacture and sell cosmetics
- make and advertise safe, nutritious infant and invalid foods
- produce individually branded remedies
- charge the accumulators (batteries) that powered the early radios.

Their clients patronised them because their expertise was trusted; they were selling their professional reputation to the public together with the photographs, the medicines and the cosmetics. Pharmacists made the greatest use of their professional qualification by counter-prescribing, now referred to as 'responding to symptoms', and it was this aspect of pharmacy that earned the public's respect for individual pharmacists. It is also an aspect of the profession that has always been grossly undervalued.

The phrase 'service provision' has been deliberately used so far as an indicator of what professions do. The manner in which this is achieved in practice is discussed in detail in Chapter 11.

Nowhere has it been suggested that professions provide their services free of charge. Every professional is a business person – they could not function otherwise. Some sell themselves directly to the public and in doing so, they must involve themselves in commerce – they may need premises, usually employ or contract staff, negotiate with commercial suppliers, often register for Value Added Tax (known as General Sales Tax in other countries), seek and exploit contacts and frequently try to maximise their income by selling products not directly dependent on their professional training. Lawyers sell insurance and mortgages as well as legal advice; surgeons depend on contacts for referrals and dentists sell dental care products in addition to professional skills. Clearly, professionalism is not seen by the public as a straitjacket on commerce and equally clearly professionalism and commerce not only can but must co-exist.

Pharmacy is more overt in portraying the marriage of profession and business than most other professions. The days are long gone when the individual proprietor pharmacist produced foods, cosmetics and remedies. The public trust in pharmacy was not lost on a few entrepreneurs who expanded the geographical reach of their own specialities which, in time, became nationally advertised products and were stocked by most pharmacies and, if the sale of the product was not restricted to pharmacy by law, by other retail outlets. This capitalisation on reputation in the manufacturing sector had its parallels in community pharmacy.

In contrast to most European practice, UK law allows corporate bodies to offer pharmaceutical services. The early manifestations of this were national companies such as Boots plc, Timothy Whites & Taylors, and a raft of Co-operative Societies. Every branch of these employed a pharmacist and each company was under the overall professional supervision of a pharmacist. The dependable image of pharmacy underpinned the commercial approach of these multiples. The example was not lost on others, with the result that the independent proprietor-run pharmacies now account for fewer than half of the total number of registered pharmacies and for much less than half the total turnover. Because the legislative and professional control is the same for both multiples and independents it is again clear that pharmacy can operate commercially within the ambit of a profession.

Client views

We have already seen that professional bodies, including the Royal Pharmaceutical Society of Great Britain, require their members to be equipped with relevant knowledge, to work within their competence and to maintain confidentiality – a seller's view of the market. Client expectations, on the other hand, are evident from a variety of sources. The National Consumer Council (NCC), together with its counterparts in Northern Ireland, Scotland and Wales, are government-funded bodies that have as their stated aim the representation of the wishes of the public.

None of these bodies has ever investigated what consumers expect from a profession or from professionals, but a report on self-regulation by the NCC in 1999[7] did include a list of basic public expectations. Table 1.1 shows a comparison of these expectations with the demands that major professions place on their members.

Table 1.1 Comparison of some of the objectives of the NCC with those of professional bodies

National Consumer Council	Professions
Access	Availability
Fairness	Integrity and confidentiality
Information – accurate and useful	Information – accurate and understandable
Safety	Knowledge, competence and CPD

More particular views of client needs are available from consumer organisations such as the UK Consumer Association through its publication *Which?* and from client surveys and focus groups. *Which?* tends towards single-issue reports on products or services that are suspected of failing to deliver as well as they might. Amongst those it has commented on are the professions of law, medicine, pharmacy[8,9] and veterinary practice, and each has been found wanting to some extent. Pharmacy was reviewed in the context of the expanding role of the pharmacist and the increasing range of effective products within the pharmacy-only (P) category that were becoming available. The results would seem to indicate that some pharmacists were not, at the time, making best use of the P range and were reluctant, in some instances, to refer clients to a medical practitioner for more appropriate investigation and treatment. The final conclusion was that 'pharmacies can't cope with the changing role'. The use of covert investigators by *Which?* has been the subject of adverse comment and it is clear that the outcomes of its investigations are often subjective; however it is equally clear that these reports serve as an indicator that there is room for improvement in order to meet the needs of clients. Despite this, pharmacists scored highly in a list of professions that were trusted by the public.

Consumer-led expectations

It is when we move to surveys and focus groups that we get to grips with what the general public – clients, customers, and patients – really expect. There is universal demand for professional competence founded on a sound knowledge base and operating under an all-embracing under-standing of professional integrity. These objective requirements are the obvious results of what the public understand by the common meaning of the word 'professional', and underpin perceptions of quality of service so important in attracting and retaining custom (see Chapter 11). They also underline earlier attempts to define public expectations and include the characteristics derived from the Roskill Report to the Monopolies Commission as long ago as 1970[10] concerning 'standards of competence, integrity and fair judgement' and which included:

- Detachment and integrity in exercising personal judgement.
- Direct, personal client relations based on trust, faith and confidence.

Collectively, professionals have a responsibility for the competence and integrity of the whole profession.

Asking the client what characteristics they would like to see in their ideal professional person brings some surprises. Within this predominantly subjective area it is to be expected that the over-riding concerns would be in the areas of personal relationships such as mutual respect, trust and accountability, and this proves to be the case. However, it is the other comments generated by the public that are more relevant to the practising professional. The following list of descriptors was picked out from amongst those used by participants in some focus groups and surveys[11] to express their views of what was expected of professional people. Professionals should be:

- approachable
- available
- caring
- communicative
- capable of lateral thinking
- motivating
- observant
- self-disciplined
- willing to liaise
- willing to listen
- willing to offer continuity.

This list reflects very personal opinions but serves as a convenient starting point to explore ways in which professional characteristics can be exploited to the benefit of client and pharmacist. There is no statistical significance in either the choice of phrases or in their order of presentation.

Approachable

This involves providing personal contact at a mutually acceptable level. Ideally, this unspoken accord should be achieved within the space of a couple of sentences by using all the usual social devices: open stance, eye contact, tone of voice, and so on, but in reality it may take longer. Direct contact should be the best advert possible and it can prevent a minor concern from escalating to confrontation. A personal relationship between the client and the pharmacist ensures that the professional is a business asset. However, quite how long this ideal can be maintained with the advent of Internet mail order pharmacy (and even remote super-vision[12]) is uncertain.

Available

The consolidation that has taken place in business practice over the past couple of decades has made it increasingly rare for the public to have access to anyone who can meaningfully be described as 'the boss', and even rarer for them to have access to someone who has specialist knowl-edge and an underlying professionalism. The longstanding requirement for a pharmacist to be present in a pharmacy to supervise sales of poisons has resulted in the community pharmacist becoming one of the few professionals with whom the public can have day-to-day random contact. The objective must become to seek ways to extract commercial advantage from this professional requirement – to capitalise on being the accessible professional on the high street.

Caring

It is to be expected that the potential clients of any health professional would expect them to be caring – after all it is a matter of self-interest to them. Focus groups have confirmed that community pharmacists are expected to be 'caring' but subsequent teasing out of the import of this word showed that it had wide implications for the practitioner–client relationship. No one quite got around to suggesting that the pharmacist should use extra-sensory perception in order to have the patient's pre-scriptions ready for collection before the client even went to the doctor, but expectations were high. For a start, there are practical aspects to the concept of caring even before the client crosses the pharmacy threshold. There is a clearly understood idea that professional excellence in terms of premises co-relates exactly with the standard of caring that can be expected. Style of premises seems not to matter – they can be traditional, retro or state of the art fashionable – but they must be brightly lit, clean, warm and welcoming. Staff are part of that welcome. If choosing the right staff is a skill, then keeping them enthused is an art form that can enrich any business (see Chapter 16). As a professional, a pharmacist should be able to identify the training needs and competence of others and doing this effectively can only increase the efficiency of a pharmacy. There is always the possibility that expensively trained staff will be lured away by competitors who are not willing to go through the training process, but it is a risk worth taking. The caring image even extends to staff uniform, an idea that goes back to the Victorian frock coat and green apron. White is traditional nowadays, but while colour is not important, image is – a view that is endorsed by multinational corporations. It does not matter how the client is dressed, their expectation is that the staff and the pharmacist will be dressed in a way that reflects the professional standing of the business. What these well-chosen, neatly dressed staff are expected to deliver is a warm welcome and a considerate, empathetic understanding of the client's needs.

Communicative

As we have seen in Table 1.1, most professions, including pharmacy, require their members to provide accurate information. Some professions go further and insist that communications with clients, colleagues or media be clear and understandable – no jargon and no buzz words. Individual members of the public have stated their preferences much more strongly; they disliked people who talked over their heads but they really loathed any professional who talked down to them in either a social or technical context. Striking a balance between accuracy and clarity often presents problems, especially if the need is to simplify a response without trivialising it. Visual clues can be misleading because anoraks, dark suits or Gucci accessories are not necessarily indicators of intellectual ability. Verbal clues are more dependable and the use of common open-question conversational gambits such as 'What can I do to help you?' provides a few seconds to formulate the response and to better judge the level at which it should be pitched.

One of the reasons for consulting a pharmacist about anything is that the client expects honesty in the reply. This might seem obvious when discussing matters such as the seemingly endless lists of possible side-effects contained in patient information leaflets, but can be more complex when the issue is something like the long-term implications of a diagnosis of a chronic condition that the patient may or may not have already probed at length with the physician. Can there be such a thing as too much honesty or is anything less than complete frankness merely evasion?

Communicating effectively with staff is equally important. Every business has its own style but staff must understand that they themselves are different from other retail staff. Many of their customers will seem to be more demanding because they have some sort of illness and because of the high standards expected from a business run by a professional.

Capable of lateral thinking

This requirement was very much a minority view, at the margin of stated needs in a professional person. On reflection, it is clear that being an expert in the technicalities and legal niceties of a profession is not the whole story. Instead, it is the sum total of a pharmacist's interests, knowledge and experience and how all this can be harnessed in the interests of both the clients and the business that is important. Lateral thinking is an appropriate umbrella term for a variety of public expectations. The pharmacist has a long tradition of being the informed repository of obscure knowledge, a guide to a host of local and national services and as an interpreter. Sometimes the response when in repository mode can only be 'I don't know the answer', but very often the corollary is 'but I know a man/agency/book/website that does'. In the role of interpreter, the pharmacist was formerly often asked to comment on the meaning of partially understood diagnoses or the implications of a particular drug regimen. Increasingly the professional is now being asked to verify or comment on information derived from the Internet. This can involve calming someone who is convinced of impending personal medical disaster or suggesting that a miracle cure is still merely a glint in some academic's research grant application. The pharmacist can also be asked to use his professional judgement to choose between the contradictory opinions expressed by two or more 'specialist' health websites. It can well be argued that fulfilling these client expectations is time-consuming and of little profit. Whilst accepting this view it must be remembered that clients talk to other people and a glowing report may result in new patronage that could generate a return.

Motivating

This is another unexpected term and it was used in the sense that the pharmacist was expected to encourage the appropriate use of prescribed medicines. Having been presented with this unforeseen word it is useful to consider it in relation to other aspects of the pharmacist's professional life. It goes without saying that, in order to register as a pharmacist, a person must be sufficiently self-motivated to go through the academic and practical training processes. The question is how to maintain that impetus throughout a life-long career in the face of organisational, educational and administrative change. The answers reside in what can be called an investment strategy.

The initial deposit is registration as a pharmacist, tax is paid annually in the form of CPD, but further investment is optional. Management training or pharmacy ownership can be seen as long-term bonds whilst specialisation in areas such as palliative care, health screening or respiratory care may be considered as equities that should yield both a fiscal and a professional dividend but which could be shorter-term investments. The choice of speciality is a very personal matter and can depend on factors such as existing interest, local demand, demographics or even a determination to stay at the forefront of practice. Every portfolio should have an insurance element and this can take the form of being aware of what is going on locally and nationally. Such awareness can be achieved by becoming involved in professional and business organisations.

Motivating the patient goes way beyond the concept of advising on the correct use of medicines and is part of the acceptance of the extended role of the pharmacist and the move into the field of public health. Cynics would suggest that health professionals have a vested interest in a population that enjoys a moderate degree of ill health. That this is a nonsense argument can easily be demonstrated by the promotion by the dental profession of the use of fluoride treatments to reduce the incidence of dental caries and the attendant fillings or extractions. The aim is now largely achieved but dentists have never been busier because people remain dentate for longer and seek more frequent check-ups and treatment. Reducing nicotine and alcohol use, promoting exercise and fluoride use and encouraging sensible diets are all attainable through the agency of pharmacy without demanding an immense use of professional time. Information loops on in-house television sets, patient-accessed computer health information websites, roller-screen adverts or even the much-maligned leaflet can all be used to improve both the quality and the length of patient life. The pessimistic view of the outcome of such a process is a reduced prescription throughput and income from a healthier population. The optimists' conclusion could be that the clients would be around for much longer, they would seek regular health monitoring and that there would be a drug-managed component to this longer, healthier life. This attitude could be considered, perhaps, to be exploitation of the pharmacy brand in a changing market.

Observant

This minority expectation of the public was suggested by a wish for professionals to look beyond the questions that were posed to them by clients who really had what they considered to be other undeclared and more awkward or embarrassing problems. Such a degree of prescience is obviously desirable but, unless the signals of distress are painfully obvious, it is often only a matter of luck if the hidden agenda is picked up. However, being observant does have some import for both the professional and the commercial interest of the pharmacist. 'Horizon scanning' for the intentions of government and local authorities can suggest the emphasis to be placed on professional services in the future and the action that needs to be taken in order to provide them in the right way, with appropriate colleagues from the correct location.

At the personal level the expectations placed on the 'observant' pharmacist can be daunting. Pharmacists are not formally trained in diagnosis, but is the persistent little sore at the hairline a rodent ulcer, is the sweet-smelling breath of a patient due to alcohol or to ketone? If a problem is suspected, how is treatment initiated? Observation can be professionally rewarding but is not without its problems.

Self-disciplined

Disciplinary matters are dealt with elsewhere in this text, but some members of the public felt it necessary to mention self-discipline as a desirable professional characteristic. Their reasons were simple and straightforward, and included punctuality, no drinking during business hours, keeping promises with regard to delivery of services and consideration for the feelings of staff and clients. Professionals are exposed to elements of discipline from their earliest student days, with academia inculcating discipline of thought and membership of a professional body imposing discipline of action. It is in the world of practice that professionalism requires a form of self-discipline which combines the freedom to exercise professional judgement with responsibility to the individual client and to society in general. This is sometimes easier said than done. In the real world we must be aware that pharmacists are not automatons and that there will be days when they are not at their best. Illness, bereavement, marital problems, financial difficulties and a host of other events can all intrude into professional life. At such times it may be necessary to 'put on a brave face' in order to continue to build that essential element of the goodwill of a business, its reputation.

Willing to liaise

The concept of seamless care has obviously not been lost on the public. There is an expectation that there will be at least an understanding between the various health professionals involved in the treatment of all but the most trivial or routine conditions and that the resultant information flow will be two-way. This is not a wish to have confidential information scattered carelessly but an expectation that relevant information can be fed into the treatment system at any point and that it will be acted upon by the appropriate practitioner.

One of the traditional roles of the pharmacist that has always been dependent on cooperation with other professionals is nowadays graced with the formal name of triage. Pharmacists have long been accustomed to advising on which minor injuries need a dressing and which need stitches, which cough can be soothed and which would benefit from further investigation. The public seek pharmacists' advice on matters such as these because they are available, informed and just possibly because they do not charge for the service. There is little room for profit here but there is the long-term prospect of professional involvement.

Willing to listen

A few clients interpret this requirement as giving them freedom to subject their chosen professional to an endless stream of conversation from which it is difficult to extract any great meaning. This must be accepted as a fact of life. In the remaining vast majority of interactions with the public, the aim of the pharmacist must be to gain the maximum amount of information as quickly as possible but in a patient and understanding manner – a seeming contradiction in terms which, when achieved, is much valued by clients.

Willing to offer continuity

When this unlikely professional requirement was enunciated in a focus group it was seized upon as a prime desire by everyone present. This almost furious response is clearly a reaction not only to the ongoing consolidation of pharmacy ownership but to the inordinate extension of the hours of service provided by many pharmacies – a provision that some consumer agencies promote as essential. Dealing first with the declining proportion of proprietor pharmacists, the emerging and expanding companies offer a career structure to pharmacists within which frequent transfers amongst branches are part of the promotion process. The resultant and often rapid succession of pharmacists can prevent a rapport developing between practitioner and client and militates against the possible development of familiarity with the treatment needs of any individual or family. The only continuity remaining, apart from any corporate image, is that provided by non-professional staff. This problem is not unique to pharmacy and is encountered in professions as diverse as law, accountancy and medicine – hence the widespread public concern.

It is with the spread of greatly extended hours of service in community pharmacy that the paradox in the public expectation of provision of professional service arises. The clients enjoy the convenience of late-night or indeed round-the-clock access and yet they still claim to experience deprivation of personal relationship with the pharmacists involved. It is obviously unreasonable to expect continuity of staffing when even 12-hour, 7-day service requires about three full-time equivalent pharmacists to be employed in order to cover work, vacation, sick leave and training. The likelihood of continuity becomes even more remote when it is remembered that the reality of staffing means that more than three pharmacists would be involved in such a set-up. The professional's concern is how to satisfy that expectation.

The above list of professional characteristics may seem slightly unexpected but are not presented as items to be ticked off as each target is reached. They are intended to convey the wide scope and all-embracing nature of the elements of professionalism in the eyes of the client – no matter if that client is an individual, an employer or a government or commercial agency. The characteristics have to be taken alongside the demands placed on every professional person, honesty, accountability, trustworthiness and the integrity of working solely within the individual's expertise.

Many public expectations are obviously time-consuming. If this time is properly used it can benefit the reputation of the pharmacist and pharmacy and in doing so can have a positive effect on salaries and balance sheets.

Professional dilemmas

Although a professional's approach to problems must be logical and should be non-judgemental there can be circumstances where professionalism and personality come into conflict.

The days of a 'job for life' are vanishing and this can create problems for the conscientious employed practitioner. The requirements and standards of large employers need not always match those of either government or profession. Employers may be large enough to set up their own training schemes, which begs the questions of who frames the content and who recognises whose standards. Company methods may prevent satisfactory adherence to some of the subjective professional requirements because personal judgement can be subsumed within an organisational protocol, personal contact can be lost within a 24-hour shift system, confidentiality becomes more difficult to maintain within a large system and narrow specialisation can make the maintenance of professional competence more difficult. Whilst there is an awareness by commerce of possible problems in employing professional people on a large scale, it is fortunate that most employers choose to use the services of the professional, not as a matter of statutory requirement but for the benefits they bring to an organisation in terms of competence and intellect.

When faced with a client whose choice of lifestyle has an adverse effect on health, be it by tobacco or alcohol use or by drug misuse, a professional should be non-judgemental about the reasons for the behaviour but does have the options of doing nothing or attempting to help to effect change. Intervention may be seen as interference or as a lifeline; it may depend on the timing of the offer of assistance as much as on the way in which it is offered.

It is when the moral, religious or cultural beliefs of a pharmacist are imported into the professional arena that the greatest potential for conflict of interest can arise. Although the service ethic that often underlies these frequently reinforce the professional attitude, belief patterns can impinge on the willingness or even the ability to take part in some professional services when certain views are strongly held. It is unfair to expect someone to compromise their personal standards by demanding that he or she work in a way they find repugnant. However, when dealing with a service that is completely legal then it is equally unfair of a professional to adopt an absolutist stance that denies the client access to any such service. The compromise judged to be the most balanced solution is for the pharmacist involved to direct the client to another service provider and to do so without comment or implied disapproval.

Concluding remarks

This chapter started by posing three questions, the answers to which can be summarised as follows:

- Not only are professionalism and business compatible, they are inextricably and synergistically linked. In order to provide professional services efficiently it is essential to use good business practices to manage finances, to provide an administrative base, to attract and retain clients, to conform to legislative requirements and to ensure that practice standards are at least current and preferably forward-looking.
- People who practice the profession in which they have trained are selling their knowledge and their expertise and thus are profiting from their professionalism. It does not matter whether they practice as individuals or as employees in the state or corporate sectors, they operate as vendors of specialised services and, like any seller, they benefit from trading in their intellectual wares for as long as there is demand. However, it is business methodology, not sentiment or instinct, which determines whether or not the services a professional provides continue to be those that the client wants and is willing to pay for. It follows that both general business and professions share the need to constantly improve and develop service standards. Failure to do so may eventually lead to unprofitability as other professions begin to compete for what they see as unexploited niche areas that they can absorb into their own field of expertise.
- Every profession depends on the core attributes of integrity, knowledge, accountability and public trust for its reputation. Every successful business has effective communications. The other characteristics we have considered rely to a large extent on personal relationships with the client and it is this that allows pharmacists to capitalise on their professionalism. Clients expect a caring and understanding approach to their perceived needs from a professional who is up-to-date and who provides services from appropriate premises, staffed by trained personnel who are aware of the ethos of the pharmacy. It is likely that, even today, there are still clients who will be faithful to a particular pharmacist if all these elements are in place and who may also spread the reputation of such a pharmacy by word of mouth. If the client can be made to feel special then, in his or her mind, the pharmacist becomes special too.

This chapter started with the claim that the concept of professionalism is not new. Hippocrates summed it up some 2400 years ago and a paraphrase of his philosophy encapsulates all that is required of a professional person:

- Do your best.
- Do no harm.
- Disseminate knowledge.

References

1. *Merriam-Webster's Collegiate Dictionary*. Springfield, MA: Merriam-Webster, 1986.
2. Ogilvie J. *The Imperial Dictionary of the English Language*. London: Blackie and Son, 1883.
3. Holloway S W F. *The Royal Pharmaceutical Society of Great Britain 1841–1991. A Political and Social History*. London: Pharmaceutical Press, 1991.
4. Pharmacy Act 1852. 15 & 16 Victoria; CAP, LVI.
5. Millerson G. *The Qualifying Associations: A Study in Professionalization*. London: Routledge and Kegan Paul, 1964.
6. Allaker J, Shapland J. *Organising UK Professions: Continuity and Change*. The Law Society Research Study No. 16. London: The Law Society of England and Wales, 1994.
7. *Self-Regulation of Professionals in Healthcare*. London: National Consumer Council, 1999.
8. Pharmacists in crisis. *Which?*, January 1996. London: Consumers' Association.
9. Healthcare on the high street. *Which?*, January 2000. London: Consumers' Association.
10. Monopolies Commission. *Report on Restrictive Practices in Relation to the Supply of Professional Services (Roskill Report)*. London: HMSO, 1970.
11. Caldwell I M. An investigation to determine the nature of characteristics which define a good professional with particular reference to pharmacy. MPhil thesis, University of Strathclyde, Glasgow, 2001.
12. Bellingham C. Remote supervision becomes a reality. *Pharm J* 2004; 272: 177–178.

Further reading

Anon. Comfort zone of the dispensary has to be challenged, says Society (Report on Unichem Convention, Mauritius). *Pharm J* 2002; 269: 499–500.

Maister D. *True Professionalism: The Courage to Care about Your People, Your Clients, and Your Career*. The Free Press (available for download from www.amazon.co.uk).

Rajani S. Professionalism: need for a strong set of core values. *Pharm J* 2002; 269: 438–439.

Rees J A. On being a professional. *Tomorrow's Pharmacist* 1999; October: 24–26.

Shulman R. Professionalism, integrity and trust on trial in clinical research. *Pharm J* 2002; 269: 27.

2

The economics of business

Alan Reeves and John P Marney

Introduction

Economics is the study of how people provide for their material well-being or, as Heilbroner and Milberg[1] starkly put it, it is the study of 'how humankind procures its daily bread'. It hardly seems that studying something as mundane as procuring bread should justify the position of economics as a key social science and as having a pivotal role in business affairs. Yet, although it might appear a simple task to produce enough for us all in a modern, advanced economy, we still live in a world where poverty is rife – a world in which there is just not enough to go round.

As a result, millions have died in famines in Africa and life expectancy in poor nations is less than half that in the rich nations. Drugs that can save lives are scarce in the developing world, where mere survival is often the aim of many people.

There are several reasons why pharmacists should know something about economics:

- It helps us to understand the world.
- It makes us all better actors in the economic game.
- It helps us to understand economic policies.
- It allows us to see why the business environment is the way it is.

Economic problems arise because wants exceed the resources available to satisfy them, giving rise to the problem of **scarcity**. If goods were as free as air or we had a replicator machine like that on the imaginary Starship Enterprise, economics as a discipline would cease to exist. It only has moment because of scarcity, and decisions about what to produce, how to produce and for whom to produce have to be made because resources are scarce. Scarcity though is relative. It is not just to do with what the Earth provides but also with what people desire. It is the balance between the two that determines whether or not there is scarcity. Desires seem to grow as material wealth increases – scarcity then becomes psychological. What is poor in one place is rich in another.

For example, poverty guidelines published by the US Department of Health and Human Services dictate that the minimum income for a family of four should be US$18100, which would be considered a fortune in many countries. Poverty then is a relative as well as an absolute phenomenon.

Society's task is two-fold: first, to develop an effective system for the **production** of enough products – products and services for people to survive, and second, to arrange for the efficient **distribution** of that production. Several questions arise from economic considerations:

- What then is entailed in producing enough for survival?
- How does the economic system ensure that enough of the right things are produced?
- What are the social institutions and business systems needed to get people into productive activities?
- Is it automatic that an economy will always produce enough and employ everyone who wants to work?

Economies of rich countries are at a very much more advanced stage of development than those of the poor. This means that the type and scale of production and distribution differ dramatically between rich and poor economies. In the advanced economy, the tendency is for each worker to specialise, then to play a very small part in the economic system. As a result, people's dependence on each other grows. Bottlenecks in such a system can slow everything down and the economy can be crippled by the failure of small groups of key workers to perform their tasks. Thus, people in the advanced economy are not self-sufficient in the way that many are in the developing countries. Ironically, by becoming more advanced, people in the developed world have become less able to produce the products needed for their survival!

Economics is traditionally divided into two main areas – microeconomics and macroeconomics. Microeconomics is the study of households and firms, how they make decisions and how they interact in markets. The first part of this chapter covers some of the basic issues in microeconomics. Macroeconomics, which is the focus of the second part of the chapter, is the study of the economy as a whole. The two are closely related. Because macroeconomic effects arise from the combined actions of millions of individuals, we cannot understand the whole economy without understanding the reasons why individual decisions are made. For example, cutting income taxes may affect the overall production of products but we need to know how it will affect households and their decision as to how much of the extra disposable income will be spent and how much will be saved. Despite the close relation between micro-economics and macroeconomics, they will be treated separately because they address different issues and often take quite different approaches.

Microeconomics

How mankind has solved the problems of production and distribution are key questions that are addressed in economics. Over time, there have been three forms of social and economic system that have been used to solve the basic economic problems. These are:

- tradition
- command
- market.

Tradition is the oldest and most common means of providing the daily bread. Societies based on tradition rely on religion, customs and codes. They have well-defined ways of distributing products based on status, position or gender. Societies based on tradition are slow to adapt to change and productivity gains are negligible. Thus, they may and often do remain unchanged for hundreds of years, with little or no progress in technology and living standards. Even in Western societies, we still see elements of tradition at work in the annual village festivals that celebrate important events, the significance of which has often been lost in time.

    Command systems are based on an authoritarian code that was often superimposed on a traditional peasant society. In Ancient Egypt, the pharaohs commanded massive legions to build pyramids. Similarly, the Romans mobilised vast armies of slaves to build the roads to speed troops and trade throughout the Roman Empire. More recently, the command economies of the Soviet Union and China were powerful forces in a world where there was sharp and often bitter division on the merits of the command system. Without doubt, the command system is highly effective in mobilising resources in times of crisis and in achieving very rapid growth from a low base. Despite this, its critics point to the lack of individual freedom and its inability to offer the levels of Gross Domestic Product (GDP) per capita attained in the West.

    Market systems, in which most of the world now live, generate economic growth so that living standards rise over time at a rate unimag-ined not that long ago, so that more products, both new and improved, are made available to the masses. Because the Western world relies so heavily on the market system, it is the focus of this chapter and in the next section we show briefly how markets work.

Markets: demand, supply and price

The **market** can be defined as 'any situation in which the buyer and seller of a product communicate with each other for the purpose of exchange'.[2] Key to this process is the existence of market demand, which is the sum of individual demands, and market supply, which is the sum of individual supplies. The interaction of market demand and market supply determine market price. Traditionally, markets were physical in the sense that sellers of products would set up stalls and wait for buyers to come to market. Of course, markets like this still exist in both developed and less developed parts of the world, and they are still the main means by which products are exchanged in many poor countries. Markets may be local, regional, national or international, depending on the product. The high street coffee shop serves the local market and the coffee beans it uses are sold on the world market by major coffee suppliers and bought by commodity buyers. Likewise, the community pharmacy will serve the local community while multinational pharmaceutical companies will market worldwide many of the drugs sold there. Markets have now developed to the extent that buyers and sellers may not actually come face to face with each other. New means of communication have allowed them to engage remotely, by telephone, fax or the Internet.

Markets are not just for products – they are also for factors of production such as labour. The demand for labour is a **derived** demand, in that labour, along with land and capital, is needed because there is a demand for the products that are made using factors of production. Thus, for example, Tesco will hire pharmacists because Tesco customers require the services of pharmacists.

The law of **demand** states that 'quantity demanded and price are inversely related, all other things being equal'. That is, a rise/fall in price leads to a fall/rise in quantity demanded. The phrase 'all other things being equal' is used because, in order to look at the effect of price on quantity demanded, it is necessary to isolate it from other influences on quantity, for example income.

We can draw a graph that shows the relationship between price and quantity (see Figure 2.1). Three demand curves are shown (note that they are called curves even when, as in this graph, they are straight lines!). A change in price causes a movement along a given demand curve. Reducing the price of a product will increase the quantity demanded, and vice versa, all other things being equal.

As well as price, there are several other determinants of demand:

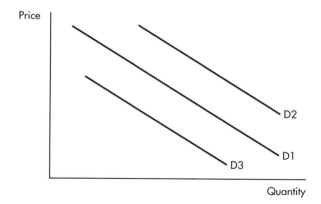

Figure 2.1 Demand curves.

- Consumer income – a rise in income causes demand for **normal products** to increase while it causes demand for **inferior products** to decrease.
- The prices of related products (substitutes and complements) – a rise/fall in the price of a substitute causes a rise/fall in demand for the product in question and a rise/fall in the price of a complement causes a fall/rise in the demand for the product in question.
- Tastes – changes in taste in favour of a product cause an increase in demand for the product.
- Demography and ageing population – as the proportion of older people in the population rises through time, there will be a rise in the demand for products demanded by old people, e.g. healthcare, and there will be a fall in the demand from young people for products such as baby clothes.
- Income distribution – taking income from the well off and giving it to the less well off (via redistributive taxes) may cause the well off to consume fewer luxuries and the less well off to consume fewer inferior products.
- Expectations – if prices are expected to rise, people will buy now at the current price rather than wait until prices have risen.

Changes in any of the determinants of demand, other than the price of the product in question, cause demand to increase (shift to the right, say from D1 to D2) or decrease (shift to the left, say from D1 to D3). Does the law of demand always apply in every case? The answer is no. There may be some exceptions to the law of demand – including the cases of prestige products, 'Giffen' products and conspicuous consumption products. The usual examples of **Giffen products** are rice and potatoes, which are consumed by people on very low incomes. Such people spend a high proportion of their income on such inferior products. When their prices fall, they are able to reduce their consumption of these products, consuming instead better ones. In **conspicuous consumption,** someone wanting others to know 'just how much they paid for something' will buy conspicuous quantities of certain products. They gain satisfaction from the apparent envy they think this may induce in others. To some, high price equals high quality, but to others it has a value that is more elitist. For more on the exceptions to the law of demand see reference.[3]

These exceptions may result in a **perverse demand curve,** as shown in Figure 2.2, but note that this is definitely the exceptional case.

The **market supply** of a product is the total that all producers are willing and able to offer for sale in a certain time period. The determinants of supply in a **competitive** industry – that is one where there are many firms selling identical products and where entry and exit are easy – are as follows:

- Price – the higher/lower the price the higher/lower will be supply. As price rises, existing firms are likely to expand production to make more revenue and profits. New firms may also be attracted to the industry, further expanding quantity supplied.
- Prices of other certain products – a wheat farmer would be encouraged to switch to barley if the price of barley rose, all other things being equal. Wheat and barley here are substitutes in production.

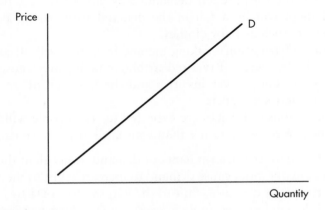

Figure 2.2 Perverse demand curves.

Substitutes in production are not always substitutes in demand and vice versa.

- Prices of factors of production – costs rise when the price of a factor rises. This may cause supply to fall as profits are reduced and some firms may lose money, forcing them out of business. As a result, supply goes down.
- Technology – innovations can increase output. A new and better machine might increase the speed of making aspirin tablets, increasing output and leading to increased profits and thus a rise in supply.
- Expectations – if firms expect prices to rise in the future they may reduce the amount they supply now so they can supply more later.
- Objectives of producers – firms can have different objectives that affect the decisions made. Traditionally, profit maximisation was the sole objective, but modern theories acknowledge that firms may have objectives such as sales revenue maximisation or managerial utility maximisation. It is hardly likely that the objectives of a corner shop would be exactly the same as those of a multinational company.

Figure 2.3 shows three supply curves. As with demand, a movement along a curve is caused by a change in the price of the product in question. A shift in the curve (for example from S1 to S2) is caused by a change in any of the other factors affecting supply. A shift to the right (S1 to S2) represents an increase in supply (at all prices), while a shift to the left (S1 to S3) represents a decrease in supply (again at all prices).

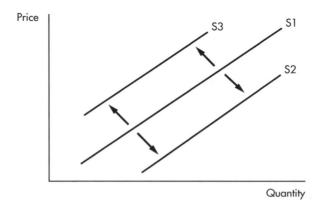

Figure 2.3 Supply curves.

Price determination

We are now in a position to see how price is determined and how it can change. By drawing both market supply and market demand curves on the same graph we can see that they intersect at price P*. This called the **equilibrium** or **market clearing** price because it is the price that equates market supply and market demand (Figure 2.4).

At P*, there is neither a surplus nor a shortage. However, suppose that price were for some reason above P*. Then Qs (quantity supplied) would exceed Qd (quantity demanded), there would be a surplus and price would fall to P* in response to excess stocks held by producers, at which point the surplus would be eliminated. Alternatively, suppose for some reason price were below P*. Then Qd would exceed Qs and there would be a shortage. Producers will respond by raising the price until the equilibrium price P* is reached, at which point the shortage disappears. If it works well, the operation of the market will automatically eliminate shortages and surpluses and restore equilibrium (Figure 2.5).

Once we have an equilibrium position, a new equilibrium can only be reached if there is a shift in either the demand curve or the supply curve, or both. This would be caused by one or more changes in any of the factors affecting supply and demand, except for the price of the product. For example, if tastes change in favour of a product, demand increases (the demand curve shifts to the right), causing both equilibrium price and quantity to rise. By way of example, consider aspirin. Suppose the demand for aspirin has increased as a result of good reports of its effects in reducing heart attacks and strokes. This would raise both equilibrium price and quantity. As usual, we have to qualify all of these effects with the statement 'all other things being equal'.

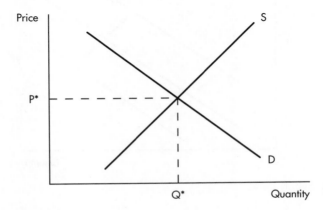

Figure 2.4 Market equilibrium.

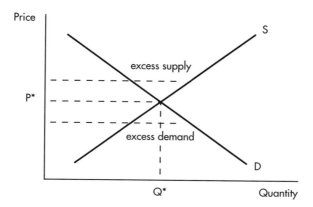

Figure 2.5 Restoring equilibrium.

In applying this theory to real business situations, a serious problem that we face is to know what is actually happening when price and quantity change. We often do not know what has caused any observed changes because there are so many variables affecting both supply and demand, any of which may change at any time. In theory, it would be possible to identify the demand curve or the supply curve if we could hold one of them firmly in position. However, we are not in the laboratory and we do not have control over any of the factors affecting demand and supply. Therefore, we cannot be certain as to what causes changes in price and quantity. This is known as the **identification problem**.

Price elasticity

A firm considering a price rise has to consider how much its sales will drop following the increase. If the law of demand applies, the firm knows that it will suffer some drop in sales, but will it be a small drop or a big drop? In addition, what happens to sales revenue – will it fall, rise or stay the same? The concept of **price elasticity of demand** is important here. This measures the sensitivity or responsiveness of quantity to price changes. Price elasticity of demand, ε is the percentage change in quantity caused by a 1% change in price. The formula is given by:

$$\varepsilon = \frac{\dfrac{\Delta Q}{Q}}{\dfrac{\Delta P}{P}}$$

where

Q = quantity originally sold
ΔQ = change in quantity sold
P = original price
ΔP = change in price

To see how it works let us take the example of a pharmacy considering raising the price of an over-the-counter brand of paracetamol. Suppose the price is currently 75p and a 10p rise is being considered. The new price of 85p is agreed and the price is changed. It is found that the new price reduces sales from 25 to 20 packets per day. Thus

$$\Delta P = +10p, P = 75p$$
$$\Delta Q = -5, Q = 25$$

then

$$\varepsilon = \frac{\dfrac{-5}{25}}{\dfrac{+10}{75}} = -1.5$$

Note that ε is always negative. Its magnitude can vary but if we ignore the negative sign and find that ε is less than 1 (but greater than zero), we have **inelastic** demand. If on the other hand it is greater than 1 (again ignoring the sign), we have **elastic** demand. So, in our example, because ε at -1.5 is greater than 1 (ignoring the sign), demand is elastic. This means that quantity is **sensitive** to price changes. A firm thinking of raising its price must then be very careful because, in our example, if it raises price by 10%, sales fall by 15% ($-1.5 = \dfrac{-1.5\%}{10\%}$). In real life, managers are unlikely to have precise estimates of price elasticities. A point to note is that price elasticity varies along the demand curve so even if a manager has a good idea as to the value of price elasticity at one price, they will not know it at a different price.

This is where knowledge, experience and instinct may be useful in gauging the effects of price changes. Generally, however, price elasticity of demand will be low/high where:

- there are few/many substitutes for the product
- the purchase price forms a small/large proportion of a buyer's income
- little/much time has elapsed since a price change.

To illustrate, again consider the case of paracetamol. Suppose that for some reason (such as a rise in the costs of raw materials), there is a rise in the price of paracetamol. Assume also that paracetamol is supplied in a competitive market (i.e. by lots of companies). By how much does the quantity demanded drop when price rises? Will it drop a lot or a little?

This can be answered by reference to the three key factors above. First, there are several close substitutes for paracetamol (aspirin, ibuprofen and combinations), so the price rise is likely to reduce the demand for paracetamol as some buyers switch to other products. Second, because paracetamol is cheap, the purchase will represent only a small proportion of the buyer's income, so little change in quantity demanded would be expected. Third, the price remains relatively constant. Thus, in this case, it takes virtually no time or effort on the part of buyers to make the switch from aspirin to a substitute. What then can we deduce from this about the likely magnitude of price elasticity of demand for paracetamol? The first and third factors would suggest that price elasticity of demand would be high while the second factor would suggest that it would be low. The actual value will depend on which of the factors is most important in the purchase decision. The likelihood is that because it is so cheap, a rise in its price of a few pence is unlikely to have a significant effect on demand and price elasticity is therefore likely to be low. In practice the situation may be influenced by a perception of efficacy or brand loyalty.

Although it is obvious for many products what the substitutes actually are, it is not always apparent. For example, it is evident that among analgesics, aspirin, ibuprofen and paracetamol are close substitutes. Altogether, the three – sold separately or in combination – comprise just about all of the analgesic market. But what about something like private medical insurance (PMI)? What are the substitutes for PMI? Until recently there were no real alternatives on the market, but the development of critical illness policies, healthcare cash plans, one-off payment for treatment and the like have provided some competition and it is therefore right to include them as substitutes for PMI. Still in the area of health and drugs, an interesting question is whether conventional medicines and complementary medicines are substitutes or complement each other. Two views are commonly held: first that they are typically used to treat different ailments and they are therefore complements, and second, they offer alternative ways of treating the same ailments and are therefore substitutes. To some extent both are true: headaches for example can be treated by an analgesic or by a herbal or homoeopathic remedy, so in this case the conventional and complementary medicines are actually substitutes. A cold's symptoms might be treated by taking an analgesic and by a complementary medicine such as echinacea, which is thought by some users to build up resistance to colds. In this case the two are definitely complementary. So it is not a simple matter of making hard and fast rules: what may be substitutes under certain circumstances may be complements in others.

There are other types of elasticity that should be mentioned. **Cross price elasticity** of demand refers to how sensitive the quantity demand for one product is to change in the price of another. The formula is:

$$\varepsilon_c = \left[\frac{\dfrac{\Delta Q_A}{Q_A}}{\dfrac{\Delta P_B}{P_B}}\right] \text{ where A and B represent different products.}$$

It is useful for firms to know how sales might be affected by changes in the prices of a competitor's products. For example, Boots having a special offer on ibuprofen may hit Superdrug's sales of ibuprofen and of substitutes for ibuprofen such as paracetamol. The same might apply to complements as well as substitutes. Complements can be a result of tastes or technical compliance. Examples of taste complements are fish and chips, strawberries and cream; examples of technical complements are drills and drill bits, DVD players and DVDs.

Income elasticity of demand is the sensitivity of quantity to changes in income, or

$$\varepsilon_i = \left[\frac{\dfrac{\Delta Q}{Q}}{\dfrac{\Delta Y}{Y}}\right] \text{ where Y is income.}$$

As alluded to earlier, a change in income can either increase or decrease the demand for a product, depending on whether the product is classed as normal or inferior. Normal products can be either necessities such as basic foodstuffs or luxuries like champagne.

Market power

Firms that are considered to have market power can set prices without fear of losing their entire market share. Firms in monopolistic competition, oligopoly and monopoly have such market power. A firm with no market power would lose the whole of its market share if it were to raise its prices. Firms that have market power are called price makers and firms that have no market power are called price takers. There are several factors that give firms market power, discussed below.

- **Lack of competitors.** Firms such as the Royal Mail, Yellow Pages and De Beers, which all have well over 70% of the markets in which they operate, face little competition from rivals. They are thus able to set prices with little fear that they will exact any sort of hurtful response from rivals. They still face a downward-sloping demand curve and have to be mindful of the effect on the market of raising prices too much even when, as with the Royal Mail, they have no direct competitors. Pharmaceutical companies whose products are protected by patent are in a very strong position because they may have no direct competitors until the patent expires. They can thus charge high prices to cover the costs of R&D and earn large profits before generics provide competition.

- **Customer loyalty.** Customers sometimes have dogged and long-lasting preferences for various products and sources of supply. They are loyal to particular products, even though they may not offer the best value for money, or to outlets that do not offer the best prices. Why should this be? Are consumers behaving in an irrational way? The answer is no – customers who go to the corner shop rather than the supermarket may do so for a number of reasons – speed, convenience, proximity and friendliness. For whatever reasons, some people are prepared to pay higher prices to benefit from one or more of the features offered by the corner shop. With certain retail activities, some people may prefer to take advantage of the expertise that shop owners have accumulated by specialising in a narrow range of products. This is true in the case of bikes and hi-fi equipment, for example, where specialist shops are the norm and where good advice can normally be obtained. The same may also apply to community pharmacies that have for many years been very supportive of the local community. Whether people will stay loyal following the abolition of resale price maintenance (RPM) in May 2001, leading to lower prices in the bigger outlets, is open to question.

- **Product differentiation.** Various features such as attractive packaging, branding, advertising and promotion are used to differentiate products from each other. By differentiating its products from those of its rivals a firm can exploit its market power and charge more for them. A small price rise is unlikely to deter buyers of products with strong brand identities from buying those products. Price elasticity is reduced by product differentiation. Firms may actively pursue what is known as 'intertemporal' product differentiation by introducing innovations through time and 'spatial' product differentiation by filling gaps in product lines. Paint manufacturers now have ranges that cover all eventualities and golf ball makers seem now to provide a golf ball for every ability and playing condition.

- **Location.** Location can be a source of market power. A prime location can give a retailer an edge over its rivals. A one-stop shopping experience that is offered by supermarkets is now more likely to include banking and pharmacy services. Supermarket chains such as Tesco and Sainsbury have in recent times moved to increase their provision of such services. The implication of choosing a location in which to open a new pharmacy is discussed in Chapter 5.
- **Ownership of natural resources.** Firms will have market power in cases where the number of producers is limited by physical factors, such as with spring water, oil, diamonds and precious metals.
- **Effects of government policies and regulation.** The provision of patents (common with new drugs), licences for mobile phones, broadcasting, professional activities (medical professions) and the like can create market power.

Achieving and sustaining market power

Achieving market power and sustaining it are quite different things. Some companies have managed to maintain their market position for many years: GE, the huge US conglomerate, has been in existence for 125 years; BP was established at the turn of the last century; Philip Morris goes back to the middle of the 19th century; and among UK companies with familiar names such as Boots and Marks and Spencer have been leaders in their field for many years. These companies have established and sustained market power over a long period. On the other hand, business history is littered with examples of companies like Courtaulds, British Leyland and Triumph whose once dominant positions crumbled. Although not as dramatic in terms of the enormous scale of the loss of market share, other prominent examples of losing market share to competitors are GM losing out to Toyota; British Airways to the low-cost, no-frills fliers such as EasyJet and Ryanair; CBS to CNN; the BBC to BSkyB; and RCA to Sony. The reasons for these shifts were manifold. They included firm or industry-specific changes, low entry or mobility barriers that allowed firms to enter from within an industry or from outside it, failure to identify early enough changes in technology or consumer tastes, lack of a correct strategic response, bad luck, etc.

Competitive advantage

Another way of approaching market power is from a business strategy viewpoint. The terminology used in the strategy literature is somewhat different and it offers some insights into the actions of firms. For instance, where economists would use the term **market power**, business strategists use **competitive advantage**.

The strategic view

If we consider a perfect market where consumers are assumed to have perfect information, entry barriers are low, switching costs are negligible, products are identical (homogeneous) and there are many sellers, customers reject that firm's products and buy from a firm offering the product at the lower (market) price. In the long run, firms cannot charge a price that is above that set in the market. This is because price is the sole factor determining whether or not a sale takes place. If the price is above the competitive level, as where products are differentiated (i.e. have some competitive advantage), the outcome is quite different. Because firms have managed to distinguish their products from those of their rivals they can increase price somewhat and not lose all of their sales to other firms.

Creation of extra value

Competitive advantage is the ability of a firm to make a higher profit than its rivals. A competitive advantage is sustainable when such high profit rates persist over time despite attempts by rivals to steal them. This creation of extra value depends on a firm's **stock of resources** (patents, brand names, key people) and its **distinctive capabilities** (activities the firm does better than its competitors). Distinctive capabilities consist of architecture, reputation and innovation. Architecture is the network of relational contracts in which a structure, style and set of routines is established to motivate employees and suppliers. Reputation matters where quality is important, such as in international hotel chains and luxury vehicles. It can take a long time to build up but can be a strong source of market power. Innovations are not always protected by patents and are better shielded when architecture is robust and reputation intact.[4] For a firm to have a competitive advantage over its rivals the implication is that resources and capabilities are not evenly distributed among firms and the asymmetry must persist through time. This resource asymmetry is the key characteristic of an important strategic framework that has emerged in the last 10 years – the resource-based theory of the firm. The main premise of this theory is that for competitive advantage to be sustainable, resources and capabilities must be scarce and imperfectly mobile so that markets to exchange resources and capabilities do not exist. Resources are immobile because:

- Knowhow and assets cannot be easily transferred from one firm to another.
- Experience is gained over time.
- Company image is intangible.
- Some assets are non-tradeable.

Competitive advantage can also be preserved by deterring market entrants by one or more of the following strategies:

- Limit pricing (deliberately charging less than profit-maximising prices in order to deter entry).
- Understating profits (by concealing profits made in monopolised parts of companies with many subsidiaries).
- Predatory pricing and 'dumping'.
- Over-investment in production capacity and extending product ranges to fill any gaps.

Threats to sustaining competitive advantage

External factors may be such that firms have little or no control over their plight. For example, the downturn in the demand for air travel after the terrorist attacks on New York has left a number of airlines and related companies in real difficulty (US Airways and three similar airlines have recently been declared bankrupt). Less dramatic but just as serious to the (short-term) fortunes of many companies are acts of God such as earthquakes and floods (most recently in central Europe).

A good example of riches to rags and to riches again (comparatively) is the tale of Domino's Pizza. First mover in the home pizza delivery business and guaranteeing delivery within 30 minutes or the pizza would be free, Domino's had 90% of the US delivered pizza market. By 1991 this had fallen to 41% and losses were experienced for the first time since the 1970s. What triggered this fall from grace? Two things: entry by Pizza Hut on the back of heavy advertising and promotion with higher quality products, by Little Caesar's offering two pizzas for the price of one; and a lawsuit where the company was ordered to pay US$78 million to a woman injured by a Domino's delivery van.

This marked the end of the guaranteed 30-minute deliveries. So, a combination of entry by powerful rivals and bad luck heralded the end of Domino's lofty position in the US delivered pizza market. However, in the 1990s, Domino's responded with a series of new product offerings, effectively diversifying its operations, and by internationalisation. In 1999 it reported record results, which were followed by even better results in 2001.

Reputation and buyer uncertainty

Consider a firm with an established reputation. It may, like some of the firms mentioned above, have been in business for the best part of a century. How do new entrants overcome brand loyalty and reputation? There are two ways, both of which adversely affect profitability – reducing price below the incumbent's price and through advertising campaigns that increase costs (see Chapter 12). Why should consumers defect from established brands that work unless they are persuaded to by (much) lower prices and/or heavy advertising and promotion? The established firm has earned its reputation and the stronger this is, the higher the 'cost' of overcoming it.

Buyer switching costs

Switching costs arise when buyers have knowledge of products that cannot be transferred to rival products. It implies that consumers face an extra cost in learning how to use new products and incumbent firms can exploit this by astute pricing. Switching costs benefit early movers who can set a price that would deter entry by new firms.

Market failure – the case for government intervention

In recent years many countries have come to rely more heavily on the market to allocate resources. We have seen privatisation and deregulation in many areas of economic life. This has meant that we now rely on the market for products that once were provided almost exclusively by the state. As long ago as 1776, Adam Smith suggested that, by pursuing their own self-interest, people are led by 'an invisible hand' to promote the interests of society as a whole. In his now famous statement he said: 'It is not by the benevolence of the butcher, the brewer or the baker and that we expect our dinner, but from their regard to their own interest'.[5]

Yet governments are still expected to build and maintain roads, to provide the legal framework, to school our young people, to run the healthcare system and to provide social protection. They are also expected to regulate businesses, which for all kinds of reasons cannot be left to their own devices. There is possibly no more regulated industry than pharmaceuticals, which is faced with a myriad of controls and regulations. These include licences for manufacturers, distributors and pharmacies; competition rulings; rules about the location of new pharmacies; price controls for OTC medicines and generics; remuneration for NHS prescriptions; and so on. If there is an invisible hand, and markets allocate resources efficiently so that consumer wants are met efficiently, then why should governments intervene in the economy? This is because markets sometimes *fail* and market failure is the main argument for government intervention in the economy.

Market failure is the inability of the market to produce a level of output that fulfils all society's needs. There are several reasons why markets may fail to produce a socially optimal level of output.

Public products

Certain products would not be provided without the intervention of the state – for example the legal system, a defence force, lighthouses, a sewerage system, schools, roads, pavements and hospitals – but much of the provision of these products is by dint of state action. A pure public product is a product or service that is consumed by everyone and from which no one can be excluded, defence being the best example. It has two characteristics – non-rivalry, where one person's consumption of a product does not reduce another's consumption, and non-excludability, where no one can be excluded from consuming the product.

This leads to the so-called free rider problem. A person who consumes a product without paying for it is a free rider. If it is easy to free ride then it is going to be difficult to get people to pay for the product. If enough people do not pay, the product would not be provided at all, hence the need for government intervention.

Immobility of factors and time lags

In the real world, factors such as capital and labour may be slow to respond to what the market needs. For instance, suppose there is an increased demand for pharmacists. The operation of supply and demand will drive up salaries. This will feed down to school-leavers, who will see pharmacy as a more lucrative career, with the result that more school-leavers will want to study it. But more pharmacists will be produced only if more places can be found in the schools of pharmacy for them to train to be pharmacists. The state can speed up the process by which more places are made available by giving more resources to pharmacy schools and/or encouraging the establishment of new schools.

Imperfect information – ignorance and uncertainty

It is assumed under perfect competition that consumers have perfect knowledge about prices and products. This may be the case in the purchase of consumer products but in the case of financial services and healthcare, full and correct information is much more difficult to obtain and the consequences of purchasing the wrong service are much more serious.

Externalities

An externality is said to exist when the production or consumption of a product directly affects producers or consumers not involved in the buying or selling of it and when these spillover effects are not reflected in market prices. Externalities may be good or bad. When people are made better off by an activity there are said to be **external benefits** – a person having a flu jab makes others less likely to catch it. When people are made worse off there are said to be **external costs** – for example, non-smokers suffer because smokers choose to smoke in confined spaces. Market prices do not take into account external costs and benefits and the state can attempt to correct externalities by taxing products that impose external costs and subsidising those that confer external benefits. Green taxes are a good example of the state's attempts to correct externalities associated with CO_2 emissions, waste, congestion, etc.

Conclusions

This brief section has barely scratched the surface of the ways in which economics can be used to inform business activity. There are many good foundation texts that will fill the gaps. For readers who want to know more about how economics is used to analyse business strategies an excellent text is *The Economics of Strategy* by David Besanko *et al.*[6] The next section looks at some aspects of the macroeconomy.

Macroeconomics

Introduction

Macroeconomics is a relatively young and imprecise discipline. Issues such as employment, inflation and growth affect everyone in the economy and all of these issues have at some time grabbed the headlines. High unemployment, rapid inflation and stagnation have given rise to concern at various times in both our recent and distant past.

It is vital for business people to have a working knowledge of economy-wide issues and, just as important, to know where to look for information on these issues. To be able to interpret the signals and messages about the economy that come every day from industry, the media and government bodies and to see the effect on their business in the coming year(s) is a necessary skill for a business manager. Understanding these signals does not mean that managers need a thorough grounding in macroeconomics but it does mean that they are able to recognise the signals, know how important they are and make sound judgements as to future courses of action.

Because governments have a pervasive influence on the macro-economy, macroeconomics and political debate go hand in hand. Governments have control over the policies that attempt to manage the rate of inflation, the level of unemployment, and so on. When the economy is doing well, governments tend to do well. However, macro-economic management by governments is a controversial area and there is a great deal of disagreement about how economies work and about the best ways to manage them.

One of the main areas of macroeconomic debate in the UK and Europe in the last few years has been whether to adopt the euro, the European single currency. While most EU countries have done so, others such as the UK and Denmark have opted to stay out of the euro zone. The decision on whether to have a common currency is a political as well as an economic one. Its impact will be political, economic and social. Macroeconomics can help us understand this debate and enable us to see the effects of staying out or going in. It can even provide various tests that must be passed in order for it to be prudent to enter. The decision to adopt the euro is one that is taken by a nation's leaders based on the full range of information.

Macroeconomics and the business manager

There is no doubt that the business manager should have a working knowledge of the macroeconomy. This does not mean that they understand all of the finer points and nuances of the exchange rate system, money and banking. Nor should the major controversies be of particular concern. Attention to these matters will only serve to distract a non-specialist from understanding the basics of the macroeconomy. A car driver does not need to know how an engine works to drive a car but it does help to be aware of the normal sound of an engine and know what flashing lights on the dashboard actually mean! In the same way, a manager should be able to interpret the economic signals that come from the media and from government publications. For instance, a stock market fall, an increase in the rate at which house prices are rising or a reduction in interest rates by the Bank of England all tell us something about the way the economy is moving and managers should be able to see the implications for their business.

To be more effective, managers operating in the UK should at least have a working knowledge of the following:

- The UK economy and its many features.
- The basic causes and implications of cycles in economic activity.
- How the UK economy interacts with other economies and how changes in other major economies might affect the UK economy.
- How the exchange rate is determined and what happens when sterling rises or falls against other major currencies such as the euro and the dollar.
- Who are the UK's major trading partners and what and why do we trade.
- How the interest rate is set and what are the effects on the economy of higher or lower rates.
- The broad effects of government fiscal policies (taxes and government spending) on the economy.
- The broad effects of changes in tax rates, interest rates and exchange rates on their business.
- The importance of economic data such as leading indicators of economic activity and the crucial role of expectations.

The above list is intended purely as a guide to what business people ought to know to be more effective managers; it is certainly not designed to be exhaustive. The intention is to focus on one or two areas that will help managers to see what is happening in the macroeconomy and to be able to judge and assess press and government reports on its future prospects. We focus on indicators and some general areas to show how some of the main features of the macroeconomy are related to each other. Many of the broadsheet newspapers and various websites provide excellent coverage of macroeconomics. The Internet has allowed everyone to find answers to the 'simple' questions such as what is the rate of inflation or how many people are unemployed. However, it does not provide answers to questions such as what is the *right* interest rate for the economy? or should unemployment benefit be raised? These questions can only be answered by resort to argument and debate informed by an understanding of the salient issues.

Forecasting

The area of macroeconomic forecasting is one where imprecision can be costly. Forecasting is one area of macroeconomics in which interest has started to grow again. In the UK, as in other countries, many major bodies like the Bank of England, the UK Treasury, the National Institute for Economic and Social Research and London Business School's Centre for Economic Forecasting produce detailed forecasts for the UK economy.

   Macroeconomic forecasters try to forecast all of the main macroeconomic variables: inflation, unemployment, growth, exchange rates, interest rates, and so on. The forecasts are used by governments and businesses to plan for the future. It is important that they base their plans on forecasts that are as accurate as possible and sometimes forecasters do provide very good forecasts, but quite often they get it seriously wrong. Simple statistics can be misleading, as the following example illustrates. Suppose economic growth forecasters run their computer models, do their sums, and put next year's growth rate at 2.5%, but it actually turns out to be, say, 1.5%. The error might only be 1 percentage point (2.5–1.5%) but this is a large percentage of the forecast value, 40% to be exact (1 in 2.5). Why do forecasters, with all of these fancy mathematical and statistical models, sometimes get it so wrong? Researchers at Oxford University suggest that it is not because of poor methods, bad models or faulty data but is the result of the impact of large unexpected events (shocks), such as the financial liberalisation of the late 1980s. The future is very unpredictable mainly 'because of the things we don't know we don't know'. The solution, according to researchers, is to rapidly adjust the forecasts once they start to go wrong.[7]

   In cases where forecasters wish to give an indication of the likely range of error surrounding the accuracy of a forecast they can provide a **forecast interval** around a **point forecast,** the point forecast being the most likely outcome. They can also use **density forecasts,** as the Bank of England now does with inflation and GDP growth. Here a **fan chart,** where forecast values fan out in the future, with colours that become lighter the further into the future the forecasts go, indicates that there is less certainty the further ahead the bank tries to forecast. Figure 2.6 shows the Bank of England inflation forecast from November 2002 (RPIX – see later for an explanation), with a point forecast of 2.5% (the target value) fanning out and becoming lighter as we go into 2004.

The cost of using inaccurate forecasts can be very high. Governments that plan to spend on the basis of a forecast growth rate that is higher than the actual growth rate will find that it does not have as much tax revenue to play with. Its spending plans may have to be curtailed or it will have to borrow to raise the extra revenue if it wishes to fulfil its plans.

We have said that governments are inextricably intertwined in the running of the economy. But what should be the aims of government with respect to the macroeconomy? The answer for a mixed economy like those in the Western world is one that almost everyone will now

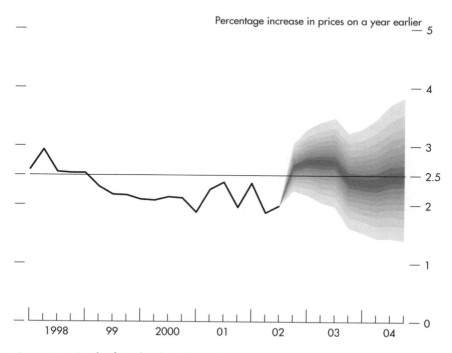

Figure 2.6 Bank of England's inflation forecasts (RPIX).

agree with: that macroeconomic management should attempt to provide stability in the macroeconomy. This means a stable fiscal framework – a tax and government spending regime to encourage firms and people to be enterprising, low and steady inflation so that the rapid inflation of the 1970s does not recur, and a steady growth rate that avoids the booms and depressions of the last century. This is the legacy of the Thatcher governments of the 1980s, which put stability, and the eradication of inflation, as top macroeconomic targets.

A brief look at the historical background will help us to see why stability is so important. It was only in the aftermath of the Great Depression of the 1930s and after the Second World War that governments took responsibility for managing economies. Before that it was believed that it was not the place of government to get involved – economies were believed to be self-regulating. In the Great Depression, when unemployment was as high as 30% and it was persistent, economists and politicians realised that markets did not work as well as they had thought. The labour market was the classic case. When wages failed to fall as a response to excess supply of labour (as the neoclassical model had predicted) and unemployment persisted, a new solution had to be found. That solution, to view the macroeconomy in a completely different way, was provided by John Maynard Keynes, who single-handedly transformed the approach of governments across the world. Keynes said that governments had to be proactive in managing the economy – in maintaining low unemployment and avoiding catastrophes like the Great Depression.

The Great Depression was indeed a catastrophe for the economies of the Western world, which had grown to become economic power-houses with unprecedented high standards of living for its people. The time before the Great Depression was one of rapid growth in many economies, notably the USA, where the preceding 100 years had seen record growth and rapidly rising living standards. This was brought to an abrupt and shocking end by the Great Depression, which saw a disastrous stock market crash and a collapse in the rate of capital formation (new housing, manufacturing plant and equipment, commercial building, and so on). Capital formation (often called capital investment) is the driving force behind a dynamic economy and when it falls, the economy suffers from unemployment and lack of output in these industries and from the knock-on effects in other industries that do not replace worn-out or obsolete equipment or do not expand by buying new equipment. The collapse in capital formation was seen by Heilbroner and Milberg[1] as the primary cause of the Great Depression in the USA.

These are the macroeconomic issues we have been talking about. Although macroeconomic factors may seem to be far removed from the day-to-day running of companies, they do have a strong influence on performance. For example, a fall in the base interest rate (an economy-wide change), which causes all interest rates to fall, may boost demand for products (especially large items financed by bank loans, such as cars and holidays) by reducing borrowing costs. It may also increase the demand for other products as householders find that lower mortgage payments release money to spend elsewhere. Finally, firms may buy capital equipment to replace or expand their current stock, as it is cheaper to borrow the money from banks.

So, the influence of an economy-wide change may be clearly felt (after some time) in the individual firm. It is up to managers to predict what might happen to sales and to have enough stocks or productive capacity on hand to meet any increase that may arise. This may mean, for example, that the company would need to hire more labour.

The Virtual Economy Model

A very good way of learning about the fundamentals of the macroeconomy is to use the Virtual Economy Model produced by Biz/ed and the Institute of Fiscal Studies (IFS) (http://www.bized.ac.uk/virtual/economy). This is a simplified version of the model used by the Chancellor of the Exchequer to chart the effects of changing tax rates, interest rates, etc. (policy instruments) on the various targets such as inflation and unemployment. Users can go in and play Chancellor and change the policy instruments to see the effect on the targets. Also on the website are sections explaining the basic theory underlying the relationships contained in the model. This is a good way of seeing macroeconomics in action and learning about the connectedness of macroeconomic variables.

This chapter focuses initially on the indexes and indicators that will help a non-specialist to interpret macroeconomic information.

Macroeconomic indexes and indicators

Economic indexes and leading indicators give a relatively simple and easily interpreted summary of the changes that have been taking place in key economic variables. Business people need to be aware of what is going on around them and the main reason why one might want to examine indexes and leading indicators is in order to assess whether or not it is the right time to invest in new products or processes. It will also help decide where to invest – either in a region of this country or abroad. Governments are also interested in these kinds of index, as a measure of how well their country is performing relative to other countries. Aggregate indicators can be thought of as falling into three main categories:

- Leading indicators and basic aggregate macroeconomic indexes.
- Macroeconomic indicators based on the actual and intended economic behaviour of individuals and organisations at the microeconomic level. These include, for example, surveys of the attitudes and intentions of samples of key participants in the economy.
- Measures of a country's overall attractiveness as a place in which to do business, both in terms of investment and production, and in terms of market potential.

The distinction can be somewhat arbitrary, as in many cases different types of data can be found in the same sources, or indeed some data, for example exchange rates, would fit into more than one category. The distinction is introduced purely in order to help readers organise the bewilderingly large amount of data they will be confronted with when they attempt to use this information.

Some examples of the kinds of macroeconomic variables and sources of information on macroeconomic data are presented below.

Leading indicators

Leading indicators are used to signal changes in the economy – specifically peaks and troughs in the business cycle. They are compiled by an organisation called the Conference Board. Two indexes are of interest:

- The index of leading indicators (called the leading index).
- The coincident index.

The indexes are weighted averages of a number of indicators, including those measuring consumer confidence, the number of house building starts and the whole economy productivity.

Figure 2.7 shows the UK leading and coincident indexes over a 12-year period. In the leading index at the top, the trend is for the line to rise over time but there were falls in 1990 and 1992 when the country was in the grip of a recession. This was followed by a general rise up to 1998, during which there was a big fall. The year 2001 saw a further fall and in 2002 the index fluctuated, and the October 2002 level is 4.5% below the February 2001 peak. The rise in the coincident index is steadier, with a continuous rise from the early 1990s. Historically, the

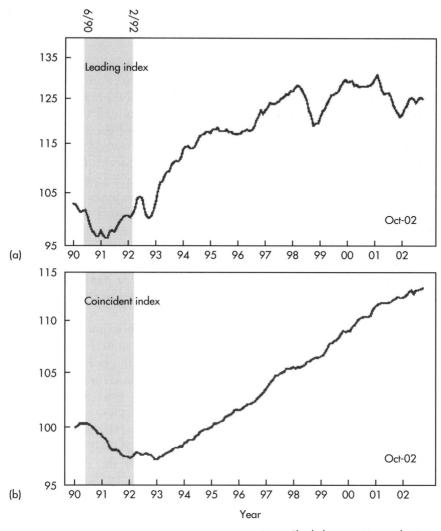

Figure 2.7 (a) Leading and (b) coincident indexes for the UK, 1990 to October 2002 (1990 = 100).

cyclical turning points in the leading index have occurred before those in the economy, while cyclical turning points in the coincident index occur at the same time as changes in the economy. A cyclical turning point can be said to occur when there is a change in direction in an index that is sufficiently large, lasts long enough and is widespread. History has shown that for the USA, a recession is likely to occur when the fall in the index is at least 2%, it lasts over 6 months and at least half of the components of the index are similarly affected.

What can be inferred from the leading indicators? Should a company considering expanding its business pay heed to leading indicators? If the indicators truly predict what will happen in the real economy, then falls in the indexes might indicate that economic activity will be dampened, people will spend less, sales will be less buoyant and profits will suffer. However, not all sectors will suffer equally. Products whose sales are not sensitive to falls in income (e.g. necessities like basic foodstuffs) will suffer less than those that are sensitive to falls in income. Large retailers are unlikely to see much change in the demand for basic foods, but demand for their premium items may fall. The demand for other 'luxury' items like yachts and holidays is also sensitive to falls in income. Therefore, a downturn will affect different sectors differently and firms need to be aware of this. The indexes will help them to see what may happen in the real economy and, knowing the income elasticity of demand for their products, what then is likely to be the effect on sales of their products.

Output, income and growth   Measures of national output include gross domestic product (GDP). GDP is calculated by summing the values added in each productive sector. A measure of GDP per head of population is often used as an indicator of living standards in a country. It also says something about how rich each person is on average and indicates the potential buying power of people in a country.

A country's rate of growth is usually taken as the annual rate of growth of GDP. A typical average rate of growth of GDP for the more mature economies ranges from 2.5% to 4%. For the more recently industrialised economies such as the Association of Southeast Asia Nations (ASEAN) economies, rates of growth of 4–8% are not uncommon. The Organisation for Economic Co-operation and Development (OECD) (http://www.oecd.org) or the World Bank (http://www. wb.org) are good sources of this sort of information.

Prices and inflation   The Retail Prices Index (RPI) (sometimes called the headline rate of inflation) is one of the main UK indexes. It is compiled by the Office for National Statistics (ONS) and shows how prices have changed month on month. An alternative index is the underlying rate of inflation (RPIX), which is the RPI excluding mortgage interest payments. This is the inflation measure that the government uses to set its target rate, currently 2.5%. The first cost of living index was compiled in 1914 while the modern RPI was first calculated in 1947. In Europe, the Harmonised Index of Consumer Prices (HICP), which was launched in 1997, measures inflation each month in the European Monetary Union (EMU) and compares each Member State on a consistent and coordinated basis. From 10 December 2003, the UK has adopted the HICP (renamed the Consumer Prices Index (CPI)) as its main measure of inflation. The CPI differs from RPIX in product coverage (the CPI excludes most housing costs such as council tax), survey method and calculation method. The current target for CPI is 2%.

Figure 2.8 shows rates for the EMU, the EU and for each country separately, allowing for easy comparisons. Generally, the lower the better, so Ireland at close to 5%, as a result of its booming economy, and others at over 3%, should be far more concerned than those economies at under 2%. However, it should be noted that these are much lower rates than those of the 1970s and 1980s. For example, average inflation in the UK during the period 1971 to 1981 was 13.9%, and in 1982 to 1991, it was 6.0%;[3] at its worst, it was 26% in 1975.

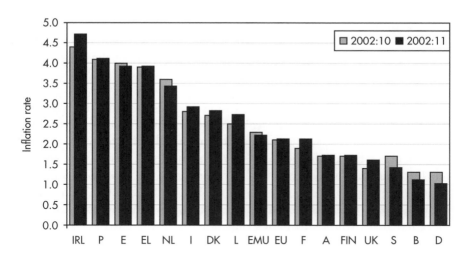

Source: Statistics Sweden and Eurostat   Data for year up to October and November 2002

EMU = Euro-zone (MUICP), EU = EU-15 (EICP), B = Belgium, DK = Denmark, D = Germany, EL = Greece, E = Spain, F = France, IRL = Ireland, I = Italy, L = Luxembourg, NL = Netherlands, A = Austria, P = Portugal, FIN = Finland, S = Sweden, UK = United Kingdom.

Figure 2.8 Inflation rate according to HICP for different countries (annualised inflation rate over the previous 12 month periods ending in October 2002 and to November 2002).

Price indexes are used by a variety of bodies such as government to determine the level of state pensions, the value of gilts and National Savings certificates and in assessing liability for capital gains tax. They are also used by employers and trade unions in pay negotiations, and by the regulators of privatised industries such as water and electricity. The HICP is used by the European Central Bank (ECB) in its evaluation of monetary policy.

Price indexes are calculated by estimating typical expenditure patterns on various different products and services in the Expenditure and Food Survey (EFS). Some 650 products make up the 'shopping basket' used to calculate the RPI. The composition of the basket is periodically changed to reflect consumers' changing buying habits as a result of busy lifestyles, changing leisure patterns and tastes. Products that people do not buy any more are dropped and new ones brought in.

It is often possible to provide rough estimates of inflation by examining monetary growth. There are various definitions of the money stock, the most basic of which, M_0, is the narrowest definition, and consists of notes and coins in circulation and the bank's operational deposits with the central bank. Usually, a wider definition, which takes account of all money deposits, is necessary to say anything meaningful about inflation. Comparative international monetary growth figures are available from the International Financial Statistics database provided by the International Monetary Fund.

Rates of interest　There are various interest rates that may be relevant. For financial institutions that deal in government debt, the appropriate rate might be the discount rate on government bills (shorter-term government debt) or bonds (longer-term government debt). Banks that deal in the Eurocurrency interbank market would pay close attention to the various interbank bid (deposit) rates and offer (lending) rates, particularly LIBOR, the London Interbank Bid/Offer Rate. LIBOR represents the marginal cost of funds to banks that borrow in the euro markets. The interest on funds that are re-lent by the banks to large corporate borrowers is usually based on LIBOR. Of more relevance to the smaller business borrower is the base rate on which interest payments tend to be based.

Employment and unemployment

Employment and unemployment are important indicators of the way economies are performing. There are two ways to measure unemployment.

The first entails doing surveys. The UK government's Labour Force Survey is done every three months and uses the International Labour Office (ILO) definition of unemployment, which is persons of working age who are without work, available for work and actively seeking employment. The second way is to use the 'claimant count', which is the number of people claiming unemployment-related benefits such as Job-seeker's Allowance. Figures for claimant count are compiled monthly.

Unemployment can be expressed as a level such as 1 million people or as a percentage, such as 5% of the workforce. The workforce is the number of people that are 'economically active'. As a rough guide to the figures, in the UK, with a population of 60 million, the workforce is 30 million and over 28 million are in work. About 19 million are 'economically inactive', of which about 10 million are over working age. The latest figures from the ONS show that for May 2004 unemployment (on the ILO measure) stood at 1.43 million (4.8% of the workforce), while the claimant count in June 2004 was 850,900. The difference arises because of the ways in which each is measured. The ILO measure is used to compare across countries while the claimant count is subject to change as the government can alter the eligibility to benefits and has frequently done so in the past, usually making it harder for people to get benefits. Each measure tells us something about unemployment. As important as the current picture is the trend – or how it has changed through time. Trend data can found on the ONS website (http://www.ons.gov.uk). The ILO website (http://www.ilo.org) is also a useful resource.

International trade

The UK is one of the most open economies in the world. It has been at the forefront of world trade for centuries and, although in the last 100 years the UK's share of world exports in manufacture, for example, has plummeted from around 33% in 1900 and 26% in 1950 to under 5% today, the UK still exports (and imports) at record levels.

International trade is necessary to provide UK citizens with the products they cannot obtain at home or prefer to get from abroad. Foreigners want to buy UK products. Britons have an almost insatiable appetite for imports, as do the citizens of many countries.

Excellent sources of international trade information are the World Trade Organization (http://www.wto.org) and http://internationalecon. com/internet-links.html, which has a wealth of links to trade, exchange rate (spot and forward), and balance of payments information.

Capital investment

Businesses may also be interested in the amount of investment (known as fixed capital formation), the ratio of investment to GDP and the amount of saving available to 'cover' domestic investment as indicated by the savings ratio. These can be found in publications such as *The OECD in Figures* (http://www.oecd.org). In addition, *World Development Indicators* (http://www.wb.org) is a good source of this kind of information.

Macroeconomic indicators based on intended or actual behaviour

Indicators based on intended behaviour

Another type of macroeconomic indicator is based on the attitudes and intentions of samples of key participants in the economy. These include sectoral surveys, such as surveys of manufacturers, on whether they expect to expand or contract, whether they plan to invest, and whether they plan to take on any additional staff.

Indicators based on actual behaviour

Stock market indexes, such as the Dow-Jones, the Hang-Sen, the Nikkei and the FT-SE, are composite price indexes that are based on a sample of (usually but not always) the most prestigious and financially sound companies listed in a particular stock market. These indexes are continually adjusting, as the buying and selling of stocks and shares respond to new information that indicates the buoyancy of the financial sector. A 'bull' market (one consisting of generally optimistic investors) is indicated by a lengthy increasing trend in stock market index numbers, while a 'bear' market (one consisting of generally pessimistic investors) is indicated by a lengthy declining trend in stock market numbers. A great deal of significance is often read into an index reaching a particular number, such as 1000 or 6000. What is probably more important is the rate at which the stock market index is increasing or decreasing, because this tells us something about the rate at which stock market prices are increasing or decreasing. So, for example, we might conclude that stock market investment is excessive if annual growth in the stock market index outstrips annual GDP growth. It could indicate financial 'overheating' and the kind of boom that is normally followed by a bust.

A light-hearted approach to macroeconomic indexes can be found in the **'Big Mac' index** published annually by the *Economist*. The idea here is to test the so-called purchasing power parity (PPP) hypothesis that, when measured in a common currency, the price of the same traded product should be the same in different countries (called the Law of One Price). This is tested by examining the price of a Big Mac, a McDonald's hamburger, in different countries.

The Big Mac index was devised in 1986 as a less than totally serious guide to whether or not currencies are at their 'correct' level. In the long run, argue PPP proponents, currencies should move towards the rate that equalises the prices of an identical basket of products and services in each country. The average US price (taken over four main cities) has fallen slightly over the past year, from $2.54 to $2.49. World-wide, the cheapest Big Mac is in Argentina ($0.78), after its massive devaluation; the priciest ($3.81) is in Switzerland. By this measure, the Argentine peso is the most undervalued currency (by 68%) and the Swiss franc the most overvalued (by 53%).

Competitiveness indicators

These are measures of a country's competitiveness and attractiveness as a place to do business. Doing business can mean various things, including simply selling to that country or setting up a subsidiary there to manufacture a product. Measures of a country's competitiveness might include supply-side measures such as relative unit labour costs, the world economic forum index of competitiveness (http://www.weforum.org), and so on. In addition to supply-side measures there are also demand-side indicators of market potential.

For most practical business purposes, macroeconomic information would have to be supplemented with sectoral information. It is surprising what can be found as a result of a few hours on the Internet, even from sources that might be considered more 'macro' than 'micro'.

References

1. Heilbroner R L, Milberg W. *The Making of Economic Society*, 11th edn. New Jersey: Prentice Hall, 2002.
2. Ison S. *Economics*, 3rd edn. London: FT, Prentice Hall, 2000, p. 15.
3. Sloman J. *Economics*, 5th edn. London: FT, Prentice Hall, 2002.
4. Kay J. *The Foundations of Corporate Success*. Oxford: OUP, 1995.
5. Smith A. *An Inquiry into the Nature and Causes of the Wealth of Nations*. New York: The Modern Library, 1937 (first published 1776), p. 14.
6. Besanko D, Dranove D, Shanley M. *The Economics of Strategy*. New York: John Wiley & Sons Inc., 2000.
7. Clements M P, Hendry D F. *A Companion to Economic Forecasting*. London: Blackwell, 2001.

Further reading

Bannock G, Baxter R E, Davis E (eds). *The Penguin Dictionary of Economics*. London: Penguin Reference Books, 2003.

Galbraith J K. *A History of Economics – The Past and Present*. London: Penguin Economics, 1991.

3

Overview of the pharmacy sector

Alan Reeves

Introduction

The UK pharmacy sector has undergone, and continues to undergo, considerable change. There are many pressures being exerted and the pace of change has, if anything, accelerated in the last few years. Not only has the structure of the industry been affected, the role of pharmacies and pharmacists is undergoing radical change. From once being seen as dispensaries, pharmacies are now being viewed as a major port of call in healthcare delivery by government and patients alike. In keeping with the change of emphasis on healthcare delivery, pharmacists will have more of a prophylactic role in promoting and maintaining good health, with patients taking much more responsibility for their own healthcare. Pharmacists will have to be aware that the future skills mix required in pharmacies will affect the roles and responsibilities of all pharmacy staff. In the future, pharmacy will be required to add more value to its products and services.

Structural change

Structural changes that are already under way or are likely to take place include:

- Increases in the concentration of sales in the hands of the big retail chains.
- Increases in the degree of vertical integration as the three main UK arms of the pan-European wholesalers have diversified into retailing.
- The threat to sole traders with the abolition of Resale Price Maintenance in May 2001 on OTC products.
- The rise in voluntary trading groups (also known as 'virtual chains') such as Numark (about 4400 members) and Nucare (about 1200 members) to attempt to strengthen the buying power and in turn price competitiveness of the sole trader sector.

- The promotion of 'one-stop shop' healthcare and the out of town retail parks as pharmacy locations.

Other changes include:

- The introduction of electronic transfer of prescriptions (ETP), whereby prescriptions written electronically by a GP are transmitted electronically to the pharmacist for dispensing. Wholesalers will need to have updated systems to deal with this if they are to be fully linked to the system.
- The setting of maximum prices for generics and reduced dispensing fees and increased clawback (discounting) by the government.
- Amendments to the control of the entry system allowing easier entry to the sector.

Table 3.1 shows that large pharmacy chains have increased their share of outlets throughout the 1990s despite the number of pharmacies staying more or less the same. The industry is not highly concentrated nationally, with the top three companies having around 28% of the total number of outlets (Table 3.2). However, judging by the increases over the 1990s in the number of outlets for groups such as Lloyds Pharmacy, Moss Pharmacy and the supermarkets, it is possible that this will increase in the future.

Distribution

The foundation of distribution in the UK is the wholesale system. There are over 10 000 prescription drugs available in the UK and retail pharmacies are not able through cost and space considerations to hold more than a fraction of these. Also, given that some 15% of ethicals make up some 80% of sales turnover,[1] it makes sense for them to hold stocks of these products and to cut down on the other less frequently prescribed medicines. Having a reliable wholesaler is therefore vital to the successful operation of a pharmacy. Wholesalers not only provide the vital distribution and stockholder functions, some will also provide technical information on the products they supply and give marketing, promotion and financial support. As well as ethicals, wholesalers will also supply OTC medicines and other goods such as toiletries. Some also offer own-label products.

In the UK, nearly four-fifths of ethical pharmaceuticals are distributed through wholesalers. The remaining one-fifth comes from manufacturers selling direct to retail outlets (retail pharmacies, hospitals,

Table 3.1 The structure of the retail pharmacy sector in 1991, 1995 and 2002

Size of chain	1991		1995		2002	
	Number	%	Number	%	Number	%
Over 50 stores	2388	20	3488	28	–	–
21–50 stores	237	2	100	1	–	–
6–20 stores	4985	4	428	3	–	–
1–5 stores	8843	74	8275	68	–	–
Total	11953	100	12251	100	11877	100

Source: Competition Commission (1996).[2]
Mulholland D. Full-line wholesaling: regionals go national, national go European, *Pharm J* 2002; 268: 107–109.

dispensing doctors) and through self-supply within the large retails chains such as Boots and Lloyds. Retail pharmacies rely very heavily on wholesalers, hospitals less so. A relatively high percentage of OTC pharmaceuticals take the direct route from manufacturer to retailer bypassing the wholesaler altogether.[2]

Wholesalers are classified according to whether they are full-line (those providing a full range of products) or short-line (those providing a restricted range of products), and national or regional. In 1990, 71% of ethical sales were made by full-line wholesalers and only 6% by short-line, which tend to concentrate on faster-moving generics. Also in 1990,

Table 3.2 Major retail chains in the UK, 2002

Pharmacy	Number of outlets	Share of total outlets (%)
Lloydspharmacy	1321	10.9
Boots the Chemists	1268	10.5
Moss Pharmacy	773	6.4
L Rowland & Co	300	2.5
National Co-operative Chemists	290	2.4
Superdrug	228	1.9
Tesco	210	1.7
Cohen's Chemist Group	107	0.9
Sainsbury's	107	0.9
Safeway	105	0.9
Asda	80	0.6
Others	7335	60.4
Total	**12124**	**100.0**

Source: Office of Fair Trading (2003). *The Control of Entry Regulations and Retail Pharmacy*. London: Office of Fair Trading.

there were some 30 full-line pharmaceutical wholesalers in the UK, most of which had regional markets (a fall from 39 in 1978). Only two (AAH and UniChem) were national, that is, they had UK-wide markets with a network of wholesale depots. Between 1991 and 1996 the number of full-line wholesalers continued to fall from 32 to 19 and the number of depots from 66 to 56. This decline continued between 1997 and 2002, when the number of wholesalers fell to 12 and the number of depots to 49. In little over a decade then the number of full-line wholesalers has fallen by 63% and the number of depots by 26%. Clearly, there has been rapid change in the structure of the wholesale sector in the UK. The number of short-line wholesalers is high, at around 4000, but many are very small, operating as sole traders, although there are some large ones. According to Farhan,[3] short-line wholesalers 'take advantage of price in the market and carefully monitor supply and demand. They listen to rumours in the market and buy and sell stock accordingly'.

The two full-line wholesalers AAH and UniChem experienced rapid change in the 1990s. In 1997 UniChem merged with Alliance Santé to become Alliance UniChem, the leading European distributor. In addition to its role as a major distributor, Alliance Unichem also has a strong presence in retailing through its Moss Pharmacies group, which is also in Italy and Switzerland. For the future the likelihood is that European expansion will accelerate as regulations prohibiting corporate ownership of retail pharmacies are softened. AAH was acquired in 1995 by GEHE (known as Celesio from April 2003), the long-established German group, which has wholesale operations in 11 countries across Europe and retail operations in seven. GEHE also owns the Lloyds Pharmacy group in the UK. In 1998, Phoenix, Germany's largest wholesaler made several acquisitions of UK regional wholesalers to form Phoenix Healthcare Distribution in the UK. It has continued to acquire UK regional wholesalers and can now be said to be the third national wholesaler in the UK. Currently the UK market share breakdown (Figure 3.1) shows that Phoenix still has some way to go to catch AAH and Alliance Unichem. Each of these companies can be described as pan-European as interests now span much of Europe.

An increasingly important trend is the drive towards more vertical integration. For wholesalers this could be forward into retailing (downstream) or backward (upstream) into manufacturing. The strategy adopted by the big distributors is to integrate forward by moving into retailing. This applies not only in the UK but also in Europe. A fundamental question for a firm is what it should make itself and what it should leave to other firms. This is called the 'make or buy' decision and

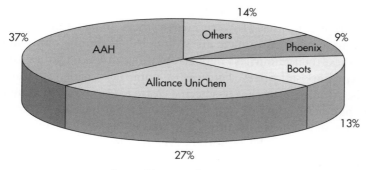

14%

37%

9%

13%

27%

Source: Various industry sources

Figure 3.1 UK distributors' market shares 2001.

will define the vertical boundaries of a firm. The make or buy decision is not a simple one. It is affected by the costs and benefits of using the market as opposed to making within a firm, the objective being to produce as efficiently as possible. The decision made by big wholesalers evidently is that efficiency will be raised by downstream integration.

Pricing of pharmaceuticals

The pricing of pharmaceuticals is a complex and contentious area. Across Europe, there are as many national pricing systems for pharmaceuticals as there are countries. In the EU, each member state has a different system. These vary from relatively free systems where pharmaceutical companies have a major say over pricing (such as the UK and Germany) to others where governments do not allow companies to have any say at all (such as France and most southern European countries). Countries that use national price controls do so by a variety of means, including national and international price referencing, in which prices are set by comparison with similar drugs at home or abroad. Each country has its own method of international price referencing. Some countries (e.g. Belgium and Greece) use the lowest EU price as a guide, while others (e.g. France and Italy) use an average of prices in selected countries. Because of the diversity of pricing systems, prices across the EU vary considerably. In the developing world the variation is even more apparent when seen as a proportion of wages. In 2000 a month's supply of ranitidine cost 13 days' wages in the Philippines, nearly 19 days' wages in Armenia and 51 days' wages in the Cameroon (http://www. essentialdrugs. org). Although these prices differ widely, they may be 'fair' in that they reflect the ability or willingness to pay for the drugs in the different countries. However, when prices are set, not by companies according to what consumers are willing to pay, but by national pricing authorities, then unfairness may creep in because companies are forced to accept imposed prices. Fairness or unfairness aside, different prices give rise to something that has been a cause for serious concern in recent years, parallel trading. In parallel trading, pharmaceuticals are bought by traders in low-price countries and sold in high-price countries. In the EU, the largest parallel importers are the Netherlands, Denmark and the UK, with parallel trade import shares of 18%, 10% and 7% respectively. In the EU as a whole, parallel trade accounts for only 2–3% of all pharmaceutical sales but this figure conceals the fact that the trade is concentrated on just 20–30 drugs and for some of these the share may reach 50% or more. In fact in the UK, IMS data (IMS Health Inc) show that about 50% of all parallel trade is accounted for by only 12 products, with only four companies shouldering the burden of 60% of all parallel imports (research.imshealth.com).

Products

Traditionally ethicals or prescription-only medicines (POMs) were dispensed under the prescription of a doctor or dentist (or vet), although the rise of nurse and pharmacist prescribing is changing this. Those dispensed without prescription are over-the-counter (OTC) products. Ethicals are dispensed by community pharmacies, dispensing doctors and hospital pharmacies. They can be either branded or generic. Branding usually occurs when the product is under patent protection but may run on when the product is out of patent. Generics are products that are out of patent protection and may be produced by any licensed manufacturer. Generics are generally cheaper and the Department of Health has encouraged generic prescribing for this reason. OTCs are divided into GSLs and Ps – the latter being sold only under the supervision of a pharmacist (see Chapter 6). A GSL or P may be treated as an ethical where it has been prescribed in a particular case.

Controls on price

Ethicals

Ethicals have no retail price competition as they are supplied by way of a prescription. But there is competition at the manufacturing and wholesale stages. In some cases pharmacists could theoretically dispense generically equivalent drugs from different manufacturers because they should be substitutes for each other; however bioequivalence cannot be guaranteed in all cases. Having considered this, the person responsible for buying in the pharmacy should then select the product with the lowest wholesale price in order to maximise income. For branded products this is not so easy to do as many are under patent and substitution is not always possible. Hence the government has had to exercise (indirect) control over branded prices. This is done through the Pharmaceutical Price Regulation Scheme (PPRS). This in fact controls profits rather than prices by setting target levels of profitability for each product. These are agreed between companies and the Department of Health (DoH) and take account of R&D spend, promotion costs and commitment to the NHS. Prices are then set to a level that should achieve the target profitability (usually measured by return on capital, but for smaller and overseas-based companies return on sales is sometimes used). Wholesalers' margins are allowed for in the calculations.

To analyse the effect of prescription charges we apply the principles established earlier to healthcare. The demand for healthcare is just like the demand for any other product in that it is affected by price, the prices of related products, income and tastes. Consumers of healthcare are patients. Different countries have different ways of paying for healthcare. If an insurance system is used to pay for healthcare (as in the USA), the price to consumers is zero and consumers would then buy the quantity of healthcare associated with zero price. If on the other hand the consumer pays a prescription charge (an example of what is known as a copayment), because now price is greater than zero we would expect the quantity demanded to be lower than when healthcare were free at point of use. Prescription charges are justified on two grounds:

- Reduction of so-called moral hazard (the tendency to be negligent about one's health because treatment in free – usually a feature of insurance-based systems).
- Raising revenue (the NHS reason for prescription charges).

The demand for prescriptions is indirectly a demand for medicines. In the NHS, doctors prescribe for patients on the basis of their health needs. The supply of pharmaceuticals is perfectly elastic because it is not determined by their price. Prescription charges are a flat rate tax in that UK governments fix the charge per prescription item. If the prescription charge exceeds the cost of the item the patient is subsiding the NHS and vice versa. Prescription charges were introduced in 1952 and, but for

1965–68 when they were abolished, they have increased steadily ever since. Between 1971 and 1979 the charge was held at 20p per item but since then successive governments have raised it 'to increase efficiency and equity' to its 2004 rate of £6.40 per item. Prescription charges have risen well ahead of inflation. Over the period 1980 to 1998 the charge per prescription item rose by 355% in real terms.[4] The charges are currently being incrementally discontinued in Wales.

A major criticism of the prescription charge is that it is a regressive tax, that is, it does not take account of people's income. People pay exactly the same charge regardless of their income. A wealthy person will pay the same as someone who just earns enough to pay the charge. There is a safety net for those on low incomes. People on income support and family credit are exempt from the charge. In the late 1990s some 86% of people were exempted for one reason or another (age, income, illness, location, etc.), so only 14% actually paid the charge.

The government believes that increases in the charges do not deter people from receiving the medicines they need. This is to say that the price elasticity of demand is zero or close to zero. Studies of the price elasticity of demand for prescriptions have estimated a range of values, but all show that demand is inelastic (less than 1 ignoring the negative sign). Examples are Lavers,[5] who estimated it as –0.22, O'Brien,[6] has it from –0.33 to –0.64, and Hughes and McGuire[7] from –0.32 to –0.37. Hitris[4] used these estimates to examine the effect of raising the prescription charge on the demand for prescriptions. Using an elasticity value of –0.33 (see Chapter 2) the rise in prescription charges from the 1997 rate of £5.65 per item to £6.20 in 2002 would have resulted in a reduction in the number of non-exempt prescriptions dispensed from £46m to £45.1m. Assuming an extra £260m revenue was generated this represented only 0.3% of total NHS expenditure on prescriptions of nearly £5.5bn in 1997 and an estimate of £8.06bn in 2002 (ABPI, http://www.abpi.org.uk). As a revenue raiser the prescription charge is not significant, and rises in the charge do not generate very much extra income, while at the same time perhaps jeopardising patients' health as they cut back on prescribed drugs.

There is also some evidence that when prescription charges rise, the behaviour of the various agents involved may change. Patients may simply reduce their demand for medicines or they may buy OTCs instead. GPs and pharmacists, who may be sympathetic to patients' needs, may alter their behaviour too. GPs may prescribe larger quantities, or pharmacists may offer cheaper alternatives to prescription drugs.

OTCs

Unlike ethicals, OTCs in principle are subject to competitive pricing at the retail level. However, until very recently in the UK, they were normally subject to retail price maintenance (RPM), though some OTCs and own labels were excluded. Under RPM, retailers were not permitted to set their own prices for medicines, but had to charge the minimum prices set by manufacturers. The background to RPM is that faced with a decline in the number of independent community pharmacies, the Restrictive Practices Court gave the independent pharmacies protection from the buying power of the large pharmacy chains and supermarkets by imposing minimum prices on OTCs wherever they were sold. This lasted from 1970 to 2001 when RPM was abolished following pressure from a number of quarters. Shortly after the abolition, Tesco, Sainsbury and Asda announced plans to cut prices of branded painkillers, vitamins and cold and flu remedies by up to 50% (personal communication trade sources). The abolition of RPM has contributed to a number of important changes in the sector, including:

- More competition in OTCs between the major supermarkets.
- Restructuring of the pharmacy market with wholesalers moving into the retail stage by acquiring independent pharmacies (this has been happening anyway).
- The establishment of more in-store pharmacies by the major supermarkets.
- Concerted efforts by smaller pharmacies to find new ways to remain competitive.

References

1. Competition Commission. *Unichem Limited: A Report on Unichem's Arrangements and Proposed Arrangements for the Allotment of Shares in its Capital*, Cm 691. London: Competition Commission, 1989.
2. Competition Commission. *Unichem PLC/Lloyds Chemists PLC and GEHE AG/Lloyds Chemists PLC: A Report on the Proposed Mergers*, Cm 3344. London: Competition Commission, 1996.
3. Farham F. Short-line wholesalers: what part do they really play? *Pharm J* 2002; 268: 112–113.
4. Hitris T. *Prescription Charges in the United Kingdom: A Critical Review*. Discussion Paper 00/04. University of York, Department of Economics, 2000.
5. Lavers R J. Prescription charges, the demand for prescriptions and morbidity. *Appl Econ* 1989; 21: 1043–1052.
6. O'Brien B. The effect of patient charges on the utilisation of prescription medicines. *J Health Econ* 1989; 8: 109–132.

7. Hughes D, McGuire A. Patient charges and the utilisation of prescription medicines: some estimates using a cointegration procedure. *Health Econ* 1995; 4: 213–220.

Further reading

Banahan B. *Marketing to Pharmacists*. New York: Pharmaceutical Products Press, 1998.

Smith M C, Kolassa E M, Perkins G, Sieker B. *Pharmaceutical Marketing*. New York: Pharmaceutical Products Press, 2002.

Kolassa E M. *Elements of Pharmaceutical Pricing*. New York: Pharmaceutical Products Press, 1997.

4

The essentials of pharmacy business

Martin McBeth and Steven B Kayne

Introduction

This chapter outlines many of the important details that need to be addressed in day-to-day business operations. Too often pharmacists become embroiled in the process of pharmacy practice and cannot find time to consider simple questions such as 'What am I selling?' and 'What are my margins?'.

Pharmacy premises

Before the introduction of the 1987 NHS Contract for Pharmacies, all qualified pharmacists were eligible to apply for National Health Service (NHS) contracts and permitted to set up retail pharmacies. With the introduction of the NHS Contract, prospective applicants had to demonstrate a need for pharmaceutical services in the location proposed. The implementation of this new requirement has resulted in a decline in the overall number of pharmacies in the UK, and this reduction in numbers, coupled with the expansionist policies of the pharmacy multiples, has virtually guaranteed that whenever an independent retail pharmacy does come on the market, the price paid reflects a substantial element in respect of goodwill (see Chapter 5).

While this goodwill reflects the underlying or potential profitability of the business, its value was boosted in the past because of the 'protected' status of the licence and the restricted opportunities in what was a tightly regulated market. Things are set to change, however, with the ending of retail price maintenance and limited deregulation of NHS contracts in England. New strategies in all the home countries are likely to create specialists in every aspect of practice.

Statutory controls regulate all pharmacy businesses. Pharmacy premises must be registered (see Chapter 6), and must pay an annual fee to retain that registration. A distinction should be drawn between pharmacy businesses and drugstores. Drugstores do not employ registered pharmacists and are limited in the range of drugs and medicines they can sell. These businesses operate as retail outlets for 'general sales listed' (GSL) drugs and medicines, together with toiletries and cosmetics. In contrast, the majority of pharmacies have a dual role, as dispensers of prescribed medicines, and as retailers of a wide range of goods, not necessarily confined to health-related items.

The law requires that whenever a pharmacy is open, there must be a qualified pharmacist in charge at all times. Use of the 'pharmacist' title requires registration of the particulars of the pharmacist by whom or under whose supervision the business is to be run. Qualified pharmacist status requires the completion of a degree course in pharmacy, covering every aspect of the structure and actions of medicines, and equipping the pharmacist with a greater knowledge of this subject than any other health professional. These studies are followed by a year's practical experience and written examination leading to membership of the Royal Pharmaceutical Society of Great Britain or Northern Ireland. The Society monitors all pharmacy premises and the professional skills and dispensing techniques of its registered members. Society inspectors visit community pharmacies once every 18–24 months.

Of 12 167 pharmacy premises registered in the UK by the Royal Pharmaceutical Society in 2002, almost 65% were owned by independents or by small chains (less than five outlets and turnover less than £1 million). Owing to the limited availability of NHS dispensing contracts in most areas, retail pharmacy chains looking to expand their presence outside UK city centres are generally able to do so only through acquisition of existing licences.

Both retail pharmacies and drugstores have experienced the effects of the overall increase in competition in the UK retail market, particularly from grocery multiples and out-of-town retail parks. The increase in out-of-town retailing – boosted by the deregulation of Sunday trading – has impacted most significantly on the pharmacy and drugstore sales of household goods and toiletries.

What does a retail pharmacy sell?

Most pharmacies sell a combination of goods and services (see also Chapter 13), the margins on which will inevitably vary. These will include some, or all, of the following:

- Drugs and medicines
- Healthcare products and supplements
- Toiletries, perfumes and cosmetics

- Photographic equipment (cameras, films)
- Film processing
- Baby foods and products
- Small electrical goods
- Health foods
- Groceries
- Pet care products
- Household cleaning products
- Jewellery
- Sunglasses
- Confectionery

In addition, registered pharmacists dispense both NHS and private prescriptions and may offer analytical services such as pregnancy testing, cholesterol testing and blood pressure monitoring. All pharmacists now maintain patient medication records and are in a position to provide monitored dosage systems to residential and nursing homes. Pharmacists are also encouraged to offer patient advice and to display health education materials, and the provision of this kind of additional service is linked to professional allowances.

Sales tend to increase during the autumn and winter because of the usual winter ailments, although this has less effect on dispensing since the blacklisting of many cough and cold remedies during the late 1980s and early 1990s. The summer months will be quieter in areas where large numbers of people regularly holiday away from home and pharmacies in tourist areas will be busier during peak holiday periods.

Counter sales of luxuries, e.g. toiletries, perfumes, gift sets, etc., are greatest during the run-up to Christmas and in some cases retail sales may be more than twice what they are during November. Sales may be held in the early months of the New Year if seasonal items remain unsold. Overall, in a well-balanced business, counter trade should be at a constant level throughout the year, but there will be seasonal peaks within the total turnover, for example antihistamines in the spring and holiday-related products, e.g. tanning preparations and sunglasses, in the summer.

Margins and product mix

Margins

To reiterate, the retail pharmacy performs a dual role. In effect there are two quite separate businesses operating from the same premises: the

NHS business in which profits are regulated by government policy, and the counter business, which is run along normal commercial lines.

The amount of NHS business carried out by the pharmacist depends largely on the location of the premises. If the pharmacy is situated near or within a surgery or medical centre, where the business effectively has an unopposed trading position, a high proportion of total turnover will come from NHS receipts (see Chapter 5). City centre pharmacies, which face competition from large multiples and offer a wide range of toiletries, cosmetics and other products, are likely to have a lower proportion of turnover from NHS business. It is estimated that the average medium-sized pharmacy depends on receipts from NHS prescriptions for approximately 60–70% of turnover, a proportion that had risen from an average of 40% before 1968. This is supported by statistics from the National Pharmaceutical Association (NPA), which reported that the typical independent contractor obtains 70% of turnover from NHS work. The precise percentage of total turnover obviously varies from business to business, and can be verified from the official forms that accompany reimbursements received by the pharmacist.

In the majority of cases, prescriptions are dispensed free of charge, but inevitably the proportion varies from location to location, depending on the socioeconomic make-up of the pharmacy's catchment. In Scotland only about 16% of patients fall into the paying group; in Wales the proportion is around 20%. Exemption from charges is available in respect of prescriptions for children, people over 60, those on low incomes, pregnant women and new mothers. The Welsh Assembly is about to discontinue all prescription charges at the time of writing.

In general terms, there has been an overall reduction in the levels of gross profit that can be achieved from NHS dispensing in recent years. Owing to the way the system is structured, the gross profit rate falls as dispensing turnover rises above the average (approximately 3500 scripts per month) and, by contrast, rises as dispensing turnover falls below the average. Gross profit percentages have also been observed to vary between rural and urban retail pharmacies. The value of individual 'rural' prescriptions also tends to be greater than urban prescriptions because the rural script is likely to be for greater quantities, say 3 months' supply as against 1 month. The overall effect is that rural pharmacies tend to achieve lower gross profit rates than their urban counterparts because of the higher average value of prescriptions.

A similar situation arises in respect of pharmacies that provide services to nursing homes, where drugs are often supplied for the nursing staff to dispense over a period of, say, 3 months. In such cases, the issue of a 3-month supply of a particular drug would constitute a single, high-value prescription.

Conversely, the proximity of a drug rehabilitation centre can substantially enhance a pharmacy's level of gross profit because significant numbers of individual prescriptions tend to be dispensed on a daily basis.

Under the current system of pharmacy remuneration, it should be clear that, in terms of gross profit percentage at any rate, the pharmacist dispensing a relatively low volume of prescriptions at lower than average ingredient cost has an advantage over a colleague dispensing higher prescription numbers with higher than average ingredient costs. That said, the higher volumes dispensed will usually more than compensate in terms of absolute gross profit.

It is possible for pharmacists to reduce their costs in respect of certain items by the use of 'parallel' imported drugs, rather than acquiring all stock from UK manufacturers. This can enhance the gross profit margin achieved. In recognition of this, many leading wholesalers now provide customers with the option of parallel imports, and the Department of Health's calculations of the discount to be clawed back from pharmacists now reflect a notional element in respect of parallel imports whether they are purchased or not.

In addition to NHS prescription dispensing, most pharmacists dispense a small number of private prescriptions (perhaps 10 a month) and the Royal Pharmaceutical Society supplies guidelines for pricing these prescriptions.

As has been noted, retail pharmacists sell a wide range of items, many with varying mark-up rates. Establishing the overall mark-up rate accurately would require calculations based on invoices sampled over a representative period. Table 4.1 details mark-up rate ranges in respect of typical products and product categories stocked by retail pharmacies.

Gross margins on counter sales in many cases fall between 25 and 33%, but this will vary depending on the pricing policy of individual retail pharmacies and the type of goods sold. Opportunities for managing margins and maximising profit are discussed in Chapter 12.

Product mix

The overall gross profit percentage achieved by retail pharmacists depends on the proportion of NHS to counter sales and on the gross profit on counter sales. A pharmacy with a high percentage of NHS turnover

Table 4.1 Typical mark-up rates for typical products stocked by retail pharmacies

Item	Mark-up (%)
Over-the-counter drugs	30–50
Agency cosmetics, toiletries	35–60
Toiletries and haircare products	20–40
Photographic	17–33
Sandals	40–50
Baby foods	10–22
Batteries	about 33
Pet products	42–50
Soft drinks, tonic wines	6–18
Small electrical goods	30–33
Sunglasses	30–40
Sanitary protection	18–26
Deodorants	about 25
Foot preparations	about 21
Gardening products	about 51
Tissues	10–25

would have a lower overall gross profit than one where turnover from counter sales and NHS receipts were approximately equal. Table 4.2 provides an example.

Government statistics show that overall gross margins achieved by retail pharmacists remained quite consistent between 1990 and 1992, but thereafter decreased substantially (see Table 4.3).

The National Pharmaceutical Association (NPA) offers its members a free, interim comparison scheme, providing an indication of how the individual retail pharmacist's trading results and costs compare with those of other pharmacies with a similar turnover.

Table 4.2 Comparison of gross profit rate in different businesses

Item	Turnover (%)	Gross profit rate (%)
NHS business	70	18
Counter sales	30	30
		Overall gross profit rate 21.6
NHS business	55	18
Counter sales	45	30
		Overall gross profit rate 23.4

Table 4.3 Gross margins over the period 1990 to 2002

Year	Gross margin (%)
1990	26.5
1991	27.0
1992	26.7
1993	23.9
1995	22.1
2000	21.9
2002	21.5

NHS remuneration

The current position

Since the inception of the NHS in 1947 in England and 1948 in Scotland, pharmacists have received remuneration from public funds for NHS dispensing and more recently for limited extra associated services, for example instalment dispensing and methadone programmes. Each month prescription forms are sent to an official Pricing Bureau that calculates the amounts due and notifies the Health Board, which then makes the appropriate payment to the pharmacist. Payment is made at monthly intervals and the make-up of the payment is shown on a form PPD9, or similar approved form. The calculation of the fees, etc. due as shown on the PPD9 is not sent to the pharmacist until 2 months after the month to which it relates, but an interim payment of 90% of the amount due is sent 1 month earlier. Thus, for prescriptions dispensed in January the pharmacist would receive 90% of the amount due on 1 March and the balance, together with the form PPD9, on 1 April.

Before 1993, remuneration was made on an 'on-cost' basis. This consisted of payment, in addition to the dispensing fees, of an on-cost allowance based on the price of the drugs dispensed. The on-cost percentage remained static at 5% between 1989 and 1991. In November 1992 it was reduced to 2.5% and it was phased out completely in October 1993. The most important current payments and allowances are explained in more detail below.

Dispensing fee

This fee is based on the number of prescriptions processed each month, and the following dispensing fees applied from the year 1990–91 until September 1995, at which date the payment changed to a single value fee.

1990–91	£1.445 for first 1400 scripts
	£0.665 for next 5250 scripts
	£0.735 for all subsequent scripts
1991–92	£1.512 for first 1500 scripts
	£0.715 for all subsequent scripts
From 1.11.92	£1.59 for first 1700 scripts
	£0.805 for all subsequent scripts
From 1.11.93	£1.35 for first 1700 scripts
	£0.945 for all subsequent scripts
From 1.8.94	£1.29 for first 1800 scripts
	£0.938 for all subsequent scripts

The rates of dispensing fees in 2003 were £0.946 for all scripts. However, at the time of writing new contracts are being negotiated and the system by which contractors are paid for dispensing may well change.

Professional allowance

A professional allowance was introduced with effect from 1 November 1993 of £500 per month per contractor provided they:

- dispensed over 1500 scripts per month;
- produced a practice leaflet; and
- displayed up to eight health promotion leaflets.

The professional allowance was increased to £720 in 1994 and £1340 in 1995. The current rate is £1575.

Other allowances and payments

In addition to those payments detailed above, a pharmacy may also be entitled to receive any or all of the following allowances:

- Containers allowance (on a per prescription basis).
- Rota service payments (hourly payments that the Health Board may pay to contractors providing services outside normal opening hours).
- Payments by patients (prescription charges paid over by patients are deducted from the payments made to the pharmacist by the Health Board).
- Expensive prescriptions allowance (all prescriptions with a net ingredient cost before discount greater than a certain amount (£100 in 2003) attract a 2% expensive prescription allowance.
- Payments in respect of pre-registration trainees (this is an allowance

payable to certain contractors in recognition of in-service training provided).

- Advice to residential homes (where a pharmacist provides advice and regularly supplies drugs, etc. to a residential home), a payment may be claimable from the Family Health Services Authority (FHSA) in respect of an initial visit to a home and thereafter an annual fee.

The difficulties

Pharmacies have historically been viewed as relatively resilient retail businesses during periods of economic recession, owing to the fact that many of the products they sell are considered necessities and most are modestly priced. However, although the number of prescriptions dispensed increases annually, the margins on NHS work have steadily declined. In addition, the independent sector continued to lose market share of sales of toiletries and cosmetics throughout the 1990s.

The viability of the small contractor, in particular, is threatened by competition from the multiples, downturns in consumer spending and the continuing squeeze and realignment of pharmacists' remuneration. A report from the Office of Fair Trading in 2003 threatened to deregulate the granting of NHS contracts to community pharmacists and was perceived as threatening the viability of smaller pharmacy outlets. Following intense lobbying by the profession the recommendations were watered down in England and dismissed in Scotland, Wales and Northern Ireland, to the relief of many.

Future developments in remuneration

For some years now, many pharmacists have criticised the inadequacy of their NHS remuneration, particularly as they have been encouraged to offer more and more services and counselling facilities to members of the public. Many rely heavily on the fact that they are able to obtain drugs at a greater discount than that 'clawed back' from their reimbursement by the Department of Health. However, in the face of an annually increasing drugs bill, the government has endeavoured to reduce the amount spent on drugs. Efforts to date have resulted in the removal of many products from the prescription-only list, and the amendment of the drug tariff (which defines the amount that contractors are reimbursed for drugs dispensed) to reflect the price actually paid for drugs by contractors rather than the gross or undiscounted price.

All the home countries have now issued health strategies for the 21st century that outline a major shift in the community and hospital pharmacists' role towards a healthcare delivery system that encompasses the promotion and maintenance of good health as well as treating disease and rehabilitation. New contracts are currently being negotiated by the Pharmaceutical Services Negotiating Committee (PSNC) England and Wales and the Scottish Pharmaceutical General Council (SPGC) for Scotland that detail a number of core services that must be provided by all pharmacy contractors and offering the option of becoming involved in the provision of supplementary services, including minor ailment and repeat prescription schemes, prescribing and medicines management (see Chapter 18), all of which will be funded. At the time of writing, the manner in which funding will be achieved has still to be finalised and is likely to differ according to the jurisdiction involved, but the exciting prospect of involvement as a full member of the healthcare team is all but upon the profession. With connection to the NHSnet and developments in IT the input of community pharmacy will advance in a way that just a few years ago would have been unachievable.

The advent of the new NHS contract referred to above is likely to stem the tide of discontent and offer a real opportunity for the re-emergence of a vibrant independent sector that can compete with the multiples on quality and range of service. Details of the NHS contract in England and Wales may be obtained on the NPA website (http://www.npa.co.uk/) and in Scotland from the SPGC website (http://www.spgc.org.uk/).

Buying from wholesalers

Pharmacy wholesalers form the distribution network for NHS drugs and appliances and offer retail pharmacies a delivery service at least daily, and often several times a day, reflecting the variable demand for prescription drugs. Wholesalers also supply toiletries, hair care products, cosmetics, etc. using the same service.

There are a limited number of major pharmacy wholesale organisations (see Chapter 4). Most pharmacies will trade with at least two wholesalers to ensure the requisite availability of prescription drugs at short notice, and also to take advantage of special offers and services offered from time to time by the competing wholesalers. The wholesale business is highly competitive, with the major wholesalers trading nationally, although a small number of independent wholesalers do survive, trading purely on price and offering little in the way of additional services such as those offered by their larger rivals. Drug and appliances manufacturers offer a further source of supply, with some manufacturers maintaining sales forces, which call directly on the pharmacists and arrange direct delivery, so bypassing the wholesaler. Alternatively, the manufacturers' representatives may call on the pharmacists to solicit business but place subsequent orders through a wholesaler with whom the pharmacist already has an account, thereby avoiding the need to bill the individual pharmacist directly.

The competition between wholesalers has benefits for the retail pharmacies. Discounts are usually available for prompt payment (within 30 days), and reductions in the region of 8–10% – depending on order volume – on most drug and surgical appliance purchases are usual. The large wholesalers who dominate the market tend to offer a combined volume and settlement discount once a certain threshold has been reached. Below the stated threshold, no discount is offered. If payment is not made within the specified period, a significant portion of the discount is forfeited. The wholesaler may also provide a further discount on goods purchased through an electronic or computerised ordering system, and possibly a retrospective annual discount in addition, based on total purchases in the course of the year. It should be noted, however, that the discount clawback scale operated by the Department of Health attempts to recover what discounts are received by contractors from their wholesalers.

Discounts on other 'over the counter' lines are less usual, apart from those for prompt settlement. That said, the NPA pays a rebate of 1% of the total payments made through their clearinghouse scheme throughout the year. This is a useful service allowing members to write one cheque to cover invoices issued by a substantial list of suppliers, saving bank charges and postage.

Pharmacists can generally expect good service from the major suppliers. Beyond the basic supply of goods, some wholesalers offer computerised ordering facilities, and others operate a loan scheme for pharmacy refurbishment and acquisition. Suppliers are usually willing to take back damaged or outdated stock and to issue credit notes for these items. Most large wholesalers offer a range of own-brand products such as baby food, vitamins and toiletries. Competition during the mid-1980s between the major wholesalers led them to offer substantial discounts for volume purchases. When this strategy began to threaten profitability, discounts offered on ethicals, i.e. on drugs and surgical appliances, stabilised at around 8 or 9% during the late 1980s and early 1990s. That said, in 1992 the supply of generic drugs became highly competitive and in certain cases discounts of as much as 46% were available off the list price.

However, the size of discounts offered is, for the most part, related to the total monthly ethical purchases made by the retail pharmacy and, to reiterate, small orders, perhaps below £2000 to £2500 per month, may well attract no discount at all. Although wholesalers offer generous inducements to encourage loyalty, most pharmacies choose to purchase supplies from more than one wholesaler, even in circumstances where the pharmacy is 'tied' to a particular supplier, in return for loans, etc.

How should the business be structured? (See also Chapter 6)

What are the choices?

The selection of the correct trading vehicle should be established at the commencement of operations and the pharmacist should seek professional advice as to the most suitable, permanent trading medium for the new business. The choice between the following business structures will largely depend on the particular circumstances of the pharmacist:

- Sole trader.
- Partnership, for example if a family member or unconnected person is to participate in the business (even where this is limited to sharing in profits).
- Limited company.

It should not be assumed that every new business should start life as a company. There are large numbers of businesses trading as companies that could operate safely and more efficiently as sole traders or family partnerships, but the taxation implications (especially capital gains tax) and costs of liquidation make a change in status impracticable. However, it is important to appreciate that many recent tax changes (including those in the Finance Act 2002) are to the advantage of the corporate entity, and this perhaps explains the significant rise in the number of sole traders and partnerships that have incorporated their businesses or are seriously considering doing so. Of most importance, a company structure usually enables retained profits to be ploughed back in the business at a relatively low tax rate (from 1 April 2002, at 19%) and, where profits are less than £10 000, without any tax at all (see also Chapter 5).

It is difficult to calculate the level of profits per partner or sole proprietor that would justify the incorporation of a business in order to save or defer tax. This is because much depends on whether profits are to be retained in the company or whether they are to be paid out as remuneration or distributed as dividends, and this is basically a personal decision for each individual pharmacy owner.

The main disadvantages of incorporation are the potential future double capital gains tax charge on assets sold by the company and on its shareholders if the company is wound up or if their shares are sold, and the high level of Class 1 national insurance (NI) contributions (payable by both the employer company and the director/employee) compared with the Class 2 and Class 4 self-employed contributions, particularly following the increase from 6 April 2003. The NI problem can be solved by paying only modest remuneration to the shareholders/ directors (subject to national minimum wage regulations) and distributing the company's profits net of corporation tax by way of dividend. However, in the past this solution created further difficulty in that a very low level of remuneration precluded the provision of an adequate company pension in retirement. Recent changes have now alleviated this problem and personal pensions can now operate adequately at low remuneration levels.

Factors affecting the choice of company structure (see also Chapter 6)

Table 4.4 offers a comparison of the various criteria that should be considered when choosing the company structure. While the risk involved with a particular trade may in effect make the isolation of that risk inside a company the only realistic option, the choice of an unincorporated or incorporated business vehicle most often depends on whether trading losses are expected in the early years of trade. Businesses that grow to a considerable size are likely to be constrained in the longer term by a sole trader or partnership structure and, therefore, if growth is anticipated, the choice for such a business is effectively between sole trader or partnership status initially, followed by transfer of the business to a company, or trading through a company from the start. If the profit levels of a business are not known initially, it is likely that the choice of an unincorporated business structure will be more beneficial, with the possibility of incorporating at a future date. At any rate, it is advisable to be prudent, as it is not a straightforward matter to disincorporate once a corporate structure is in place.

If losses are anticipated in the early years, and the proprietors have other taxable income, an unincorporated business allows them to achieve the earliest relief for the losses. By contrast, company losses are effectively

Table 4.4 Comparison of various business structures

	Sole trader	Partnership	Company
Direct taxes on the 'business'			Corporation tax Class 1 NI on 'earnings', and 1A on most benefits
Direct taxes on the 'individual'	Income/capital gains tax Classes 2 and 4 NI	Income/capital gains tax Classes 2 and 4 NI	Income/capital gains tax Class 1 NI on 'earnings'
VAT	No special rules to distinguish the choices		
Drawing profits	Automatic	Depends on profit-sharing ratios	Dividends will normally be paid, but are discretionary
Outside investment	Bank etc. finance, otherwise not usually beyond the principal/partners		May be easier to attract outside investment via equity or loan finance
Attraction to employees	Difficult to share profits other than by additional remuneration		Potential for share schemes may make more attractive
Legal status	No distinction between business and the owner, who is personally liable for the debts of the business	Partners are jointly and severally liable for all debts Partnership has a continuing existence (subject to the partnership agreement)	Company has a separate legal persona, and is liable for its own debts Shareholders liability limited to unpaid share capital (but subject to personal guarantees for credit)
Pensions	Stakeholder pensions and retirement annuities	Stakeholder pensions and retirement annuities, and potential for annuity from partnership	Stakeholder pensions, retirement annuities or company scheme as required
When usually utilised	Small and/or new business	Small to medium sized, or new businesses, or where rules prevent incorporation (e.g. solicitors)	Any size business, but particularly larger businesses where not prevented from incorporation
Loss issues	Losses available to offset against personal income and gains of principal/partners		Losses only available to offset against other income in company

locked into the company. Because a new company is unlikely to have other income against which to relieve the losses in the short term, they must be carried forward for relief against trading profits when and if these materialise.

Value added tax (see also Chapter 10)

History

In the UK, goods had been subject to purchase tax as a way of raising money for the Exchequer, but by the late 1960s products as a proportion of economic output had declined and with it the indirect tax base. The anomaly that products should be taxed but not the burgeoning service sector became increasingly obvious. The government eventually decided to introduce a value added tax (VAT) in 1973 at a standard rate of 10%. A year later this was cut to 8% and an additional 'luxury rate' of 25% introduced on a range of items in 1975.

The wide disparity between the two categories led to the 25% rate being reduced to 12.5% in 1976. However the administration of the two rates remained difficult and further revenue was required to permit reductions in income tax. In 1979 the two positive rates of VAT were amalgamated at 15%. These frequent changes and constant repricing of OTC products caused difficulties for pharmacy staff.

Following the widespread evasion and subsequent repeal of what came to be known as the 'poll tax', a substantial slice of local government taxation was replaced by a further increase in the rate of VAT to 17.5% in 1991. Thankfully the government has not tinkered with the rate since, although the VAT base has been extended steadily over the last 30 years. An early change was that the original concession for food and drink did not seem to be quite so appropriate for confectionery, ice cream, soft drinks and potato crisps, and they were duly subject to VAT from 1974. VAT is known as general sales tax (GST) in some countries.

VAT rationale

Although a whole range of reasons for introducing VAT have been put forward at one time or another, the main ones are that it:

- is a broadly based tax
- is a tax on consumption
- promotes tax harmonisation
- makes a contribution to balance of payments policy
- is self-enforcing.

Charging VAT

With a few exceptions (see below) VAT is charged on the value of supplies of taxable goods and services made in the UK, including some exports to EU countries. It is also chargeable on imports of goods from outside the EU. All businesses must register for VAT within 30 days where the value of taxable supplies in the previous 12 months was more than £58 000 (April 2004 budget), or is likely to exceed this annual limit within the next 30 days. Failure to notify on time attracts penalties.

The rates

The various rates for VAT are as follows:

- Standard rate – The standard rate is 17.5% and is applied to most products and services.
- Reduced rate – A reduced rate of 5% applies to domestic power and fuel supplies, child car seats, cycle helmets and – most import-antly as far as pharmacy is concerned – women's sanitary products.
- Zero-rated – If a business offers zero-rated goods, it must pay input tax to its supplier but does not charge output VAT to the customer. The input tax can be reclaimed. Zero-rated supplies include medicines dispensed on prescription.
- Exempt supplies – Books and most other publications, clothing and footwear for children and most foods are exempt from VAT.

Keeping records (see also Chapter 10)

Every business registered for VAT must keep records that satisfy the requirements of HM Customs and Excise. These records will include till rolls, cashbooks and bank statements, as well as original VAT invoices for all purchases and expenses. Normally these records have to be stored for a minimum of 6 years. The choice of business structure has no bearing on these requirements. An inspection is carried out by the Customs and Excise every 12–18 months and, in the case of an independent pharmacy contractor, the inspector will often insist on visiting the premises rather than going to the accountant. In these circumstances all records since the last inspection have to be made available. Any subsequent queries can be directed to your accountant.

Paying VAT

The value of VAT collected (output tax) can be offset against the VAT due to Customs and Excise (input tax) and any net balance due is paid.

Depending on the ratio of dispensing to counter trade the large amount of VAT paid out to wholesalers to cover the monthly drug bill will more than compensate for the tax collected from OTC sales and a repayment will be claimed. Over the busy Christmas trading period, however, this position may be reversed and tax due (see Chapter 10). VAT on purchases of cars, except those bought wholly for business purposes after 31 July 1995, and business entertainment expenses cannot be reclaimed.

Substantial businesses that allow clients to run credit accounts have to account for VAT at the date that the invoice for the supply is raised (as opposed to when the products or services are actually delivered or paid for by the customer). VAT on bad debts that are more than 6 months old and have been written off may be reclaimed. However businesses with a turnover of not more than £600 000 may account for VAT when the cash is received from the customer rather than on an invoice basis, thereby obtaining automatic relief for any bad debts.

VAT is normally paid to the Customs and Excise quarterly, on a special form, but pharmacy businesses that are usually in the position of claiming repayment may account monthly. Penalties are charged for late or incorrect VAT returns. For further details on VAT regulations see the UK Customs and Excise website (http://www.hmce.gov.uk).

Pay as you earn taxation

History

The core of pay as you earn (PAYE) taxation is deduction of tax at source. This means that employers deduct tax when they make wage or salary payments to employees.

Deductions from pay by employers have been part of the income tax system for more than two centuries. For example, in 1803, tax on emoluments from public offices and employments of profit was actually assessed on the employer who was entitled to deduct it from the salary. However the real history of PAYE started during the Second World War. In 1939, many employees paid tax directly to the collector at half-yearly intervals. Manual workers were permitted to spread the payments over 13 weeks by buying 'income tax stamps'. Employers were not involved in this system. The war saw a big increase in both the number of employees paying tax and in the rates of tax. Many found this hard to budget for and it led to the introduction of arrangements for employers to deduct tax from pay. These arrangements were widened in 1942 to all weekly wage-earners. The tax was still assessed every 6 months by the Inland Revenue, who then told employers how much to deduct. A government White Paper in 1943 proposed the current PAYE system. Crucially it involved deductions based on the *cumulative* pay and tax deducted in the year. This is still the feature that distinguishes PAYE in the UK from the systems in most other countries. The system was initially proposed only for weekly wage-earners and pensions paid by their former employers, but the scope of PAYE was subsequently extended much more widely through a system of codes and deductions. New Income Tax (Pay As You Earn) Regulations were introduced in 2003. The main purpose of these Regulations was:

- to make the existing documentation clearer and easier to use
- to bring the legislation into line with practice
- to make it more consistent.

Calculating PAYE

The amount an employer deducts from an employee's wages depends on:

- PAYE tables issued by the Inland Revenue.
- A PAYE code issued by the Inland Revenue (or decided by the Regulations) for the employer to use for the employee.
- The amount of wages the employer pays and (usually) the total of previous payments in the tax year.

Record-keeping

The Inland Revenue requires every business that employs staff to keep proper records for PAYE and for calculation of tax liabilities. Certain returns are required monthly and annually. Again, the choice of business structure does not affect the requirements.

Paying PAYE

Employers are obliged to pay the PAYE that has been collected from employees to their local tax office promptly, on a monthly basis, and there are penalties for late payment. Further details on the 2003 PAYE Regulations may be obtained from the Inland Revenue website (http://www.inlandrevenue.gov.uk).

Income tax and corporation tax

The Inland Revenue requires every business to maintain transaction records sufficient to support the reported results of the business. Annual returns are required by the Inland Revenue for both income and corporation tax purposes.

The Companies Act places additional requirements on the directors of a business operating as a limited company, and annual returns are required to be made to Companies House, in addition to an annual audit of the records for companies above a certain size. The audit thresholds were increased substantially by statutory instrument for accounting periods ending 31 March 2004 and thereafter. The new limits of turnover above £5.6 million and net assets above £2.8 million eliminate the requirement for all but the very largest pharmacy companies to carry out an audit.

Accountants (see also Chapter 10)

Pharmacists will benefit from the services of a professional accountant both at the outset of a business venture and also on an ongoing basis. The accountant will be able to offer advice on the following:

- The appropriate structure of the business.
- Obtaining tax relief on the purchase price of the business.
- Preparing cash flow and profit forecasts.
- Raising the appropriate finance (see also Chapter 5).
- Setting up and maintaining appropriate financial systems.
- Monitoring performance.
- Exit routes.

An accountant can advise on the best way to raise additional finance either through bank overdrafts or loans or from other sources (see Chapter 5). Importantly, an accountant can ensure your financial systems are effective and able to cope with company expansion. Adequate working capital, good controls over stock, invoicing, credit control, and cash collection are among the most important aspects of good financial management in a growing business. As a business expands, the volume of transactions will inevitably increase and an accountant should be able to assist in such tasks as payroll preparation and additional book-keeping.

Obtaining tax relief

Given the significant values attributed to goodwill in the acquisition of a pharmacy it is important that professional advice is sought in advance of purchase. Recent tax law changes have created the opportunity to obtain tax relief by writing off goodwill purchased over its estimated useful life. This has a major benefit in terms of tax cash flow and it is crucial to obtain professional advice on this matter.

Further reading

Tootelian D H, Gaedeke R M. *Essentials of Pharmacy Management*. St Louis, MO: Mosby, 1993.

National Pharmaceutical Association's Pharmacy Business and Practice website (http://npa.atalink.co.uk/welcome.phtml).

5

Acquiring and financing a pharmacy

Kirit Patel and Steven Kayne

Introduction

The quickest method of entry to the market is to acquire an existing pharmacy, together with its NHS contract. This chapter explores the various factors that need to be taken into account when considering the acquisition of a pharmacy.

Essentially there are two questions to be addressed in assessing the business risks associated with acquiring a pharmacy business:

- **Do I want to be in the community pharmacy business?** In answering this question it is necessary to realise that healthcare delivery is a highly competitive industry and a largely evolving one. Retail pharmacy is facing immense pressure for change from a number of sources: political, professional and economic. This competition has resulted in an enhanced reliance on NHS dispensing and a need to develop new services by pharmacy contractors.
- **Do I want to acquire a particular pharmacy?** This second question relates to factors that affect the profitability of a particular pharmacy that is the target of an acquisition.

Having carefully evaluated the risks involved by answering the two questions, a well-informed decision can be taken to proceed (or not) with an acquisition.

Competitive risks in the whole (macro) market environment

Government policy – The OFT Report

In the UK the award of NHS Contracts has been investigated by the Office of Fair Trading (OFT). It is possible for a pharmacy to be opened anywhere; however there are currently limitations on the award of a contract to dispense prescriptions under the NHS. In a report published in early 2003, the OFT recommended deregulation, but this was quickly rejected in Scotland, Wales and Northern Ireland. The government eventually made some modifications to the recommendations that were accepted in England.

Supermarkets

Following the loss of Retail Price Maintenance (RPM), supermarkets have begun to sell General Sales List (GSL) medicines at reduced prices and this has further increased competition. Around 500 supermarkets have entered the market by obtaining new contracts or by relocating an existing pharmacy into their premises. They have better merchandising, and provide convenient one-stop shopping with extended hours. As a result they have far more customers passing through their doors.

The split of NHS to non-NHS business in community pharmacies has moved from the commonly quoted 60:40 to 80:20 or even less. Products such as toiletries and nappies – long the basis of pharmacy income – have largely disappeared from our shelves, mainly as a result of good merchandising in supermarkets. Proprietor pharmacists often tend not to concentrate on important marketing issues like layout, category management and better merchandising.

Dispensing doctors

Dispensing doctors in rural areas can often apply for a dispensing contract to cater exclusively to the rural patients registered at the surgery. In urban areas, some doctors' surgeries own their own corporate body and operate a pharmacy by employing a superintendent pharmacist. More commonly, an existing surgery will rent out part of its premises so that a contractor can relocate into the surgery; this can have a major effect on local pharmacies, whose prescription volume may decline drastically. It is not uncommon for developers to charge high rents and premiums to allow pharmacies to relocate into the surgery.

The Internet

Although trading of medicines on the Internet is increasing at a much slower rate than anticipated during the Dot.com boom, it will gain momentum. With electronic transfer of prescriptions (ETP) and web literacy of patients improving, patients are able to source from anywhere in the country. Competition could also come from pharmacies further afield, or even across borders. The local pharmaceutical services will more likely be funded from the funds devolved from the global sum, thus there is a distinct possibility of the current contractors losing out. This threat to community pharmacies is not only from new entrants but also from national chains that are better placed to bid for these local services.

Mail order pharmacy

Mail order pharmacy has gained over 15% market share in the USA. Pharmacy2U (http://www.pharmacy2u.co.uk) is one of the largest companies operating on the warehouse model and provides yet another source of competition.

One-stop healthcare centres

The 750 Primary Care Centres proposed by the NHS Plan (see Chapter 12) will create one-stop healthcare centres with pharmacies in-house, which may become a significant threat in the future. With part of the global sum of money from central government devolved to Local Health Authorities and Primary Care Trusts, manufacturers will be able to bypass wholesalers and local pharmacists, and approach fund-holders directly. The sourcing of high-priced vaccines and injections from pharmacies is also rapidly decreasing in some areas of the UK, with doctors able to secure direct supply. Oxygen deliveries through pharmacies have greatly declined because gas suppliers can now make direct deliveries.

GP prescribing habits

The prescribing habits of GPs have a direct influence on the number of prescriptions dispensed and the drug cost – for example whether a GP prescribes for 28, 56 or 84 days and whether for a brand or a generic. Pharmacists may have little control over these decisions. Prescription collection and delivery has proliferated not only as part of a health in the community initiative but also to ensure a steady flow of prescriptions.

Assessing the micro-environmental risks associated with acquiring a pharmacy

Identifying a target

Finding a pharmacy to buy could be a problem, because only 100–200 are sold each year in Britain. Information on pharmacies or NHS Contracts for sale can be obtained in several ways, including:

- Registering with national pharmacy agents such as Henry Perlow, Ernest J George, George Orridge, Keith May or Alan Orme.
- Advertising in trade journals such as *Chemist & Druggist*, the NPA's *Pink Supplement*, *Pharmaceutical Journal*, or in other pharmacy press in the 'Business Wanted' section of the classified ads.
- Enquiring through national wholesalers, whose extensive network of representatives often hear about pharmacies for sale.
- Networking with fellow pharmacists.
- Identifying the city/town and then approaching pharmacy owners directly, or asking an agent to enquire directly from proprietors.
- Consulting the register of pharmacies maintained by the Royal Pharmaceutical Society.

Starting a new business may be preferable to buying an existing one because of the high cost of goodwill. However, in pharmacy this is complicated by the extremely bureaucratic process of obtaining a new NHS Contract, which could drag on for 2 years or more because of objections from existing businesses. Many of the factors involved in starting a new business are similar when buying an existing one. In either case initial research is crucial.

Factors relating to the acquisition

In deciding whether to proceed with an acquisition it is important that an orderly approach is adopted. Table 5.1 provides an example of a checklist of items used by the author that should be carefully evaluated before arriving at a realistic purchase price.

It is beyond the scope of this chapter to cover each of these items in detail, and when intending to acquire a pharmacy it is important to seek advice from professional advisors. Some of the more important issues are dealt with below.

Choosing a location

The three golden rules of owning and running a successful retail business are location, location and location. Because a pharmacy derives most of its income from prescriptions, the most attractive location is often within sight of a doctor's surgery.

When buying an existing business, it is important to identify the locations of surgeries from which the majority of prescriptions are likely to come. There is always the possibility that a pharmacy could relocate

Table 5.1 Pharmacy acquisition checklist

General	Vendor name and address
	Pharmacy name and location
	Reason for sale?
	Years of ownership; freehold or leasehold
	Surgeries, pharmacies, residential homes, nursing homes, supermarkets, in the local neighbourhood, their addresses, maps
	Prescriptions – monthly average, collection and delivery
	Copies of last 24 months' FP34s supplied?
	If purchase agreed, *all* FP34s received by vendor after initial contact must be forwarded to Day Lewis even after completion
	Opening hours
	Computer system
	CCTV + type of alarm, name of company
	Details of any other on-going contracts, hire purchase or leasing agreements
	Staff and locum details – hours worked, rate, entitlement, staff benefits and contracts
Financial	Annual sales for last 3 years, give year-end date
	Weekly takings sheet for the last 52 weeks supplied
	Gross figure to include VAT and levy
	Copies of last 12 months' VAT returns supplied
	Stock value and condition
	Due diligence – writing letters of enquiry to local GPs, PCT, local authority planning department, change in ownership
Contracts and licences	Nursing home contracts (copies)
	RPSGB registration certificate
	Homes contracts
	NPA registration certificate
	Methylated spirit licence
	Data protection licence
	Vendor to confirm destruction of extemporary preparations and disposal of obsolete stock, galenicals/powders/poisons

between your pharmacy and the surgery from which most prescriptions originate (known as 'leapfrogging'). Applications to the appropriate authority for relocation within the defined neighbourhood are usually favourably considered.

In the interests of clinical governance, especially after the Shipman, Bristol Infirmary and Alder Hey cases, the government has indicated its intention to merge many single- and two-doctor surgeries and there is already a strong movement in this direction. The development of Primary Care Centres will speed up this consolidation of surgeries. Care should thus be taken before buying any pharmacies near small surgeries because they may be relocated. These risk factors should be reflected in the valuation of the business.

The size and condition of the surgery premises and the facilities available need to be evaluated. If there are space constraints then there is a chance that the surgery might be redeveloped, possibly some distance from the pharmacy, thus making it more vulnerable. Many developers tender out for pharmacy owners to relocate within the new development, often at a substantial premium or rent, or both. With larger corporate bodies making better-covenanted tenants, the independent pharmacy owners often lose out in this bidding process. One also has to consider local competition. The larger supermarket chains have started incorporating pharmacies within their premises and so a large supermarket currently without a pharmacy in the vicinity is a future threat. They may be able to buy an existing contract and relocate a pharmacy within the supermarket. Should the control of entry be relaxed then this threat will be increased.

A final check should always be made with the planning department of the local council. Future developments within the location could affect business in a positive or negative manner, e.g. installation of red routes, waiting restrictions and yellow lines would have detrimental effects. Conversely, relocation of doctors' surgery or construction of new houses and parking facilities might have a positive effect (see 'blight notice' below).

The NHS Contract (see also Chapter 6)

Each of the various options for buying or setting up a pharmacy come with their own legal complexities. With the existing control of entry, the first step would be to obtain an NHS Contract, either by buying the pharmacy and the NHS Contract from an existing pharmacy owner, or by acquiring shares in a corporate body owning a pharmacy, or you might be fortunate enough to successfully obtain a new contract. The legal implications are different in each case and not all lawyers will be conversant with the complexities, so it is a good idea to choose a legal firm with relevant experience.

Survey of premises

Structural survey

It is important to have a structural survey carried out by a chartered surveyor to ensure that there are no potentially expensive long-term problems, whether the property is being bought outright or is the subject of a leasehold arrangement. In addition, if the property is being bought then an independent valuation is necessary. This will take into account the condition of the premises and the locality. The banks do not usually insist on a full structural survey. It is up to the purchaser to protect the investment.

Business rates

A survey of the premises is also important for the purposes of assessing rates. Every property is assigned a rateable value by the District Valuer, which is reviewed in April every year, and the rates of X pence for every pound of rateable value have to be paid annually. It is important to seek the advice of a chartered surveyor to evaluate the rateable value. Properties are sometimes over-valued by the District Surveyor, and if this is the case, an appeal can be lodged. However, it can take the District Valuer 6 months or more to consider the case. It is therefore important to lodge the appeal as early as possible, because for successful appeals the credit is backdated to the date of the appeal. Any changes in the locality that adversely affect trading in the area can lead to a reduction in rateable value, and similarly, extending a property can lead to an increase.

If the premises are vacant then no rates are payable for 6 months. Depending on the local council, only half rates might be payable, but in order to qualify for this the building has to be completely vacant and have no furniture of any kind. Lastly, if any building is vacant and under repair then no rates are payable during the period of the building works, provided the local council is notified. The general rule of thumb is that the higher the rentable values in the locality the higher will be the rateable value of the property, and vice versa.

Moving to a leasehold premise

Taking on an existing lease

When contemplating a move to leasehold premises it is important to have the lease carefully scrutinised by a surveyor or lawyer, to highlight any contentious clauses. For example, a repair covenant requires a person taking over a lease to be responsible for all repair liabilities for the rest of the lease, including those incurred before the lease was assigned.

The surveyor can be asked to evaluate the rateable value and advise on the likely outcome of the future rent review. There may be some clauses that could make it difficult to sell the business in the future.

Negotiating a new lease

Often a retiring pharmacist wishes to sell the pharmacy business but wants to retain the property as an investment. It is crucial to negotiate the terms of a lease in principle before deciding on the goodwill (see below). Goodwill – the premium paid by the purchaser to reflect the intangible value of the business – is affected by a number of factors including rental values.

Rental values have a direct effect on the goodwill value of the business. The other factors to bear in mind are those that could enhance or reduce the value of the goodwill. Is there a break clause in favour of the landlord? Is the lease too restrictive in its user clause? Are there restrictions as to what can be sold from the premises? Are there restrictions as to what signage is allowed outside the shop?

Purchasers often agree the rent and the terms of the lease and leave the rest to the lawyers. This can lead to extra legal costs as the lease is shuttled between lawyers, each adding and deleting clauses. Solicitors charge for each letter received or sent. The memorandum of understanding with the vendor, or Heads of Term, should be sent to lawyers.

Leases are often 15 to 20 years long and there is no certainty that the pharmacy will be in the same location for this time. In fact it is often better to take a 10-year lease and leave the option open to relocate if necessary. A break clause in favour of the tenant is desirable for longer leases, although landlords are unlikely to offer one. However, at the time of negotiating the purchase of the pharmacy the landlord may agree if they feel they are cashing in on the goodwill. The other factor worth considering is whether to avoid having to give a personal guarantee for the lease by purchasing the pharmacy in the name of a limited company and giving a quarter's rent as a rental deposit. Leases issued prior to changes in legislation regarding the privity clause means that the guarantee could be called upon the lifetime of the lease, even if the pharmacy has been sold on to someone else. Lastly it is important to make sure that the lease does not prohibit any other business use – the landlord should not be able to withhold change of use for the lease, in case you wish to relocate the pharmacy and assign the lease for some other use.

Anti-competitive clauses   Often a parade of shops is owned by the same landlord and, because it is in his/her interest to have successful tenants, he/she may put anti-competitive clauses in the lease. These prohibit other traders on the parade from selling items that would normally be sold in a pharmacy. If there is a breach of this covenant, i.e. a neighbouring shop starts allocating a large amount of display for toiletries or medicines, then it is important to notify the landlord as soon as possible. Failure to do this could make it difficult for the landlord to take prohibitive action.

Assignment of lease   When selling a pharmacy, the landlord's consent is required to assign the lease and use the premises as a pharmacy. The landlord will also demand payment of their legal costs for the assignment and could refuse the assignment if they feel the guarantees offered by the new lessee are not strong enough. The landlord usually requests bankers, accountants and other landlord's references before agreeing to the assignment. Many first-time owners may experience difficulties because they do not have references from other landlords, however this can be overcome by giving personal guarantees and a rent deposit. Most leases include a clause to protect the tenant, that the landlord would not unreasonably refuse the assignment of the lease. There has to be valid ground, e.g. poor covenants offered by the new tenant, or breaches of the repairing obligations on the premises.

Dilapidation   It is usual for landlords to serve a dilapidation order on the tenant at the rent review period, but most certainly when the lease runs out. This enables the landlord to force the tenants to carry out all repairs and redecoration to the whole property, interior and exterior. The dilapidation schedule will also include the tenant's own improvements. Not painting windows and other woodwork often means having to replace them at a later date because of their poor condition. Ignoring leaking gutters can lead to subsidence and cracking in structural walls. Ignoring leaking roofs can result in rotting roof timbers. It is better to take preventative action. Finally, if the lease is not renewed then all fittings attached to the building, e.g. suspended ceiling lights, plumbing, etc. belong to the landlord and cannot be removed. It is therefore important to maintain the property, as any neglect could prove to be costly in the long run. The electrical wiring also forms part of the landlord's premises and may have to be replaced at the tenant's expense.

Disclosures   All contracts of employment of existing staff should be reviewed for any onerous conditions. Solicitors will carry out a local search to satisfy the mortgagee, as they will take charge of the lease. The lease itself has to be mortgageable and all information disclosed before the purchase agreement should form part of the disclosure. The disclosure should include any information that might be detrimental to the business, such as relocation of doctor's surgeries or application for a new contract. Disclosure should also include nursing home business, or loss of any large account customer.

Blight notice   The law allows the tenant or the landlord to make a 'blight notice' claim on the local council for any loss in trade from major government-initiated development in the area. This could be a major alteration in the roads or a traffic diversion, for example. A blight notice can also be served if the property falls under compulsory purchase order. The cost of retaining a surveyor to lodge the claim is also paid by the local council. The claim can include all losses due to forced sale of goods, cost of relocation, cost of new fittings and loss of profits for 3 years. The laws relating to blight notices are complicated and it is important to seek expert advice from a chartered surveyor and solicitor.

Insurance   Under the Landlord and Tenant Act 1988 and the Commonhold and Leasehold Reform Act 2002, the tenant could be responsible for all insurance and repair to the premises rented from the landlord and the landlord can serve notices on the tenant for any breach of this contract under the terms of the lease. In practice the landlord may pay the premium and reclaim it from the tenant. In order to reduce the cost it is worth obtaining an independent quote and comparing it with the landlord's premium. It is worth asking the landlord to allow you to insure the property and have his/her interest noted in the policy. This way the landlord is protected and you can shop around for the cheapest insurance. Most leases make it the tenant's responsibility to insure the plate glass and tenant improvements – suspended ceilings, flooring, wiring, extensions, etc. The occupier is also responsible for insuring the fixtures, fittings and stock.

It is important to ensure that the property is not under-insured and it is worth asking a valuation surveyor to indicate the value at which the property should be insured. Insurance companies are also able to send an agent to advise. There is no need to insure the land itself.

An insurance company will often demand an alarm system and five-level mortice locks on all exit doors. The back door usually requires a metal plate to be fitted to it. Failure to do this could nullify any claims arising from a burglar alarm activation. It is important to ensure that the insurance covers subsidence and damage caused by riots. There is public liability insurance for third-party claims. If the premises, or its contents, are under-insured then the loss adjuster appointed by the insurers will cut down the claim on a pro rata basis. For a full discussion of insurance matters please see Chapter 9.

Landlord covenants   All leases contain conditions that the tenant is obliged to fulfil. It is often not permitted to sublet parts of the premises or assign the lease without landlord consent. Similarly all planning permission applications and building alterations need landlord consent – removal of any load-bearing walls could cause subsidence or damage to the property. The property must be maintained in good condition and usually has to be painted every 3 to 5 years. Any change of user clause needs the landlord's consent. Affixing fascias, especially illuminated, would also require the landlord's consent. Any serious breach of these conditions might cause the landlord to seek termination of the lease or refuse to renew the lease at the end of its term.

Lease renewals   Under the relevant Acts the tenant has the protection of having the lease renewed. The lease will allow for regular review of the rent, but landlords are required to serve a notice indicating an increase in rent and by law the tenant has the right to appeal if this does not reflect the going market rate. It is important to retain the services of a chartered surveyor to advise and agree rental increases. In the event the two parties do not agree, there is recourse to apply to the Royal Institute of Chartered Surveyors, who can appoint an arbitrator whose finding is binding on both parties.

The only grounds on which the landlord can refuse to renew the lease are (a) if the tenant has seriously breached any covenants; (b) the landlord wants the property for their own use; or (c) the property is to be demolished or redeveloped.

At the end of the lease the landlord serves a notice terminating the lease and the tenant has to file a counter-notice in court to renew it. Whenever such a notice is received, legal advice must be sought to file for protection. Respective lawyers would then negotiate a new lease. A surveyor must be appointed to agree the new rental and any changes in the terms of the lease, e.g. length, permission to sublet the flat upstairs, etc.

Rent reviews   Under the terms of the lease the landlord has to serve notice of a rent increase and the tenant has the right to appeal. Advice must be sought from a local chartered surveyor before agreeing to any rental increase. The landlord has to justify any rental increases and they must be based on the current rents charged in the locality. The premises are zoned into different categories and valued accordingly, e.g. the front of the shop is Zone A and it is worth more rental value per square foot than the storerooms which could be say Zone D. The chartered surveyor has good knowledge of the area and can use comparable figures in the locality to help mitigate rent increases. Under the Landlord and Tenants Act both parties have recourse to have the matter determined by an arbitrator appointed by the Royal Institute of Chartered Surveyors. The arbitrator has the final say and bases his judgement on the evidence presented by each party. Most leases contain a clause that prevents rents from going down. Some leases, especially the pharmacies located in doctors' surgeries, are often index-linked. In a high inflationary period these could prove to be detrimental. One has to take a view before accepting an index-linked rental revaluation clause. The frequency of reviews is usually 3–5 years and so one must ensure that there are no onerous clauses, which favour the landlord.

Safety Once a new lease is taken on from the landlord, it is the responsibility of the tenant to comply with all legal requirements. The property must comply with all aspects of health and safety regulations.

Transferring the NHS Contract (see also Chapter 6)

The special nature of the pharmacy business makes it different from the other retail businesses. It is important to ensure that the lawyer acting on your behalf has a clear understanding of the intricacies of NHS laws. Apart from carrying out legal assignment of leases, freeholds and transfer of undertakings of staff, the contract needs to provide for the pharmaceutical needs as well. It needs to ensure that the contracts are signed subject to transfer of the NHS Contract, which is vested in the vendor's name. The premises itself should also be registered with the Royal Pharmaceutical Society of Great Britain (RPSGB).

Purchase of a limited company

Due diligence

In the case of a purchase of a corporate body, it is important to ensure that all the unknown and known liabilities of the company are warranted by the vendor. Any fraudulent claims from the Prescription Pricing

Authority (PPA) could also jeopardise the NHS Contract and this should also be a part of the warrantee. Because all the liabilities are passed on to the purchaser, it is important to ensure that more emphasis is given to the disclosure and warranties. The purchaser inherits the historic goodwill value (see below) and the deferred capital gain tax, and this future liability, along with the legal and professional costs, should be taken into account before agreeing to the purchase in this manner. The valuation of the business should reflect this.

In spite of the disclosure and warranties, it is important to ask a chartered account to carry out an inspection of accounts (known as 'due diligence') before completion. All necessary enquiries should be made with PCTs, planning departments and GP surgeries. The new owners of the company need to ensure that they retain all records for 6 years, including PAYE. The Inland Revenue and HM Customs & Excise can demand records up to 6 years old and reclaim any unpaid taxes. All unpaid debts of the company are inherited by the purchaser and hence need to be disclosed.

Process of transfer

The contracts for sale and transfer of companies are very complicated and reflect the risk the purchaser is taking when buying the company. The transaction also requires the auditors of both the vendor and the purchaser to liaise in order to reconcile the assets and liabilities of the company, and establish a final value for the shares.

The vendor's accountant prepares projected interim accounts showing the anticipated value of the company and the sale proceeds on this basis. Solicitors normally hold up to 10% of the purchase price as retention to cover any liabilities that might emerge.

After 3 months, once the final value of the NHS debtors has been established, completion accounts are jointly prepared by both accountants in order to establish a final value of the company. This value will establish all future liabilities, such as PAYE and tax, as well as creditors and debtors.

The solicitors would then release part of the retention and ownership of the company is transferred over to the purchaser. The balance of the retention is held jointly by the two solicitors for approximately 2 years to cover for any eventualities. If no undisclosed claims are forthcoming, the retention is released to the vendor.

The Superintendent Pharmacist appointment has to be notified to the RPSGB. All bank mandates also have to be cancelled by the outgoing director and new ones put in place by the purchaser.

Calculating the cost of a business

The purchase price of a business comprises four main elements in addition to the cost of the property or lease:

- Goodwill
- Value of turnover
- Stock (inventory)
- Equipment, fixtures and fittings

In addition a buyer should make provision for the cost of stamp duty on the purchase and have sufficient working capital.

Goodwill

Goodwill represents a premium paid in respect of certain competitive advantages enjoyed by a business due to a combination of factors including:

- geographical location;
- reputation built up over many years;
- some special service or product provided by a business.

The cost of all investments is determined by the potential return on capital and in retail pharmacy this is no different. Goodwill paid for a pharmacy would need to generate sufficient revenues in order to repay its liability to the banks and give an adequate return on capital. There is a direct relationship between the risk taken and expected returns.

Therefore any uncertainty in the future viability of a pharmacy would increase the risk and hence reduce the value of investment. The goodwill value therefore falls if the future looks bleak and likewise increases in periods of optimism.

The valuation of goodwill is often a matter for negotiation between parties; there is no fixed formula. A figure is arrived at with the help of advisors, according to circumstances prevailing at the time of sale. A common method is to use a multiplier (e.g. $\times 5$) on the average net profit. The following factors would decrease the goodwill.

- High level of nursing home business – not guaranteed to be retained.
- Scripts from single or small surgery (likely to be relocated in the future).
- Existing doctor's surgery in a poor state of repair or cramped – likely to move.
- Extended trading hours – difficulty in obtaining pharmacist cover.

- Short lease – reduces bank security.
- Condition of property – potential dilapidation.
- Condition of shop fittings – additional investment necessary.
- Low level of dispensing – less than 60% of total sales.
- Local planning – supermarkets, red routes, parking restrictions, etc.
- Area where pharmacist and staff recruitment is difficult.
- Business focused on many deliveries – expensive and not easy to manage.
- High agency sales, cosmetics, perfumery – cost of stock investment high and no guarantee to retain agency.
- Local large supermarket does not have an in-house pharmacy – future threat under government's deregulation agenda.
- Major buyers leave the market affecting the demand, e.g. Unichem, AAH and Phoenix, sourcing shops in mainland Europe due to regulation.
- Higher Bank of England base rate – high loan repayments.

Factors contrary to the above will increase goodwill valuation:

- Location within or adjoining a surgery – long-term security.
- High NHS dispensing – easy to manage.
- Badly managed pharmacy – potential to increase sales.
- Lower margin shop – potential to increase profitability.
- Strategically located near existing shops – will increase traffic.
- Well-trained staff – can help build up the business.
- Competition in the area – potential to increase sales.
- Only pharmacy in a rural setting – no competition.
- Doctors relocating in the area –potential to increase business.
- The local surgery being recently renovated – unlikely to relocate in the near future.
- Short working hours – easy to manage and potential of increasing hours.

Calculating the value of turnover

At one time pharmacy was valued as a percentage of turnover or annual sales, but this is no longer the case. A pharmacy, like any other business, is valued on the multiple of net profitability before cost of finance. As a general rule of thumb, 20% return on capital is reasonable when owning and running a pharmacy, and so the net profitability of a pharmacy needs to be calculated and multiplied by five, ignoring all the interest charges (borrowing costs). This is a rule of thumb valuation and other factors that would increase or decrease the goodwill need to be taken into consideration.

Often the financial account of the vendor does not paint a true picture. It is important to add back or take away costs depending on the nature of the particular business. Self-employed pharmacist owners often do not consider their own salaries as an expense, which would appear as profits. On the other hand, the pharmacy owned through a corporate company has to show the owner's salaries in the form of directors' remuneration and this then reduces the profit. To compare on a like for like basis, it is important to ignore all drawings or salaries by the proprietor and replace it with the cost of substituting the vendor with another pharmacist at a market salary. The same is true for spouses, as often their salaries are distorted.

The most practical way of calculating the professional salary of the pharmacist is to use the equivalent locum rate for the hours that the pharmacy is open. Other matters to be considered are verification of income, staffing costs and property overheads.

Calculating the value of stock (inventory)

Stock should be valued at the lower of cost and market value, as near to the handover date as possible. In practice there may be a fair amount of 'horse-trading' about what will be taken on by the new owner and what is considered 'dead' and outdated stock. A competent pharmaceutical stock-taker will be happy to arbitrate in such situations.

The vendors should be responsible for the cost of disposing of old unwanted medicines.

Value of equipment, fixtures and fittings

All equipment purchased should be unencumbered and of free title and the ownership titles should be available to pass to the purchaser. All hire purchase agreements relating to CCTVs, PMR records and even the shelving should be disclosed. The warranties should also cover the accuracy of all financial and other trading information provided by the vendor. With regards to the stock, it is important to include the basis for pharmaceutical and toiletries stock and that any non-saleable and short-dated stock is excluded.

Fixtures and fittings are charged at the written-down value in the profit and loss account, but again a consensus view of the value usually emerges.

Other costs to be financed

Initial operating capital

The NHS pays 60 days in arrears (although a 30-day advance is given) and in order to fund NHS debtors and VAT, the pharmacy will require 3–4% of turnover in addition to the purchase price.

It is also common practice to negotiate extended credit from wholesalers for the first few months' purchases. This helps to cover other overheads like legal, professional and unforeseen costs.

Stamp duty

Stamp duty is payable on purchase of assets but not the goodwill element of the pharmacy and so it is important to negotiate apportion of the purchase price effectively. Stamp duty is payable if the purchase is by way of transfer of shares and also on the purchase of freehold property.

Sources of finance

Buying a business requires substantial investment, and an individual's savings are often insufficient. Business loans are available from a number of sources, which vary with respect to factors such as size, length of loan, available security, interest rates payable, etc.

Gerry Green (Green Pharmacy Consultants), addressing a joint Institute of Pharmacy Management and Young Pharmacists' Group Conference in 2000, warned colleagues that before taking steps to buy a pharmacy, pharmacists should be aware of all the costs involved. The stock would require an upfront payment of £20000 to £30000, and fixtures and fittings could have a book value of £10000. The goodwill would be five or six times the business's net profit figure. On top of that, the purchaser would need to allow about £10000 for various fees and start-up costs.

Wholesaler guarantees

Ideally, personal capital should be used to fund a purchase. Borrowing directly from a bank involves all sorts of personal guarantees – which the bank would have no hesitation in enforcing – and interest charges at base rate plus 2.5–3%. The most common and often preferred way of purchasing a pharmacy is to use the loan guarantee scheme offered by the three large national wholesalers – Alliance-Unichem, AAH and Phoenix. The wholesaler guarantees up to 80% of the purchase value, including the stock, to the bank, and in turn would expect the pharmacy owner and spouse to personally guarantee this loan to them. The 20% contribution expected from the purchaser would come from savings or be borrowed from family and friends. Subsequent purchases of any more pharmacies by the purchaser may require less cash input because of the equity build-up by the first business.

There is an advantage to the borrower in that, because of the nature of the wholesaler's guarantee, the interest rate itself is lower than might otherwise be expected – 0.5–1.0% above base rate – and it is repayable over 10 years. The interest is usually added to the principal and the repayments are made by 120 equal monthly instalments. The bank would also take a fixed charge on the lease or freehold and fixed assets of the company as their security.

In most cases the bank would expect the business to retain its trading account with them. There are, however, some exceptions, including Medical Finance Ltd, which provides a loan to a pharmacy owner on wholesaler's guarantee and allows the proprietor to have an overdraft facility with a clearing bank. In this case the wholesalers would expect 70% of purchases to be made through them under their agreed terms and conditions. This allows some purchases to be made elsewhere if a better deal can be struck.

Advances against NHS receipts

There are other companies, such as Pharmacy Partners, who advance money against the NHS debt, bearing in mind that the NHS pays up to 60 days in arrears and money is owed to HM Customs & Excise for VAT. Although suppliers are paid VAT on purchases, Customs & Excise treat dispensing sales as an exempt item and therefore the NHS does not reimburse VAT. This has to be reclaimed from Customs & Excise. The combined figure could be in excess of £50 000 for an average pharmacy. The cost of borrowing offered by Pharmacy Partners would be higher than that offered by clearing banks (see *Pharm J* 2000; 265: 189).

The Small Firms Loan Guarantee Scheme

An estimated £8 billion is available in the UK for small and medium enterprises (SMEs) from the DTI, EU, Business Link and Business Angels. The Small Business Service (SBS) Small Firms Loan Guarantee Scheme guarantees loans from the banks and other financial institutions for small firms that have viable business proposals but who have tried and failed to get a conventional loan because of lack of security. The loans are available for periods of between 2 and 10 years on sums from £5000 to £100000 and also up to £250000 if a business has been trading for more than 2 years. The SBS guarantees 70% of the loan, which could be up to 85% if a business has been trading for more than 2 years. In return for the guarantee the borrower pays the SBS a premium of 1.5% per year on the outstanding amount of the loan. The premium could be reduced to 0.5% if the loan is taken at a fixed rate of interest.

Other sources

There are also banking subsidiaries such as Lombard, HSBC Commercial Finance, etc. offering asset finance, helping to finance fixed assets – fixtures and fittings, computers, shop refurbishment, etc. This can be by way of a straight loan or by leasing or hire purchase over 3 to 5 years at a higher interest rate than a straight bank loan. Vehicles for business can also be funded in this manner.

The National Pharmaceutical Association (NPA) financial services division also offers finance for fixed assets over a similar period for a maximum of £30000 per owner. It is important not to use short-term working capital, e.g. an overdraft, to purchase fixed assets.

Cost of financing

The cost of financing the purchase must not be forgotten. The following example shows how to calculate loan repayments.

The monthly loan repayment for a business purchase including stock of about £45000 might be calculated as follows:

Goodwill	£266000
Stock	£45000
Total cost	£311000
Deposit 20%	£62200
80% borrowing	£248800

At a rate of 1¼% over base rate over 10 years with interest to principal at a base rate of 6%, i.e. on a fixed repayment basis would be £1250 per every £100000 borrowed. Therefore the repayment for the above loan, including interest, is

$$\frac{£248\,800}{£100\,000} \times 1.250$$

= £3110 per month

= £37320 per year

The loan interest rate and repayment would depend on the Bank of England base rate at the time.

The profit of £53 200 leaves approximately £16 000 positive cash flow. This is a useful buffer. This is after having received a pharmacist salary of £30 000.

Structural alterations

It may be that alterations are necessary when taking over a new business. Planning permission is necessary for any exterior changes to the property or change of use from one class to another, i.e. storeroom to a flat or offices. All illuminated fascias and extensions need consent from the landlord and local council. Similarly, removal of any main structures must conform with building and health and safety regulations. For changes to listed properties and in conservation areas, local government consent is needed. VAT exemptions and grants are available for certain types of properties. Any changes to the shop front, and the facade of the shop, would also require planning permission.

Further reading

Anon. Buying and selling pharmacies. *Pharm J* 2004; 273: 11.

A guide to buying and selling pharmacy businesses has been produced by the law firm Charles Russell. The guide covers aspects such as structuring the sale and purchase, identifying assets to be transferred, steps in the transaction and tax allowances and reliefs. Free copies can be obtained from Stephanie Palmer (tel 020 7203 5065, email stephanie.palmer@charlesrussell.co.uk) or downloaded at www.charlesrussell.co.uk

Holland-Brown N. Buying a pharmacy: A guide for the first-time buyer. *Pharm J* 2003; 270: 578–580.

McQueen J. Pitfalls in business and how to avoid them. *Pharm J* 2001; 266: 403.

Pitfalls in acquiring a pharmacy business. Report of Institute of Pharmacy Management International/Young Pharmacists Group Joint Conference, Brighton April 2000. *Pharm J* 2000; 264: 634.

Wang L-N. Raising capital – The wholesaler's guarantees schemes. *Pharm J* 2003; 270: 581–582.

6

Legal aspects of pharmacy business

Gordon Appelbe

Introduction

Ever thought of buying a pharmacy or establishing a new one? If you have, or intend to, then a few legal hints might come in useful. Probably the first question to answer is who is going to own the business – you personally as an independent owner, a partnership, or a private limited company? All three of these legal owners can own a pharmacy business or in Medicines Act phraseology be 'a person lawfully conducting a retail pharmacy business'. However, the only person who can individually own a pharmacy business is a pharmacist on the register in Great Britain (see also Chapter 4).

Individual ownership

An individual pharmacist may own a retail pharmacy business and as such take all the profits. However he must also accept all the liabilities that, if the business fails, could result in bankruptcy.

Partnerships

A partnership is defined in the Partnership Act 1890 as the relationship that exists between persons carrying on a business in common with a view of profit. In contrast to a company (see below), a partnership, or **firm**, is simply a number of individuals each of whom has a responsibility for the affairs and liabilities of the firm as a whole.

In England and Wales a partnership (firm) does not have a legal status of its own as does a company. This means that the private assets of each partner can be called upon to satisfy any of the firm's debts – jointly and severally. All the partners are liable for any debts incurred by one partner acting on behalf of the firm.

In Scotland a partnership has a status similar to that of a body corporate, i.e. it is a legal person distinct from the partners of whom it is composed. It is for this reason that in a partnership owning a retail pharmacy in England and Wales all the partners must be pharmacists, whereas in a Scottish partnership only one partner need be a pharmacist. A partnership can arise in either of two ways: by express agreement, or by implied agreement between two or more persons. A partnership can be implied if two or more persons work together in such a way as to fall within the definition as set out in the Act. Generally, if they share in the management of the business and share the profits, then the law will recognise them as partners.

When a partnership is formed to run a retail pharmacy, it is invariably a partnership of express agreement, and the conditions of the partnership should be set out in a partnership contract or articles. The articles can be altered at any time with the consent of all the partners, whether this is express or implied. The only exception is where the articles restrict the right to vary, e.g. that no change may be made for 2 years.

A partnership can be formed where one of the partners may limit their responsibility for the firm's debts, leaving the other partners to share the unlimited liability. This partner is often referred to as a **sleeping partner**, as they take no part in the management of the firm. Partnerships of this type are not common and are governed by the Limited Partnerships Act 1907. If a person wishes to limit their liability in this way today they are more likely to invest in a limited company. Once again, it is stressed that before contemplating forming a partnership pharmacists should take legal advice and have any partnership contract drawn up by a solicitor.

Companies (see also Chapter 4)

If you wish to limit your liability then you can set up a private limited company with yourself, and others, as shareholders and/or directors of the company. A company – or corporation aggregate – is a body of persons combined or incorporated for some common purpose. The most common example is a registered trading company, that is, a company that has been incorporated under the Companies Act 1985 (as amended). These Acts are a consolidation of the law relating to companies contained in a number of earlier statutes, including certain sections of the European Communities Act 1972. The notes given here can only outline the general principles of company law, with some special reference to certain aspects that particularly affect pharmacy businesses.

Incorporation as a company enables a group of people to act and to trade in the same way as an individual owner. It also enables them to trade with limited liability to the individual shareholder. Once incorporated a company is a legal person and quite distinct from its members. It can own property, employ persons, and be a creditor or debtor just like a human being. This is the fundamental principle of company law.

The promoters of a company must file the following documents with the Register of Companies:

- Memorandum of Association.
- Articles of Association.
- List of directors and name of secretary.
- Statement of the nominal share capital.
- Notice of the address of the registered office.
- Declaration by a solicitor or a person named in the articles as a director or secretary that all the requirements of the Companies Acts in respect of registration have been complied with.

If all the documents are in order the registrar will issue a certificate of incorporation, which is conclusive evidence that the company has been registered and that the requirements of the Act have been complied with.

There are at least three types of company: a public company; a private limited company; and a private unlimited company. Most pharmacists will be concerned with the private company, whether limited or not. A **private company** needs only one director, although there may be more than one. If there is a sole director he/she cannot also be the company secretary. Shares and debentures in a private company cannot be offered to the public. An **unlimited company** is one where there is no limit on the members' liability to contribute to the assets in order to satisfy the company's debts.

A company must appoint a pharmacist as its superintendent who is responsible for the keeping, preparing, selling and dispensing of medicines and for ensuring that the business as far as it concerns the sale of medicines is under his/her control or subject to his/her directions, under the control of another pharmacist.

Memorandum of Association

The Memorandum of Association regulates the external affairs of the company and must include five clauses, namely, those relating to the name, registered office, objects, liability and capital of the company. It must be signed by each subscriber.

The name of a private limited company must end with the word 'limited'. For a public limited company the last words must be 'public limited company' or 'plc'.

There is a general freedom of choice of the company name, but a company cannot be registered under the Act by a name that includes, otherwise than at the end of its name, the words 'limited', 'unlimited' or 'public limited company' or the Welsh equivalents, e.g. 'cfyngedig'. Where 'cfyngedig' is used, the fact that the company is a limited company must also be stated in English and in legible characters on all official company stationery and publications, and in a notice conspicuously displayed in every place where the company's business is carried on.

No name may be used that the registrar considers offensive, or which, if used, would constitute a criminal offence. In the latter category would fall a retail company that is not conducting a retail pharmacy business but wishes to use the title 'chemist'. However this restriction is applied in the Medicines Act 1968.

Certain words and expressions may only be used in company or business names with the approval of the Secretary of State or other relevant body specified in regulations (SI 1981 No.1685, as amended). For the word 'chemist' the Royal Pharmaceutical Society of Great Britain is the relevant body, but, when 'chemist' or 'chemistry' is used in an industrial sense, it is the Royal Society of Chemistry. Similarly, for the word 'apothecary' the relevant body in England and Wales is the Worshipful Society of Apothecaries and in Scotland, the Royal Pharmaceutical Society of Great Britain. Some titles are totally prohibited, e.g. the word 'Royal'.

Articles of Association

The Articles of Association regulate the internal affairs of the company, i.e. the rights of shareholders and the manner in which the business of the company is conducted. A model set of articles is set out in regulations made under the Act, which may be used by a company as it is, or adapted as required. If no articles are submitted with the application for registration the statutory ones will apply. The articles of a company are freely alterable by special resolution of the company, subject to certain safeguards.

The legal effect of the Memorandum and Articles is that they bind the company and its members as if they had been signed and sealed by each individual member and contained covenants on the part of each member to observe all the provisions of the Memorandum and Articles.

Directors

The first directors of a company are usually appointed in accordance with the articles; if not they are appointed by the original subscribers to the company. Subsequent appointments are usually governed by a procedure laid down in the articles. It must be stressed that a pharmacist becoming a director should be fully aware of the contents of the Memorandum and Articles of Association of the company he/she joins. Directors must exercise their powers as directors for the benefit of the company. A director has a duty to the company to exercise such skill and care as he/she possesses. If appointed in a specific capacity calling for a particular skill, e.g. a pharmacist who is a director of a body corporate, must exercise that skill in a reasonable manner for the benefit of the company. Directors are not bound to give continuing and unremitting attention to the company's affairs and are justified in trusting the officers of the company to perform their duties honestly.

A pharmacist who becomes superintendent chemist of a company will almost invariably be appointed a director, and a knowledge of the powers and duties of directors is essential. For example, if a company fails to make its annual return then the company and/or any of its officers or directors is liable to a default fine. A pharmacist who resigns as a superintendent chemist should ensure that they also resign as a director. Instances have occurred where a pharmacist, some years after having resigned as a superintendent chemist, has been prosecuted for failing to make an annual return because he/she had remained a director of the company.

Registration of pharmacy premises

Having made the decision to own the business and having acquired premises the next step is to register the premises with the Royal Pharmaceutical Society of Great Britain (RPSGB). The provisions for registration are laid down by the Medicines Act 1968 and a form for this purpose is available from the Society. The Society's Registrar has to inform the appropriate Minister at the Department of Health and may not register the premises before the end of two months unless the Minister consents for such registration. The registration form has to have the name of the owner, the full postal address of the premises, a brief description of the premises and two copies of a sketch plan, drawn to scale, showing where medicines are prepared, sold, dispensed, supplied or stored together with a statement that there are arrangements so as to enable supervision to be exercised by a pharmacist of any dispensing and sale of medicines at one and the same time. In the case of a company the name of the superintendent must be on the form and a declaration made by him/her as to whether or not he/she is on the board of directors. If the superintendent is not on the board the company may only use the title 'pharmacy' in connection with its business. Before registration there will be a visit from the Society's inspector, unless it is an existing business, who will verify the particulars submitted.

In the case of new premises, the proposals submitted have to include layout of the dispensary, etc., should comply with the Society's Code of Ethics and in order to comply with the Misuse of Drugs Act 1971 there should be a controlled drugs cupboard that conforms with the legal specification and which must be bolted to the floor or wall – not a partition wall.

Employment legislation (see also Chapter 8)

Conducting a successful business, of course, depends on the employment of staff. There is a massive volume of legislation concerning the employment of staff and only a hint can be given in this chapter. Difficulties and misunderstandings frequently arise between employer and employee because the terms of the employment have not been put in writing. It is advisable to ensure that all the conditions of service are set out either in an exchange of letters or in a formal contract. More details are included in the references at the end of the chapter.

An employer is required to give an employee, not later than 8 weeks after commencement of employment, a written statement identifying the parties, specifying the date of commencement of employment and giving, among other particulars, details as to the scale or rate of remuneration; terms and conditions relating to hours of work; holiday and sickness entitlement; and the length of notice the employee is obliged to give and is entitled to receive in order to terminate their employment. Each statement must specify the person to whom an employee can apply for the purpose of seeking redress of any grievance relating to their employment and give details of any disciplinary rules which apply to them. There is no requirement to give a written statement if the employee normally works less than 16 hours per week. Note that the written statement is *not* a contract of employment.

Changes in the terms of employment have to be notified in writing by the employer to the employee within 1 month of such a change.

The amount of notice an employer must give to terminate the contract of employment of a person who has been continuously employed for 1 month or more varies with the period of continuous employment – 1 week if employment has been for less than 2 years and 1 week for each year of continuous employment after 2 years.

Statutory Sick Pay (SSP) is payable to all staff between 16 and 65 years of age who earn more than the lower earnings limit for National Insurance contributions. SSP cannot be claimed until the employee has been absent for more than 3 days. There are special detailed requirements for any pregnant employee.

There are detailed requirements regarding conditions of employment relating to working time and require employers to consult with their employees and set up procedures to monitor and record working hours. Shop workers are permitted to refuse to work on a Sunday and cannot be dismissed, made redundant or subject to any prejudicial action for so refusing.

Working conditions (see also Chapter 8)

The legislation requires that there is provision for a comprehensive system for securing the health, safety and welfare of all people at work and there is a duty placed on employers, and employees, to ensure that this is carried out. In addition, other legislation requires certain conditions to be maintained in the workplace. These include four areas – namely the working environment, safety, facilities and general housekeeping. These areas cover such matters as working room temperatures, ventilation, lighting and space; safety not only for staff but also for customers; facilities for washing and toilets; and disposal of waste materials. Special provisions are laid down for the disabled.

There are special provisions regarding the disposal of controlled waste. The Controlled Waste Regulations 1992 define clinical waste as, amongst other things, 'waste arising from . . . pharmaceutical or similar practice . . .' and describes clinical waste that arises from a private dwelling or residential home as household waste, as distinct from that from any other source. It is unlawful to deposit controlled waste in, or keep it on, any land, or knowingly cause or permit such waste to be deposited unless a waste management licence authorising the deposit is in force. The Water Resources Act 1991 prohibits a person from causing or knowingly permitting any noxious, poisonous or polluting matter to enter any inland waters.

Controlled waste includes household, industrial and commercial waste of any kind, whether conventionally thought of as polluting or not. A pharmacist whose actions give rise to controlled waste, including a decision to discard such material, is fully bound under the legislation as a producer of controlled waste and carries the corresponding duty of care, including where medicines are returned by patients. A clear interpretation as to how the code of practice should be applied to medicines returned by patients is not available. It is clearly wise to contact the local office of the Environment Agency for specific guidance on compliance with the code.

There are special restrictions on the destruction of controlled drugs. Controlled drugs returned by patients are subject to the same considerations described above for other returned medicines and advice should be sought from the relevant Environment Agency. Unwanted stocks of controlled drugs are still subject to the requirement for witnessed destruction on the site of their production but disposal via the sewage system does not comply with the Water Resources Act. Accordingly, the practice has developed that the pharmacist will arrange denaturing: the resultant product and its container is then treated as a special waste.

The Special Waste Regulations 1996 provide that waste falling within certain descriptions should be designated as special waste and subject to more extensive documentation than is required for non-special waste before it may be removed from premises. Special waste means controlled waste containing substances listed in Schedule II to the regulations and that has specified hazardous properties as set out in the regulations or is a prescription-only medicinal product.

Other aspects of a pharmacy business of which owners should be aware relate to weights and measures; trade descriptions, which include advertising; and consumer protection, which includes product liability, safety of goods and price controls.

Certain activities are unlawful. The legislation renders unlawful discrimination on the grounds of sex, marriage, race or disability. It also requires that a woman shall not be treated less favourably than a man in the same employment in respect of pay and other terms of her contract where she is employed on the same or similar work as a man.

National Health Service Contracts

Most owners of retail pharmacies will want to provide pharmaceutical services, which includes the dispensing of medicines, under the provisions of the National Health Service, and will have to apply for a contract with the local health authority and comply with the chemist's terms of contract.

Sale or supply of medicines

All pharmacies are permitted to sell certain medicines over the counter. Those medicines that are on the General Sales List (GSL) may be freely sold but those that are Pharmacy-Only Medicines (P) may only be sold from a pharmacy and even then only by, or under the supervision of a pharmacist.

A Prescription-Only Medicine (POM) may only be sold or supplied in accordance with a prescription given by a practitioner. To meet that requirement, certain conditions must be satisfied. The prescription must be signed in ink by the practitioner giving it; must be written in ink or otherwise so as to be indelible and must include the following particulars:

- the address of the practitioner giving it;
- the appropriate date;
- such particulars as whether the practitioner giving it is a doctor, a dentist, district nurse/health visitor or extended formulary nurse prescriber, or a veterinary surgeon;
- the name, address and the age, if under 12, of the person for whose treatment it is given.

Prescriptions cannot be dispensed more than 6 months after the appropriate date, unless it is a repeatable prescription.

A **repeatable prescription** means a prescription containing a direction that it may be dispensed more than once. A **health prescription** means a prescription issued by a doctor, dentist, district nurse/health visitor or extended formulary nurse prescriber under the National Health Service Act.

Records have to be kept, in a bound book or electronically, of all POMs except those written on a health prescription.

Controlled drugs are also classified as POMs but are more strictly controlled. The prescription writing particulars are similar but records must be kept in a particular way and health prescriptions for such medicines are not exempt from the record-keeping procedures.

In addition, certain controlled drugs are subject to safe keeping regulations and have to be stored in a special cupboard, secured to the floor or wall, which has to comply with the specification laid down in the regulations. The destruction of controlled drugs has to be supervised by a person who has the authority to witness such destruction.

Poisons

A pharmacy is also permitted to supply poisons that are listed in both Part I and Part II of the Poisons List. Such sales on pharmacy premises may only be sold by, or under the supervision of a pharmacist. Certain poisons may only be sold under certain conditions, e.g. Poisons in Schedule I of the Poisons Rules. In these cases the purchaser must be known to the pharmacist to be a person to whom the poison may properly be sold, a record must be made in a special poisons register and the entry must be signed by the purchaser. A purchaser who requires a Schedule I poison for the purpose of his trade or business may give the pharmacist a signed order in lieu of a signature. The signed order must contain certain particulars including the name and address of the purchaser, his trade or business, the purpose for which the poison is required and the total quantity. Certain poisons are subject to additional restrictions. These poisons include strychnine, cyanides, thallium and zinc phosphide.

Code of conduct

In addition to the legislation, both pharmacists and persons lawfully conducting retail pharmacy businesses must comply with the RPSGB's Code of Ethics and attendant guidelines. This Code can be found in the *Medicines, Ethics and Practice* guide issued by the Society annually.

Summary

It will have been seen that opening a business is complex and surrounded by legislation, both pharmaceutical and general. This chapter has only touched on the many issues, but there are organisations and much literature available to those who wish to contemplate conducting a retail pharmacy business. Some of these are listed below.

Further reading

Appelbe G, Wingfield J. *Pharmacy Law and Ethics*, 7th edn. London: Pharmaceutical Press, 2001. In particular Chapters 5–7 Sale of Medicines; Chapter 16 Controlled Drugs; Chapter 4 Registration; Chapter 17 Poisons; Chapter 25 General business.

Appelbe G. Legal requirements for the sale and supply of veterinary medical products. In: Kayne S B, Jepson M, eds. *Veterinary Pharmacy*. London: Pharmaceutical Press, 2004, 159–173.

Judge S. *Business Law*, 2nd edn. Basingstoke: Macmillan, 1999.

MacMillan M, Lambie S. *Scottish Business Law*, 3rd edn. Harlow: Pearson Education, 1997.

Medicines, Ethics and Practice No. 28. London: Pharmaceutical Press, July 2004.

Merrills J, Fisher J. *Pharmacy Law and Practice*, 3rd edn. Oxford: Blackwell, 2001.

National Pharmaceutical Association, leaflets on employment, etc. (http://www. npa.co.uk/)

Booklets from the Health and Safety Executive (http://www.refit/hse.gov.uk)

Department of Trade and Industry. *Your Guide to the Working Time Regulations* (available from http://www.dti.gov.uk/er/work_time_regs/wtr0.htm (accessed 7 July 2004)).

7

Consumer law

Adrian Spooner

Introduction

This chapter is based on consumer law as it applies in England and Wales. The situation prevailing in other jurisdictions in the UK and overseas may vary in detail or interpretation but similar principles will generally apply.

Consumer law covers a range of matters regarding the rules that apply when goods or services are supplied to the public. The rules that apply are derived from a mixture of legislation and common law. Legislation is law produced by Parliament, usually as Acts of Parliament or Statutory Instruments. Common law is that developed by the courts over the years, for example, the law of negligence.

The application and effect of consumer law will depend on the nature of the interaction with the consumer:

- Where transactions with consumers take place, contract law generally controls the consumer relationship, i.e. where the sale of goods takes place. Depending on what is said or done, the law of negligence can also apply, but more importantly, a raft of consumer rights derived from legislation will be implied into the consumer contract.
- Where advice or services are provided, the law of contract will usually be relevant but the general law of negligence will almost certainly apply. Again, consumer rights derived from legislation will also apply.

Whether the sale of goods is taking place or services are being provided, legislation has been introduced that overlays the common law to increase the level of protection of consumers' rights. Many of these rights cannot be taken away and will only apply to consumer transactions, as opposed to business-to-business transactions.

Consumers and contracts generally

The general law of contract applies to consumer transactions and a basic understanding of this is important for community pharmacists. Contracts will be formed where goods are sold or services provided under an agreement with a customer. A contract is a legally enforceable agreement that can be oral, written, or a mixture of both. Certain criteria need to exist for a contract to arise:

- The parties must intend to create legal relations (this will usually be the case where the sale of goods or services takes place in a retail context).
- There must be an offer in respect of the contract that is communicated to the other party. Where goods are bought that are on open display in a shop, the offer is made by the customer selecting the goods and going to pay for them. The display of goods is not actually an offer but something known as an 'invitation to treat'.
- The other party to the contract must accept the offer. In this respect it is important to be clear what is actually being accepted and when. It is possible to respond to an offer with a counter-offer that alters the terms of the contract that is formed.
- There must be 'consideration' for the contract, which usually takes the form of money paid by one party in return for goods and services supplied by the other party. A contract will not be present where no consideration is provided, for example where free advice is given. However, this does not remove liability under the general law of negligence or other professional or regulatory rules.

The above are the main elements of a contract and all need to be in place for a contract to exist. This will generally be the case in the context of a consumer contract for goods or services. It should be noted that there are specific consumer protection measures that relate to the nature of formation of contracts entered via e-commerce methods and distance selling. However, this type of transaction is relatively rare in pharmacy.

Contract terms

Contract terms set out how a contract is to operate and the benefits given and obligations undertaken by each party to the contract. The standard terms of contracts are usually set out in a written contract agreed between the parties. Usually, the terms will be more complex where businesses are entering into agreements with other businesses. Contracts with consumers generally set out little or no express terms. However, this can vary depending on the size of the retailer and what goods or services are being sold.

Where terms are expressly set out, these establish the duties of each party. For a consumer contract, the consumer will usually be obliged to pay a certain amount of money for specific goods or services. In community pharmacy, where goods are sold, it is normally not necessary to expressly set out terms. However, where more complex service-type arrangements are concerned, for example where a community pharmacy supplies a range of professional services, it would be advisable to develop and apply express terms setting out clearly the obligations of each party (subject to statutory controls on what can be controlled by the contract). From a practical standpoint, setting out clearly the terms of the contract and thereafter elements of its performance to the required standard usually proves invaluable in successfully defending claims that might arise.

In consumer contracts, certain terms will be implied into the contract and these provide the consumer with significant rights. There are restrictions on the ability for the seller to exclude these implied terms in consumer contracts. These provisions are set out in legislation that applies to all consumer transactions and these implied terms vary depending on whether goods or services are being supplied.

Terms implied in consumer transactions

Sale of goods

Where goods are sold to a consumer, the Sale of Goods Act 1979 (and other legislation not detailed here) will apply. This sets out a number of terms that are implied into the contract with the consumer and are concerned with the condition of the goods sold and the right to sell them. These act in the consumer's favour. The terms include:

- That the goods sold will be of satisfactory quality.
- That the goods will correspond to the description given to them by the seller. This will normally be taken for granted in consumer sales in pharmacy.
- That the seller has the right to sell the goods and that they are free from third-party rights over the goods. This will almost certainly be the case in consumer pharmacy sales.
- That, where the buyer makes known to the seller his purpose for buying the goods, the goods will be fit for that purpose.

- That, where the goods are sold by sample, they will comply with the sample. For example, where a customer requests 50 g of aqueous cream, which might be measured and sold from a 500 g container.

The implied terms, which are most likely to be raised by consumers where complaints are made, are those relating to satisfactory quality and being fit for the purpose. Satisfactory quality will exist if the goods meet the standard that a reasonable person would regard as satisfactory, taking account of any description of the goods, the price (if relevant) and all other relevant circumstances. When looking at quality of goods, the state and condition of the goods must be considered and also the following aspects of goods, as appropriate to the circumstances:

- Fitness for all purposes for which the goods of the kind in question are commonly supplied.
- Appearance and finish.
- Freedom from minor defects.
- Durability.

A consumer will not be able to claim that goods were not of satisfactory quality, in respect of any matter, where, for example:

- The matter is specifically drawn to the buyer's attention before the contract is made.
- The buyer examines the goods before purchase and the examination should have revealed the matter in issue.

Where a consumer makes known, either expressly or by implication, any particular purpose for which the goods are being bought, there will be an implied condition of the contract that the goods are reasonably fit for that purpose. The exception is where the buyer does not rely on, or it is unreasonable for him to rely on, the skill and judgement of the seller.

Contracts relating to services

Where services are supplied to consumers under a contract, legislation implies terms into the contract that govern three aspects of such contracts:

- The quality of the service. The supplier of the service must perform it with reasonable care and skill.
- The time of performance of the service. If not fixed by agreement, the service must be performed within a reasonable time.
- The price of the service. As with timing, if not fixed, the price must be reasonable.

As will be discussed below, where advice is supplied outside a contractual relationship, the general law of negligence (and professional obligations for pharmacists) will still be relevant when supplying such advice.

Breach of consumer contracts

As already stated, consumer contracts can relate to the supply of goods and/or services. There are several ways in which a breach of these contracts can occur. Generally, a sufficient breach will mean that the party suffering the breach has the right to claim damages in respect of the loss suffered or caused by the breach. Where the statutory implied terms of consumer contracts are breached the consumer might have the right to:

- reject the goods sold and terminate the contract;
- have his or her money back;
- sue for damages.

Types of liability and the supply of advice

Where advice is provided to consumers, the common law of negligence can apply whether or not a contract is in place. Under the law of negligence, where it is found that:

- a duty of care is owed (to use reasonable care and skill in advice provided) (see also Chapter 8);
- the duty of care has been breached;
- the breach has caused damage to the party to whom the advice has been provided;

then the party suffering the damage will have a right of action against the provider of the advice under the law of negligence. The right of action would take the form of a claim for monetary damages, and in the context of community pharmacy could relate to death or personal injury, but could extend to other types of damage, i.e. to property.

Given the activity and standing of pharmacists, there is usually a clear duty of care owed by the pharmacist for advice given. Such advice is regularly provided in community pharmacy and **it is important to appreciate that liability for incorrect advice can provide a right of action against the supplier of the advice** for damage that is caused by it. In the case of a pharmacy the damage might relate to death or personal injury. There are also professional obligations concerning provision of advice that pharmacists give. It is advisable that standard protocols and record-keeping should be used in order to reduce the risk of error when providing advice to consumers, especially where the service or advice given is complex. Hopefully, this is an area that will be addressed by adherence to **Standard Operating Procedures** (SOPs) the requirements for which are being introduced by RPSGB (see Chapter 8).

Limiting liability

Where sale of goods legislation applies, a retailer of goods to consumers cannot expressly exclude the statutory implied terms. In fact, it is a criminal offence to include a term, or display a notice, which purports to exclude the statutory implied terms for sale of goods or restrict liability for their breach.

The party supplying goods or services under a consumer contract of any type cannot exclude or restrict liability for death or personal injury resulting from negligence.

With regard to liability for other losses or damages caused by negligence this can only be excluded if the exclusion or restriction on liability satisfies the test of reasonableness. Negligence in this context means any breach of any contractual or common law duty to take reasonable care and skill, i.e. where providing a service to a consumer.

The consumer protection regime

Where a defective product is supplied, consumers have a statutory right to claim damages in respect of the harm caused by the defect. Where a defect exists in a product supplied, there are various ways that the consumer could claim in respect of the defective goods. In the consumer context these will usually be:

*   against the supplier under the sale of goods regime;
*   against the supplier, or someone higher up the supply chain, such as the manufacturer of the goods, where it can be shown that the defect was present when the goods were supplied by the relevant entity.

The second alternative arises from consumer protection legislation and allows a consumer or other person damaged by the defect to claim losses caused by the defect in the product (even if the claimant does not have a contract with the person/entity from whom he wishes to claim damages). It is important to appreciate that liability for defective products under this regime can be passed up the supply chain to the manufacturer of goods and that the liability here is strict, i.e. no fault needs to be shown.

CASE STUDY

The following scenario is designed to raise some thought-provoking points about consumer issues that are common in the community pharmacy environment. However, note that pharmacists should also be aware that, as well as complying with consumer law when interacting with consumers, other factors must be taken into account that arise from professional and regulatory sources, for example the RPSGB Code of Ethics.

Mrs Jones, an elderly lady in her late sixties, requires something to treat an allergic eye reaction. Following a discussion with pharmacy staff to check usual matters about medicines she has taken and previous history, etc., commonly used antihistamine eye drops are recommended. She also purchases a gas refill for her hair curling tongs, but no discussion is had about this.

Later the same week Mrs Jones returns, angry because she wanted to use the hair curling tongs and had opened the packet of refills only to find that they were for a different brand of tongs. Mrs Jones now demands her money back so that she can go elsewhere. She also indicates that she has been using the eye drops and that this has resulted in an eye infection. An examination of the product confirms that the expiry date of the drops passed some time ago and it appears likely that the eye infection was caused by the drops.

Firstly, looking at the gas refill purchased by Mrs Jones, it is clear that she did not make clear any particular use to which the gas refills were to be put, and pharmacy staff made no express comment as to the suitability or otherwise of the gas refills for any particular purpose. There is nothing defective about the refills per se. In such circumstances, Mrs Jones does not have a right to claim for a refund for the refills she bought. If the pharmacy staff had indicated that the refills were suitable for the type of curling tongs Mrs Jones used, then the pharmacy would be liable to provide a refund because the goods supplied would not have been fit for the purpose sold, as requested by Mrs Jones.

Turning to the medication supplied, it is obvious that goods sold past their expiry date are not of satisfactory quality or fit for the purpose sold. This gives Mrs Jones the right to ask for her money back and to sue for damages. The product supplied would also be deemed defective under the consumer protection regime and Mrs Jones could have a right to claim damages in respect of the physical injury she has been caused. It is also the case that the person selling the product could have acted negligently in supplying eye drops that were past their expiry date, and liability could arise under the general law of negligence. Therefore, we can see that this one type of transaction can lead to liability arising from a number of sources.

continued

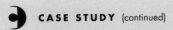

It is possible that the goods might have been defective when supplied to the pharmacy, and that some liability could be displaced up the supply chain under the consumer protection rules. However, this would probably not remove liability for the pharmacy arising under other heads.

Following the unfortunate injury caused to Mrs Jones, the pharmacy implements and validates the operation of a number of checks in the pharmacy to ensure that product expiry dates are checked. These include a rolling programme to check expiry dates of stock by staff, including stock rotation and a short educational programme for staff on checking expiry dates and matters that should be brought to a customer's attention with respect to certain types of product, i.e. eye drops.

Further reading

Ervine W C H. *Green's Consumer Law in Scotland*, 2nd edn. Edinburgh: W Green and Son, 2000.
Schulze R. (ed.) *A Casebook on European Consumer Law*. Oxford, Hart Publishing, 2002.

Websites

Citizens Advice Bureau http://www.adviceguide.org.uk
Citizens Advice Scotland http://www.cas.org.uk
English Consumer Law http://www.compactlaw.co.uk/consum.html
Scottish Consumer Law http://www.scottishlaw.org.uk/lawscotland/consumer.html

Useful addresses

The Office of Fair Trading, Unfair Contract Terms Unit, PO Box 2, Central Way, Feltham, Middlesex TW14 0TG (tel: 020 8398 3405)
The Office of Fair Trading Consumer Information Line 0845 7224 499 (calls charged at local rate)
The Director General of Fair Trading, Field House, 15–25 Bream's Buildings, London EC4A 1PR
The Data Protection Registrar, Complaints Department, Wycliffe House, Water Lane, Wilmslow, Cheshire SK9 5AF

8

Practical risk management

Charles P Butler

Introduction

This chapter will examine the concept of risk management, highlighting the relevance and importance to both individuals and to organisations of adopting a rigorous but realistic assessment of risk. It will provide a business case and the basis for a scientific model of designing risk management strategies that are intended to maintain or improve quality of services. The process of change management will be explored, together with its relationship to clinical governance, corporate governance and risk management.

Risk is a fact of life. Managers and healthcare professionals should not be discouraged from taking risks if by doing so they develop more effective ways of managing the business or of providing improved care for patients. It is important that risk-taking follows from a deliberate decision, taken on the basis of good information and with a thorough understanding of the possible consequences and likely outcome. If risk has implications for others (staff, customers, patients), then their needs must be taken into account, with careful consideration being given to whether or not their informed consent is required.

What went wrong?

There are a number of noteworthy milestones in history where disasters have occurred that took people by surprise. In most cases, nobody need have been surprised if only the theory of risk management had been applied objectively to everyday situations. With the benefit of hindsight, most of the disasters could have been avoided, often by applying inexpensive measures, by not relying on someone for advice who had conflicting interests, by not cutting corners, or by not slavishly following custom and practice.

Why did the Titanic sink? Why do pharmacists occasionally make dispensing errors even when the prescription is simple and unambiguous?

Why . . . ? Why . . . ? Why . . . ? Would the application of a risk management process have made a difference?

Another consideration is to ask searching questions about what was learnt and what is now being done differently as a result of something going wrong. What was learnt from the Zeebrugge ferry disaster? What difference did the Kings Cross fire make to the future safety of London Underground passengers and staff? What changes were introduced as a result of deaths of patients being injected with strong potassium chloride solution? What . . . ? What . . . ? What . . . ? Have the inherent risks been managed in such a way that the chance of a similar adverse event happening again has been reduced to any significant degree?

 CASE STUDY

The Titanic disaster
Valuable lessons can be learnt from any one of the disasters that have happened throughout history. A study of a disaster, undertaken of course with the benefit of hindsight, quickly shows how risk management is such an obvious and natural a process that it makes one wonder how things could have gone so wrong. A close examination of the sinking of the RMS Titanic during its maiden voyage, when it struck an iceberg in the North Atlantic on 14 April 1912, is no exception. The perception was that Titanic was unsinkable, although White Star Line, its owners, never claimed this. What they said afterwards was that the vessel was as safe as could be built and that the accident, which took place in calm seas, was simply bad luck.

Attention was drawn at the time to human failings – proceeding at full speed despite repeated warnings of icebergs, a lack of binoculars on the bridge, inadequate wireless procedures and poorly trained operators (wireless was a relatively new invention). The wireless operator on another ship in the vicinity that could have provided timely assistance was asleep in bed when eventually an SOS message was sent from Titanic.

Questions were raised over some of the Titanic's safety facilities, such as an insufficient number of lifeboats, and further questions about the suitability of the steel used for the hull. It was thought that the steel might have been of a particularly brittle nature, although that claim has since been disproved by the use of modern materials science techniques.

At first, the damage caused when Titanic hit the iceberg was thought not to be serious and this presented the crew with problems in persuading disbelieving people to take their places in lifeboats. Few of the crew were adequately trained in evacuation procedures and to start with, passengers did not consider their lives were in danger. Lifeboats left the side of Titanic, many with

→

CASE STUDY (continued)

spare seats because the crew had been told to evacuate women and children first. Because of this, male passengers as young as 13 years old were refused access to seats on the lifeboats, and although this procedure was corrected later, it was only after many partly full lifeboats had left the ship.

The collision was not head-on but instead the iceberg slid and ground along the side of the vessel. There was no single large gaping hole in the side, merely a series of tears in the metal hull along a 100-metre length of the starboard side. The damage seemed inconsequential. Nevertheless, some 3 hours later the Titanic had sunk 4000 metres to the bottom of the Atlantic and more than 1500 passengers and crew had perished.

Putting these facts into a modern context, what were the causes of the terrible death toll?

- A belief that nothing could go wrong.
- Faith in the custom and practice of construction.
- Warnings being ignored.
- A lack of vision.
- Poor communications.
- Inadequate networking.
- Stakeholders not being involved or kept informed.
- Insufficient safety equipment.
- Badly developed procedures and protocols.
- No appreciation of the likely outcome.
- Badly trained staff and poor performance monitoring.

However, the situation was more complex than that.

Doing it right first time

Doing it right first time is the ultimate goal of a successful risk management programme. It improves services and guarantees quality; it makes a job professionally satisfying; it avoids the possibility of legal action being taken; and it maximises business opportunity.

The most effective managers are those who are prepared to take calculated risks, deliberately choosing to make such judgements from a range of fully detailed options. Risk is everywhere in a pharmacy setting:

People: employees, visitors, customers, and contractors.
Equipment: portable electrical equipment, stepladders, computers, handling equipment.

Materials:	medicines, chemicals, packaging materials, and aerosols.
Services provided:	professional services, advice, sales of medicines, general sales, the design of new services.
Buildings:	internal and external structures, fixtures and fittings, electric and gas supply, air conditioning units, pollution control.
Management systems:	communications, reporting structures, accountability, skill-mix, leadership.

In many of these areas, the law provides a framework within which the risk management process can be managed (see also Chapter 6). For example, the Control of Substances Hazardous to Health (CoSSH) regulations, Manual Handling Regulations, Fire Precautions (Workplace) Regulations, Reporting of Injuries, Diseases and Dangerous Occurrences (RIDDOR) regulations, etc. Although the legislative list is long and daunting and will include a number of different regulatory bodies, it naturally makes sense to comply with the law in order to avoid prosecution. In some prosecutions, particularly under health and safety legislation, company directors can be made personally liable and the company can be so severely penalised as to cause its closure. Few small- or medium-sized employers or businesses will have sufficient in-house expertise or knowledge to deal effectively with anything other than a proportion of the regulatory burden. In many instances, specialist outside help will have to be obtained, perhaps through a professional organisation or from a commercial concern, and this outsourcing will need to be built into the overall risk management programme.

Preventing adverse events before they happen may have cost implications and may at first appear to be a distraction away from running a business. However, wise managers will take a wider and more positive view. An accident may result in one or more members of staff being absent from work for a period of recuperation; this in itself may lead to lost sales; a customer may have been adversely affected and that person's goodwill could be lost forever. By providing a safe environment for all and good working conditions for the staff, managers can concentrate on maximising the return on the overall investment made in that business. A risk management programme will greatly assist in reaching this objective.

In a business setting, a financial risk management programme will not merely safeguard the business but will provide senior management with the tools they need to improve profitability. If appropriately designed, a financial risk management programme will detect trends such as adverse trading conditions or an unexpected escalation in costs. During the process, clues will soon become apparent as to how the financial risk facing a business can be mitigated or even turned to a commercial advantage.

As organisations grow, their risk management programmes will need to adapt to fit the needs of the moment. They also need to become involved in matters of wider interest, not merely levels of sales, profitability and cash flow. The process of financial risk management becomes more complex and wide-ranging if outside interests are involved in the business, such as banks, outside shareholders, charitable trusts or other stakeholders. Those with legitimate interests in a business must be made aware of any conflicts or duality of interest, they have to be consulted before major decisions are taken, they may have to be involved in advising on contracts or appointments, they must be provided with progress reports at appropriate times, and they may require regular financial reports. Therefore a financial risk management programme should assess and encompass the needs of all these stakeholders to ensure they remain on-side with the directors, otherwise there is a risk of investors withdrawing their funding, their expertise and advice, or their voting power. This process is recognised as being an integral part of **corporate governance**.

Within the evolving world of community pharmacy, when new services are being put out to contract, both the purchaser and the provider will want to reduce their exposure to risk to an absolute minimum. Both parties will attempt to shift the risk in the direction of the other – this is commercial logic. Whereas there is little scope for a provider to shift any risk associated with a defect in the professional service aspects of the contract, there is considerable benefit to be gained if as much as possible of the organisational and financial risk remains with the purchaser.

In the clinical arena, implementing a risk management programme indicates a commitment to delivering high-quality care. This is part of **clinical governance**, a system through which organisations are accountable for continuously improving the quality of services and for creating an environment in which care of a high quality will flourish. Stung by criticism and against a background of some high-profile court cases and enquiries, in 1993 the NHS published its definitive work on risk management,[1] producing its own model of total quality management, which is based on a process of medical audit, clinical audit and risk management. More recently, the Department of Health in England published *An Organisation With a Memory*[2] and *Building a Safer NHS for Patients*.[3]

It is obvious that government places great store by the contribution that clinical governance (risk management) can make to improving standards of care and to reducing costs.

Risk management – making a difference

The principles behind managing risk are a key focus within quality assurance and total quality management. This should be viewed positively as an evolving process, not as a one-off or stand-alone programme that is completed and then filed away.

Within the specialist field of controls assurance, Charles Vincent defined **risk** as 'the probability that a particular adverse event occurs during a standard period of time'.[4] The Collins Concise Dictionary gives a lay definition that is similar, 'the possibility of incurring misfortune or loss'. Put simply, risk is the potential for an unwanted outcome. It can be anything that has the potential to prevent an individual or an organisation from reaching its goal.

Risk management involves **risk assessment** (that is the making of decisions concerning identifiable risks) and is concerned with the subsequent implementation of decisions to eliminate or minimise the impact of risk. Risk assessment flows from the application of a realistic and objective process of **risk estimation** and **risk evaluation**. Quality is the outcome of a successful risk management programme; getting it right first time is its ultimate goal.

All risks are related to the circumstances that apply at the time. For example, during a 7-day period the risk of a randomly selected individual dying while sky-diving is small, but the risk will change significantly according to time of year, weather conditions, and the age, experience and degree of training of the individual concerned.

It is all too easy for a layperson to become confused and mesmerised by terminology that the experts take for granted. However, when seen in the context of historical or newsworthy events that are familiar to all, the process of managing risk through all its component parts becomes easy to understand and can then be adapted to all manner of different settings.

Mechanical systems will fail from time to time; human systems will fail more frequently. These are inescapable facts of life and risk should not be seen as an evil but as part of the process. Risk management is about identifying and then balancing the risks against the benefits.

All new projects, whether the construction of an ocean-going liner, setting up a small sterile products manufacturing plant for a hospital pharmacy, or planning the introduction of a new service in a community pharmacy, should include a rigorous and objective study of the risks involved. By the same token, activity in established fields should also be subjected to the same rigours, with previous assumptions being tested against knowledge gained from experience.

Risk estimation: Risk estimation includes the identification of outcomes, an estimation of the magnitude of any associated outcomes and consequences and an estimation of the probabilities of those outcomes actually happening.

The first step is to identify the risks to which the process will be subjected. Managers should start the process by considering the organisation's objectives and the factors that may prevent it from reaching those objectives. This should provide a 'top level' review of risks, looking at the overall scene, both inside the organisation and externally. From this, management and staff will be able to focus on more detailed operational risks and begin to consider appropriate actions. A framework for identifying risk is given below:

Failure to . . .	Inability to . . .
Loss of . . .	Inappropriate . . .
Concentration of . . .	Reliance on . . .
Non-compliance with . . .	Disruption to . . .
Lack of . . .	Inadequate . . .
Reduction of . . .	Increase in . . .
Conflict between . . .	Delay in . . .

Risk may be financial in nature, it could arise from attempts to introduce new ways of providing a service, it could be a result of plant or machinery being used in an unconventional manner, it could be because staff have inadequate skills or that they just lack confidence. In other words, risk assessments must be wide-ranging in the areas they consider and must be firmly rooted in honesty. Some of the risk categories that should be taken into account include:

People	Information
Operational	Property
Financial	Reputation
Strategic	Regulatory
Funding	Technology
Social	Political
Competition	Governance
Management	Naturally arising

This process of risk estimation is likely to produce an extensive list but any temptation to prune the list at this stage should be strongly resisted. Some ranking of the identified risks is needed before the least significant ones can be put on one side. These 'lesser risks' may in time become of greater significance as the process of implementing a new project progresses. Continual audit, evaluation and review are needed to ensure the risk management process can do its job effectively.

A **risk profile** can be obtained, for which the key factors are:

- probability
- impact
- level of concern.

This prioritises risks that have been identified, so that the long list becomes more manageable. The focus moves to the risks with the highest ranking and a scoring system can be set up for risk evaluation.

Risk evaluation: Risk evaluation is a complex process of determining the significance or value to be placed on the risks that have been estimated, for example as shown in Table 8.1.

One thing that must never be overlooked is the effect that a change in working practices, or the introduction of a new service, may have on the risk profile of any of the other activities within the organisation.

Individuals working on their own will need to use their judgement, a risk in itself. Undertaking this as a collective exercise will focus the organisation's attention on a key issue – **risk appetite**. One person might score a potential event as low probability, whereas another person may perceive the risk as highly likely. The process of evaluating the risks can be a positive exercise in sharing the different perceptions of risk. In large organisations this procedure will provide ample opportunity for small-scale wars to break out between the finance director and the director of operations, between the sales manager and the marketing director. As part of the overall process, the organisation will have to reach a reasonable consensus about the level and types of risks it is prepared to accept.

Table 8.1 A scoring method aimed at providing consistency in evaluating risk

Score	Probability	Impact	Concern
1	Very unlikely	Insignificant	Unconcerned
2	Unlikely	Fairly serious	Mildly concerned
3	Possible	Serious	Concerned
4	Likely	Very serious	Very concerned
5	Highly likely	Major disaster	Gravely concerned

An example, using a few of the many risks associated with the introduction of a new computer-based medicines management service, can be used to identify the significance of the inherent risks. Each risk is scored, with the scores being multiplied across the grid, to produce a risk profile for the service at its current stage of development and roll-out, as shown in Table 8.2. This illustration shows that now risks can be prioritised or ranked by using this graphic illustration of key areas of risk.

Table 8.2 Risk profiling: a worked example (using the system in Table 8.1) to ascribe a score to each identified risk

Identified risk	Probability	Impact	Concern	Total (P × I × C)
Database crash	4	3	5	60
Key person leaves	3	2	2	12
New procedure fails	4	3	3	36
Competitor activity	2	5	3	30
Poor market uptake	1	5	2	10
Inability to demonstrate benefit of the system	2	5	5	50

Risk assessment: Risk assessment brings together the two strands of the process, risk estimation and risk evaluation. It is possible to draw up a 'risk map', as shown in Figure 8.1. The aim is to achieve a situation where all risks fall in the bottom left-hand quadrant and none in the top right, a situation that is unlikely ever to happen. Circumstances may change over time, or at particular times of the day, so the relative

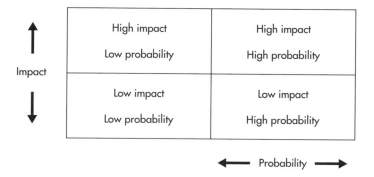

Figure 8.1 Risk map: used for prioritising elements of a risk management strategy, both at the developmental stage and for review purposes.

positioning of risk may alter – perhaps whilst a locum pharmacist, unfamiliar with the operating procedures of the organisation is left in charge with insufficiently experienced staff to assist.

Health and safety – risk and benefit

There is huge financial and human cost attached to accidents and ill health due to work in the UK – 187 million days are lost a year and the economy loses nearly £17 billion annually as a result.[5] Complying with health and safety law should be viewed as a positive process that can benefit both the individual and the organisation. Administering a risk management programme is an organisational function but before anything can be done, the organisation has to adopt a risk management philosophy. Clearly, if the organisation comprises a proprietor and two members of staff, the matter is a relatively simple one but the thought processes and rationale hold true no matter what size the organisation is.

The flow chart shown in Figure 8.2 shows the elements required to manage the risk management process.

An organisation requires a risk management philosophy that should be a clear statement of where the organisation stands on the issue of risk and its management and is usually referred to as a risk management

Figure 8.2 Corporate risk management – the process of 'managing risk management'.

statement. From this the organisation can write its **safety policy**, a legal requirement if it employs five or more people.

An important concept in health and safety legislation, provided for within the Health & Safety at Work Act 1974, is the **duty of care** (see Chapter 7). This is a legal duty under common law (which has become extended under health and safety legislation), requiring both individuals and organisations to avoid carelessly causing personal injury or damage to property. Under statute law, employers have a duty to take care of employees and others and can be tried under the criminal justice system. If found guilty, employers can be liable to pay a fine or in serious cases can be sent to prison. In the event of an accident an employer can be found criminally liable and ordered to pay a fine, as well as being civilly liable and obliged to pay damages. While organisations can minimise the financial risk by insuring against claims for damages through negligence, they cannot insure against punishment and the payment of fines. It should also be noted and understood that employers have vicarious liability for acts of negligence on the part of their employees, meaning that an employer could be liable even if they did not authorise the employee's act or knew nothing about it.

A health and safety policy is a legal requirement. It should be a working document to be used in the induction and training of staff and should be regularly revised to ensure it remains relevant. Importantly, it must be communicated to employees and anyone else working under the organisation's control. Organisations such as the National Pharmaceutical Association (NPA) are invaluable sources of help and advice for the beleaguered and the bewildered or a local solicitor, preferably one with specialist knowledge, will advise. Although reticence amongst employers is understandable, the local enforcing agency for health and safety (usually the local authority environmental health department) is also there to help and can be approached for guidance.

Three essential matters need to be covered in the safety policy:

- **Part 1: General statement of policy:** committing the organisation in writing to tackling health and safety issues. This should be signed and dated by someone with management responsibility at the highest level.
- **Part 2: Responsibility for carrying out the statement of intent:** people with specific areas of responsibility (e.g. fire procedures, first aid, etc.) must be identified.
- **Part 3: Arrangements and procedures:** giving outline detail of how the policy will operate, for example how to report accidents, what to do if there is a fire, etc.

A health and safety risk assessment

Under the Management of Health and Safety at Work Regulations 1999 there is a requirement to undertake a risk assessment, and this must be written down if an organisation has five or more employees. Organisations with fewer than five employees would also be strongly advised to have a written assessment and in all cases it is worth including the document within Part 3 of the safety policy.

Certain individuals have specific needs that should be taken into account when undertaking risk assessments as part of the development of health and safety policies and procedures. For example, the needs of new and expectant mothers, of young employees and of disabled staff must all be assessed and any particular risks identified must be appropriately managed.[6]

From information contained in earlier sections of this chapter, the process of risk assessment can be seen as a relatively simple one, being considered against the background of two basic definitions. A **hazard** is something that has potential to cause harm, e.g. faulty stepladders, broken guttering, or items left on stairways. **Risk** is the possibility of a hazard causing harm. Then, risk assessment becomes a routine process of:

- **Identifying** hazards arising from the organisation's activities that could affect anyone.
- **Assessing** the risk of the hazards occurring.
- **Evaluating** the likely severity of the outcome.
- **Eliminating** the hazards or reducing them to the lowest level of risk that is reasonably practicable.

Assessing risk properly relies upon the person undertaking the assessment having a thorough understanding of the work carried out by the organisation. It cannot be done effectively without a strong lead from management, nor without the active cooperation of employees who should be consulted, either as individuals or through someone considered to be a representative of them.

A written risk assessment can be started, as follows:

- **Step 1**: Look for the hazard.
- **Step 2**: Decide who may be harmed and how.
- **Step 3**: Evaluate the risks and decide whether existing control measures are adequate or whether more should be done.
- **Step 4**: Record the findings as part of a risk assessment document.
- **Step 5**: Review the assessment from time to time.

Figure 8.3 is an example of a suitable format for a written risk assessment.

Risk Assessment Document

Premises: .... Carried out by: .... Date of assessment: ...../...../20..... Next review due: ...../...../20.....

Hazard	Risk of	Risk from	Risk to	Control, preventative and protective measures	Residual risk	Action needed
Roof tiles, chimneys, gutters	Injury	Falling masonry and ironwork	All visitors and staff	Regular inspection and report; immediate repairs if necessary. Rolling programme of maintenance.	Low	Replace cast iron gutters and downpipes with PVC when next repairing or painting.
Entrance mat	Injury	Tripping	All visitors and staff	As above	Very low	None
Stepladders	Falling	Losing balance or being knocked over	Staff	Staff training: steps to be used only when fully extended; avoid stretching or leaning. 'Guarded' by another member of staff if used in shop area. Regular inspection of steps for damage.	Low	
Body piercing	Infection and injury	Skin prick; contaminated blood	Staff	Trained staff only to do piercing in designated area. Staff to have hepatitis vaccination. Protective gloves and washing facilities provided. Sharps container for disposal.	Low to medium	Check latest advice and requirements with local authority.

Figure 8.3 An example of a suitable risk assessment form.

The results of a risk assessment will be useful in identifying gaps in skills and knowledge within an organisation and will therefore inform the training needs assessment of staff.

Whilst conducting the assessment the manager responsible should ideally walk around the premises – inside and out – with an employee (whose opinions must be taken into account), looking critically at the surroundings to identify what has the potential to cause harm or injury to staff, customers and any others who may visit the premises.

Risk assessment should not be limited only to areas of risk inherent to the structure and buildings of the workplace – it must extend to more nebulous topics such as conflict in the workplace. By law, employers must undertake a systematic examination of all work activities, including the threat of violence to staff, and must record the significant findings in their risk assessment. Violent behaviour is not just physical assault or the threat of it. The Health and Safety Executive's working definition of violence is 'any incident in which an employee is abused, threatened or assaulted by a member of the public in circumstances arising out of the course of his or her employment'.

Because of the nature of the services provided and the stock held, all pharmacy premises and the staff working in them are at potential risk from violent acts occurring. Many community pharmacies operate in areas of the country or in parts of cities where there is a greatly increased risk of violent acts occurring, or they provide services to client groups under circumstances that may frequently be expected to give rise to conflict. Employers must not ignore this and must assess and manage the risks according to local circumstances.

Other health and safety issues requiring an assessment of risk

There are many different regulations that place a duty upon the employer to assess and document risks in the workplace and to provide appropriate methods of managing those risks. At first sight the list appears daunting but, by applying the principles contained in this chapter, the task of risk management is made relatively straightforward. In addition to the basic statutory requirements provided for under the Management of Health and Safety at Work Regulations 1999, examples of other legislation where risk management techniques must be applied are provided by the following.

Provision and Use of Work Equipment Regulations 1998

The risks of using equipment should be assessed and measures taken to protect against potential hazards. This would apply to mixing machines used in small-scale manufacturing, to portable heaters, etc.

Manual Handling Operations Regulations 1992

A risk assessment is needed in all cases where employees have to lift, carry, push or pull items. If such an operation cannot be avoided then employers need to take steps to reduce injury, provide information and provide a safe system of work.

Personal Protective Equipment at Work Regulations 1992

After an assessment of risk, these regulations require that adequate protective equipment and clothing must be available in cases where risks to health and safety cannot be controlled by other means. In a pharmacy, typical examples of protective clothing include gloves, goggles and dust masks.

Health and Safety (First Aid) Regulations 1981

All workplaces must have appropriate first aid provisions that differ according to the nature of the work and the number of employees. In most pharmacy settings it is necessary only to have an appointed person (possibly 'the pharmacist on duty') and to have a simple first aid kit. In all cases, the needs and risks have to be assessed and adequate management controls put in place.

The Health and Safety (Display Screen Equipment) Regulations 1992

There are wide-ranging considerations needed for managing the risks to employees that are associated with visual display units (VDUs): the equipment, the work environment, heat emission and radiation, the software itself, the user. It is unlikely to become much of an issue in a typical pharmacy setting but prudent managers will still apply the key principles of assessment and management of risk.

Fire Precautions (Workplace) (Amendment) Regulations 1999

All premises to which the public has access must have either a fire certificate or an exemption certificate issued by the local fire brigade. Except for large store pharmacies, most community pharmacies will be exempted from needing a fire certificate but all pharmacies will have had to carry out a risk assessment and to have put in place appropriate control measures and staff training.

Electricity at Work Act 1990

There are two main areas of concern with electricity – the supply and individual appliances. In terms of risk assessment there is a need to protect users of electricity from hazards such as electric shock, fire or explosion. Trailing wires can cause people to trip and may result in the equipment itself being accidentally damaged. A faulty connection, an incorrect fuse rating, or an overloaded circuit can cause a fire. Problems with the supply or with a plug may result in loss of vital data from a computer and could have an adverse effect on a business.

The Electricity at Work Act 1990 requires employers to arrange for someone who is suitably qualified to undertake appropriate checks at appropriate intervals. Clearly, only a qualified electrician would have the skills and equipment necessary to test the mains supply, distribution board, fuses and circuit breakers, ring mains, sockets and light fittings. The electrician who undertakes the test should provide a certificate confirming the inspection, together with any recommendations for remedial work and a suitable interval before a re-test is needed.

Someone from within an organisation can inspect equipment. Individual appliances should be listed before a visual and 'user' test is undertaken. A decision is also needed on the relative risks of a dangerous fault developing; this will inform a decision on when a re-test is needed. In the case of an item that is static – a computer, cash register or printer – an annual inspection of cable, fuse rating, etc. is all that is normally necessary. In the case of an electric kettle, in constant use in a very busy work environment, a more frequent inspection of the cable, plug and wall socket plate is needed, together with a check for water leaks.

On the face of it, the Act places a huge burden on small- and medium-sized businesses, which the faint-hearted may be tempted to ignore, at their peril. However, by applying the principles outlined in this chapter the process becomes altogether more manageable. Figure 8.4 gives an example of a suitable form to use when carrying out routine checks on portable electrical equipment.

Portable electrical appliances: Inspection checklist

Premises: .... Inspection by: .... Inspection date: ....../....../20......

Appliance: Type and Make (incl. model no.)	Serial no. (or code no.)	Mains plug (condition/fit)	Fuse (Amp rating fitted)	Condition of flex	Appliance plug – if separate from mains plug (condition/fit)	Test of working function	Outer casing (condition etc.)	Notes	Next inspection due
Vacuum cleaner ~ Sebo Auto. X1	SE/9321/0 03	Good	13 amp	Average ~ discoloured near plug	N/A	OK	Undamaged but handle getting loose	Ask users to report if cleaner becomes temperamental	6 months
Philips fan heater	HD3341/C	OK: one of the pins getting worn	13 amp	Good	N/A	Good – Turns on/off with thermostat	Good		6 months
Morphy Richards jug kettle	M2196/53	Good	13 amp	Good	Good	Good – switches off automatically	OK – plastic at spout getting discoloured	Kettle getting old. Consider replacing within 12 months	6 months
Stag desk lamp (brass)	39/CAS/but	Good	3 amp fuse and 60 watt bulb – OK	Good	N/A	Good	Good	Replace bulb with low energy type	1 year

Figure 8.4 Inspection checklist: an example of a suitable form for creating a database of electrical equipment and for recording the results of routine inspections.

The CoSHH assessment

Most pharmacists will feel relatively comfortable about assessing risks in areas where they have specialist knowledge and skills, such as chemical compounds and medicines. Integral to a risk management programme is an assessment under the **Control of Substances Hazardous to Health (CoSSH) Regulations 1994**, something that must be conducted in respect of all premises where employees work. The regulations charge an employer with a responsibility to assess the workplace for risks from substances used, stored or found there, and for taking all necessary steps to control any identified risk. A hazardous substance can be solid, liquid, powder, gas, dust or an organism that may damage health if it comes into contact with skin or eyes, if it is inhaled, swallowed or if it enters the body by transference to the mouth by contaminated hands or through the skin. It will be seen that the Regulations take a CoSSH assessment well beyond consideration of chemical compounds and medicines, although this would be a useful and logical starting point for pharmacy managers.

Many substances found in a typical pharmacy are hazardous to health, even in an era where unit packaging and specialist small-scale manufacturing by specialists have removed much of the need for compounding or assembly by repackaging from bulk. Consideration must be given to any potential hazard arising from accidental spillage or from a packaging failure. Neither should the assessment merely take account of substances used in the normal course of the business – for example cleaning materials, typewriter correction fluid, sharps containers for contaminated injecting equipment, dump bins for returned pharmaceutical waste, photocopier toner, solvents, remnants of paint, paraffin for heating an outhouse, are all relatively commonplace and could present a significant hazard to health.

The process of undertaking the assessment is identical to that for the basic health and safety risk assessment:

- **Step 1**: Look for the hazard.
- **Step 2**: Decide who may be harmed and how.
- **Step 3**: Evaluate the risks and decide whether existing control measures are adequate or whether more should be done.
- **Step 4**: Record the findings on the CoSSH risk assessment document.
- **Step 5**: Review the assessment from time to time.

Once assessed, the risk management of these hazards will include a review of working practices, considering whether less harmful substances can be substituted, reviewing staff training needs, providing more information to staff and visitors on avoiding harm, and deciding whether a potentially hazardous situation could impact adversely on the safety of other business activities, such as dispensing services.

Often the training and information needs of employees are overlooked but it is of the greatest importance not to take knowledge for granted – for example that mixing certain detergents with common bleach is likely to result in the release of chlorine gas and can be dangerous, especially in the confined area of a WC cubicle.

Insurance – a tool of financial risk management

Insurance forms an important part of the financial risk management strategy for any business. It is covered in detail in Chapter 9. The level of cover should be regularly reviewed and any changing insurance requirements must be considered as an integral stage to be taken into account when planning some new business venture, when introducing changes to existing services, or when there is some change in external factors. All the main areas where there is a risk of substantial damages being assessed or awarded are usually included within the scope of normal commercial and buildings insurance policies, such as:

- **Employers' liability insurance**: Under the Employers' Liability (Compulsory Insurance) Regulations 1998, employers are required to have insurance in place to compensate their employees for illness, injury or death caused by the employer's negligence or that may arise during the course of employment.
- **Public liability insurance**: Although not a legal requirement, good risk management will include insurance to compensate a third party where loss has arisen through the negligence of someone acting with the employer's authority.

Good commercial insurance policies will include cover for a wide variety of occurrences, possible claims and potential losses. Mostly, the need for insurance will be obvious to the proprietor or manager but, despite having insurances in place, all risks should be managed appropriately to reduce the possibility of a claim having to be made. If the insurance company believes an insured party knew it was acting negligently and recklessly it may repudiate a claim, or seek to reduce the level of compensation. In such cases it may be difficult to arrange cover in the future.

Specialist policies will be needed for **professional indemnity insurance**, to indemnify the individual pharmacist and to protect the public on those occasions where there is a failure of quality in a professional service that results in a claim. It is an ethical requirement in many professions, including pharmacy, for practitioners to carry professional indemnity insurance with sufficient cover to meet claims made against them. As part of a change management process, the amount of cover and the scope of the policy should be checked with the insurance company in advance of undertaking any 'new roles', because the insurance company could perceive its exposure to a potential claim is about to change. Any proposed task that is not already included in the cover must be discussed openly and in depth with the insurer so that they can consider whether to extend cover within the existing policy or whether additional insurance is required.

As an additional safeguard for any business, the advice of a good insurance broker should be sought on areas of insurance such as life assurance, to provide payment during periods of sickness, cover for long-term illness and disability. Even small- and medium-sized companies should consider whether they are at substantial risk if a key member of staff dies or becomes incapacitated. These employers may wish to insure the life and health of the individual so that the company receives the benefit of the policy in the event of a claim. Although the payment will not replace the skills and expertise of a former employee, the company might be able to buy in temporary help that it otherwise could not have afforded, whilst a suitable replacement is recruited.

Clinical risk management

Clinical risk management, a key component of clinical governance, is a matter of considerable importance and of concern to all those involved in patient care. Risks increase rapidly whenever changes in practice are taking place, at busy times, when there are shortages of skilled staff, when lines of communication become disrupted, when staff are still under training and when there is a lack of clear leadership.

A pharmacist's clinical *raison d'être* is to manage risks on behalf of both patient and prescriber. However, society sees it differently, principally because lay opinion does not like to admit that there are any inherent risks in 'simple' clinical procedures. Everybody knows that an organ transplant carries risks; few patients recognise the risks within pharmaceutical care, preferring instead to apportion blame if things go wrong. If clinical risk management is to take its rightful place in patient care, then it is essential that patients come to understand the nature of risk and that pharmacists are accepted as specialists who can help them manage their own risks. The result will be better concordance and improved clinical outcomes (see also Chapter 18).

The influence of government

Because of the potentially complex nature of clinical risks, sometimes brought into focus only when something goes wrong, it is often necessary to learn from the mistakes of others. The Department of Health report, *An Organisation With a Memory*,[2] recognised the risks inherent in healthcare delivery and that patient safety was improved by learning from mistakes. Their further report, *Building a Safer NHS for Patients*,[3] laid out the government's plan to incorporate this principle into the delivery of NHS services.

The Toft Report, published following the thirteenth occasion over a period of 15 years when a vinca alkaloid was administered intrathecally instead of intravenously, concluded '. . . the incident . . . was not caused by one or even several human errors but by a more complex amalgam of human, organisational and social interactions'. Systems of record-keeping, error reporting and dissemination of anonymous information is rapidly becoming accepted as a method of improving patient care.

The National Patient Safety Agency (NPSA), set up as part of the government's safety agenda, has made a serious attempt to move public opinion in the direction of 'self-risk management' with the following advice to patients:

- Speak up if you have any questions or concerns.
- Keep a list of all the medicines you take.
- Make sure you get the results of any test procedure – ask what they mean for your care.
- Talk to your doctor and healthcare team about your opinions if you need hospital care.
- Make sure you understand what will happen if you need surgery.

The professional viewpoint

As pharmacists become engaged in a wider range of clinical services the exposure to risk increases:

- A risk to the pharmacist.
- A risk to the pharmacy staff.
- A risk to the patient (and carer).
- A risk to the commissioning organisation.

To be effective, all four partners need to understand the nature of the risks within a procedure and how it is intended that they should be managed. In practical terms it is often only the commissioning organisation (government, local care agency, Primary Care Trust, etc.) and the pharmacy owner or pharmacist in charge who will be involved in considering risk. Pharmacy staff and patients will be relegated to the status of involved bystander. Broadly, considerations can be generically classified into a number of essential categories:

- **Process design**: in-building quality and safety features, keeping matters simple.
- **Leadership**: setting standards, writing procedures, explaining.
- **Stakeholder involvement**: engaging people in the process as equal partners.
- **Training**: ensuring the correct skill-mix and that skills are maintained.
- **Communications**: open-channel communications for all stakeholders.
- **Performance measurement**: incident reporting and assessment.
- **Review**: peer review; stakeholder assessment; audit; incident reporting.
- **Disaster recovery**: clear unambiguous procedures if things go wrong.

Many of the tasks undertaken in a clinical setting, whether dispensing repeat prescriptions in a community pharmacy or an eye surgeon undertaking a cataract operation, vary little from day to day or from patient to patient. Therefore, for routine procedures, a standardised approach is often adopted by setting up a stepwise methodology by which the simplest of tasks is undertaken in a uniform way. Known variously as clinical guidelines, protocols, pathways or **standard operating procedures** (see Chapter 7), they are firmly embedded in a risk management programme. During their design, the key elements of risk estimation and risk evaluation will have been considered, in turn providing a risk assessment from which a large part of the risk management programme (i.e. the protocol) can be laid down.

Protocols have their supporters and their detractors: 'Extreme positions tend to result from naïve expectations of their impact and oversimplification of the process required for their development and implementation'.[4] Protocols have been criticised as 'cookery book care', compromising clinical autonomy and reducing the role of clinical judgement in patient care. However, anyone trying to recreate a culinary masterpiece using recipes from a cookery book soon realises that cooking in practice is a lot more complicated and messier than it is on paper. Following a recipe does not guarantee a quality outcome – that requires judgement. The BBC cookery expert, Delia Smith wrote in her book '. . . it is also unwise to assume that learners already possess the basic skills, knowledge and experience to follow a recipe'.[7]

The development and implementation of protocols potentially carries both costs and benefits, some of which can be anticipated whereas others cannot. Clinicians and clinical managers need to decide whether their introduction is likely to provide improvements in quality of care at a cost that is reasonable.[8]

In the world of medicine and nursing it is now more common to talk of care pathways (also defined as protocols), which are structured multidisciplinary care plans, detailing the essential steps in the care of a patient. There is ample evidence that the world of pharmacy has changed and continues to change, and that it is engaging with clinical risk management, almost by stealth. Pharmacists have become involved with their staff in designing protocols for the sale of medicines by suitably trained staff and for the giving of advice to members of the public; standard operating procedures for prescription dispensing in community and hospital pharmacies are to be a professional requirement of the Royal Pharmaceutical Society of Great Britain (RPSGB); incident recording and error reporting are to be an NHS requirement.

So far, pharmacy has been rather introspective. There is a greater contribution that pharmacists can make in the arena of clinical risk management and they should not hesitate to become the champion of patient safety – dealing with other health professionals from a position of strength, given to them by their specialist skills and expertise. As a starting point, pharmacists should work in partnership with others to get rid of ambiguous prescriptions, to minimise errors in dispensing, and to improve concordance through fewer administration errors and by improved information. There are many challenges facing pharmacists today, for example:

- The design of safe repeat dispensing services.
- Dealing with increased demands for advice and information.
- Deciding how best to supervise dispensing and the sale of medicine by staff.
- Specialised hospital services, e.g. oncology, paediatrics.
- Involvement in clinics.
- Working in partnership with other professions.
- Palliative care services, care of the older person.

It has been clearly established there are risks whenever a service is provided. In terms of risk management in all its various guises, and the problems associated with managing change, a careful application of the principles in this chapter should achieve the correct balance between risk and benefit.

 CASE STUDY

The Titanic disaster – the epilogue

On 27 August 1862, some 50 years before the Titanic sank, Brunel's ship SS Great Eastern hit an uncharted rock in heavy seas off the coast of Long Island, USA. The impact ripped a hole in her side that was some 3 m wide and 30 m long, far more extensive than the damage sustained by Titanic. However, the Great Eastern not only remained afloat but she sailed into New York the following day, with no reported injuries amongst passengers or crew. How could the outcome be so different when apparently the surviving vessel was damaged to a greater extent and was in perilous waters?

A far less charitable interpretation of the Titanic disaster than the one given by its owners was that it resulted from cost-cutting exercises in the design and construction of the vessel that rendered the ship unsafe. The Titanic's owners claimed that bad luck had played an important part in the ship's demise, but an alternative view is that it was fortunate there had been no similar accidents years earlier with ships of a similar design. White Star Line displayed an unbending faith in the custom and practice at the time that had evolved around shipbuilding.

The Great Eastern had a double hull with a second skin about 70 cm inside the outer shell. Inside that, the ship was divided into 32 compartments by 15 transverse bulkheads situated 10 m above the waterline and one further bulkhead running longitudinally. Watertight lower decks further divided those compartments. The Titanic also had 15 transverse bulkheads and was designed to keep afloat with any two of its compartments flooded – or even if four of the smaller compartments, situated at the bow, were breached. White Star Line believed customers would be attracted to Titanic because of the opulence of the ship and its magnificent open spaces – lofty lounges, ballrooms and restaurants – but they took no account of the difficulty faced by designers in providing adequate watertight compartments.

One significant difference from Great Eastern was that the transverse bulkheads in Titanic were only 3 m above the waterline. When the crew of Titanic began to examine the damage they found the first five compartments were flooded and the sixth was leaking. It soon became apparent, as the front compartments filled, that the sixth compartment would drop below the waterline by

→

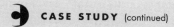

CASE STUDY (continued)

more than 3 m, thus allowing water to spill over into the next compartment, making the ship sink further. The end point was inevitable. What were the additional factors that contributed to the Titanic disaster?

- Cost pressures.
- Custom and practice remaining unquestioned.
- Perception of customer demand.
- Adoption of part but not all of a proven design model.
- Lack of fail-safe features.
- Poor appreciation of the 'what ifs'.

Dispensing with risk

This chapter has deliberately drawn on the world outside pharmacy, in an attempt to inform and encourage the reader to think about his or her own working practices, so that a tailor-made risk management strategy can be individually tailored to that environment. Nevertheless, there is one professional task with which most pharmacists are familiar that deserves mention – prescription dispensing.

Without doubt, dispensing is a high-risk activity. Risky to the patient, to the NHS, to the professional indemnity insurers, to professional reputation, to business goodwill and to the self-confidence, livelihood and well-being of the staff involved when things go wrong. Why is this, when to the uninformed, modern dispensing seems so simple? An examination of some of the major risk areas shows how wrong this perception is.

Continuing professional development

It should not be necessary to remind pharmacists of the need to keep abreast of therapeutic developments and to be aware of the introduction of new products, changes in licensed applications for established medicines, the usual doses of medicines and of their more specialised use in areas such as palliative care, paediatrics and psychiatry. Modern therapeutics is a fast-moving world, one that the pharmacist must keep under constant review. As the duties and responsibilities of pharmacy support staff evolve, it will be necessary also to ensure that their knowledge is maintained and that they are also fully engaged in a staff development process. This applies equally to all staff – dispensary assistants/technicians, medicines counter assistants and prescription reception staff – each has an important role in providing a safe and reliable service to the public.

Pressure of work

Inevitably, dispensary staff who are working under pressure and at speed are likely to be more at risk of making an error. Tiredness, thirst, hunger and repetitive work all affect performance, with an increasing chance of errors occurring the longer someone has been at work without a break or a change in routine. The supervising pharmacist has a professional duty to ensure staff levels are adequate for the predicted workload, including a proper consideration of known seasonal pressures and busy periods before public holidays, and that staff are allowed adequate rest periods. Standard operating procedures are a vital tool in reducing the error rate, with action being taken to address any shortfall after an assessment of the competence and training needs of dispensary staff, but they will be of little use if the staff cannot reasonably cope with the workload expected of them.

Dispensary environment

A good manager will ensure that the dispensary has good lighting with no dark corners, an uncluttered dispensing bench, an accessible and flexible storage system for stock, adequate heating and ventilation, a high standard of properly maintained equipment (computer, refrigerator, scales, etc.), and access to a range of up-to-date reference sources. Continual interruption by the telephone is a source of irritation that can induce errors, and thought should be given as to how best to overcome this. Without the basic requirements of an orderly and pleasant working environment being fully satisfied it is unlikely that even the best staff will be able to provide a reliable and safe dispensing service.

Reading the prescription

Jokes about the quality of doctors' handwriting are still abundant, despite the almost universal use of computers for prescribing. Whereas the occasional handwritten prescription, from a hospital outpatient department or after a GP's house call, can cause havoc, so can a worn printer ribbon or depleted ink cartridge. The pharmacist must decide how to minimise the risks of an interpretation error: use of a magnifying glass, contacting the prescriber, seeking verification from the patient and from previous patient medication record (PMR) entries. The choice or combination of choices of action will depend on individual circumstances but clearly nothing can be dispensed without certainty.

Computer errors

Computers are (generally) error-free; humans are not. Established suppliers provide software that is free of major errors but even so, when new or changed products are introduced (changes in formulation, changes in strength etc.), the dispensary staff must be trained to be extra-vigilant for these and to watch for product codes that are similar to established ones.

Typographical errors, incorrect selection of product codes from the computer drug file, and transposition of labels, are all common sources of operator error, as are the errors caused by dispensing from a pile of labels that have been prepared for a batch of prescriptions. Repeat prescriptions can cause additional problems if the dispensary staff assume there have been no treatment changes and then proceed to produce labels with reference solely to the PMR rather than to the prescription itself. This must never be done.

Product selection

Prudent stock purchasing policies, attention to dispensary stock layout, consulting with dispensary staff, training, and the design of robust checking procedures are prime tasks for the pharmacist to undertake so that selection errors are minimised.

Products bearing similar or similar-sounding names (e.g. lofepramine/ loperamide; bisoprolol/bisacodyl; carbamazepine/carbimazole) or those with a 'co-' prefix (e.g. co-dydramol, co-proxamol) contribute to a large number of dispensing errors. Awareness of the extent of the problem can be obtained by referring to a leaflet that is produced and regularly updated by the NPA.

Although the pharmaceutical industry is keen to play down the influence their corporate style of packaging has on the frequency of dispensing errors, those involved in dispensing frequently cite the similarity in pack design within a range of drugs from one manufacturer as a major contributor. Sometimes the strength of a medicine is poorly displayed on the box in pastel shades which, coupled with an identical style of font, pack size and overall colour, makes one drug look very much like another. Until the needs of both industry and dispensing pharmacist can be reconciled, dispensary staff must attempt to separate and mark such products on their shelves, and the pharmacist should consider whether choosing a different supplier is feasible.

Checking procedures

Incorporating robust checking procedures into the dispensing process is not difficult, especially if experienced dispensing staff are employed. Because two pairs of eyes are better than one, no pharmacist should feel it beneath his or her dignity to be checked by a dispensary assistant, provided that the assistant has the self-confidence to speak up if a mistake is discovered. Many dispensaries are 'single-handed', and this presents a significant problem when it comes to checking work. It can be difficult to ignore and override the original understanding of a prescription, product selection, etc., and this will largely dictate the outcome of a self-check. The only way of trying to overcome this is to set aside the dispensed items and to undertake another task – perhaps dispensing another prescription, transmitting an order, counselling a patient – before returning some minutes later to perform the checking process.

Bagging and handing out

Handing out medicine to the wrong patient is not infrequent and can be caused by a lack of proper process for receiving prescriptions over the counter from patients. The situation is made worse if a pharmacy has a large number of patients with the same or similar names, and the introduction of a numbered docket system, with the prescription reception staff being required to ensure the patient's address is correctly shown, will certainly help to eliminate a number of mistakes. Staff should not allow themselves to become intimidated by patients who appear impatient and in a hurry – they must follow whatever procedures the supervising pharmacist has laid down – including asking the patient to confirm the address before handing over any medicine. Inside the dispensary, staff must always be vigilant to ensure the correct PMR is recalled on the computer, that the medicines for each family member are correctly labelled and bagged separately and that the full name and address appears on the bag before it is put aside for handing out.

An analysis of 7000 reports of dispensing errors from 89 UK hospitals between 1991 and 2001 reveals where the majority of problem areas lie within the dispensing process. The error rates that occurred when dispensing from in-patient drug charts, discharge prescriptions and outpatient prescriptions are listed below:[9]

Wrong drug supplied	23%
Wrong strength (of the right medicine) supplied	23%
Wrong quantity	10%
Wrong warnings or directions	10%
Wrong drug name or details on label	9%
Wrong strength on label	8%
Wrong dosage form	7%
Wrong patient name on label	7%

Amongst the recommendations contained in a Department of Health report[3] are those for safer dispensing:

- Check the clinical appropriateness of the prescription before dispensing.
- Carry out an accuracy check of the dispensed medicine, if possible by a second person.
- Dispensing should be in line with the RPSGB's practice guidance.
- Staff should be suitably trained and demonstrate competence to dispense and, if appropriate, to carry out the final check.
- Dispensing errors and near misses should be reported by all pharmacists through the NPSA reporting scheme.
- Environmental conditions in the dispensing area should support safe practice, and minimise fatigue and distractions. Facilities and staff should be appropriate for the workload.
- Use the RPSGB's **HELP** mnemonic for accuracy checking:

  How much has been dispensed
  Expiry date check
  Label check
  Product check

- Labels should be read at least three times: on selection, on labelling, and when issuing – to confirm the drug name, strength and formulation.
- The patient's or carer's understanding of the medicine should be checked on issue.

Concluding remarks – risk management and quality

The processes of risk management and change management need to be firmly embedded in any business, being linked by sharing the common strands of seeking to provide something of quality, meeting the established needs of the customer, whilst also satisfying the professional aspirations of the provider. It is the responsibility of management to ensure the progressive survival of its business, forever looking for new and improved ways of fulfilling the business objectives of the organisation.

When asked what measurables they seek from a typical pharmacy, most customers surveyed will mention three aspects – price, access and quality – and out of these three, quality is the most important. The quality of service on offer in a pharmacy will be used to judge whether the price is reasonable and whether that pharmacy will be chosen in preference to one that is more conveniently located but where the service is believed to be of an inferior quality. Quality can only be achieved by setting standards and by using performance indicators, then by using an audit cycle where risk management strategy is firmly embedded as an integral part.

An additional factor to take into account during a time of change is whether any of the proposed changes, maybe a new service, will destabilise any part of the existing business. New risks may be identified and the risk profile of existing risks may alter, thereby requiring a reassessment of the entire strategy. It is better business to delay the implementation of a new service rather than to sacrifice quality – 'doing it right first time' is the ultimate goal of a successful business as it maximises the business opportunity.

All those who are engaged in dispensing will be able to think of examples of dispensing errors with which they are familiar. Part of the risk management process that dispensary staff ought to undertake every time there is an error is to analyse it carefully in an attempt to identify the major causative factors.

Individual pharmacists, in conjunction with their staff, will adopt their own way of working. Once a sensible and logical approach has been implemented to minimise the effects of major risks in both the dispensary and shop areas, as well as in the dispensing process itself, then two watchwords must always remain – REVIEW and CHECK – to ensure that the ultimate goal of successful risk management is achieved – doing it right first time.

References

1.   Department of Health. *Risk Management in the NHS*. London: DoH, 1993.
2.   Department of Health. *An Organisation with a Memory*. London: DoH, 2000.
3.   Department of Health. *Building a Safer NHS for Patients*. London, DoH, 2001.
4.   Vincent C (ed.). *Clinical Risk Management*. London: BMJ Publishing Group, 1995.

5. Barlow J (ed.). *The Health & Safety Handbook*. London: Directory of Social Change, 2001.
6. Department of Trade and Industry. *Maternity Rights – A Guide for Employers and Employees* [DTI/HSE PL958 (Rev. 3)]. London: DTI, 2003.
7. Smith D. *Complete Cookery Course*. London: BBC Worldwide Publications, 1989.
8. Field M J, Lohn K N. *Clinical Practice Guidelines*. Washington, DC: National Academy Press, 1990.
9. Audit Commission. *A Spoonful of Sugar – Medicines Management in NHS Hospitals*. London: Audit Commission, 2001.

Further reading

Maguire T. Managing risk. Part of *Mind Your Own Business*. Booklet provided free from *Chemist & Druggist Online* (details available from http://www.dotpharmacy.com/matters.html)

Managing current risks in community pharmacy. Report of National Association of Co-operative Executive Pharmacists Meeting Cork 2001. *Pharm J* 2001; 267: 564–565.

Managing risk (leading article). *Pharm J* 1999; 263: 695.

Reason J. *Human Error*. Cambridge: University of Cambridge, 1990.

Reason J. *Managing the Risks of Organisational Accidents*. Ashgate, Aldershot, 1997.

Royal Society. *Risk: Analysis, Perception and Management*. London: Royal Society, 1992.

Royal Society. *Science, Policy and Risk*. London: Royal Society, 1997.

Vincent C. *Clinical Risk Management: Enhancing Patient Safety*. London: BMJ Books, 2001.

9

Insurance

Alan B Watson

Introduction

Insurance should be seen as an integrated part of risk management, which is covered in detail in Chapter 8. The intention of this chapter is to focus on insurance for pharmacists in community practice and to address their specific problems and concerns. It will be impossible to detail all available cover, conditions and rating factors in such a limited format, however the major elements and issues and common features will be identified. The chapter will assume that the pharmacy will require fire, special perils, employers, and public liability, and theft/burglary insurance for buildings, stock, contents, fixtures and fittings, as well as liability insurance.

The introduction will explain the nature, function and benefits of insurance and the theory behind pricing and rating. The insurance 'hard and soft' market operation is described as well as the link with the 'insurance underwriting cycle'. A simplistic approach to the importance of insurance for the individual is presented through a hypothetical situation. This example can be applied to the largest business concern and the effect of uninsured risk on any organisation, but usually with more serious consequences to life and property.

The chapter then comments on the factors that may affect the proposer's decision to insure and the insurer's decision to offer insurance; numerous standard exclusions and conditions are also described.

Nature, function and benefits of insurance

The nature and function of insurance is to protect individuals, society, industry and commerce from the effects of risk by providing a form of financial protection through the provision of an insurance contract, a form of risk transfer device. This is undertaken by the insured normally paying a fixed amount known as a premium to an insurer, in return for financial protection or indemnity in general insurance and liability insurance. Indemnity is not available in life insurance contracts.

Value to individual, industry, commerce and the state

Insurance provides financial security in the event of loss, damage or liability, and also acts as a means of saving and investment. The industry invests in industry and commerce by means of research and development in technology for the health service, fire and security, engineering, motor aircraft and marine sectors. This research and development in the long term provides safer equipment, plant and machinery, reduced risk environment and claims. In addition to financial protection, the individual benefits from peace of mind and availability of valuable information from the industry on many aspects of loss reduction in the fire, security, motor and liability sectors. This data bank of practical advice is provided through brochures, pamphlets, reports from fire and security surveyors and motor, marine and aviation engineers.

Economic and financial benefits

The insurance industry in the UK provides employment for approximately 300000 individuals in the industry and auxiliary fields. The industry settles claims of approximately £200 million for life insurance-related claims and £40 million in non-life claims each day. Insurance contributes some £2 billion towards the UK economy. These benefits are only a fraction of the total contribution of insurance towards the well-being of the UK economy.

Hard and soft markets

The insurance market is subject to the normal fluctuations of any commercial market. These fluctuations result in the increase and decrease of prices or premiums. It may help the reader to appreciate the activities of the industry related to the hard and soft market. In a hard insurance market, insurance companies adopt a less flexible attitude by imposing harsher conditions and higher premiums, and often removing the marginal insured who has an optimal premium which if reached will no longer insure. As premiums increase and the selectivity of the insurers results in improved claims and increased premium funds, competition enters the equation. Competition drives premiums down, the marginal insured enters the market with poorer loss experience, premium rates reduce and conditions are more flexible. This forms part of what is known as the underwriting cycle and forms undulating trends over a 5-or 6-year cycle. The astute insurance purchaser may read the cycle to their advantage, from the viewpoint of the individual or corporate organisation.

Pricing and rates

Insurance pricing and rates are dependent on a variety of factors for each of the forms of insurance underwritten; this is described in further detail on page 164. Pricing and rates are important to both the insured and the insurer. From the insurer's viewpoint, an insufficient premium or rate results in an inadequate contribution to the insurer's funds, which may in future years lead to an increase in premium. From the insured's viewpoint, one of the objectives is to obtain the most inexpensive quotation. This attitude may be self-defeating as with this quote may come inadequate cover and service. It has been said that an individual or company should purchase insurance at a reasonable price and the object of this purchase is a fair and equitable, efficient and effective claims service. Knowing that your claim will be paid in full as efficiently as possible is desirable. This can prove to be exceedingly difficult in today's financial world, because of the variety of intermediaries and forms of insurance available – insurance brokers, consultants, agents, direct line operations, direct insurers, and the Internet. Further development of the factors that constitute the rating/underwriting mechanism will be discussed under the individual forms of insurance later in the chapter.

To insure or not to insure, that is the question

Consider the practical effects of the following series of incidents. A pharmacist is approaching the shop premises one morning only to see the fire services attending a fire at the adjacent premises. This would not appear to be a problem, however part of the fire has spread to their property and caused £10 000 of damage to the building, £10 000 smoke/water damage to the stock and prevented access to the shop for 24 hours. On return to the shop they are confronted by the broken front and rear doors, the alarm system has been disabled and £5000 of stock has been stolen. The following day an elderly lady trips on a frayed carpet and falls through a glass display cabinet resulting in serious injury, not to mention the damage to the cabinet and the glass impregnated stock. On day 5 the shop is totally destroyed by an earthquake.

Consider the plight of the pharmacist and the resultant financial, legal and practical implications if the premises were not insured or insurance as a risk transfer had been removed from the global financial market place. A motor premium of £1000 is expensive unless you drive into a bus queue. The above represents a highly improbable situation, however many individuals and organisations are without insurance through accident or design. The risks and hazards inherent in society have the potential to injure, damage and destroy life and property on an individual, national or international scale. The provision of adequate insurance at a reasonable price is desirable and essential and it is hoped that this chapter will provide some insight into various insurances, cover, conditions and underwriting/rating factors and practices.

The insurance process

Insurance cover is dependent on the following.

The proposal

The proposal is an important document as it details the risk to be insured and contains a number of questions that are subject to the insurance principle of Utmost Good Faith, which requires honest and truthful answers to questions presented in the proposal form by any authorised insurance official. Non-compliance with the principle may result in future non-payment of claim, the policy being void, legal action for damages, and court action. The proposal form will be considered by the insurer/underwriter when calculating the rate/premium. This is normal for smaller risks that may require additional input from a specialist surveyor, e.g. fire, theft, liability; composite should the risk be complex, technical or expensive.

The survey

The survey may be considered as a detailed proposal completed by a specialist from the insurer or from a specialist agency or consultancy. The survey is technical and detailed, time-consuming and may involve the use of architect plans, reports from alarm companies, surveyors or any other experts. The surveyor's report is collated with all other available information to provide a pictorial view of the risk proposed. This should include the surveyor's report, plans, photographs, video and any other relevant information that will allow the underwriter to make an informed decision as to the acceptance or refusal of the risk.

Previous claims

Knowledge of previous claims is very important to the underwriter, to indicate the level, frequency and severity of past claims and provide evidence of a claims pattern or trends. This data will also indicate the attitude to risk management and loss prevention of the proposer/insured.

Small and frequent losses will indicate a particular attitude and large and infrequent losses another; should losses be significant or unusual, the insurer may contact previous insurers to make further enquiries. Obviously future terms, conditions, rates and premium will be based on the proposer's previous claims history, in particular where this experience is adverse and indicates a level of negligence on behalf of the individual, company or organisation.

Previous insurance history

This information may link with the previous heading, as the proposer's previous insurance history will have a bearing on the proposer's attitude to insurance. Regular and frequent change of insurer may indicate an awareness of the market, broker knowledge or constant monitoring of the market, or merely a movement to identify the least expensive form of cover available. If the history indicates a degree of loyalty to a limited insurer it may indicate willingness to form stronger bonds with the insurer, to be familiar with the company, staff, etc. either directly or through a broker. This attitude may also indicate an indifference to the market and a lack of understanding of premiums, rates, contracts and conditions. Obviously the previous claims and insurance history inform the underwriter of several factors, only a few of which have been identified above. It is the underwriter's function to draw all information together and to examine and analyse the material in order to make a sound judgement that produces an acceptable premium for the proposer/insured and a profit for the insurer.

Specialist insurers

Knowledge of specialist insurers and the contracts on offer may provide a more acceptable contract to the proposer; this may be so in the case of specialist risks such as pharmacists. There may be distinct benefits to examining the market personally or through a broker, preferably one who is familiar with the specialist risk. These insurers or brokers target specialist risks and are aware of the potential losses and the risk management control methods that will provide the greatest level of protection for the most appropriate premium.

Underwriting factors

An underwriter will consider many factors when making an informed decision about whether to accept or decline, or to accept subject to warranties or conditions. It is impossible to identify all the factors in a chapter such as this, as each form of insurance requires specific as well as general factors to enable the underwriter to come to a satisfactory decision. The intention is to make the reader aware of a limited number of these factors or elements that will be considered by the underwriter. This list is by no means exhaustive, however it may go some way to informing the reader about some of the more common indicators, including exclusions and conditions, and the rationale for inclusion in the chapter.

The structure of the policy

Standard exclusions and conditions

Exclusions

Exclusion is a term in an insurance policy that identifies an area or set of circumstances in which the insurer will not be financially responsible should a loss occur from the subject of the exclusion. There are many exclusions throughout the various forms of insurance available, however they normally fall into two categories, general and specific. General exclusions normally apply to the majority of accident and liability insurances. Specific exclusions apply to specific forms of insurance, e.g. motor, liability, fire and special perils, etc. The following exclusions represent a number of general exclusions that apply to accident and liability policies.

War and kindred risks   Insurers are not inclined to accept potential major catastrophic losses – war, riot, civil commotion, rebellion, revolution, etc., all fall into this category. A number of perils such as riot, civil commotion, etc. may be covered on payment of additional premium, providing the risk is not exacerbated by location of the risk to be insured, i.e. near a football ground, nuclear installation, newspaper office or party political headquarters. This form of event should normally be covered by the state.

Sonic bang   With the advent of supersonic flight, insurers were reluctant to cover the results of 'sonic explosion' from an aircraft and the concomitant difficulty of proving the loss. Insurers withdrew from this market for general and liability business, any loss being directed for payment by the state.

Riot and civil commotion, locked out workers, etc. As mentioned above, insurers are not inclined towards the provision of cover unless for additional premium. Losses from this source are often difficult to prove and settle and involve legal complications under statute. Proposers for insurance or brokers requesting this form of cover often do so with the implication that the cover is required for some specific reason, i.e. the possibility that the risk could manifest itself as a claim in the future. Should a pharmacist be located in areas of potential unrest, a specific request should be made to insure against riot, etc. This may be included at an additional premium, possibly subject to a survey. If the risk is considered to be above average then cover may be denied.

Radioactive contamination Radioactive contamination of individuals or property has potentially serious repercussions for the insurance industry, with long-term implications. Insurers may insure radioactive material that is properly protected and stored against the normal perils of fire, theft or damage by perils of nature, however the insurer will not be responsible for the release of potentially harmful substances that may contaminate individuals or property. The use and storage of radioactive material is governed by statute.

Conditions

A condition is an insurance term that imposes a duty or responsibility upon the insured to abide by a given set of circumstances or to be aware of situations that may result in non-payment of claims, voiding of the policy or civil damages. Similar to exceptions, conditions are either general or specific. General conditions apply to most accident and liability policies, specific conditions only to specific policies. A set of general conditions is provided.

Subrogation This condition is normally evident on all property and liability policies. Subrogation is the right in law that the insurer has of standing in place of the insured and availing all the rights and remedies the insured has against any negligent third parties. For example, should a painter or decorator be in the course of redecorating a pharmacist's premises and negligently causes £10000 of damages to stock and property, the insurer has the right of pursuing the negligent decorator after attending to the claim. The subrogation condition is normally found in the policy section headed Claims or under a separate heading of Subrogation.

Contribution This condition concerns the insurer's interest in the number of policies effected on the risk to be insured because evidence of multiple policies on a single property or stock, etc. may indicate an intention to defraud. The proposal form may also request similar information. Legally the insurer has the right to recover a rateable proportion of any loss from other insurers who may have an interest in any loss or claim. Contribution is one of the six main principles of insurance, together with subrogation above, and with the principles of Insurable Interest, Utmost Good Faith, Indemnity, and Proximate Cause.

Claims The claims condition is essential to all insurance contracts as it details the circumstances under which the insured should claim. The method of notification/intimation is detailed, for example by phone or letter, as is the period required for notification, e.g. 7, 14, 28 days, or immediately in the case of motor, theft and liability claims. The insured must supply all material to substantiate the claim, estimates, tenders and accounts. The claims condition may also include a subrogation condition, and states the rights of the insurer in the event of loss, i.e. the right and authority to enter the premises, instruction to mitigate the loss of property or to take any action that may reduce any further potential loss. Contravention of this condition may result in the insurer cancelling the claim or policy.

Arbitration The arbitration condition is normally invoked when the insurer and the insured are in dispute over the quantum (amount) of the claim not liability; arbitration operates after liability has been admitted. Arbitration is an action that is normally less expensive and more efficient than court action. The case is heard by an arbitrator from the Institute of Arbitrators and is subject to the Arbitration Act, which details the rules, procedures and conditions under which the arbitration may take place. This condition is normally found in all property and liability insurance contracts.

Indemnity Indemnity, although not a condition in its own right, pervades the entire range of the property and liability insurance contracts – it is the substance of insurance. Simply stated indemnity should place the insured in the same financial position after a loss as they were immediately before the loss (indemnity does not apply to life contracts). The principle is linked to a formula (current market value, less wear, tear and depreciation, CMV – W/T/D). The current market value is the value at the date and place of loss. Should the proposer or insured not wish to suffer the reduction of the claim by wear, tear and depreciation, they may wish to consider a reinstatement contract, which dispenses with the application of wear, tear and depreciation. In the case of household insurance this may be called 'new for old', and is normally more expensive than its indemnity counterpart.

Types of policies

The following policies have been chosen as they represent the most popular forms of insurance available. However, this list is not exhaustive.

- Fire insurance
- Special perils insurance
- Employer's liability insurance
- Public liability insurance
- Theft/burglary insurance

Each policy will be described, with the basic form of cover, the rating structure and the various underwriting factors that will affect the rate and premium.

Fire insurance

Cover

Cover is normally in respect of property, including buildings, stock, contents, fixtures and fittings, machinery and plant. The insured perils are:

- **Fire:** (conditional) basically damage or destruction by fire from any cause whatsoever not excluded.
- **Lightning:** unconditional damage or destruction caused by lightning to the insured property.
- **Explosion:** (conditional) damage or destruction to the insured property caused through the explosion of boilers or gas used for domestic purposes, e.g. baths, showers, kitchens, etc.

Rating

Rating is normally based on the sum insured for the property to be insured applied to a rate calculated by considering a number of underwriting factors, some of which are detailed below. The sum insured may require input from specialists and consultants, property valuers, architects, surveyors, engineers or accountants.

Underwriting factors

- Building construction
- Building occupation
- Location
- Machinery/plant
- Physical/mechanical and electrical fire protection and security
- Insurance survey
- Sums insured
- Previous claims
- Employees
- Surrounding property and occupation

Another important form of insurance, consequential loss insurance (loss of profits), would normally be considered should the risk warrant both fire, special perils and consequential loss insurance. Consequential loss insurance is not covered in this chapter because the description and explanation of this form of insurance requires a more extensive understanding of insurance policy contract cover. Pharmacists should be aware of the following when considering fire-related insurance cover. Shop stock such as paper and cardboard containers, alcohol-based products, perfume and after-shave, toiletries, and pressurised/aerosol canisters may be more susceptible to fire. Consideration should also be given to risk control measures, with minimum protection being provided by adequate fire extinguishing appliances, smoke blankets, smoke and fire alarms and first aid equipment. For further information on risk prevention, see page 169.

Special perils insurance

Cover

Perils include explosion, riot, civil commotion, storm and flood, aircraft and motor impact, landslip subsidence and heave, and earthquake. This form of insurance is normally effected in addition to fire insurance because the fire insurance policy is limited in cover.

Rating

Rating is normally based on the sum insured for the property to be insured applied to a rate calculated by considering a number of underwriting factors, some of which are detailed below. The sum insured may require input from specialists and consultants, property valuers, architects, surveyors, engineers or accountants.

Underwriting factors

- Building construction, roof, walls, guttering
- Building occupation
- Location, earthquake (recent Manchester event), flooding subsidence, landslip
- Proximity to sea, river, reservoirs, dams
- Proximity to gradients, hills, airports, football grounds
- Condition of property
- Exposure of property including stock and contents
- Previous claims
- Detail of stock, contents, fixtures and fittings
- Sum insured

This form of cover is reasonably extensive with regard to the range of perils covered, however each of the perils is followed by a number of exceptions and conditions. In addition, the policy document contains specific and general conditions; the general conditions apply to the entire document. The interpretation of the fire and special perils policy should not be undertaken lightly but with a competent insurance broker, loss assessor or loss adjuster. In addition to the exceptions and conditions the insured must consider the effect of excesses/deductibles, average (the penalty for underinsurance) policy limits and warranties that may apply. Pharmacists should be aware of the following when considering special perils insurance cover. Shop stock such as alcohol-based products, after-shave, toiletries, pressurised/aerosol canisters, etc. may be more susceptible to explosion. Location of property is extremely important when considering special perils insurance, for example proximity to airports, rivers, sea (flooding), gradients, mines/underground geological faults, and urban and rural services.

Employer's liability insurance (see also Chapter 8)

Cover

The insurer will indemnify the insured in respect of a claim by an employee who dies or is injured or is affected by any disease in the course of their employment. The insurer will compensate the employer for any associated court costs including solicitor's fees and expenses. The policy will not pay for any damage to an employee's property. This form of insurance is compulsory for the majority of employers in the UK, and a certificate of insurance must be displayed in a prominent position at the employer's place of work.

Rating

Employer's liability premium is normally calculated on the workforce wage or salary figure, taking into consideration the following underwriting features.

Underwriting factors

- Number of employees
- Class of employee
- Nature of business
- Previous claims
- Machinery, plant other equipment
- Working conditions
- Compliance with health and safety legislation
- Compliance with other specialist legislation
- Work away from own premises
- Salaries/wages amount

Employer's liability policy exclusions normally include claims related to public and product liability policies. Pharmacists should be aware of the following when considering employer's liability insurance cover – employee access to machinery and equipment, sources of heat and cold, microwave or X-ray equipment or other energy sources. Employers must be aware of health and safety procedures and other employment legislation pertaining to their own business. Liability claims are often contentious and costly in terms of compensation and reputation and can cause irreparable damage to small business organisations with a close working relationship between employees and the employer. The use of chemicals and drugs that may come into contact with hands must be carefully monitored and the risks assessed for adverse reactions.

Public liability insurance (see also Chapter 7)

Cover

Public liability insurance is issued in respect of an organisation's liability at law to indemnify members of the public and other third parties (apart from their own employees) against death, injury or disease and damage to their property occurring as a result of the organisation's negligence. The policy will also cover the costs and expenses of any court case that may result from the claim, with the insurer's permission. Examples of claims include customers being injured or their property damaged by worn carpeting, accidental spillage of liquid on floor, or stock on high shelves falling on customers. Pharmacists must be aware of children, partially sighted and the disabled who may be more vulnerable to accidents and/or injury.

Rating

Premium is normally calculated on a per capita basis per employee for small business concerns, or a flat rate or nominal premium is charged where the risk element is low. Turnover may be considered as a factor in rating, particularly in product liability risks. Premium may be adjusted at the end of the policy year to reflect actual turnover against nominated turnover at the commencement of the period of insurance.

Underwriting factors

- Condition of buildings, shop, etc.
- Public access
- Nature of business
- Work away from the insured's premises
- Previous claims
- Survey, if considered necessary
- Factors depend on risk, e.g. pharmacy, department store, shop, school, university, industrial/commercial
- Sum insured
- Related legislation
- Number of years business established

Public liability policy exclusions normally include claims related to employer's liability insurance. A number of public liability policies are available, such as business risks policy, product liability insurance, professional liability, personal public liability (may be included in the household policy), and director's and officer's liability insurance. Pharmacists should be aware of the following when considering public liability related insurance cover. Risks that may affect customers must be monitored, points of entry and exit, doors, condition of carpets, access to shelves, corners, lighting and storage or stock on higher shelves.

Burglary insurance

Cover

Theft insurance is normally in respect of theft or burglary to the premises resulting in the theft of property, usually by forcible and violent entry to or exit from the property. This form of cover is more limited than that provided by statute and will not include for example claims for shoplifting and collusion and fraud by staff to remove stock from the premises.

Rating

Premium rates are normally based on the proposer's or insured's valuation of the stock as the sum insured times the appropriate rate for the nature of the business and the following underwriting factors. The base rate is determined normally by the nature of the trade or business linked to the location and the experience of the proposer or insured.

Underwriting factors

- Nature of business
- Detailed description of stock
- Physical protection, electrical and mechanical
- Nature and quality of physical and electrical protection, extensive
- Location
- Stock values as the sum insured
- Previous claims
- Nature and description of safes, drug cupboards, protected areas
- Staff history
- Hours of business

Burglary or theft policies are normally subject to a variety of conditions and warranties that may complicate an otherwise normal risk. Pharmacists should be aware of the following when considering burglary or theft related insurance cover – certain types of shop stock may attract burglars and thieves (opportunistic or premeditated), including drugs, cameras and equipment, cosmetics (ladies and gents), perfume, batteries, etc. This stock may be of medium to high value and can be packed and transported in a short period of time and sold in pubs, on market stalls, etc.

Risk management (see also Chapter 8)

Risk management is another major consideration for any organisation operating in today's business environment. This discipline relies on a tested practical base, an academic methodology based on risk identification, analysis and control through risk elimination, reduction and transfer, monitor and risk review. The discipline of risk management is covered in greater depth in Chapter 8; this section of the book concerns only those aspects of insurance relating to risk management. Insurance is a tool of risk management and can be an effective method of risk transfer, if undertaken with caution and thought. Discussion with a responsible and competent insurer and/or broker is essential to securing a quality contract. Such discussion may also include a lawyer, accountant, architect and surveyors. Health and safety issues must be considered because they impinge on most organisations today and have implications for employers and public liability related insurances.

Methods available to reduce premium can be as follows:

- Accept an excess/deductible.
- Installation of fire and theft control and prevention measures.
- Installation of physical, electrical and mechanical protection.
- Acceptance of warranties/conditions.
- Long-term contract agreement.

Risk control

Part of any risk management or insurance survey function is to make recommendations regarding risk control. Methods of risk control apply broadly to three areas, i.e. fire, security and liability. A considerable amount of material is available from various sources relating to the protection of property, e.g. the Association of British Insurers, police and fire authorities, ROSPA, the Health and Safety Executive and a multitude of other bodies and associations, however a number of broad-based pointers to risk control are provided. Due consideration should be given to the following. A list of improvements, recommendations and requirements from insurers depend initially on a number of factors, which dictate the level of risk control expected:

- The location of the premises is paramount, town against country risk.
- The nature of the risk presented – large, medium, small.
- Nature of stock and values, individual and total.
- Previous claims record and existing protection.

Considering a town centre pharmacy as an example, basic risk control measures under the headings fire, security and liability, may include the following.

Fire

Fire extinguishing appliances for water, chemical and electrical fires, all colour-coded for clarity and identification. The installation of fire/smoke/heat detectors of varying degrees of quality and cost should be considered. Fire blankets should be placed near any source of naked flame. The installation of fire doors for staff protection and containment of fire should also be considered. Chemicals in stock used in the pharmacy may act as a retardant or accelerant, perfumes, aftershave or any alcohol-based product. Fire exits should meet industry standards and the owner must consider liability aspects by maintaining clear access and having the doors regularly maintained.

Security

Security is also dependent on location and the nature of stock and values. Isolated risks provide the burglar with a delay advantage. Two factors may deter thieves/burglars – the degree of difficulty in entering the property and excessive noise. The more difficult to gain access and the louder the alarm when entering the property, the more likely the amateur will be deterred. Basic security protections may include:

- Locks, to British Standard, should be fitted to front and rear doors. Often good-quality locks are fitted to substandard doors with 50%/90% glass panels, which defeat the purpose of the lock.
- Bars/grilles should be fitted to rear sections or extensions and should be *securely* anchored to the surrounding masonry, brickwork, etc. (burglars have been known to fish stock through widely spaced bars).
- Safes should be seriously considered; decisions have to be made as to the type of safe required, depending on the purpose. Consider the options available, free-standing or anchored to the floor, strength, thickness and quality, single or double key locks or single or double combination locks, connected to alarm system, etc.
- Alarm systems – quality and cost need to be considered. A quality system will be expensive but to cut corners may be a false economy. The insurer may recommend an appropriate alarm company. Alarm

systems may be 'bells only' or connected to the local police station, although requires authorisation and it is uncommon for the police to support this option except in exceptional circumstances. The alarm may also be connected to the alarm company's 'central station' facility. The choice and quality of alarm system is detailed and technical and would require a chapter alone to describe the various features involved in the decision-making process. However, part of the alarm system should include a panic button facility for staff; this can either be audible or silent (as used in banks, etc.). Panic buttons must be easily accessible remembering that staff may not necessarily be located behind a counter or desk. This facility should be linked to a cash handover policy/strategy, and staff should be made aware of the policy, as any loss will be covered by the insurer providing the appropriate policy has been effected. Any drugs cupboard should form part of the alarm system and should have a panic button situated in close proximity, as unobtrusively as possible.

Liability

Liability risk control should be considered under two main headings, employee and third party liability, where third parties would include customers, delivery men, representatives, contractors, etc. Third parties will also include children, the elderly and the disabled, who require special consideration. The owner must take a number of simple precautions, such as replacing worn carpets, possibly replace glass counters and display cabinet glass with a safer alternative. Stock should be maintained at a reasonable height and doors should be simple to operate for the elderly or disabled (although the door also has to act as security for the property). Customers should not have access to areas where drugs are stored or prepared and all guidelines for handling drugs or chemicals should be adhered to. Staff must follow health and safety procedures and any protective clothing prescribed by rules or procedures must be worn. Any non-compliance may result in non-payment of any claim.

How to make a claim

The intimation of a claim to an insurance company may appear to be a simple task and may for many insured prove to be simple, however many individuals who claim find it fraught with problems. Initial advice is to contact your broker, agent or financial adviser, or contact the insurer to obtain details of the correct claims procedure. It is often in the insured's interest to contact the insurance company directly with details of the claim, to confirm that the event is covered. A quality insurer will inform the insured directly if the event is insured or not. If the claim is valid then a claim form will be issued, or in the case of an Internet company a form can be completed over the web or a claim can be intimated over the telephone. A number of options are available should the claim be repudiated, and one should not necessarily give up at this point, but contact a broker, loss assessor or solicitor, as they will have more experience of claims management. It may prove valuable to read the policy document to confirm that the loss is covered. This may not be a simple process, as the policy must be read as one document and due consideration must be given to warranties, conditions, exceptions and excesses. The claims condition should also be studied, as specific action must be taken in respect of each form of insurance, e.g. fire, burglary and liability. The insured must appreciate that with conditions, warranties, excesses and penalties for underinsurance, etc. it is unlikely that they will recover 100% of the claim. If the loss is serious in nature and cost, it may be advisable to consult a loss assessor to act on your behalf. This may complicate the situation when settling the loss with the loss adjuster, who is independent but is instructed by the insurer, and may lead to conflict.

Having confirmed that the event is covered, either personally, or by using an insurer, broker, etc., the next step is to ensure that the correct authorities have been advised, i.e. for a theft claim the police must be notified, for liability the insurer must be advised as soon as possible to defend its position and appoint a solicitor to act on their behalf or to attend to the claim in-house. If the claim is a relatively simple, intimate claim, complete claim form, carry out insurer's instructions, await investigation and then hopefully the cheque should follow. As stated earlier, the pursuit of cheap insurance is not the objective in the search for the perfect policy, but the most effective and efficient claims service, one which pays out promptly and with the minimum of fuss.

Should the claim be potentially serious and expensive then expect delays from the time the claim form is submitted by the insured to the insurer, as the company must realistically investigate the claim thoroughly. A loss adjuster should be appointed immediately and a visit to the insured or to the property will follow. The relevant authorities will be contacted; police, fire brigade, medical, hospital and the necessary reports will be submitted in due course. The insurer or their agents have certain rights of access to the insured's property and this is one reason for reading the policy claims conditions, to become familiar with the duties, rights and responsibilities of insured and insurer in the event of a claim being made under the policy. After the initial inspection or visit, the loss adjuster will prepare a preliminary report for the insurer, to inform them of the circumstances surrounding the event. The report will detail the sums insured, property values, estimates of the estimated maximum loss figures, and confirm that warranties and conditions have been complied with. The application of any excesses or penalties such as average in respect of underinsurance will also be covered. With liability claims, employers, public and products the circumstances surrounding the loss will be investigated to ascertain liability. Discussions with the insured and the third party, employees, other third party, or customer will be arranged together with any witnesses present at the time of the event. For property losses, the insured will need to obtain estimates or tenders for repair, rebuilding, construction, etc. This documentation should be forwarded to the loss adjuster for registration, confirmation and evaluation and on instruction by the loss adjuster or insurer work can proceed. For liability claims, all documentation from employees, third parties and customers must be passed immediately to the insurer, together with letters, documentation, etc. from solicitors, and for lawyers acting on behalf of the third party. If the property claim proceeds without impediment, the loss adjuster will visit the property to confirm that the work has been carried out to the satisfaction of the insured. A form of satisfaction note will be signed, the final report will be prepared and submitted to the insurer and a cheque should follow in due course.

Complaints – concerns and procedures

Should there be concerns regarding the negotiation, management of the claim or with regard to the settlement amount, a number of avenues to resolution are available. If the claim is being managed by the loss adjuster, they should be contacted initially. It may be necessary to employ a loss assessor to discuss the situation with the loss adjuster and ultimately the insurer concerned.

Should this route be unsuccessful you must undertake the escalator method, by contacting various individuals within the company hierarchy, beginning with the claims manager at the local branch, who may be willing to negotiate the claim with authority from head office. If this is unsuccessful, proceed to the branch manager, who may be more amenable to protect the branch reputation or image without having to resort to head office, particularly if the claim is dubious as to liability or content with the bias towards the insured. Should this course of action be unsuccessful next proceed to the head office claims department, as they should be aware of the problem and be in a position to provide a definitive answer to the concern. At this point the majority of technical arguments will have been exhausted and the company's attitude to their reputation/image must be relied upon with other factors such as the amount of the claim and status of the insured and their ability to process the claim further and ultimately through the courts. One must consider the value of progressing the claim through each stage in the insurance company hierarchy. Each new individual may adopt a different approach to the liability aspect and amount. When negotiating at head office level the company appreciate the determination to pursue the claim to the courts if necessary. If the claim amount is considerable the case may proceed to executive management and be argued before senior management who will be the final arbitrators within the insurance company.

Should these methods fail, settlement may be pursued beyond the insurance company, firstly through the Institute of Arbitrators, who will only consider the amount of the settlement in dispute as liability will have been admitted by the insurer. Providing the claim meets the criteria, the Insurance Ombudsman could be approached. One final avenue may be to instigate court proceedings against the insurer; this can be expensive and time-consuming but may result in a court award in your favour or an out of court settlement that may meet the approval of both parties (or at some point in the proceedings the newspapers may be approached, if the loss has some personal or unique angle – insurers tend to avoid this form of negative reputation enhancement or pure bad publicity).

In all circumstances, reasonable and regular contact should be maintained with the insurer or loss adjuster or any of the insurer's representatives, either independently or in conjunction with the broker or insurance consultant at all times.

Other policies

Many policies have been omitted because of the space constraints of this chapter, in particular consequential loss/loss of profits, which is a major consideration in any business organisation, and product liability. The range of available insurance is diverse and is dependent on individual business operations and stock priorities. With the range of policies available, and the number of loadings, warranties and conditions applied by insurers, it is impossible to examine each in relation to specific risks or businesses. The proposer or insured must also consider the range of attitudes adopted by insurers depending upon whether the property is situated in a rural or urban location, whether town or suburb, and whether good, medium, poor or disastrous risk area/sector.

Finally, for the purchase of insurance the cheapest is certainly not always the best. In the insurance market you are paying for the most effective, efficient, courteous, professional claims service available, for all forms of claim, whether large or small.

Further information

The Chemists' Defence Association (CDA) is a wholly owned subsidiary of the National Pharmaceutical Association and provides professional indemnity cover of up to £10 million for those members, their employees and engaged locums unfortunate enough to make a professional mistake. CDA has a policy for all individual primary care pharmacists, under the name of Pharmacists' Professional Indemnity Limited (PPI). The cover provides:

- Professional indemnity
- Public liability
- Legal defence costs
- Confidential legal advice, tax advice and counselling

Professional indemnity insurance specifically for locum pharmacists is also available. Further details can be obtained from: National Pharmaceutical Association, Mallinson House, 38–42 St Peter's Street, St Albans, Hertfordshire AL1 3NP (email: npa@npa.co.uk).

Further reading

Chartered Insurance Institute Textbook, Associateship 655 Risk Management.
Chartered Insurance Institute Textbook, Associateship 760 Personal Insurances.
Association of British Insurers, Annual Reports and Accounts, 2002.
Association of British Insurers Facts and Figures, 2002.
Association of British Insurers Insurance Trends, 2002/2003.
Davis M, Hood J, Stein B. *Insurance Non-Marine, an Introduction*. London: Witherby, 1997.
Dickson G C A, Stein B. Risk and Insurance, Study Course 510, Chartered Insurance Institute, 1995.

Part Two

Putting management into practice

10

Financial management

Steven B Kayne

Introduction

The health of a business is dependent on effective financial management, which takes the form of:

- recording
- analysing
- planning
- control.

Recording financial data (in profit and loss and balance sheets) is required for several external and internal management reasons, while analysing (using financial ratios), planning and control (budgeting) are used to ensure that the business generates enough money to allow it to operate and provide the professional services deemed necessary by the owner or manager. It is important for the manager to be aware of basic accounting principles to be in a position to carry out these functions.

Financial management is all about using business assets efficiently, maximising the ability of resources to generate profit. In pharmacy, there is another dimension; that of providing service (see Chapter 11), and in some circumstances there may appear to be a conflict of interest. For example, does one deliver the balance of an antibiotic prescription that was not in stock when the patient called at the pharmacy, even though the cost of doing so will far exceed the dispensing profit? Questions like this are encountered daily in the pharmacy and cannot be addressed solely in terms of profit.

It is too enticing, and often too easy, to use 'blue sky' thinking in planning business activities. It is even easier to spend money without fully realising the return one is getting for it. Thus, a basic understanding of the four elements of financial management is essential for anyone in business. These are:

- recording financial data
- analysing
- planning
- control.

Accounting – an introduction

The main tool that is used to assist in the financial management process is known as 'accounting'. A general introduction to some of the main aspects of accounting is provided in this chapter. It is by no means exhaustive but will highlight some of the more important issues that can be pursued in greater depth in specialist textbooks or in conversations with financial advisors.

Accounting may be defined as the designing, recording, analysing, reporting and auditing of information systems or models that transform data into information for the following internal and external purposes:

- The measurement of income.
- As an aid to management decisions.
- As an aid to the planning and control of business activities.
- As an aid to meeting external reporting requirements.

The system should:

- satisfy both internal and external recording requirements
- be easy to understand and apply
- be adaptable to future changes in operations
- be inexpensive to maintain
- not be time-consuming.

There are a number of excellent electronic accounting packages on the market and theoretically, a competent business proprietor should be able to carry out most of the accounting needs. However, the services of an accountant will remove much of the worry associated with tax computation, as well as providing access to a range of other services (see Chapter 4). It is useful to choose an electronic package that is compatible with the package used by the accountancy firm looking after the business affairs, for it facilitates greatly the exchange of management information. It is also possible to employ book-keepers to carry out day-to-day recording processes and even prepare accounts in some cases.

Accounting principles

All aspects of accounts are governed by the following two principles.

- Dual effect – Every transaction has two effects, e.g. if a pharmacy purchases OTC medicines for sale, it has more stock and less cash. If it now sells a medicine to a consumer, it has less stock plus an amount of cash equal to the retail value of the item.
- The accounting equation – The two effects mentioned above are equal and balance each other. The ultimate accounting equation is represented by:

    net assets = proprietor's funds

    where:

    an **asset** is defined as something owned by a business, available for use in the business and **net assets** are defined as a business's total assets less total liabilities. A **liability** is defined as the amount owed by the business, i.e. an obligation to pay money at a future date. **Proprietor's funds** represents the total amount that the business owes to its owner or proprietor. Proprietors' funds comprise **capital** (the amount a proprietor has invested in the business) and **profits** (funds generated by the business), minus **losses** (any funds lost by the business) and **drawings** (amounts taken out of the business by the proprietor(s)).

Accounting process

The way in which the necessary elements of the reports are derived and the format of the reports is governed by accounting practice, in turn based on a number of standard procedures and controlled by audit (see below).

The major disadvantage of the financial reporting process is that it is historical. In some cases a considerable time may elapse between the end of an accounting period and the presentation of the accounts, making the results so far out of date that they may be of little or no use for future planning.

Accounting conventions

Four conventions are used in preparing financial reports:

- Objectivity – In preparing accounts data that is objective and as reliable as possible must be used. Objective data should be capable of independent verification and must not be based on personal opinions.

- Prudence – In preparing accounts it is normal to err on the side of conservatism. Profits are only included if they have been realised while losses are recorded immediately they become visible.
- Materiality – In preparing accounts, attention must be given to those items of particular importance to the business, and their values clearly disclosed. The items will obviously depend on the size of the business. Other less important items can be combined. It is usual to supply a list of notes to the annual accounts highlighting any unusual trends.
- Consistency – There are different ways in which information can be assembled in the construction of financial reports. For example, the method used to calculate depreciation (see above) may vary. It is important that the same methods are used from year to year. If changes become necessary, they must be fully documented.

Two assumptions are also made with regard to accounts. These are that the monetary unit is stable; there are special techniques to deal with times of high inflation. The second assumption is that the business is a 'going concern', i.e. it will continue to exist in future accounting periods.

Accounting standards

The Financial Reporting Council (FRC) with its subsidiaries, the Accounting Standards Board (ASB) and the Financial Reporting Review Panel (FRRP), together make up an organisation whose purpose is to promote and secure good financial reporting.

The role of the ASB is to issue **accounting standards**. It is recognised for that purpose under the Companies Act 1985. It took over the task of setting accounting standards from the Accounting Standards Committee (ASC) in 1990.

Accounting standards developed by the ASB are contained in Financial Reporting Standards (FRSs). Soon after it started its activities, the ASB adopted the standards issued by the ASC, so that they also fall within the legal definition of accounting standards. These are designated Statements of Standard Accounting Practice (SSAPs). Whilst some of the SSAPs have been superseded by FRSs, some remain in force.

Accounting standards apply to all companies, and other kinds of entities that prepare accounts that are intended to provide a true and fair view. The Foreword to Accounting Standards explains the authority, scope and application of accounting standards.

The ASB's objectives are set out in the ASB's Statement of Aims.

One of these is to develop principles to guide it in establishing accounting standards. These are contained in the ASB's Statement of Principles for Financial Reporting. The statement typically describes views on:

- the activities that should be reported on in financial statements
- the aspects of those activities that should be highlighted
- the attributes that information needs to have if it is to be included in the financial statements
- how information should be presented in those financial statements.

The ASB's Statement of Principles for Financial Reporting can have a variety of roles. Its main role is to provide conceptual input into the ASB's work on the development and review of accounting standards. The Statement is not, therefore, an accounting standard, nor does it contain any requirements on how financial statements are to be prepared.

Unlike its predecessor body, the ASC, the ASB can issue accounting standards on its own authority, without the approval of any other body. The ASB's policy is to consult widely on all its proposals. Generally, the development of a new accounting standard involves at least two formal consultation documents, a Discussion Paper and a Financial Reporting Exposure Draft (FRED).

The ASB collaborates with accounting standard-setters from other countries and the International Accounting Standards Board (IASB) in order to ensure that its standards are developed with due regard to international developments.

Auditing (see Chapter 4)

An audit is an in-depth examination of the information system to determine if, or to what extent, the management's financial statements fairly report the economic performance and financial condition of the company. The audit will include miscellaneous tests of the accounting records, usually verifying assets and liabilities. It also involves examining the internal control systems (including the computer information system) to determine how they prevent fraud and errors in general.

Recording and reporting financial data

A pharmacy proprietor may well question the necessity of providing financial reports and using separate banking accounts for the business. After all, it is my money anyway – surely I can do what I like? Why are records necessary?

The answers to these questions relate to both internal and external reasons. Not only is it important to know whether a business is making sufficient profit to enable it to pay its bills when they fall due but the Inland Revenue has more than a passing interest in business operations! Being able to justify business expenses becomes almost impossible if personal and business banking is one and the same thing.

Further, if the business is being operated as a limited company it is considered to be a completely separate entity and all monies flowing between a company and its directors need to be properly recorded.

Keeping records for internal reasons

Internal records generally centre around recording income and expenditure and are vital to enable informed decisions to be taken. For example, it may be beneficial to track sales at the cash point by coding items to identify fast movers or giving assistants identification numbers to monitor their activities and decide on bonus payments. Private prescription clients may be identified and their frequency of visits to the pharmacy noted so decisions on stock-holding may be taken – medicines for repeat prescriptions can be obtained on a 'just-in-time' basis. Looking at last year's Christmas sales might help in deciding on a budget for the following year.

Decision-making

To decide which option to choose amongst several it is necessary to obtain as much relevant information as possible and establish some criteria on the basis of which, the best alternative can be chosen. Some of the factors affecting the decision may not be expressed purely in monetary terms, particularly where staff or clients are directly affected. A key member of staff may want more time off to spend with the family; this will have financial implications but the request is granted anyway to keep them contented. This is a 'qualitative' judgement.

A 'quantitative' decision can be made when the various factors to be considered, and relationships between them, are measurable. A quantitative decision comprises seven steps:

- **Identifying the objective** Sometimes referred to as 'choice criterion' or 'objective function'. Examples include increasing turnover or providing new services (e.g. pharmaceutical care).

- **Identifying constraints** Many decision problems have one or more constraints, e.g. limited space for a consultation area, or lack of skilled staff.
- **Considering the range of alternative courses of action** under consideration. For example, improving profit could involve increasing sales at current cost levels or maintaining existing sales volume but decreasing costs.
- **Forecasting** the benefits of each alternative course of action and estimating the benefit foregone by choosing one opportunity instead of the next best alternative. This is known as the opportunity cost.
- **Applying** the decision criteria in 'what if?' models and ranking the alternatives.
- **Making** the choice of preferred alternatives.
- **Implementing** the decision.

Keeping records for external reasons

As well as for the internal uses detailed above, records on revenues and expenses need to be maintained for the following external sources:

- Inland Revenue, to enable tax responsibilities to be met.
- Profit and loss and cash flow statements are often required by banks and other commercial lenders before renewing or increasing facilities.
- Suppliers in fixing credit limits and terms.
- Staff members (e.g. managers) whose pay is linked to profit generation.
- Shareholders, directors and partners (depending on the structure of the business).
- Investors use accounting information, as well as other information, to make decisions to invest, or decrease their investment in a business.

Financial reports

The two principle statements that form a set of accounts are:

- The profit and loss account, defined as a summary of a business's transactions for a given period.
- The balance sheet, defined as a statement of the financial position of the business at a given date (usually the end of that period).

There are other reports that may be seen in company reports, including the Funds Flow Statement, useful in decisions concerning availability of cash in a business (liquidity).

The profit and loss or income statement

The profit and loss or income statement reports on the business transactions in financial terms over a defined period of time. For external reporting requirements this has to be produced annually but many businesses instruct their accountants to produce the reports quarterly or even monthly, when they are usually referred to as 'management accounts'. Read alongside cash flow predictions and budgets a comprehensive picture of business operations may be gained.

A simplified version of a profit and loss statement is shown in Figure 10.1. The following terms are used:

Sales	Value of sales less VAT
Cost of purchases	Cost of buying stock: calculated by taking value of stock at start of accounting period less value of stock at end of accounting period (physically counted) minus any discounts allowed from suppliers
Gross profit	Sales minus cost of purchases
Expenditure or overheads	Staff wages, establishment costs (heating, lighting, etc.), car expenses, telephone, postage
Financial costs	Banking and hire purchase costs
Net profit	Gross profit minus overheads
Depreciation	Depreciation represents the spreading of cost of capital expenditure (computers, cars, furniture and fittings) over a period of time equal to the expected useful life of the asset. There are several ways of calculating depreciation and an accountant will offer advice. Accounting convention dictates that the method used is consistent (see above).

It is important to include a comparison with the previous year in order that large deviations may be identified. In some large companies up to five years; results may be given, with any major variations explained as notes to the accounts.

An Independent Pharmacy

ANYTOWN

Profit & Loss Account for the period January to December 2003

	Year end 31 Dec 2003		Year end 31 Dec 2002	
	£		£	
Income				
Counter sales	147500		120000	
NHS Income	227000		186000	
Other sales	1000		750	
		375500		306750
Cost of Sales				
Opening Stock	31000		30000	
Purchases	240500		187000	
	271500		217000	
Closing Stock	−33000	238500	−31000	186000
GROSS PROFIT		**137000**		**120750**
Expenditure				
Wages	50000		44000	
Locum fees	3500		4200	
Pensions	5250		4200	
Telephone	1200		1400	
Printing, postage & stationery	675		598	
Motor expenses	5166		4069	
Accountancy fees	2950		1950	
Hire of equipment	3088		4155	
Depreciation of equipment	2578		2555	
Depreciation of vehicle	3500		4000	
Rent & rates	5750		5250	
Insurance	950		945	
Heat & light	495		534	
Finance costs				
Bank interest	2297		2000	
Bank charges	1800		2020	
Hire purchase	2801		2900	
		92000		84776
NET PROFIT		45000		36026

Figure 10.1 Profit and loss account.

Balance sheet

The balance sheet is a report that represents a snapshot of the financial
condition of a business at a given point in time. It summarises what a
business owns (assets) and owes (liabilities) and the amount of money

the proprietor has invested in it (capital). In terms of the accounting equation (see above):

assets = liabilities + net worth

Thus, anything owned by the pharmacy business is either owed to suppliers (creditors) or to the owner (net worth). A number of terms are found in a balance sheet, as shown in Figure 10.2:

Fixed assets	Assets acquired to provide a medium- or long-term benefit to a business. Tangible assets are buildings, machinery, furniture and fittings and vehicles; intangible assets include goodwill. Goodwill has not been included in the example; its calculation is explained in Chapter 5.
Current assets	Assets that form the basis of business trading. They include stock, amounts owed to the business by customers (debtors), payments made in advance of the due date (e.g. rent).
Intangible assets	Assets that are not in any physical form. They include goodwill.
Current liabilities	Liabilities that may have to be met in the short term or theoretically on demand. They include outstanding invoices from suppliers (creditors), and bank overdrafts. Current assets should always exceed current liabilities otherwise it is likely that the available cash will run out during a period of heavy expenditure.
Long-term liabilities	Liabilities needing to be met at times in excess of one year.
Drawings	The amount taken from the business by the owner.

Capital account

The capital account reports on the amount of money left in the business to fund day-to-day operations; in computer terms it is the business 'RAM'.

An Independent Pharmacy

ANYTOWN

Balance Sheet for the period January to December 2003

	Year end 31 Dec 2003 £		Year end 31 Dec 2002 £	
Fixed Assets				
Tangible assets: fixtures, computers and vehicle (value less depreciation)		52500		39040
Current assets				
Stock	33000		31000	
Trade creditors (money owed to business)	5500		3200	
Items paid in advance – prepayments	5240		2445	
Cash in hand	1950		867	
Total	45690		37512	
Current liabilities				
VAT due for payment	300		400	
Trade debtors (money owed to suppliers)	2750		3450	
Taxes and Social Security due for payment	5460		3450	
Overdraft	15180		12000	
	23690		19300	
		22000		18212
Long term liabilities		74500		57252
Bank loan		24500		0
Capital in the business		50000		57252
Capital Account				
Balance brought forward		57252		52000
Add Net profit		45000		36026
Total		102252		88026
Less Drawings		52252		50000
		50000		38026

Figure 10.2 Balance sheet and capital account.

Publishing accounts

In the case of limited companies, rules for the publication and disclosure are laid down under various Companies Acts or, if publicly quoted, the Stock Exchange.

Analysis of accounts

Ratios are the means of presenting information, in the form of a ratio or percentage, which enables a comparison to be made between one significant figure and another. Often the same ratios of like firms are used to compare the performance of one firm with another. A 'one off' ratio is often useless – trends need to be established by company ratios over a number of years.

The great volume of statistics made available in the annual accounts of companies must be simplified in some way. Present and potential investors can therefore quickly assess whether the company is a good investment or not.

Financial ratio analysis is helpful in assessing an organisation's internal strengths and weaknesses. Potential suppliers will, for example, want to judge credit worthiness.

Ratios by themselves provide little useful information; they only indicate where further study may improve company performance. Management can compare current performance with previous periods and with that of competing companies. Four key areas are generally used for analysis:

- profitability
- liquidity
- leverage (ratio of own capital to borrowed capital)
- management effectiveness.

Financial ratios provide an important yardstick to gauge the performance of the business and its ability to meet its short- and long-term commitment. Examples of some common ratios are as follows.

Liquidity ratios

Two ratios are commonly used – the **acid test ratio** (or insolvency ratio) and the **current ratio**

$$\text{acid test ratio} = \frac{\text{current assets} - \text{stock value}}{\text{current liability}}$$

Current assets include stock, cash in hand and cash due to the business from debtors. Current liabilities include items such as cash due to suppliers, overdraft, and short-term loans. A ratio significantly less than 1 would necessitate close scrutiny for it could be associated with insolvency.

$$\text{current ratio} = \frac{\text{current assets}}{\text{current liabilities}}$$

Depending on the type of business and the value of stock-holding, the aim should be to have a ratio here in the region of 2:1.

In order to be able to pay bills a business must have ready access to cash when they are due. This is known as **liquidity** and is provided by the working capital augmented by an overdraft if necessary. Liquidity planning may be achieved with the aid of a cash flow projection (see below). The overdraft requirement of a pharmacy business should be not more than around 5% of sales under normal circumstances although this may be higher at certain times of the year, e.g. when buying in Christmas stock. The bank would normally expect to see a fluctuation in cash flow with the account moving into credit from time to time – for example just after the NHS payment has been received. Overdrafts are not designed for long-term lending. Any long-term lending or 'hardcore' overdraft should be converted to a loan with fixed repayments. It is recommended that capital investments (e.g. new windows, shop fittings or equipment) should be funded by long-term loans and not paid for out of trading capital, unless the business is cash-rich. Such action will have a positive effect on the acid test ratio and improve solvency.

Profitability ratios

Gross profit (GP)

$$\text{GP }(\%) = \frac{\text{sales} - \text{cost of sales}}{\text{sales}} \times 100$$

The gross profit percentage of an average pharmacy would be approximately 25–30%, depending on the mix of dispensing to OTC business.

Return on capital employed (ROCE)

$$\text{ROCE }(\%) = \frac{\text{net profit after interest}}{\text{capital employed}} \times 100$$

This is an indicator of return on capital investment. It can vary widely, depending on the amount of money borrowed to finance the investment.

Profit on cost and return (POC, POR)

$$\text{Profit on cost (\%)} = \frac{\text{profit}}{\text{cost price}} \times 100$$

$$\text{Profit on return (\%)} = \frac{\text{profit}}{\text{selling price}} \times 100$$

These two ratios are used in price setting and often give cause for confusion. An item costing £1.00 and sold for £1.50 will have a POC of 50% and a POR of 33.3% before addition of VAT.

Gearing or leverage ratio

The **gearing ratio** (GR) is a measure of the degree to which an investor or business is utilising borrowed money and reflects long-term stability. Companies that are highly geared may be at risk of bankruptcy if they are unable to make payments on their debt; they may also be unable to find new lenders in the future.

$$\text{GR} = \frac{\text{long-term loans}}{\text{total capital}}$$

Gearing (or 'leverage') is not always bad, however it can increase the shareholders' return on their investment and often there are tax advantages associated with borrowing. It is unlikely that lenders would be willing to contribute more than 50% of the total capital.

Management effectiveness

The **stock turn ratio** is an example of a measure of management effectiveness.

$$\text{Stock turn} = \frac{\text{sales}}{\text{stock}}$$

It is important that stock value is monitored and not allowed to 'creep', for this uses up cash resources. Ideally the whole stock should turn over 10–12 times a year, but this will vary according to the items involved.

Frequent deliveries from wholesalers mean that a fine balance can be struck between holding essential stock and purchasing 'just-in-time'.

Other ratios in this sector include the **ratio of stock to cost of sales** (indicates the number of weeks' stock being held) and **sales to fixed assets,** showing how much sales revenue has been generated for every pound invested in fixed assets.

Investors' return

A range of ratios are available to measure investors' returns in public companies, including **earnings per share, dividend and earnings yield** and **price earnings ratio.**

Planning and control

One of the most important business tools is an internal planning and control device known as the **budget.** This should be kept updated regularly according to environmental developments. The budgeting process provides a mechanism through which management can design activities and attach costs and revenues to their implementation.

The budget looks like a profit and loss or income statement in format, although it differs from the latter in that the figures presented refer to a prediction for the future rather than a report on what has already occurred. In its simplest form it forecasts expected sales, costs of sales, overheads and the likely profit. However it is usual to break down each of the categories into subgroups; thus the entry for 'Sales' might be broken down into prescription income (and then further into NHS, private prescriptions, veterinary prescriptions, etc.), OTC medicines (pharmacy-only, general sales list, dressings, etc.) and toiletries (cosmetics, hair care, etc.). This would in turn affect decisions on buying stock and offers opportunities to reflect increases in the amount of sun preparations or antihistamines that have to be bought in during the summer months.

In many cases it is possible to produce a number of budgets relating to different sets of circumstances, for example at three different levels of sales activity. Higher sales often reflects higher overheads and purchases. This may be particularly appropriate for pharmacies operating in resorts or tourist locations with turnover significantly affected by the weather. This process is known as **flexible budgeting.**

Although comparison of activities against a budget and the identification of positive and negative variances are useful in establishing how a business is performing, the process can be time-consuming and can, if taken too seriously, restrict a manager's entrepreneurial skills. This may deny him or her the ability to exploit an unexpected opportunity. Further, one can become obsessed with continually checking against the budget every week; the fortunes of a business do vary regularly so the budget should normally be set annually unless there are compelling reasons to carry out the procedure more often.

The **cash flow statement** (Figure 10.3) is a form of budget constructed to show how cash moves in and out the business, usually on a

An Independent Pharmacy 2

ANYTOWN

CASH FLOW Jan–June

	Jan	Feb	March	April	May	June
	£	£	£	£	£	£
Income						
VAT Repayment			1200			1200
Counter sales	15000	13000	13000	14000	15000	15500
NHS Income	20000	17500	18000	19000	18500	18500
	35000	30500	32200	33000	33500	35200
Purchases	28000	22000	20000	19500	21000	21500
Cash generated	7000	8500	12200	13500	12500	13700
Expenditure						
Wages + NIC	4200	4200	4450	5000	5250	5500
Locum fees	350	350	500	350	350	600
Pensions	425	425	425	425	425	425
Telephone			290			290
Printing etc	50	0	350	50	25	0
Motor expenses	400	400	500	200	200	300
Accountancy fees			1250			1250
Hire of equipment	250	250	250	250	250	250
Rent & rates			1500			1500
Insurance	950					
Heat & light			200			200
Tax payment	5000					
Finance costs						
Bank interest			1000			1000
Bank charges			100			100
Hire purchase	250	250	250	250	250	250
	11875	5875	11065	6525	6750	11665
Cash flow	−4875	2625	1135	7005	5750	2165

Figure 10.3 Cashflow statement.

monthly basis, and reflects the ability of the business to pay its bills when they fall due. The full budget may identify that the business will be able to purchase a new computer system but it does not tell the manager exactly when the cash is available. There may be a number of unexpected overheads to deal with, or delays in collecting income, for example problems with the prescription pricing authority computer system might mean their cheque arrives late. Further, as a business expands it needs more cash to support the infrastructure and in many cases proprietors do not have sufficient liquid funds to support this expansion. In these circumstances it is particularly useful to keep a running cash flow analysis each month so that decisions can be taken at appropriate times without incurring extra overdraft charges.

In Figure 10.3 a quarterly repayment of VAT is shown in the income column. VAT is described in Chapter 4. Most pharmacies, particularly those with a high NHS to OTC ratio, will normally receive VAT refunds because of the zero-rated status of prescription drugs, except perhaps in December when standard-rated counter sales are high. Depending on the accounting system chosen, refunds may be received monthly or quarterly. Purchases may be higher in some months than others because the business may be restocking after stock-taking (the stock should be at its lowest when the stock is counted for the annual accounts required for tax purposes) or there may be extra stock bought in for Christmas. Expenditure varies because some payments are due quarterly or even annually, putting some strain on cash flow at these times if appropriate arrangements have not been made. Tax is paid in the UK at the end of January and July and again if the business does not have a separate tax account into which regular amounts are paid in anticipation of the tax bill, then the cash has to be taken out of the business on these due dates. It should be noted that the cash flow is only concerned with cash accounting and items such as depreciation are not included.

Use of Internet banking can assist in keeping daily track of the bank balance and also cheques being presented for clearing. It is a useful tool in order to ensure that a cheque that cannot be honoured by the bank is not sent to the supplier. Each company feeds constant information to credit check companies and any unpaid cheques become public knowledge very quickly and could lead to withdrawal of credit by other suppliers and an inability to open new accounts. Internet banking is also cheaper to use and more convenient than writing and posting cheques to pay bills.

Other planning and control tools are the profit and loss statement and balance sheet provided by accounting procedures, outlined below.

Tax planning

Information required by accountants should be provided promptly at the end of the accounting period and efforts made to ensure that undue delays in producing the tax returns do not occur. There are severe penalties for not paying tax on time. It may be necessary to pay an interim payment to the tax authorities that is far in excess of what is necessary if correct figures are not to hand.

In the UK, tax payments are made at the end of January and July and allowance should be made in the cash flow projection.

It is necessary to plan for personal as well as business taxation. Proper tax planning can save many thousands of pounds. Personal tax planning is also important.

Further reading

Dyson J R. *Accounting for Non-Accounting Students*. London: Pitman Publishing, 1989.

Fleming I, McKinstry X. *Accounting for Business Management*. London: Harper Collins Academic, 1991.

Harrison J, Dawber R. *An Introduction to Business Accounts*. London: Pitman Publishing, 1984.

Holmes G, Sugden A. *Interpreting Company Reports and Accounts*, 3rd edn. Cambridge: Woodhead-Faulkner, 1986.

Rice A. *Accounts demystified. How to understand financial accounting and analysis*, 4th edn. Harlow: Pearson Higher Education, 2002.

Van Horne J C. *Financial Management and Policy*. Englewood Cliffs, NJ: Prentice Hall, 1986.

11

Managing service delivery

Ian Harrison

Introduction

This chapter deals with establishing service levels and ensuring they are maintained. This may mean striking a balance between quality and cost to ensure a value for money outcome. A mindset change is involved in moving from the management of 'assets and resources' to the 'delivery of services'. The transition does not necessarily involve dramatic changes in what people do; it has more to do with constant re-valuation of why people do what they do.

Managing assets and resources at its simplest level is about applying resources to manage assets to the highest standard possible within the constraints of the resources available. Delivering services is more about focusing on the customer's needs.

The service organisation

Pharmacy is generally work done in the context of a service organisation. That may be in a retail context, in a general medical practice support context, in a hospital context, industry context or academic context.

A **service organisation** is when two or more people are engaged in a systematic effort to provide services to a customer, the object being to *serve* a customer.[1] This begs the question 'What is a customer?' We generally think of 'the public' (external customers). In fact we can have 'internal' customers who may see our role as an essential in enabling them to fulfil their own role. In this way anyone we react with in our professional and managerial capacity can also be a customer.

The service is 'delivered' by a service process – a set of interrelated tasks that are appropriately sequenced. If we asked someone who ran a dispensary about their aims, their response would include something about the accurate dispensing and supply of medicines. They would probably go further and include the counselling and advice given to patients. A number of tasks must be performed in a set sequence to 'fill' the script and give appropriate support to the person who presents the script.

Customer expectations

Customers make assumptions about the quality of service provided. Zemke,[2] quoting Berry's Texas A & M University study, identified five service quality factors important to customers:

- Reliability – the ability to provide what was promised, dependably and accurately.
- Assurance – the knowledge and courtesy shown to customers, and the ability to convey trust, competence and confidence.
- Tangibles – the physical facilities and equipment and the appearance of staff.
- Empathy – the degree of caring and individual attention shown by staff.
- Responsiveness – the willingness to help customers promptly.

'Good' service processes (service 'inputs') create satisfied customers (service 'outputs'). Improving services to be 'good' requires giving attention to financial issues so that the organisation has the minimal equipment and staff to fulfil the service tasks. At the same time four characteristics of services must be met by the processes of the organisation:

- Simultaneity. Patients and pharmacists must be brought together. The 'generation' of counselling advice and its transfer to the patient occur virtually simultaneously. Although it may be possible, via information technology, to establish some degree of remote contact with customers, services are often historically limited to discrete geographical territories to achieve economies of scale.
- Heterogeneity. It is difficult to establish standards for the OUTPUT of a service organisation and even harder to ensure that such standards are met each time a service is delivered. Because it is not appropriate or possible to monitor every aspect of a professional's role, assurance is given by the job holder having attained a certain knowledge level supplemented by a skill level in competencies such as interpersonal skills. Working procedures and standards backed by a legal framework complete the requirement for homogeneity.
- Intangibility. A large buyer of medicines, raw materials or medical devices is able to subject them to objective tests. This is not so for the buyer of services. Intangible services are difficult to describe to

potential buyers. An understanding of customer psychology is needed and marketing will generally place emphasis on the benefits that the service can bring. In practice referrals by satisfied customers are extremely important.

- Perishability. Whilst we are familiar with the concept of expiry dates, plus the demand and supply factors in stock turnover, an advisory service cannot be subjected to 'stock control' procedures. A clinical pharmacist cannot increase their workload from two wards to six wards in a given time constraint, without a radical reduction in the time and quality devoted to each patient. Advice is not generally manufactured to build up stock. It may be thought that an exception would be the compilation of information sources, such as the *British National Formulary*. However professional advice requires the real-time interpretation of that information in an individual patient context.

Added value

One of the most difficult concepts for those who have not studied marketing is that of 'added value'. In a test of cola drinkers, pre-test drinkers said they preferred Coke to Pepsi in a ratio of 3 to 1. When the taste tests were conducted 'blind' the preferences of the same group were slightly in favour of Pepsi.

Pharmacists know that patients and doctors can be 'sold' on appearance and brand image. Whilst such 'added value' occurs on an emotional level, the perceptions are 'real' for the particular patient or doctor. So value is added in some cases by building brand image. In other cases the level of service quality is a factor that can lead to a customer changing from one service provider to another.

For any service there is a core component and relating this to, say, total parenteral nutrition, the IV feed tailored for an individual patient may account for 30% of the impact, but 70% of the cost. The added value comes from the product 'surround' where the knowledge of the nutrition team and the preparation skills of the pharmacy staff may result in 70% of the impact of the service but account for only 30% of the true cost (see Figure 11.1).

Value is 'added' to medicines in the way we handle them, manipulate them and advise on them. Each pharmacy has a greater or lesser scope to add value to their core service. The perception of added value depends on the type of 'customer'. Considering a hospital pharmacy outpatient section:

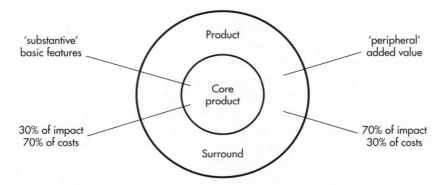

Figure 11.1 Added value is perceived around the product or service.

- The outpatients are external customers.
- Their perception of added value may include the shortness of the waiting time, the friendliness of the staff and the ambience of the waiting area.
- The internal professional perspective of doctors and pharmacy section heads. These would include:
  - The selection of the correct medicine and strength.
  - The checking of pharmacy concerns with prescribers.
  - The questioning of patients to ascertain familiarity with their treatment and to reinforce compliance.
  - The inclusion of compliance aids and patient information leaflets.
  - The handing of the medicine to the correct patient.
  - Managerial perspective.

The management's perspective of added value could be the provision of performance indicators proving (a) good systems of work are in place, (b) appropriate skills mix and training are used and (c) a low level of complaints is received.

Staff roles in service delivery

Whilst many people get excited about changing processes it is actually the staff who make the change and the staff who carry on making the new process work. Failure to clarify staff roles, involve staff and give them appreciation for a job well done, will soon result in the abandonment of the new service delivery process.

Role conflict

When staff are given additional duties to improve the perceived quality by the customer, they can mistakenly be given responsibility for cutting waiting times, etc. These objectives are mutually incompatible. Another type of role conflict occurs when the staff member views the new role as demeaning. This may then be reflected in cynical comments to the customer.

Role ambiguity

Poor leadership and supervision can put staff in the difficult position of not knowing the reasons behind what is expected of them. When anything occurs outside a 'scripted' response they are ill-equipped to respond extemporaneously.

Applying discretion

Figure 11.2 shows a graphic illustration of the employee discretion model.[3]

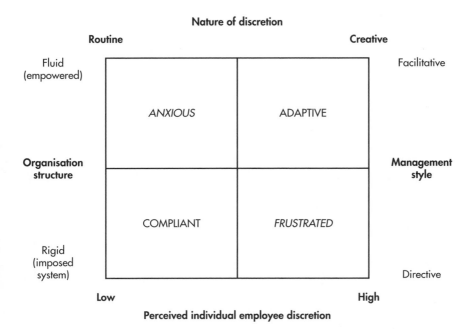

Figure 11.2 Employee discretion model.[3]

Organisations whose service offerings are characterised by the term **compliant** (lower left quadrant in Figure 11.2) include multiples/supermarkets with:

- an emphasis on consistent service delivery;
- good procedures and training on handling a variety of customer situations;
- high volumes appropriate for automation or low cost labour;
- directive management style due to high turnover and low motivation;
- short-term performance measures such as response times.

Local innovation is not encouraged because it may lead to customer expectations that it should be fulfilled at each location run by the multiple or supermarket. The challenge is to get employees to 'own' problems and creatively help in their resolution.

Process ownership is engendered by good top-down communication, participative involvement, teamwork and creating rituals that celebrate employee success in difficult transactions with customers.

Adaptive organisations typically have:

- high degrees of creative discretion in developing new processes;
- frequent dependence on key individuals' skill and knowledge;
- resistance to standard processes, leading to inconsistency;
- facilitative management styles which maximise individuals' performance;
- long-term performance measures.

It is important that individuals exercise a high degree of collaboration and that customers know more than one person in the organisation, to avoid losing that customer when a key employee leaves.

The **anxious** quadrant is 'being empowered but not feeling it'. If their role is not clarified, management may write the employee off as 'not being up to the new task'.

In the **frustrated** zone staff are vocal about perceived or real concerns. They feel the system inhibits them from operating in the most effective way. They may feel they are 'above' the system and what they do on an ad hoc basis is really in the customers' interest.

It might be thought that the route from **compliant** employee to an **adaptive** employee can be direct. In practice this is often not the case. Junior pharmacists and chief technicians who have assumed new hospital responsibilities may in fact not have assumed a new level of accountability with the corresponding degree of discretion. They understandably become **anxious**.

Junior technicians may feel constrained by a system imposed by legal requirements and professional standards. Professional managers in small organisations are often in the **adaptive** quadrant. However, the imposition of a clinical governance system exerts a new type of imposition that can lead to **frustration**.

Motivation is not just a function of discretion (self-determination). It arises when there is (a) also a feeling that the work has a purpose (easy to see the link in healthcare), (b) a feeling by employees that their work uses their competencies satisfactorily, and (c) employers recognise that everyone seeks rewards, but the type of rewards can be varied to match individuals' reasons for being at work. To take an extreme example, the person who goes to work to get respite from domestic problems may not take kindly to being given time off!

The emergence of e-service may give some customers a greater feeling of control. However many customers are frustrated by poor service levels in the start-up phase. Companies who have invested in the technology are sometimes puzzled by the slow uptake of their innovative style of service delivery.

Analysing services

There are a number of key components that can usefully assist in the analysis of service delivery:

- Customer requirements
- Resources, ranging from staffing levels to high-tech equipment
- Configuration of processes in relation to one another
- Process flows
- Strategic leadership
- Communication
- Standards and procedures
- Key performance measures
- Training and reflective learning
- The extent to which quality assurance and continuous improvement is applied.

These will all be helped by considering 'best practice' in comparable activities, not necessarily in pharmacy.

Resource mapping

Using medicines information in a hospital pharmacy as an example, the process flow may be as indicated in Figure 11.3. By listing the service

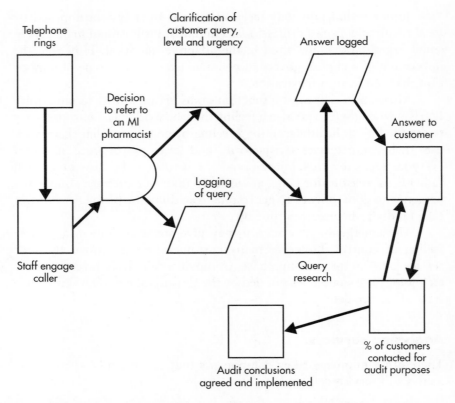

Figure 11.3 Resource map (medicines information in a hospital pharmacy). It is a flowchart convention to use squares for tasks, D for decision points and rhomboid shapes for data collection/collation.

flow elements horizontally and the cost drivers vertically we can create a resource audit matrix. Table 11.1 depicts a resource audit matrix of the medicines information process.

This simple analysis only encompassed two activities: dealing with a medicines information question and auditing responses. From the completed matrix we can identify the activities that consume the greatest resources. By creatively linking certain boxes we may be able to identify ways of enhancing the service. It appears that time and money can be saved by linking the completed query data directly to professional audit software if the two are designed to be compatible. Furthermore it should not be necessary to have hard copy data if findings can be typed directly onto a template on the computer.

Table 11.1 Resource audit matrix of a medicines information process

Resources/tasks	Call handling	Query research	Answer handling	Professional audit
Facilities		Office/unit (cap£)		
MI staff		Professional staff*	Secretarial support	Internal/external pharmacy auditors
Logs	Clear design			
Database		Access to 'experts' Evidence texts* IT equipment		
Configuration	Customer-facing	Internal	Customer-facing	Customer feedback Internal/external
Revenue cost	££££ (funding of staff relates to usage of service)	£	£	
Capital cost		£££ (cost of rooms and equipment)		£

Note: Critical resources are asterisked. Capital costs are typically buildings. Revenue costs are annual costs of manpower, overheads and IT equipment (the latter being divided over 3–5 years for depreciation purposes).

Configuration

In most service activities there are some staff and activities visible to the customer, with others generally out of sight. In a large hospital pharmacy there can be staff in a number of specialist sections and medicines management technicians at ward level who are generally not brought face-to-face with patients unless asked by nurses to counsel a patient on how to optimise therapy such as inhaler use.

In a community pharmacy, the relative position of OTC medicines, cosmetics, baby goods, counselling area, dispensary and storeroom must be carefully planned. Elsewhere in this book (see Chapter 13), attention is drawn to the science and psychology of enhancing purchasing decisions. Those goods positioned at eye level are far more likely to generate an opportunistic sale. Shops should ideally be designed to allow easy switching of merchandise location. Each location can be coded so that the EPOS system can give management reports showing from where the greatest volume is selected. Higher margin goods can then be relocated to those 'hot spots'.

CASE STUDY A

The 'one-stop shop' concept was pioneered for neurology outpatients at Leicester Royal Infirmary. A special unit was designed to allow patients to be seen by their consultant soon after arrival. Appropriate X-rays and tests were then carried out in the unit by multi-skilled technical staff. The consultant then saw the patient again with a diagnosis and treatment plan. Previously, the need to revisit for results placed great strain on the patients and so the new system is proved.

Enhancing process flow

At points on our process flow 'maps' we can identify the following:

- Where value is added or not added. This then gives a basis for minimising non-value-adding tasks.
- Where a number of people are handling a different aspect of the same task. These multiple 'hand-offs' (really handing-ons) can be overcome by multi-skilling fewer individuals in the process chain.
- Identification of bottlenecks, before which work builds up at busy periods. This gives the option of doing certain tasks in parallel or adding specialised staff or equipment at certain busy times.
- Check/measurement points. We need to ask 'What happens to the measures?', 'Are the checks/measurements relevant?', 'Who acts upon them?', 'Can we reduce their number?'
- Are there any tasks that can be streamlined?

Walk-through

A walk-through is a necessary step to make sure that what you think happens (or what you are told happens) really does.

- Familiarise self with relevant existing process documentation.
- Arrange with the section head that you can interview some staff.
- Interview a sample of staff to understand what really occurs.
- Compare how different people perform the same tasks to determine what the best operating standard should be.

A walk-through checklist (modified from Harrington[4]) should ascertain many of the following outcomes:

- Differences between the documented process and the present practice.
- Differences between the way employees are performing the same task.
- Identification of employees needing retraining.
- Suggested improvements to the process (generated by the people performing the process).
- Process measurement points and measurements.
- Activities that need to be documented.
- Process problems.
- Roadblocks to process improvement.
- 'Suppliers' that have input into the process.
- Internal process requirements.
- Time to perform a cycle of work (plus delay times between such work).
- New training programmes required to support the present process.
- How 'suppliers' should receive feedback data.

Service transaction analysis (STA)

Customer input is also needed at this stage. Five steps are needed:[3]

- The service process to be analysed is specified and agreed.
- Mystery shoppers (if a retail process) or external consultants score whether transactions were pleasing (+), satisfactory (0) or unsatisfactory (−).
- A written explanation is noted alongside the score.
- The scores are joined up to give a visible profile of a transaction.
- Managers can use the feedback to inform them what to prioritise.

Table 11.2 shows a community pharmacy STA that shows a poor outcome. Following such a procedure is of great benefit in identifying areas of deficit in service delivery.

Overhauling service delivery

We can now look at seven steps used to overhaul service delivery:

Table 11.2 A community pharmacy STA

SERVICE TRANSACTION ANALYSIS SHEET				
Organisation	*Community pharmacy*		*Concept:*	
Process	*Handing in prescription*		Prestige pharmacy premises	
Customer	Purchaser		appealing to higher socioeconomic groups	

Transaction	*Score*			*Message*
	+	*0*	–	
High street location	x			We are accessible and available
Good facilities	x			Expensive but competent
Ignored			x	You are not worth the trouble
Way greeted		x		We want to help you
Fill in back of script		x		You are just another punter
No pen			x	We don't really care
Medicine unavailable			x	What business are they in?
Call-back slip	x			They've locked me in, but it won't get mixed up with anybody else

Overall evaluation: Poor service design with exception of call-back slip. Pharmacy is not customer-oriented. Customer service is a sham.

- Define the service concept precisely, identifying 'core' components as well as 'peripheral' or value adding perceptions. 'What are we trying to accomplish?'
- Focus on each component and sub-process and referring to the Enhancing Service Processes and the STA above, decide whether tasks could be done in a different way to yield a better outcome. The cost of change is governed by value for money or quality enhancement considerations. 'What change can we make that will result in improvement?'
- Consult fully with all internal staff and those to whom the service is marketed.
- Diplomatically challenge the logic of customers' previous expectations and how these have been met. Customer focus groups are used by supermarket chains. It is usual to have conducted a preliminary brainstorming process with staff to develop potential alternative processes.
- Consider the benefits and cost of incorporating information technology to give greater control than for the process being replaced.

- Design and test a new service delivery process, then extend the implementation.
- Incorporate a quality assurance scheme with the setting of standards and how the service outcome can be directly or indirectly measured. 'How will we know that a change is an improvement?'

Capacity considerations

Service capacity has been defined by Slack *et al.*[5] as being: 'The maximum level of value-added activity, over a period of time, that the service can achieve under normal operating conditions'. We are all familiar with the difficulties for restaurants meeting food demands on a Saturday evening (or pubs at Sunday lunchtime). We therefore recognise the balance between demand and capacity.

When a patient goes into renal failure their creatinine levels rise. This is a direct consequence of the falling capacity of the kidneys to filter water, urea and salts from the blood.

It is tempting to conclude that kinetic formulae may be applied to service process flow. However, in practice there are too many variables and it may take longer to reach 'steady state' than the timeframe available.

Before end-stage renal failure is reached the clinician has a number of available options. Similarly, we may influence the demands on a pharmacy service when capacity levels vary.

A shift in the balance can result in:

- The loss of perceived (value-added) quality by not meeting customer standards.
- There is little time to question, listen, think and respond appropriately in our professional capacity. The customer may not feel valued and a retail manager will be aware of a reduced chance for a complementary sale.
- Failure to meet output targets (and consequently income).
- Waiting times suffer – those waiting for dispensed medicines in a community pharmacy, hospital out-patient department, or patients waiting for treatment doses on the wards.
- Loss of customers who may not return.
- A shop where there is a queue at the counter may lead some to go elsewhere. However, before pharmacies were common in supermarkets, Cartwright found that almost 80% of the elderly always used the same pharmacy.[6]
- Stressed staff.

- An initial effect is that staff become curt in their responses or, paradoxically, may make inappropriately long explanations. The long-term effect is staff absences and ultimately burnout or resignations.
- Staff transfers from other sections. This can then have a detrimental knock-on effect in the sections now expected to perform with a slimmed staff.

Capacity strategies

Johnston and Clark[3] identified four main capacity strategies, explained below.

The level capacity

Strategy: In this case scarce or expensive resources are maintained at a constant level, and the organisation must manage the consequential issues for service quality. This is the historical method adopted for appointments with GPs or hospital consultants. In recent years the NHS Modernisation Agency has championed a number of new approaches (see Case studies A and B). These may be summarised as queue management or booking systems.

The chase

Strategy: The service organisation attempts to match supply to demand as much as possible by building flexibility into the operation. The prime objective is to provide high levels of service availability or fast response, in the most efficient manner. This is now generally used by service organisations like banks and supermarket check-outs. Once queues reach a predetermined level, multi-skilled staff working behind the scenes are temporarily allocated to a till.

The demand management

Strategy: Rather than change the capacity of the service operation, the organisation influences the demand profile to 'smooth' the load on resources. A pub can have a 'happy hour' pricing strategy to encourage off-peak business. Some restaurants offer limited menus at lunchtime, effectively restricting their service range. The use of promotional offers at certain times of day or applying only on quiet days is another demand

CASE STUDY B

A Devon general practice found that demand was greatest on Mondays for patients presenting with a new problem. They scheduled those coming for follow-up visits to quieter days. This produced a much smoother demand between Monday and Friday.

CASE STUDY C

Many hospital pharmacies, when adequately staffed, place more staff on the wards, where the treatment decisions are made. By being part of the therapeutic team, they can have a significant impact on demand. They are increasingly communicating prescribing decisions to the pharmacy using hand-held computers over a hospital IT network. This means dispensing can be scheduled and results in patients having quicker access to intended medication.

management strategy. It is difficult to see how such demand strategies may be applied to pharmacies.

The 'coping'

Strategy: When demand surges and the result is overload many organisations 'cope' (or may not cope) with more demand than the system was designed to deal with routinely. This has to be the most common strategy for the small pharmacy. It is an environment that suits staff that can 'move up a gear' when demand is high. They must also be trained to identify fill-in jobs that should be undertaken at quiet times.

Because this service capacity strategy is common in pharmacies, and healthcare in general, we will identify some pointers that may help in the management of such situations.

- We can note that the pressure on most public services has been aggravated by management targets that can often be inspected by an outside body such as the Healthcare Commission or the National Audit Office. The staff drawn to working in healthcare have values that mean they want to contribute effectively to society. Their behavioural style may be predominantly that of a 'relator', effectively caring for others and not driven by financial rewards. However, such rewards become critical below a certain threshold.
- The result is a tension between (a) a management imperative to increase throughput, e.g. to meet waiting time targets in order that yet more patients can be treated in the system in future and (b) a professional and internal ideal to meet a set of quality standards for the benefit of the patients under current care.

  - The tension may partly be reduced by a mutual understanding of the two opposing pressures. This may then be used as a creative basis for finding solutions or partial solutions.
  - Alternative approaches are (a) to change the skill mix by devolving work presently undertaken by a pharmacist to a non-pharmacist, (b) for the pharmacist to delegate certain work to another, possibly more junior, pharmacist.

- It is often said that 'if it moves, it can be measured'. In practice there are too many measures that are no longer relevant and probably inadequate attention to measures that can, if properly communicated, make a difference.
- For a professional we need some way of measuring the actual load on the pharmacist plus some measure of the outcomes from their interventions.
- Some of your internal or external customers may value seeing you at a different time of the day or week than occurs presently. It should be possible to prioritise those who require you at the busiest times and reschedule part of your working day.
- Understand the nature and impact of the coping zone.

  - Patients/customers will wait longer.
  - Medicines are more likely to be out of stock.
  - Patients/customers may feel too rushed to remember what they want to ask.
  - Staff may be too pressured to be courteous, and may look for another post.
  - Errors and complaints may increase.

Managing bottlenecks

They can be recognised by the volume of work built up in front of them at a busy period. In severe cases these may include some work required on a previous day.

Goldratt's work[7] has identified a number of rules applicable to bottlenecks (modified from Johnston and Clark[3]):

- Ensure that only essential work passes through the bottleneck.
- Be ruthless in taking away non-essential activities from the bottleneck.
- Ensure that no substandard work passes through the bottleneck.
- Once you have established where the bottleneck is, devote proportionately more management attention to it to ensure maximum throughput and therefore maximum effectiveness for the process.
- Do not attempt to move a bottleneck in a complex system.
- Dealing effectively with a bottleneck in one location often reveals a 'new' bottleneck at a different point in the process.

 CASE STUDY D

In London, it can sometimes be difficult to recruit hospital pharmacy technicians because higher-paid jobs are available without formal training. One process that took up an inordinate amount of staff time was dispensing for outpatients and in-patients. Delays in dispensing were leading to queuing, missed doses and further pressures being exerted on an already over-worked staff. The hospital was the first in the UK to install the ROWA automated equipment, now colloquially known a 'robotic dispenser'. This has largely solved the dispensing bottleneck. The high cost can be justified by the savings on scarce technicians.

CASE STUDY E

Now that most lines are available as 'ready for issue' original packs, only requiring selection and labelling for the individual patient, space-efficient storage is vital. Assuming there is space to install a round stack with adjustable shelves, which can rotate independently of one another (Sintek Carousel), a number of staff can access the items concurrently. By separating the dispensary from the OTC counters and providing a bow-fronted NHS dispensing counter with computerised labelling dispensing stations, a carousel can be installed immediately behind. This enables seated or standing staff at the counter to deal with most patient's needs without leaving their workstation. There may be ten or more carousel shelves, sloping towards the front from the axis at an angle of about 25°. This ensures that stock is always ready at the front of the shelves.

A pharmacy dispensing around 2000 lines per week will typically have three forward workstations for use at the busiest times. These can access 800 or more lines from the carousel. The concept is less suited to a large repeat dispensing business.

Converting demand to output

A useful framework has been devised by Johnston and Clark[3] to show the inter-relation of demand and capacity issues in a service organisation. It is graphically represented in Figure 11.4.

- *Service output* is an indicator of capacity over a period of time, e.g. dispensed items per month, drug costs per prescriber.
- *Service resource* indicates the essential resources for the service process, e.g. pharmacist, labelling computer, floor space.
- *Service demand* is an analysis of the impact on capacity demand from say (a) a community pharmacy merchandise promotion, or (b) the appointment of a new hospital consultant with new prescribing habits, or (c) the implementation of new National service Framework (NSF) or National Institute for Clinical Excellence (NICE) prescribing advice. It can thus deal with demand fluctuations in addition to work volume.
- *Service capacity management* will look at the effects of various techniques to increase or 'flex' the capacity, e.g. bringing in extra staff to cover known busy periods. It also involves forecasting,

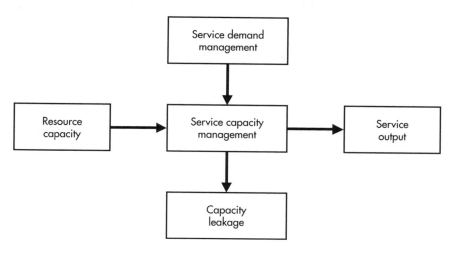

Figure 11.4 Service capacity management framework.[3]

prioritisation, and scheduling. *Capacity leakage* is a concept that recognises that sometimes capacity can in reality be less than anticipated, e.g. staff correcting errors, waiting for stock replenishment, waiting for a supervisory check, staff delay in returning from breaks, staff sickness/absenteeism, slower working as a backlash against a controlling management style.

  CASE STUDY F

A Director of Pharmacy Services in a large general hospital prepared a business case for a new staff member without factoring in the effect of training and annual leave absences. The consequence was that staff had to 'cope' when the new pharmacist was absent. Staff grew resentful that their own work suffered at these times. The relevant clinical directorate sent complaints to the Director of Pharmacy Services.

A case for new staff should request funding for (a) the 'on cost' of a company pension, national insurance (state pension), employer contribution to PAYE (income tax) and (b) the 'man year' that will give full cover due to legitimate absences. Rather than 1.0 whole time equivalent (WTE) person the case should be made for 1.15 WTE.

Quality counts

Generally it is the lower-paid members of the organisation who will be physically interfacing with the customers. This may be in-service trained counter assistants in a retail environment or dispensary receptionists in some hospital pharmacies. They should not be neglected in any consideration of how customers perceive the organisation.

A problem with many service delivery departments is that they are often not managed as systems and processes. They are typified by a series of fragmented and uncoordinated activities. Each activity may be separately supervised, with little attempt at integration. Some large hospitals have restructured their pharmacy staff into work teams serving specific groups of clinical directorates (consultant-led teams with an overall budget). This aids communication and responsiveness.

Departments where service delivery systems are haphazard and poorly managed will be characterised by high levels of service failure. For example, failure to respond with a medicines information query answer before a decision is made on a clinical intervention.

In any department comprising professionals, the consistency of output can mainly be assured by the selection of appropriately qualified staff and by paying attention to their continuing education. Let us take as an example a service delivery process that involves ten tasks in series. If an error occurs in each task 1% of the time, more than 10% of the final output will be adversely affected. An error, which in isolation seems insignificant, can be quickly compounded.

In addition to assessing the probability/likelihood of service component failure, the criticality/seriousness of such a failure as a prioritisation tool should be addressed. Figure 11.5 is a quality matrix for a hypothetical out-patient dispensary:

- Even error 'criticality' depends on individual perceptions (see Chapter 8).
- It will usually be more critical for an individual patient to be out of stock of a new medicine (item 1 in Figure 11.5).
- Patients and staff may view the long and cramped waits as the norm.
- Interpersonal skills must be tailored to individual behavioural styles and conducted in an adult non-patronising manner.

Quality standards are being examined by the National Patient Safety Agency. At the moment there are inadequate data. This is changing and in a few years it may be possible to apply Six Sigma controls, aspiring to accuracy of six standard deviations.

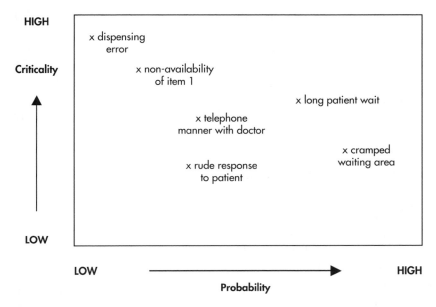

Figure 11.5 Quality matrix for a hospital outpatients department (hypothetical example).

Wright[1] extrapolates UK data to give three dramatic health-related examples of 99.9% conformance to quality:

- One hour of unsafe drinking water per month.
- 300 incorrect surgical operations per week.
- 15 000 babies dropped by the doctor at birth each year.

Quality improvement techniques such as the Ishikawa cause and effect 'fishbone'[8] and benchmarking are outside the scope of this chapter but have been used in the NHS.

Recovering from poor service

Anderson and Zemke[2] give five axioms for dealing with disappointed or even angry customers:

- Recognise that customers have specific recovery expectations. These vary but may include receiving an explanation and having access to someone in authority.
- Successful recovery addresses psychological as well as physical issues. It is therefore important to focus on the person, using listening skills, before addressing the problem.

- Involve the customer in finding the solution turns 'my problem' into 'our problem'.
- Remember that customers react more strongly to 'fairness' failures than 'honest mistakes'. 'I'm sorry this has occurred and I'll make sure it is cleared up right away' is as close to a magic bullet as there is in service recovery.[2]
- Effective recovery is a planned process. Customers remember the skills of the person delivering the solution more than the actual solution.

The top skills to promote effective recovery are:

- conflict management
- apologising
- displaying humility and poise, rather than defensiveness
- follow-up, not just a promise to follow up
- problem-solving.

The NHS clinical governance agenda has led to more openness and recognises that prompt, specific and sincere responses generally avoid lawsuits, rather than precipitating them.

Quality management model

The most rounded model for quality management in a service delivery context is that of the European Foundation for Quality Management's (EFQM) Excellence Model.[9,10] The nine sections neatly tie together many of the service delivery topics we have covered:

- Strategic leadership
- Management of staff and other resources
- Adoption of standards
- Development of efficient processes
- Application of professional competency
- Minimisation of errors and wastage
- Attainment of patient satisfaction
- Yield of value-for-money patient outcomes.

A modified version of the EFQM is shown in Figure 11.6. Note that the first three groupings are drivers labelled *enablers*, with the right hand drivers being *outcomes*. A feedback loop is shown at the top to indicate that we learn from not getting things quite right and we innovate to achieve continuous improvement.

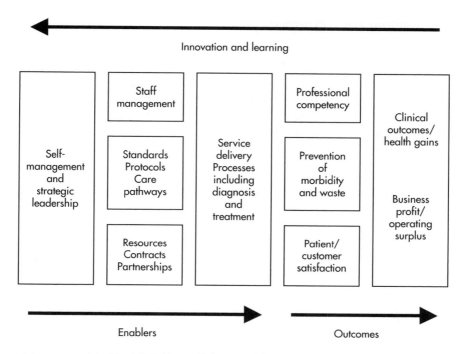

Figure 11.6 Modified EFQM excellence model.

Waste

One topic that we have not encountered so far is 'waste'. We know that many prescribed medicines are never used. Waste is also a useful concept in the context of service delivery. There are seven types of waste to consider when designing-in value:

- Excess service – delivering a service level far greater than customers need.
- Delay, for example staff not using quiet times to the benefit of the organisation.
- Double-handling – the use of IT and the Internet (see Chapter 15).
- Inappropriate processes – insufficient pre-packs, excess checking.
- Unnecessary stock – excessive buffer stock.
- Unnecessary motion – reaching, bending, walking, etc.
- Defects – the cost of corrective action.

Controlling performance

Peters cautions against an over-emphasis on the collection of data ostensibly to inform management decisions.[11] He recommends that section heads or managers of small organisations consider only 4–6 key measures with which they will be continuously up-to-date.

Based on the work of Kaplan and Norton[12] many companies' service operations managers now devise measures under four headings (adapted from Wright[1]):

- External or Customer
  Market share and new customers
  Customer satisfaction (and increasingly, loyalty)
  Customer retention rates
  Number and type of complaints
- Operational
  Equipment, staff and space availability
  Throughput and waiting times
  Number of customers by type
  On-time and accurate deliveries
  Error rates
- Financial
  Total costs and breakdowns by labour and processes
  Total revenue and operating surplus/profit
  Cost and revenue per customer
  Profit/operating surplus per customer
  Sales per square metre
- Developmental
  Number of suggestions
  Number of improvements/innovations
  Employees involved in training
  Employees involved in improvement group/teams
  Staff satisfaction and turnover

The more key staff understand how these four types of measure interlink with the organisation's strategy, the more competitive advantage they will generate.

The main factors to bear in mind when choosing measures of productivity/output are:

- Simplicity of measurement and presentation.
- Identification of a series of inter-related measurements, weightings being added to reflect ranking/priority.
- Highlighting of trends over time, as well as discrete values.

- Measures that reflect the effect of a local task on a subsequent stage. This is valuable in dealing with a bottleneck.

Points to remember

- Obtaining the views of customers is important before attempting to improve service delivery.
- Do not assume that what you consider adds value will be perceived in the same way by customers.
- Processes can be greatly enhanced by hard work on the part of the manager and staff.
- Service improvements without staff involvement is a short-sighted strategy. However involvement of selected staff will bring pressure to those staff as they learn new approaches to making work more effective and efficient. Those staff that have to cope with the added workload implicit in any change must feel their needs are being met.
- Proven techniques to improve service delivery include resource mapping, redesigning process flows, walk-through and service transaction analysis.
- Quality is driven by management not the customer. It is important to have processes for measuring errors and interpreting their root causes. In this chapter we have covered a number of useful models, which integrate key aspects within service delivery plus relationships with the wider business.

A case study depicting a service delivery scenario is presented in Case Study G, together with two questions to consider.

 CASE STUDY G

In a recent annual report, the Chief Executive of Superstore plc stated that customer satisfaction and loyalty were the real drivers of the company's profit and growth. These were influenced by how the staff felt about their work, rewards and management. The same theme was reflected in company training programmes.

To test these assertions a senior human resources employee collected and correlated the following performance data. Statistically significant correlations are in bold type.

continued

CASE STUDY (continued)

	Sales per sq. ft.	Employee turnover	Employee absence	Quality of working life	Service delivery value	Share of grocery budget	Average trolley value	Customer referral	Customer satisfaction	Employee referral	Employee satisfaction	Satisfaction with supervision
Profit margin	+H	+L	–L	–H	+H	+H	+H	+H	+M	–L	–H	–M
Sales per square ft		–L	–L	–H	+H	+H	+H	+H	+M	+L	–M	–L
Employee turnover			–L	–L	–L	+L	–L	–L	–L	+L	+L	+M
Employee absence				+L	–M	–M	–H	–M	+L	–M	+L	–L
Quality of working life*					–H	–H	–H	–H	–H	+L	+M	+M
Service delivery value						+H	+H	+H	+H	–L	–H	–L
Share of grocery budget							+H	+H	+M	–L	–M	–L
Average trolley value								+H	+M	–L	–M	–L
Customer referral									+H	–L	–M	–L
Customer satisfaction										–M	–H	–L
Employee referral (a good place to work)											+M	+M
Employee satisfaction												+H

[*The quality of working life performance indicator was based on the assumption that as planned working hours increase, the workplace became more stressful and quality of working life diminished.]

→

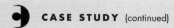 **CASE STUDY** (continued)

Questions
(a) What conclusions can you draw from the data?
(b) Are there any implications for the supermarket chain?

[adapted from a case study by a manager now working for Boots the Chemist[3]]

Conclusions drawn from the data
Caution is always needed when trying to interpret correlations.
We are not informed whether the store is a large one on an out-of-town site or has a smaller urban location.

- The least profitable stores have the happiest employees and the most dissatisfied customers!
- Quality of working life has a strong negative correlation with:

  - perceived value of service delivered/customer satisfaction/customer referral
  - share of grocery budget spent at that store/average trolley value

- Employee satisfaction has a moderate positive correlation with:

  - employee satisfaction/satisfaction with supervision

Where planned hours were greater than actual a level capacity policy had been used. When busy this gave a perception of poor service value, leading to customer dissatisfaction. When quiet however the staff appreciated breaks and liked having regular hours that were not re-scheduled for anticipated busy periods.

The managers at the store had a hunch that staff satisfaction did not drive customer loyalty – contrary to the line fed from head office. Such observations as these have supported the trend towards greater self-service, self-scanning and internet shopping.

References

1. Wright J N. *The Management of Service Operations*. London: Cassell, 1999.
2. Performance Research Associates. *Delivering 'Knock Your Socks Off' Service*, 3rd edn. New York: Amacom, 1998.
3. Johnston R, Clark G. *Service Operations Management*. London: Pearson Education, 2001.
4. Harrington H J. *Business Process Improvement*. New York: McGraw-Hill, 1991.

5. Slack N, Chambers S, Harland C, *et al. Operations Management*, 2nd edn. London: Pitman, 1998.
6. Cartwight A, Smith C. *Elderly People, their Medicines, and their Doctors*. London: Routledge, 1988.
7. Goldratt E M, Cox J. *The Goal*. New York: North River Press, 1984.
8. Ishikawa K. *What is Total quality Control? The Japanese Way* (translated by Lu D J). Englewood Cliffs, NJ: Prentice Hall, 1985.
9. European Foundation for Quality Management (EFQM) (1999). http://www. efqm.org (accessed 14 July 2004).
10. Lugon M, Secker-Walker J. *Clinical Governance: Making it Happen*. London: Royal Society of Medicine Press, 1999.
11. Peters T. *Thriving on Chaos*. London: Pan Books, 1989.
12. Kaplan R S, Norton D P. *The Balanced Scorecard*. Boston: Harvard Business School Press, 1996.

Further reading

Standard textbooks on service operations

Johnston R, Clark G. *Service Operations Management*. London: Pearson Education, 2001 (especially Chapters 6 and 7 on processes and capacity).
Wright J N. *The Management of Service Operations*. London: Cassell, 1999.

Customer care

Performance Research Associates. *Delivering 'Knock Your Socks Off' Service*, 3rd edn. New York: Amacom, 1998. (Developed by Kristin Anderson from an earlier book of the same title by Ron Zemke.)
Quinn F. *Crowning the Customer*. Dublin: The O'Brien Press, 1990. (A jargon-free writing style by an author from the retail sector.)

Analysing systems and constraints

Senge P, Kleiner A, Roberts C, *et al. The Fifth Discipline Fieldbook*. New York: Doubleday, 1994. (Especially the section on Systems Thinking – Chapters 13 to 24.)
Goldratt E M, Cox J. *The Goal*. New York: North River Press, 1984. (A management novel in which a new manager is given 3 months to save the company.)

Performance improvement

Fitzgerald L, Johnston R, Brignall T J, *et al. Performance Measurement in Service Businesses*, London: The Chartered Institute of Management Accountants, 1994. (Especially Chapter 3: Measuring Service Quality; and Chapter 5: Measurement of Resource Utilisation.)
Rumler G A, Brache A P. *Improving Performance*. San Francisco: Jossey-Bass, 1990. (Process mapping using flow charts giving particular attention to measurement points.)

12

Managing profit

Kirit Patel

Introduction

This chapter builds on the basic introduction to running a pharmacy business presented in Chapter 4 and outlines the opportunities for maximising profit.

The management of profit involves a preliminary analytical process. This allows an informed decision to be made on the way forward for the business. No business has unlimited resources. Making best use of resources is all about careful targeting to ensure one's efforts bring the most advantageous outcome. There are three main stages to be considered:

- The analytical stage
- The planning stage
- The managing stage

The analytical stage – answering the question 'Where are we now?'

There are micro- and macroeconomic factors that affect the business environment (see Chapter 2), some of which may occur without prior notice. Carrying out some 'what if' modelling may be useful to identify the ability of the business to function effectively under different environmental positions. To move forward one must know the base level from which progress will be made. There are two popular tools for answering the question 'Where are we now?', the SWOT and the PEST analysis:

- The **SWOT** analyses the business's *strengths, weaknesses, opportunities* and *threats* in a given period.
- The **PEST** analysis looks at the *political, economic, social* and *technological* factors.

These analyses should be applied at both macro and micro level. The information derived will assist in drawing up a business plan and making appropriate decisions.

SWOT analysis

The following example of a typical SWOT analysis relates to community pharmacy as a whole. A similar exercise at the business level would reveal factors relevant to an individual pharmacy business. It is not exhaustive.

Strengths

- Pharmacy is a well-liked and respected profession by the general public.
- Community pharmacists tend to adapt easily to the needs of the local community.
- Historically pharmacy numbers have remained static, implying that there is a long-term future in the industry.
- With ever-increasing pressure on the NHS and secondary care, there will always be a demand for primary care.
- Accessibility; a network of healthcare delivery outlets throughout the country.

Weaknesses

- Pharmacists often tend to compete with each other and undervalue their services. An example of this is delivery and supply of monitored dosage boxes at no extra cost.
- There is heavy reliance on one paymaster, i.e. the government. The reliance on NHS dispensing has increased for most independents, which tend to polarise near doctor's surgeries.
- Pharmacies tend to operate for longer hours because of competition.
- The professional nature of the pharmacist tends to make them compromise on business skills at times.
- The large companies opting for online warehouse pharmacy model can have a detrimental effect on pharmacy, especially after the introduction of Electronic Transfer of Prescriptions (ETP.)
- The government pressure on the NHS and secondary care leads to shrinking margins. Once identified, these weaknesses can be worked on to turn them to opportunities.

Opportunities

- The ever-increasing competitive pressure to offer new services, coupled with long waiting at surgeries, offers an opportunity for pharmacy to enhance pharmacist prescribing in the future.
- Pharmacists should proactively consider relocating into surgeries, especially when a surgery relocates, or expands due to consolidation.
- The provision of fees from the government's global sum for local pharmacy services is an opportunity for those willing to undertake extended roles.
- A recent minor ailments study has identified the role the pharmacist can play in reducing the pressure on doctors.
- A continuation in the trend to reclassify more Prescription-Only Medicines (POMs) to Pharmacy-Only (P) should be seized as an opportunity when advising patients about healthcare.

Threats

- A recession and downturn economic cycles can be a threat.
- Changes in employment and health and safety regulations could increase bureaucratic burdens on the business.
- The current flow of products from P to General Sales List (GSL) will increase competition, as there are many thousands of outlets currently selling GSL medicines. The government's drive to make medicine freely available has led to deregulation of many products.
- The relocation of single- and two-doctor surgeries in larger premises may affect the viability of the pharmacy.
- Increased competition from the supermarkets following the abolition of RPM and the reclassification of some medicines from P to GSL.
- Relaxation in the control of NHS Contracts bringing new entrants to the market following recommendations in the OFT report.

There follows two examples of events affecting community pharmacy.

Government policy – the NHS Plan

The NHS Plan was announced in July 2000 and is a plan for investment in the NHS in England, with sustained increases in funding and far-reaching reform. It is available at www.nhs.uk/nhsplan.

The purpose and vision of the NHS Plan was to give a health service fit for the 21st century: a health service designed around the patient. The NHS has delivered major improvements in health but still currently falls short of the standards patients expect and staff want to provide. The gap in expectations offers pharmacy an opportunity. Similar opportunities exist in the other UK jurisdictions.

The Case study below provides an analysis of the NHS Plan in terms of opportunities and threats.

CASE STUDY 1

The NHS Plan – Opportunity or threat?
On the whole, the 'NHS Plan – Pharmacy' will result in more opportunities but will inevitably bring some threats with it. The Plan specifically mentions that those providing better pharmaceutical services should be rewarded at the expense of others. Pharmacists willing to undergo change and adapt to the new working conditions will therefore be able to benefit from the various objectives of the NHS Plan.

Medicines management will enhance the pharmacist role, from dispensing to helping the patient take ownership of their own health. The pharmacist can strengthen relationships with the patient through prescription intervention and 'brown bag' reviews. There is also scope for help and advice on compliance and concordance. In any business, it is only by understanding the customer and fulfilling their needs that can bring business. In pharmacy, these customers are the patients. The local pharmaceutical services will enable pharmacists to tender for additional revenue at local level.

Repeat instalment dispensing will minimise the number of visits the patient has to make to the doctor. Pharmacists should be able to manage repeat prescriptions on behalf of the patient. Workforce development has since been taken a step further. There will inevitably be changes in the Medicines Act to enable dispensing and supply of medicines by support staff without pharmacist supervision. This should be viewed only as an opportunity, freeing time for other roles. It should be seen as scaling up of support staff rather than descaling of pharmacists.

NHS Direct, a nurse-led telephone help line has since developed by directing patients to the pharmacy. The electronic transfer of prescriptions, high on the government's agenda, will help strengthen the e-connectivity with the doctor and the patient. Use of modern technology will help improve communication and avoid duplicating data entries on PMR, by accepting data electronically. This helps reduce errors and speeds up the dispensing process. The deregulation of certain medicines from POM to P will enabled them to counter-prescribe better. At the same time, the deregulation from P to GSL will increase competition from non-pharmacy outlets and possible loss of sales. The

→

CASE STUDY 1 (continued)

minor ailment study has shown that pharmacists can reduce workload by counselling and prescribing medicines for minor ailments.

E-commerce can be an opportunity as well as a threat. E-prescription breaks the boundary and will increase the threat from mail order pharmacy. E-commerce in pharmacy has not made in-roads. Inevitably, as younger generations come through, there will be further potential for development. The NHS Plan does mention the need to revisit the control of entry in rural areas. Since then the OFT has also started an enquiry. Perhaps the greatest threat comes from the 750 Primary Care Centres, many of whom will possibly have in-house pharmacies.

The second Case study is a rather different proposition; it relates to the operation of a veterinary pharmacy during the foot and mouth epidemic that occurred in the UK in 2001. The substantial threat to the business caused by events totally outwith the proprietors' control was mollified to some extent by seizing on an opportunity to change the focus of supply.

CASE STUDY 2

Resilience through adversity
It could never happen to us. North Cumbria is a quiet place where the daily routine never changes. An area totally dependent upon livestock farming, but with many deep and rich characters that make one really understand where the true value of community pharmacy lies; the people.

Longtown Auction Mart is the largest sheep auction in England, trading up to 20000 sheep in a single day. Sometime between 15 and 22 February 2001, some infected sheep passed through the auction, mixing with sheep and farmers throughout the area and triggering a disaster. We can still only guess at the extent of the implications for the whole economy of North Cumbria; an area with sparse population and little opportunity to diversify into tourism.

We wake each morning to hear the names of farms confirmed with foot and mouth disease, whose owners are friends as well as customers. As the numbers of our customers confirmed grows to exceed £200000 worth of turnover, and

continued

the continuation of the cull threatens to exceed half of our turnover, one turns to some fundamental SWOT analysis and 'out of box' thinking.

During this crisis, my pharmaceutical skills continue to be called on to solve the most varied practical problems. How do you change the pH of 500 000 gallons of slurry outside of the range 6 to 9, so that it can be safely disposed on the land of an infected farm? More to the point, how do you relay that information to a man who has not only lost his livelihood (and remember the compensation only reimburses him for the value of his livestock), but also participated in the destruction of cows that he's nurtured for years? How do you degrease livestock handling equipment ready for sterilisation? All this whilst consideration of other fundamental questions. How do you coordinate other businesses in the town to effectively lobby MPs and Ministers to attract funding for the local economy? Which of the many important points do you emphasise in a time-limited meeting with Rt Hon Michael Meacher MP who is heading up the Rural Task Force? But most fundamentally, what is to happen to our staff when there are no livestock left in North Cumbria for them to treat?

Well, virtually all the businesses in the town have very little option to realign. The feed company can only sell bulk feed to farmers, how does the auction trade if there are no sheep or cattle? Even the doctor can only treat human patients. But the pharmacist has a broad scientific training and is qualified in many areas. Most specifically he has greater knowledge than any other on the High Street in pharmacology and therapeutics, be that for human or animal medicines. In fact most animal medicines are identical in formulation and use to human medicines. And he/she has communication skills and high numbers of pet owners passing through his/her premises.

If this crisis has taught me anything, it is to have as many strings to my bow as possible, otherwise there'll be a bleak future. A fact that my father-in-law realised too late when he was forced to close his butcher's shop when Asda opened up round the corner.

If a community pharmacy is to provide a comprehensive pharmaceutical service, it should be an ethical obligation to provide that service to animals as well as humans. Every community pharmacy in the land can, and should, provide a range of pet medicines, whether that pharmacy be rural or urban. Pharmacists already have the breadth of knowledge to advise and sell these products. With RPM under imminent threat of being abolished and no certainty to restriction of contract protection, the more strings the better.

It could never happen to you? That's what I thought!

Phil Jobson (Veterinary Pharmacist, Longtown, Cumbria)
This article first appeared in The Veterinary Pharmacists' Group
Newsletter Issue 8 (Summer 2001)

PEST analysis

The second commonly used tool to analyse the environment in which a business is operating is known as a PEST analysis. Considering that a community pharmacy is reliant on government policies, the political and social factors, coupled with technological advances, have a greater effect. Therefore a PEST analysis is perhaps an equally relevant tool. This considers social, technological, economic and political factors that affect pharmacy.

Political factors

- As a result of government policy to bring pharmacy into the NHS team as a full member, involvement in healthcare delivery will expand markedly. It is all about increasing the availability of healthcare and creating equal opportunity for the entire population. This has led to a number of extended roles, including pharmacist prescribing and medicines management (pharmaceutical care in Scotland).
- Following the Shipman incident the government has clearly stated its intention to promote clinical governance in the community pharmacy.
- The mandatory generic price cuts and the Pharmaceutical Price Regulation Scheme has reduced drug costs and hence revenues for pharmacies.
- The government regulations on employment and health & safety, planning, taxes, VAT and even the EU regulation are factors that affect daily business. Political decision in some European countries following deregulation of community pharmacy, in Italy and Holland has diverted the major players currently acquiring pharmacies away from the home English market. This reduced demand has been the cause of a drop in goodwill values.

Economic factors

- Factors such as interest rate, exchange rate, GDP, money supply, and economic cycles affect both the stock market and the disposable income of the general public. Property rents and valuations are also affected.
- Costs of utilities are influenced by the general state of the economy.
- Higher inflation means a higher wage bill.
- A good economy creates full employment and this makes it difficult to recruit good staff in certain areas.

Social factors

- The baby boom of the 1940s has led to an ageing population of over 65s.
- Computer literacy has created opportunities for e-commerce.
- Health awareness is now probably at its highest among the general public.
- Social factors affect the behaviour of consumers as well as employees in a pharmacy and this has an effect on efficient running of the pharmacy.
- The demographic profile of the area in which the shop is located determines the shopper's behaviour and has an influence on the inventory.

Technological factors

- Recent technological advances have brought about the use of the Internet and Intranet, improving communications. Connection to the NHSnet is spreading in Scotland.
- Pilot studies on Electronic Transfer of Prescriptions (ETP) are nearing an end and, once implemented, will help connect the pharmacy's PMR systems to those in doctors' surgeries and improve the manner in which prescriptions are handled.
- The Intranet of professional bodies, such as NPAnet, PSNCnet, etc., has improved information flow.
- In the USA, voice recognition technology has made management of repeat prescriptions much easier for pharmacies to handle.
- The advances in EPOS tills have made stock management easier. Swipe terminals and bank lines have helped reduce costs.

The planning stage – answering the question 'What are we going to do?'

Setting objectives

Having evaluated the current position of the business within the chosen environment, realistic objectives need to be set, together with a strategic plan to achieve them.

Larger companies tend to have a mission statement, which clearly states the direction the company must take. In order to stay focused, the mission statement should have objectives that need to be visited regularly, to ensure the company does not deviate in achieving its goals. Examples of possible objectives are:

- increasing the number of prescriptions dispensed
- achieving sales targets
- increasing gross margin within a clearly defined period.

In order to achieve these objectives, a well-defined strategy is necessary, for example:

- The strategy for increasing the prescription numbers could be the introduction of a collection and delivery service.
- The strategy for increasing counter sales might be better merchandising (see Chapter 13).
- The strategy for increasing gross margin would be to sell the product at optimum price and negotiate the best deals from suppliers as well as minimising pilferage and wastage.

In the case of an existing business, the competition, the size of the premises and the demographic profile of the local area need to be taken into account. It is not a good idea to have an unrealistic vision or objectives, as failure at a fairly early stage can be demotivating.

Drawing up a strategic plan

To draw up a strategic plan every action needed to achieve objectives within the predefined period should be detailed. At this stage it is important to ascertain that the financial and human resources required to implement the plan are in place. Financial management and human resources are considered in Chapters 10 and 16 respectively.

After a realistic strategic plan has been developed, the implementation stage can begin. Re-evaluation should occur at regular intervals using an audit circle approach that identifies performance and makes any required changes to the plan.

The managing stage – answering the question 'How do we do it?'

Profit may be optimised in three ways:

- Increasing revenue by enhancing sales in both dispensary and OTC.
- Improving gross margin.
- Reducing costs.

Increasing revenue

Dispensing (see also Chapter 13)

Remuneration from dispensing makes up the core of the business of almost all community pharmacies with NHS Contracts. The four UK National Health Strategies have all clearly indicated the direction pharmacy needs to take. The pharmacy of the future should be service-focused. Dispensing a prescription should be seen as the delivery of healthcare with the medicine being the by-product.

Examples of ways in which an increase in prescription numbers may be secured include the following actions. Remuneration may be available under the Dispensing Contract for those items marked with a*.

- Having adequate stock. Keeping common drugs appropriate to the season or current local disease patterns.
- Ensuring that patients' special requirements are ordered in time for prescription repeats.
- Offering sympathetic counselling services in a private area; having suitably trained female staff available if requested.
- *Offering medicines management and medicines review. In order to capture any error or identify drug interactions that could take place or improve concordance and compliance, the patient may be asked to bring in all medicines for a thorough review. This is sometimes called 'a brown-bag review'. Apart from improving patient care, the brown bag would help strengthen the bond between the patient and the pharmacy further. This is likely to reduce the likelihood of the patient having prescriptions dispensed elsewhere.
- Collection of prescriptions from surgeries and delivery of prescriptions.
- Prescription reminder service. Elderly or forgetful patients can be reminded following a PMR printout at the end of each week to highlight repeat prescriptions that should be presented. This also helps with stock control.
- *Follow-up enquiries for recently discharged hospital patients to ensure medication is readily available and/or being used appropriately.
- Diagnostic testing, as part of medicines management, to monitor drug requirements.
- *Supply of concordance aids.
- *Offering domiciliary visits.

Enhanced services

Pharmacists and suitably trained support staff in future will be obliged to take on additional roles. Pharmacists should also invest time in training support staff to free up their own time, which can be valuably spent discussing other aspects with patients. This can be achieved through appropriate training and the implementation of WWHAM protocols so that the patient is made to feel that the pharmacy should be the first point of call for all their health needs.

The developing role for pharmacy technicians and dispensing assistants will assist greatly in this area of practice.

Enhanced services should be advertised through local newspapers, leaflets in the pharmacy or posters in the local surgery's waiting area.

Healthcare and lifestyle advice

A public health role for pharmacists is emerging, particularly with respect to smoking cessation, head lice and cardiovascular disease. Involvement in such schemes will bring increased custom.

Assisting surgeries

The importance of building the bridge to the surgery from which prescriptions are generated is paramount. This can be further strengthened by assisting the doctors with their formularies, prescribing data analysis and generally helping to improve patient care in the doctor's practice. Prescribing advice and supply of drug information may also be appropriate.

Interaction with the patient

With the introduction of ETP by 2005, the patient will be able to nominate a pharmacy that will receive and handle their prescriptions through an electronic link with the surgeries. In order to proactively build that connectivity with the patient it is important that everything possible should be done to ensure that the patient chooses your pharmacy. This concept can be put into place right now using email, or paper questionnaires (see Figure 12.1) and the setting up of discussion groups. This is a cost and time-effective manner of communicating instead of writing letters. It is also necessary to use patient records for Customer Relationship Management and use the route of network marketing. Effective time management, as discussed later, would certainly help develop these services and aid in establishing a link proactively.

Healthcare Information Mailing List Form

Name

....

Age

....

Address

....

Email address

....

Telephone

....

Which of our pharmacies do you frequently visit? ....

Would you like to join a discussion forum? ....

On which of these topics would you like to have information?

    Asthma ☐

    Coronary Disease ☐

    Smoking Cessation ☐

    Diabetes ☐

    Hypertension ☐

    Mental Health ☐

    Other, Specify .... ☐

Would you also like to receive information on promotions on your email? ....

Please feel free to contact our shops for advice on any of these.

Signature ....   Date ....

Figure 12.1 Example of a mailing list form for healthcare information.

Improving profit margins

Dispensing

Drug supply

With such a large proportion of income coming from dispensing, even the slightest improvement in gross margin can make a substantial improvement in the cash generated. It is important to shop around to obtain the best deals possible, particularly for generic drugs that now account for over 75% of all prescriptions written in the UK. There are many generic manufacturers, short-line and full-line wholesalers competing with each other and as a result the prices for many generic products can vary substantially.

Using licensed parallel import products has also helped improve margins. Furthermore, those who make more use of parallel imported products rather than dispensing UK brands can substantially increase profitability.

Prescription forms

Prescriptions are valuable items and should be treated with care. Patients who are exempt from the prescription charge must sign the forms, otherwise the fee will be deducted from the pharmacy remuneration. It is possible that cross-border supplies will be restricted across the countries of the UK altogether – at the present time there are differences as to what may be supplied on the NHS. Forms should be checked carefully, particularly in border areas. There are still difficulties with blacklisted products being supplied.

Most Prescription Pricing Authorities have electronic scanning of prescriptions for pricing purposes, but there are items for which endorsement is necessary. These commonly include dietary foods, products needing certain storage conditions (e.g. in a fridge) and controlled drugs, and should be marked zero discount (ZD), otherwise an average of 10% of the value of these products will be clawed back each month, regardless of whether or not the discount is obtained. Where a hosiery item has been measured and fitted, a payment should be claimed. Some products such as ACBS can only be dispensed if prescribed in the correct manner by the GP and a clear instruction from the GP is needed. There are rules for claiming broken bulk on a minimum pack that contains more than has been prescribed.

The Drug Tariff is difficult to understand and yet forms the basis on which pharmacists are reimbursed. A working knowledge of the tariff will ensure that profits are not compromised.

There is also a special fee payable for expensive drugs (see Chapter 4) and emergency prescriptions but these claims need to be endorsed on the prescription.

Enhancing counter sales

Merchandising

Enhancing counter sales is all about layout, merchandising and category management, which is discussed in Chapters 13 and 14. The pharmacy needs to keep the right stock in the right place, with the right merchandising, it needs to be acquired at the right price. Purchasing and stock management are also vital.

Adding profit to the sale

There are a number of ways in which the profit of a pharmacy can be increased:

- Linking sales such as Vitamin C with paracetamol-based products being counter prescribed for cold remedies.
- Patients with cold and flu are prescribed antibiotics but rarely other products for immediate comfort and relief.
- Sales of specialist skincare products and alternative therapies can be enhanced when handled by a trained counter assistant.
- Counter-prescribing of own-brand products improves gross profit and creates repeat sales. This will help generate repeat business. Nationally advertised brands may have lower margins for retailer due to heavy advertising costs. The strength of the retail pharmacy is the ability to intervene and recommend on counter medicines. Pharmacists may choose to counter-prescribe similar products to the national brand leaders made by other companies who may not have such overheads and offer better discounts to the retailers.
- Pharmacist owner can ensure that without compromising patient care, staff could be trained to sell larger sizes of non-medicinal lines. This would offer value for money for the patient and larger margins for the pharmacy.
- Promotion of special offers, three-for-two, etc. can increase sales.

Pilferage

Customer and staff pilferage account for a small drop in the gross profit. Implementation of protocols and discipline can help reduce the seepage, as well as provide better security.

Cash pilferage, dishonoured cheques or forged notes all contribute to losses. Acceptance of cheques that are not honoured because of failure to record guarantee cards or stolen credit cards, would also reduce gross profit margin.

Stock control (see also Chapter 14)

Damaged and out of date stock also leads to losses. Expiry dates should be checked regularly and stock rotation carefully monitored. 'Dead' stock should be cleared out and not left on the shelves.

Most community pharmacies provide a photographic developing and printing service and money is lost through unclaimed photographs – this can be avoided by taking a deposit.

Reducing expenses

There are four main expenses in any business:

* wages
* premises cost
* finance
* general expenses (including legal and professional fees).

Wages

Salaries and wage costs ideally should not exceed 14% of annual sales. The rate of hourly pay may be market driven in the locality where the business is trading or a minimum wage rate fixed by the government. In planning staffing requirements, opening hours and fluctuating demand should be considered. Each pharmacy needs to track the hours of the local surgeries from where the main business is derived and any deviation too far away from surgery opening hours would not usually generate sufficient revenue in that period.

Closing the pharmacy on Saturday afternoons and during lunch hours are options, especially if paying for a locum pharmacist. Often the dispensing business generated on Saturday afternoon and during lunch hours is negligible and yet constitutes 15% of the wage cost. It is unnecessary to trade with extended hours as this simply increases the wage cost without the corresponding increase in the business being justified. Use of a regular locum helps maintain good customer service and efficient running of the pharmacy.

Premises cost

There are many factors connected with the cost of maintaining premises (see Chapter 5), of which the rental element is usually the most important. The size of premises may be inappropriate for the business conducted. If too small, it inhibits the potential of increasing revenue prompting thoughts of a building extension or moving to a larger site. If the premises are too large there are a number of possibilities for reducing costs, for example subletting to related professionals – a chiropodist, homeopath, physiotherapist, reflexologist or nutritionist. In some cases this may help generate extra revenue and increase sales and dispensing. If this is not possible then it is prudent to relocate appropriately to reduce overheads. Any surplus space on the upper floor can be converted to residential use and sold off or rented on the open market. It is important to optimise the usage of space within the premises.

The property should be maintained on a regular basis, despite the strain on resources that this may cause. In the long term any neglect on the maintenance could be picked up by a 'schedule of dilapidation' (see Chapter 5) that a landlord normally serves on the tenant at the time of rent review and definitely when the lease comes up for renewal. These schedules of dilapidation can often result in a substantial amount of money being spent on repair and restoration.

Utilities cost

The cost of utilities can be mitigated by the following:

- Proper insulation and correct heating to avoid wastage. Use of storage radiators for off-peak heating. Use of gas heating, making sure that the heaters are strategically located and insulating the roof, etc.
- With the deregulation of the utility companies shop around for suppliers of electricity and gas.
- The same is true for telephone expenditure. Restrict unnecessary use but also shop around for competitive rates. Put a bar on international and premium call lines.

- Installation of water meters.
- Use of timers on fascia lights and heating.

Finance costs

Finance costs may be reduced by making more use of swipe terminals, and encouraging cashback. The cost of handling hard cash is far higher than electronic banking. More use should be made of electronic payment systems rather than writing cheques and using NPA clearinghouse, where one payment can settle many suppliers' invoices. One should also negotiate with the banks the interest rate charged for loans and overdrafts and also the bank charges for the annual reviews. Use of Girobank for clearing cash can help mitigate costs. Efficient stock control with prudent stock levels will benefit cash flow.

General expenses

One can shop around for the best rates for other services – stocktaking, accounting, etc. Keeping proper accounting records reduces auditing compliance costs. Reducing stock levels also reduces cost of stocktaking and insurance, thus being a double benefit.

Further reading

Armstrong M. *How To Be An Even Better Manager*, 5th edn. London: Kogan Page, 1999.

Berman B. *Retail Management*. New York: Macmillan Publishing Company, 1986.

Bingham F G, Raffield B T. *Business Marketing Management*. Cincinnati: South Western College Publishing, 1990.

Hagel H, Rovers J P. *Managing the Patient Centered Pharmacy*. Washington, DC: American Pharmaceutical Association, 2002.

Maguire T. Managing marketing. Part of *Mind Your Own Business*. Booklet provided free from *Chemist & Druggist Online* (details available from http://www.dotpharmacy.com/matters.html)

Tootelion D H, Gaedeke R M. *Essentials of Pharmacy Management*. St Louis: Mosby, 1993.

13

Marketing within the pharmacy environment

Mel Smith

Introduction

Why is anyone in business? The answer to this question must be to attract customers. Customers are the reason for anyone being in business – even those who are altruistic and do not wish to make a profit must attract customers.

The customer is the common thread throughout this chapter. A business offering services or products that are not required by customers will soon fail. By understanding customers and potential customers and offering them products and services they value, a business will succeed. Expansion of a business relies on meeting new needs of existing customers, or attracting new customers to the present offering. When attracting customers to a business their expectations have to be met or exceeded. This will ensure that the customer visits the business again. To do this, staff are needed who believe in and promote the business. Motivated staff who understand the marketing strategy are essential to the success of the business. This chapter looks at what marketing is. It will soon become clear that in any marketing strategy, the customer is king! Methods that can be employed to understand the customer and the way that they make their decisions to purchase both services and products are discussed. By understanding who the customers are and how they make their decisions the chapter then looks at how this can be built into the business strategy or plan. Within the business plan the tactics which can be employed to grow the business will be covered. Finally the chapter reviews how to market ideas to staff. This involves communicating the strategy to staff, training them in new ways of working to ensure that the benefits of marketing the business are maximised.

In the independent community pharmacy, the largest amount of work and most of the turnover is usually generated by NHS prescriptions. The reduction in the profitability of dispensing by successive governments means that while the volume of work generated has increased, the profit expressed as a percentage of each prescription has decreased. It could now be argued that the most profitable areas of pharmacy are the over-the-counter (OTC) medicines, toiletries and general sales goods. These are the very areas that are being targeted by the major players in the grocery sector.

If community pharmacy is to prosper in the present environment, it is now more important than ever before that pharmacists develop their business skills. Through the aid of marketing skills it is possible to maximise the opportunities for community pharmacy to compete. To achieve the best within a business, you need to look at how to market yourself. What does the business (customer) need from you in terms of product and service? How can you best meet the demands of the business? Creating a demand for the services that you provide will ensure that you are still required by the business. If you understand the direction of the business then being aligned with this will help development within the business.

What exactly *is* marketing?

Kotler[1] defined marketing as: 'The social and managerial process by which individuals and groups obtain what they need and want though creating and exchanging products and value with others'. This definition is broad and shows that marketing can be applied to more than just the commercial environment. It can be applied to those whose 'products' are professional services, i.e. GPs, dentists and clinical pharmacists. It can also be applied to the provision of services, to other departments within an organisation (internal marketing). This is discussed in Chapter 11.

What is a want and what is a need?

Maslow described the different needs of a human being as being hierarchical[2] (see Figure 13.1). Basic needs are those required to survive. These Maslow referred to as physiological needs. When these are met then new needs apply, the need for security and protection. As more of the basic needs are met then the motivation is to fulfil 'higher needs' or wants. Marketing can provide the motivation to fulfil these needs.

Drucker wrote:[3]

> The aim of marketing is to make selling superfluous. The aim is to know and understand the customer so well that the product or service fits him/her and sells itself.

Wants

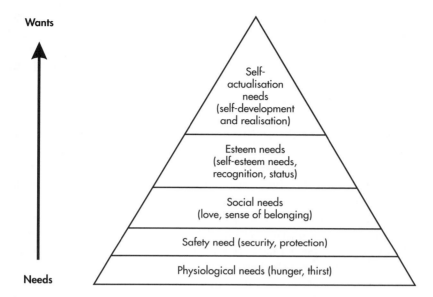

Needs

Figure 13.1 Maslow's hierarchy of needs.

It is clear from both these statements that the centre of any marketing theory is the end user of the product or service. The end user can be described as the customer or consumer. Customers are the people that buy the product or service; consumers are the people that use the product or service. For this chapter, we will assume they are one and the same. It is therefore clear that in any marketing-led organisation that the customer is King!

Drucker shows this in the following quote:[3]

> True marketing starts out with the customers, their demographics, related needs and values. It does not ask, 'What do we want to sell?' It asks, 'What does the customer want to buy?' It does not say, 'This is what our product or service does.' It says, 'These are the satisfactions the customer looks for.'

The marketing concept is not new, in fact the idea of exchanging products or services, which are of value to others, is how trade took place for hundreds of years. The importance of marketing is dependent on the availability of products or services. The Industrial Revolution provided the means to mass-produce products. Products could be produced more cheaply. The reduction in the price of products increased demand. As demand outstripped production and the emphasis was therefore on increased production. Choice is therefore limited to what is available and marketing and selling are less important. A similar growth was seen in the pharmacy dispensary during the 1950s and 1960s, with the rapid development of new treatments, penicillins, tetracyclines, beta-blockers and oral contraceptives. These increased the number of prescriptions and the growth in the profitability of community pharmacy. This growth was a general market growth and benefited all pharmacies.

Generally, during the 1920s, production was beginning to outstrip demand. To secure market share industry switched from pure production to development of products with advantages over the competition. Variation of similar products began to emerge and the selling of the product became important. Within the pharmacy dispensary, this market has not been well developed as the competition between various products tends to take place within the medical sector as this is where the decisions have been made. It is, however, visible within the OTC trade as manufacturers sell their variation of similar products.

When the market is saturated, that is production outstrips demand, the number of variations of products has increased to a level where the demand for the variations is diminished and the development of new products slows, any increase in market share is taken at the expense of someone else within the market. Customers become more sophisticated, and understanding and meeting the needs of these new customers is all-important. Within pharmacy this is the stage we are at now. The market is made more complicated by the ingress of new players, looking to expand out of their present stagnant markets. These new players already understand the needs of the customers, and marketing philosophy.

An illustration of the changes in customer's expectations can be illustrated by the automobile industry. During the early 1900s the saying, 'You can have any colour as long as it's black' was associated with the automotive industrialist Henry Ford. The implication of this was that, as Ford was the main producer of cars, then if you wanted a Ford car, you had to accept the colour Henry Ford produced – not only the colour, but also the model, because the Model T was the only mass-produced car available. During the 1950s and 1960s, as the number of producers increased, the types of cars increased. The range and colours were limited; when the Mini first came on the market, there was only one engine size and one body shape. Today a customer purchasing a new car not only has the choice of body (saloon, hatchback, estate), but also engine size, body colour, wheel type, gearbox type and the opportunity to specify a large array of factory-fitted extras. Companies now compete to personalise the experience for the consumer and the consumer now expects these choices as standard. Although at the moment the consumer is generally limited to where they can purchase a particular make of car within a region, this will change over the next few years. With increased competition, the future of motorcar retailing will continue to change. Those who best respond to their customer's needs will be the retailers who survive.

This also illustrates the dynamic nature of wants and needs. When the original need of a vehicle, which can transport individuals from one place to another has been met, then the wants of air-conditioning, audio systems and global satellite positioning systems are introduced.

Marketing strategy as part of a business plan

Information about customers and their needs and motivations should be built into the business plan. From your own research you will know what type of customers you have, you will know what their needs are and how they can meet those needs in your area. It is your decision on the customers you want and the products or services you are going to provide. It is important if you are going to stay in business that the customers you wish to serve exist in the location you serve and that the products and services you offer are required by these customers.

The **marketing mix** is probably the most famous phrase in marketing. The elements are the marketing 'tactics' that assist in achieving the chosen strategy. Also known as the 'four Ps', the marketing mix elements are **price, place** (location), **product** and **promotion**. Some commentators will increase the mix to the 'five Ps', to include people. Others will increase the mix to 'Seven Ps', to include physical evidence (such as uniforms, facilities or livery) and process (i.e. the whole customer experience, e.g. a visit to Disneyworld). It represents a co-ordinated programme to obtain the most favourable response from potential customers. While putting things in named boxes is a convenient way of understanding the salient features of each it should be realised that there really are no boundaries surrounding the various topics for all the elements of marketing blend into each other if a business is going to prosper. The most important factor in setting strategy are the characteristics of your customers and how they may be expected to behave.

Understanding your customer

From the discussions above it is clear that a 'customer' is anyone to whom you offer products or services. Thus, the patient who presents a prescription is a customer of your service, the person who purchases an item within your pharmacy is a customer, the GP to whom you provide information is also a customer, as are the primary care trusts (PCTs) to whom you may provide services. It is also clear that customers may change if the products or services you offer change.

As mentioned earlier, the reason for being in business is to attract customers. The collection of data on the opportunities and problems in attracting customers is known as market research. The function of market research is to generate information, which will aid marketers in making decisions. The data can be primary data collected by your own research or secondary data, available from other sources (see Chapter 13).

To understand your customers, you need to understand your product offering, and vice versa. These two are interlinked. You need to know where your customers come from – this is the catchment area of your business. You need to know the type of customers within your catchment area. There is a practical guide called *Understanding your Community* (see further reading), which will help you to identify who your potential customers are. You can easily find out who your present customers are, by conducting an in-shop survey. On a piece of paper and on one day of the week record every customer who enters your shop. Record their approximate age, their gender and whether or not they purchased a product from your shop. You could also record whether they brought a prescription into your shop to be dispensed (a sample chart can be found in the booklet *Understanding your Community* mentioned above). Do this on different days of the week over the next two months. This will give you primary data on the type of people who visit your shop.

You should know:

- How many people visit your pharmacy on an average day.
- The age bands of the people.
- The gender of the people.
- How many people buy products in your shop.
- How many people enter your shop but do not purchase anything.
- How many people only have their prescription dispensed in your shop.
- How many people have their prescriptions dispensed and make a purchase.

These are your present customers. These customers usually know what services they require from you and if they leave empty-handed then you are not meeting their needs with the services you offer. You can obtain information about this gap by keeping a record of all the requests that you cannot meet. Note every time a customer asks for something that you cannot supply.

This is the first piece of market research. The present customers, and to a certain extent their product/service needs, have been identified. This information is useful as far as it links present customers' needs with the services they expect to be provided.

This does not address the customers who require your services but who do not enter your business. How do you find out who these customers are? Why do they not feel that you offer a product that they need? You can find out how many people – potential customers – pass by your shop by simply counting the number of people who pass the door of your shop. You can do this over several weeks at different times of the day on different days. If you wish to obtain more information, you could collect the data on the gender and approximate age of the people who are passing you by.

Geographical catchment area

You need to identify your catchment area. A start for this can be your present customers. Where do they come from? On a local map of the area, a street or Ordnance Survey map of approximately 1:2500 would be ideal, locate where customers bringing prescriptions to you come from. You can find this information from the address on the prescriptions. Also locate on the map areas where your potential customers could come from – housing estates, nursing homes, industrial works, schools, shopping centres, etc.

Do you have people visiting your business from all the areas on your map? If not, do you know why? Is it difficult to reach your business from some areas (maybe a major road runs between you and some of your customers)? Are there other geographical reasons why people do not visit your shop? Once you know your catchment area, you can do further research and can add information on your potential customers. The local census (available from your library or town hall) can provide a great deal of information. From your own surveys, you know the gender, age range and distance they have to travel. Mark on your map areas that attract people to your location – schools, shopping centres, factories, bus stops, car parks, etc.

Customer characteristics

There is a great deal of work done on the behaviour of customers.[4] By identifying the types of customer in your area you can extrapolate what types of services they would be interested in purchasing from your business. Thus cash-rich but time-poor customers may be attracted to your business if you offered them a telephone order and delivery service.

Customer types

Customer type is a way of segmenting the market to identify discrete target groups. An accepted method is by social class:

A	Higher managerial, administrative or professional
B	Intermediate managerial, administrative or professional
C1	Supervisory and clerical
C2	Skilled manual
D	Semi-skilled and unskilled manual worker
E	State pensioners, widows, casual and lowest grade earners.

In more recent years the use of socioeconomic groups as a segmentation variable has been criticised. However in 1981 the Market Research Society published the findings of a joint industry working party[5] and the following points were reported:

- Social grade provides satisfactory discriminating power.
- No other classification variable could provide consistently better discriminatory power.
- No evidence was found to show a decline in the discriminatory power of social grade over recent years.

A more complex segmentation using computer models and data based on where a customer lives (geography) and a variety of socio-demographic variables, such as occupation, home ownership, size of family, etc. has been developed. This segmentation is referred to as the 'geodemographic technique'. Using this technique various models have been developed. ACORN (A Classification of Residential Neighbourhoods) segments customers by the housing characteristics within a particular area. Large multiple retailers use this system to determine store locations, by comparing the potential buying power of various ACORN locations. Information on the ACORN geodemographics for an area can be found at the website www.upmystreet.co.uk.

Other methods using education and benefits analysis are also used to segment the market. The aim of all these systems of analysis is to refine the list of customers, so that the product or service offering is 'tailored' to the customer's need.

A type of segmentation may also be used to find the answers to two important questions about your existing and potential customers:

'What type of customers do I *have*?' Are they:

- young, middle-aged or old?
- money-rich but time-poor?

- time-rich but money-poor?
- local?
- passing trade?

What type of customers do I *require*? Does the business plan highlight any of the following?

- An increase in customers using your business?
- Increases in 'spend' for each customer using your business?
- An increase in sales to the customers using your business?
- An improvement in the image of your business?

These are not mutually exclusive, however you should focus on one. This will inform you of the type of services they require. It is pointless trying to build a business selling baby items, nappies, baby milk, etc. in a business that is situated next to sheltered housing for senior citizens. Similarly it is likely to fail if you specialise in appliances for the elderly on a development for working commuters. Although these are two extremes, and any business has to cater for more than one profile of customers, these considerations should be taken into account when looking at all the services the business offers. You will have had the experience of going to the bank during your lunchtime and standing in a long queue at a single cashier counter. How do you feel? This is an example of how not to meet your customer's needs. Some businesses are now trying to influence different types of customers to shop at different times. Thus some stores offer senior citizens discount if they shop on certain 'quiet' days and times. Others encourage a buying frenzy by announcing one-day sales or extra discounts at weekends when the whole family can influence purchases.

Retaining existing customers and attracting new ones

As a result of your market research and your decision about what your core business is, you will know if you are serving the maximum number of customers available to use your business. Your aim should be to encourage more of your target customers to use your business, while retaining and encouraging your present customers. Research shows that there is a higher cost associated with gaining customers than with retaining customers. Thus changes to your services should take into account the needs of your present customer base. Your aim should always be to develop a loyal customer base, i.e. one who would not think of purchasing the service you offer from any other source. Kotler[5] has researched customer brand loyalty and divided customers into four groups:[1]

- Hard-core loyals – customers who always buy the same brand.
- Soft-core loyals – customers who usually divide their purchases between two or more brands.
- Shifting loyals – customers who purchase one brand for a period of time, but then change to another brand completely.
- Switchers – customers who show no brand loyalty at all and switch brands on every purchase.

It has been shown that the industry can attract the switchers – at least in the short term – by offers and sales promotions. Analysis of data from shifting loyals may tell a company the inadequacies in the marketing programme, which are causing the customer to change brands. Why people's shopping patterns are changing. Is the offering of a competitor failing to meet the customer's needs? Can you fill this gap?

Are you failing to change to meet the changing needs of your customers? If this is the case, are your competitors changing their strategy to meet your customer's needs?

It is clear that once you have decided on your customers and your business area, you need to understand who are targeting the same customers as you, by supplying the same services as you. This is known as the competition. Others who are targeting the same customers as you but with different services could become competitors, if you decide to extend your offering to include their services. They could become your allies, as is seen in some department stores and supermarkets.

Dealing with competition

You can look at competitors within your geographical catchment area, but this will not give you the full picture. You need to understand where your customers go for the services you provide. This may include out of town one-stop shopping, mail order or convenience purchases made near work. All these are competitors. To understand your competitors it is useful to visit them. Information is available on the philosophy of publicly quoted companies in the form of annual reports. Advertisements, either on the television or in newspapers or magazines, will show you how they aim to attract their customers. While it is interesting to try and understand the marketing philosophy of major players, for you it is important to see where you can offer their customers a better service than they can. Remember that multinational retailers will look at the global market and not at the local one. Wal-Mart, the world's biggest retailer, has not had the same success in Germany as they have in the

USA. It can be useful to do a SWOT analysis on your and their businesses (see Chapter 12). Can you turn one of their weaknesses into one of your strengths? For example a 3 for the price of 2 offer may be useful to someone who uses a large amount of a product, but for an occasional user this will not be an incentive. Lower everyday prices may be of value if your customer is able to purchase on a trip to an out-of-town centre, but the additional cost of travel may make it poor value if the single item can be purchased locally.

Are your competitors' customers *your* customers? Well, by the definition we have used of a competitor the answer must be yes, however if the customers they attract are not the ones you are trying to attract, then they are not your competitors and you need not alter your strategy to include them. We have said that the market is dynamic and so in future, they may become your competitors. Much time and effort can be expended in trying to compete against a business that is no direct threat to you. Are customers visiting a pharmacy outside your catchment area, really going to use your pharmacy if their present pharmacy closes? Is this pharmacy really a competitor?

If your competitors are successful, what are they doing different to you? How are they meeting their customers' needs? If your analysis shows you how they succeed can you use similar methods?

Factors affecting customer purchasing decisions

Income

Money – or rather the amount of money one has to spend, usually referred to as disposable income – has an important effect on purchasing decisions. Looking at the family income identifies the economic resources of the family group. Over the last decade there has been a gradual increase in economic resources and a movement in the way that these resources are spent. There has been a decrease in the percentage spent on food and clothing and an increase in the amount spent on housing. Overall, there has been an increase in disposable income. The type of expenditure is reflected by the economic climate, thus the housing market is buoyant when people have confidence in the future. Quality and quantity of consumables purchased are determined by current income.

Those in the high income group, usually dual-income families, tend to work long hours and value time greatly. In their purchases they value quality and service rather than cost. The idea of 'quality' of service is explored in Chapter 1.

The 'down market' group includes those who are time-rich but have lower disposable incomes. This comprises a sizable proportion of the market, including young, old, single and divorced, who tend to spend more on education, prescription drugs, tobacco, milk and laxatives. They tend to respond to 'no frills' marketing and have been successfully wooed by a marketing strategy that convinces them they are 'smart and special' rather than 'poor and worthless'.

It is clear from our own experiences that our amount of disposable income is dynamic. It depends not only on how we earn or receive our income, but also on the demands made on our income by others. It is also true that your customers' needs change over their lifetime. A typical model is the family life cycle:

- Single
- Married no children
- Full nest I (youngest child < 6 years)
- Full nest II (youngest child 6–12 years)
- Full nest III (youngest child > 12 years)
- Empty nest I (still working)
- Empty nest II (retired)
- Alone (partner deceased)

Thus 'Married with no children' and 'Empty nest I' will probably have more disposable income than the full nest categories. It is also expected that children will play an important part in making decisions about what to purchase. If your research shows that the majority of people in your area are in the first or last two groups then a product offering biased towards babies and children is going to be ineffective. Similarly a product and service offering of aids for the elderly is unlikely to work if your customer base is made up of young single people or couples with young families.

The age cycle has an effect on purchasing as the married with no children will spend much of their income on housing, whereas the 45–55 age group spend more on clothes and eating out and the 65+ group spend more on healthcare.

Price of product or service

In all cases the absolute cost of the product is not the main driver – value for money is more important. This is best expressed as the value that the customer places on the purchase. Thus the time-poor customer will not value an out of the way journey to purchase a product a penny cheaper. Similarly the down market group may spend more time on shopping, but tend to purchase in a locality where they perceive value. This is true for everyday consumables. On high-value one-off purchases, although price may be important if the discount is large enough, service plays a more important role. Purchases like houses and cars, which are infrequently made, involve a high level of research by the customer and a high level of technical input by the sales staff. The level of service provided by the seller is important in these transactions and is usually considered as part of the 'value package' by the customer.

The absolute cost of a product is not the only indicator used by a customer. With the exception of items like toilet rolls, bread and baked beans, which are known as KVIs (known value items), most customers have little idea of the actual cost of a product. They do, however, have an idea of an acceptable price range. If the products you are offering fall within this range they will consider purchasing them. This range can vary – for instance, people tend to spend more on products if they are an emergency purchase, rather than a planned purchase. You will find that major multiples charge more for their products in their convenience stores than for the same products in their supermarkets.

The perception of value for money is a different concept to price. It will be noted that a well-known supermarket chain expresses its advertising as rolling prices back and giving value for money. A closer look at the advertisement will show that the prices are not related to particular goods and are therefore meaningless. The concept however is strong and customers who shop at these stores believe they are receiving value for money.

For certain products customers will consider price as an indicator of quality. At the extreme, they consider it a mark of exclusivity – an example of this is Omega watches. At the other end of the market, they may consider 'cheap' products as substandard.

Ease of purchase

The customer that feels time constraint, especially when purchasing consumables, will be more inclined to purchase products and services that save time in a time-efficient way. Thus ready meals purchased at handy locations are more appealing than fresh ingredients purchased at an out of the way store, even if the former are purchased at a premium price.

Quality of service

Reliability, fitness for use and service are considered by the customer as much as price and the price only becomes important if it is outside the range the consumer believes is acceptable (see Chapter 1). If the product is a leading brand then the consumer will still purchase, despite the price premium (see Chapter 14).

If customers can go to various locations to purchase the services you supply, why are they choosing to come to you? If it is because they believe that they will obtain good advice, the message conveyed by the 'Ask your Pharmacist' campaign, how are they going to feel if this service is below standard, or not offered at all? Similarly, no price reduction is of value if the lack of advice that self-selection offers leads to the purchase of an inappropriate product.

Research shows that customers will choose where to shop on the basis of convenience, experience and urgency. This is similar to brand loyalty (Table 13.1). Customers will decide on the amount of advice they need based on their knowledge of the symptoms and experiences.

It can be seen from Table 13.2 that customers will choose a pharmacy for semi-serious conditions of which they have little knowledge. Again if the customer's service expectations are not met, then they will feel cheated and this will influence their future decision-making. Decisions are also made based on urgency (see Table 13.3).

Table 13.1 Reason for store choice (%)

	Boots	Superdrug	Tesco	Asda
Regular store/always shop here	58	29	74	72
Convenient/closest	29	25	12	19
Needed something I knew they sold	12	25	2	0
Passing/in the area	8	23	4	2
Other	12	18	10	14

Table 13.2 Customer decision tree (symptoms and experience)

Symptoms	Experiences	Choice
Serious	Not applicable	Doctor/hospital
Semi-serious	Little knowledge	Pharmacy
Moderate	Knowledge	Regular/most convenient
Buy for stock or replacement	Knowledge	Regular/most convenient

Table 13.3 Customer decision tree (symptoms and urgency)

Symptoms	Urgency	Choice
Serious	Very	Doctor/hospital
Semi-serious	Very	Any pharmacy open
Moderate	Very	Any store open
Moderate	Can wait	Regular/most convenient
Buy for stock or replacement	Can wait	Regular/most convenient

If we look at this at a practical level, let us assume you are on holiday and develop the symptoms of allergic rhinitis, to which you are periodically prone. The symptoms are not serious enough to require the services of a doctor, but are spoiling the holiday for you and your family. You make the effort to find the nearest pharmacy, but on arrival you find it closed. What do you do? Do you suffer the symptoms until the pharmacy opens? Alternatively, do you look for the nearest store that is open and likely to sell a product that may relieve the symptoms, even though you realise that this is probably not the product you usually use?

The features of the products and services on offer (see also Chapter 4)

What type of product are you offering? Does the product or service meet the needs of your identified customers and the needs of your business plan? What is your core business? Your core business is what products or services you wish to offer to your customers. Major companies usually encapsulate this in their vision statement and strategy. A marketing-led company will include their customers at the heart of their business strategy. Thus the products or services they offer are dictated not by what they produce, but by how they believe they will best serve their customers. The following are examples of vision statements. Which is marketing led?

> To provide our customers with safe, good value, point to point air services. To effect and to offer a consistent and reliable product and fares appealing to leisure and business markets on a range of European routes. To achieve this we will develop our people and establish lasting relationships with our suppliers.

> Company X is a leading health and beauty retailer and combines quality with exceptional value for money in both branded and own-brand products.

So what is your core business? Is it:

- dispensing prescriptions?
- providing healthcare advice?
- improving the health and well-being of your local community?
- to sell OTC medicines?
- to protect the public?
- to put your competitors out of business?

You should now have some idea of the type of customers who use your business and the types of products and services they require. Is your business geared to meet their requirements?

If your aim is to dispense prescriptions, does your business have:

- a large dispensing area;
- procedures in place to accurately receive prescriptions;
- efficient facilities for dispensing;
- an area to advise your customers on how to use the dispensed medicines?

To this you could add a collection and delivery service. Maybe an 'on-call' out of hours service for prescriptions generated by deputising services could be considered. The employment of more than one pharmacist and several qualified technicians may be desirable if cost-effective. The introduction of electronic transfer of prescriptions could make the need for customer contact minimal. The dispensing service could take place in a location away from the customer and the dispensed medicines could be delivered to the customer at their home or at the surgery. The information for the patient could be computer-generated and sent to the customer as a printed sheet. Do you think your customers would be happy with this?

The need for a large front of shop space is questionable. Opening hours need to be focused around the surgery opening hours, with less staff being employed in the quiet periods and at weekends. The whole layout and ambience of the business should be focused on the prescription process (see Chapter 12).

This analysis can be carried out for your business. The aim is to align what services you wish to offer with the needs of the customers you wish to serve, in the geographical area where they seek the service. The service that you offer must offer value for money to both yourself and your customer. This is where pharmacy differs from most other businesses in that the dispensing service is not paid for by the customer, nor is it a free market where development of premium services attracts premium prices. It is therefore important that you view the development of your service in this area, in the light of the remuneration, which you are likely to receive.

Place – the location chosen for displaying goods or services in the pharmacy

Merchandising and layout

Merchandising and layout are covered in detail in Chapter 14 so will be mentioned only briefly here. Take a look at your business in light of your information on your customers and services. Does the layout of your business reflect what you wish to offer? It should be appreciated that marketing is about conveying a consistent message to your customers. If your message is that the service I offer is 'I care about the health of the community' then a display of sweets or stationery at the front of the business does not reinforce this message. In the modern business, analysis of the market place is important. If your customers are early adopters, people who like to try new ideas, then ensure you have a section of the latest products on display. If you have customers that are traditionalists then avoid the desire to introduce new products too quickly (see also Chapter 14).

Category management

Rather than look at a product the preference is now to look at the category in which the product is located. The management of products by this method is called category management. The way that a category is viewed can be different depending on who is doing the viewing. The consumer, the retailer or the manufacturer can define the category. It is usual for the retailer and the manufacturer to agree what constitutes the category. They will then test their understanding by collecting and interpreting consumer data. When the category has been defined it is possible to look at the position of various brands within the category. In a category, which has a strong leading brand, the category strategy will be dominated by the leading brand strategy. Some retailers call such a brand leader 'a category captain'. It is usual in a consumer-led company for this strategy to be based on the assessment of the consumer's beliefs for the dominant brand. If the retailer and the manufacturer share information on their belief in the category, the synergy not only serves each group well but also grows the category.

A small retailer may have difficulty in developing a category strategy. By understanding the strategy of the major player within a category and aligning your strategy to theirs, it should be possible to lever benefits. This requires an understanding of your own definition of a category and information on the market leaders and market share.

Information on the market category is available from a variety of sources. Independent information is available, but this usually has to be paid for. Information from manufacturers can be biased towards their products, but wholesalers, representatives and specialist magazines will all provide information on the state of the market, and how products are doing within a particular category. Your own sales data will also tell you which items your customers prefer. With the development of electronic point of sale (EPOS) data, it is possible to identify which items your customers prefer; this should be used to develop a buying policy, which ensures that you stock only those products on which you are going to make a profit. The data should also inform you on which pack sizes that you need. If you look at the successful retail businesses you will see that the range of products is not as large as it appears. Within a category the 'brand leader' is stocked and maybe the second brand and an own label, but third or fourth in the market are rarely stocked.

The place and way in which products are displayed in categories is described in Chapter 14.

The importance of brands The brand name is the vehicle through which the manufacturer establishes the product's identity. Customers' knowledge about a brand is often quite high, they will know a brand, but they will have little idea what the ingredients of the product are. They will, however, trust a brand. They buy the image, which is maybe all that differentiates brands. Manufacturers will spend large amounts of money on developing a brand's image and developing the image over a period of time. A company will seek to communicate the desirable and believable benefits of a brand by advertising. The advertising strategy is designed to differentiate the brand from others in the market and to move the customer towards purchasing the brand over others. The strategy for achieving this is long term and usually involves establishing a brand identity. The customer relates to this identity and is moved towards purchase. The launching of new brand names is expensive and risky. This can be seen with the failures of rebranding initiatives such as Consignia from The Royal Mail.

The use of **umbrella branding** or **family brands** is cheaper and less risky. Within the pharmacy environment, however, the regulatory authorities can limit this. The importance of this can be seen when brand names associated with one active ingredient are used for an entirely different ingredient. Thus a brand based on paracetamol which is safe for asthmatics, may be contraindicated for asthmatics if an ibuprofen variant of the brand is launched. This can be overcome by using the phrase 'from the manufacturer of', or a variation of the brand name may be used. This can be seen when the manufacturers of the antihistamine brand Piriton (chlorphenamine) launched a cetirizine-based product as Piriteze.

The other advantage of launching products under an umbrella brand name is that advertising for the new product can have a halo effect on the other products in the brand range. Thus the launch of a new variant may increase sales of the whole range. The disadvantage of umbrella branding is that if adverse publicity is directed at the new product then it may affect other products in the range. This is the reason why diverse multinational industries tend to promote product brands rather than their corporate image as a brand.

Promotion and selling

Advertising

Advertising can be defensive as well as proactive. Manufacturers of brand leaders who are not launching new variants will still heavily advertise the brand, especially if they know that a competitor is about to launch a new product. The aim of this advertising is to negate the effect of a competitor's advertising. Advertising that raises awareness of a category may benefit the brand leader more than other brands. As with all marketing, it is important for the marketer to know what the customer's needs are and what the competition is doing to meet these needs. For advertising to be effective it must be related to these needs.

It can be seen that manufacturers spend a considerable amount of time and money building brands and market share. This is reflected in the premium price paid for brands. It is also clear that customers 'buy' into brands as customers demand branded items. Stores that specialise in their own label products, like Body Shop, Boots and Marks and Spencer, spend as much money as the manufacturing industry on building their own brands.

Unless you have the capital to put into building your own brand, then the selling of branded products is the most effective way of building your business. It is important to understand the marketing message of the brand so that you can maximise the message and reinforce the customer's motivation to purchase the brand. The distributor or manufacturer will supply point of sale material in line with their brand message. This does much of the work for the retailer. It is important that any point of sale material enhances the message that you wish your business to convey to your customers.

If brands are important to your business, should you stock a brand range or a range of brands? If brands are about differentiating products from those of competitors and this is achieved by highlighting the difference so as to motivate customers to purchase, then it is clear that different brands will appeal to different customers. If you are appealing to different types of customers then a range of brands may be needed, however the more brands you stock, the more diverse and diluted your marketing message becomes. The major retailers will stock very few brands, but will stock many of the variants within the brand range.

Generic advertising is useful to convey the message that a certain commodity or service is available. The National Pharmaceutical Association with its 'Ask your Pharmacist' campaign has successfully achieved this. The campaign was initiated in 1982. The National Pharmaceutical Association (NPA) commissioned research that showed that the general public in Britain did not appreciate the extent and depth of knowledge of the community pharmacist. In 1983, the NPA launched a national advertising campaign carrying the slogan, 'Ask Your Pharmacist – you'll be getting good advice'. Although the campaign has an effect on increasing the awareness of the public about all pharmacists, this is not a problem as the NPA represents the majority of community pharmacists in the UK. The campaign has been so successful that the government is now encouraging the public to seek advice from their pharmacist, rather than their doctor, for the treatment of minor ailments. Individual community pharmacists could build on this with adverts in local publications. Generally a single supplier does not undertake this type of advertising, as it benefits competitors as well as the individual supplier.

In all cases, the aim of advertising is to affect customer's behaviour. Advertising is aimed at people's emotional level. Psychological research shows that 75% of a purchasing decision is emotion and only 25% is logical. Although you may feel that you are doing the customer a favour by suggesting a cheaper generic equivalent to the requested product, you may undermine the whole purchasing experience. An illustration of this is the advertisement for Coca Cola, where customers are buying the product because of the lifestyle it portrays. The vision statement of the Coca Cola company reinforces this:

> The Coca-Cola Company exists to benefit and refresh everyone who is touched by our business. Founded in 1886, our Company is the world's leading manufacturer, marketer, and distributor of non-alcoholic beverage concentrates and syrups, used to produce nearly 300 beverage brands. Our corporate headquarters are in Atlanta, with local operations in nearly 200 countries around the world.

Selling skills

If the aim of your business is to provide customers with the service they need, then customers will use your business if you meet or exceed their expectations. It follows that to meet a customer's expectations you must know what they are. We have discussed how to tailor your services to attract the customers you require, but each customer will have their own specific requirements. It follows that a customer will go to a business selling cars if they wish to purchase a car. Once there, however, their needs will be unique to them. They will have their own ideas on colour, style, extras, etc.

To find out the customer's needs it is important to communicate with the customer. This communication is part of a selling skill. It is essential to ensure that you supply the customer with the correct service. What are the important skills that are required to succeed in selling? They fall into three areas: knowledge of the product or service you are selling, an understanding of the customer and an ability to communicate.

Pharmaceutical knowledge is the pharmacist's speciality, the emphasis on keeping up to date with changes in treatments, new products, etc. is the basis of both continuing education and continuing professional development.

The understanding of the customer is something that is not taught to pharmacists. Although the skills required to understand customers and to communicate are not taught in the undergraduate course, by the time the pharmacy student graduates, they are expected to have a competence in these skills, which can be assessed during their pre-registration year.

To understand the customer's requirements, you must communicate with the customer. Communication takes place in a variety of ways, the most obvious one is by talking. However, remember that communication is a two-way process and listening is at least if not more important than talking. Both are less important than the attitude of the salesperson. This is usually communicated non-verbally. It will show in dress, actions and 'body language'. It is important to ensure that you and your staff portray the right message. Major stores have a dress code or uniform. Educate your staff that the customer always comes first. Work, which has to be done without interruption, should be out of sight of the customer or after the business is closed. The customer has the ability to go elsewhere for the service you offer. Similarly the customer is not interested in the seniority of the staff that is serving them. If a customer is waiting to be served, then the first free member of staff should serve them.

There are two types of questions which can be used: open or soft questioning. These questions are used to elicit information and start with the words; what, why, when, how, where and who. Examples are shown in the Case study below. Questions starting with other words are called closed or hard questions. They can be answered with a yes or no. Although they do not elicit information they are useful if used at the right time, e.g. to close the sale.

CASE STUDY

The use of closed and open questions
The following illustrates the use of these types of questions:
'Can I help you?'
This is a closed question and usually elicits the answer *'No, I'm only looking!'*
'How may I help you?' This is an open question and cannot be answered by *'Yes'* or *'No'*
'Which of these two items would you like?' This is an open question, which could elicit the answer *'Neither of them thank you'*
'Would you like the red item?' This is a closed question, which will decide if the customer requires the red item or not!

The incorrect use of closed questions can lead to verbal 'ping-pong', with little information being gleaned. In such a conversation neither the customer nor the salesperson feel satisfied.

When you have asked a question it is necessary to wait for an answer. This can be difficult, especially if you are inexperienced. It may take time for the customer to digest what you have asked them. It is important that you listen carefully. Do not spend this time formulating your reply or your next question. You will miss what the customer is saying. If you find that the conversation is getting complicated, at an appropriate point, stop and summarise what you believe has been said:

> As I understand it, you require something to treat your husband's cold. He has had it for five days and it is now causing him to cough. The cough is a tickly one and it is keeping him awake at night. Is that correct?

Again you need to wait and see if the customer agrees with what you have said. The answer will be 'yes' or 'no'. If the answer is 'no', then you need to ask another open question asking for information on where you are incorrect in your summary, before you ask for more information.

If you need to refer the customer to someone else, give the person to whom you are referring as much information as possible. You will have experienced the scenario, where you have phoned a company with a query, explained what the problem is, only to be told that this is handled by another department. You are passed to the new department and have to start the explanation from the very beginning again. If this happens more than once, how do you feel? If you are the person to whom the customer is referred, then begin the conversation by summarising what you believe you know about the problem. This gives the customer the chance to correct any information, which you have interpreted incorrectly.

Although people will tell you they like choice, most people really only like to decide between two items. The more choice they have, the less likely they are to make a decision. By the correct use of questioning and a good knowledge of the products, services and benefits to the customer that you offer, it should be possible to narrow down the choices for the customer. This is not to reduce the choice the customer has, but to help them clarify what they need. If a patient in the pharmacy is allergic to gluten, then narrowing the selection of products to those that do not contain gluten is not doing the customer a disservice. Similarly, if the information the customer gives you shows that they will need other products in addition to the one they wish to purchase, you are not meeting their needs if you do not supply these as well. This is known as linked selling. An example of this is batteries for an electrical product. If the customer spends time purchasing the product, only to get it home and find that until they purchase some batteries, it will not work, how do you think they will feel? Do you believe that you have met your customer's needs? Within pharmacy the suggestion that tissues, may be useful if you are recommending some medication for a cold may mean that the customer can go straight home, rather than having to make a detour to another shop to purchase their tissues elsewhere. It also shows the customer that you are interested in their welfare.

If we look at the quote from Drucker stated at the beginning of this chapter, we see that he states:

> True marketing starts out with the customers, their demographics, related needs and values. It does not ask, 'What do we want to sell?' It asks, 'What does the customer want to buy?' It does not say, 'This is what our product or service does.' It says, 'These are the satisfactions the customer looks for.'

The last part of the quote can be stated that customers buy benefits, not features. What do we mean by benefits? A customer buys a product or service for what it does for them, not for what it is made of. For instance, customers do not buy screwdrivers because they like screwdrivers, they buy screwdrivers because they have a need to screw a screw into a wall so that they can put up a picture. Why then do pharmacists and many manufacturers sell their products on features? Buy this because it contains ibuprofen in a sustained release form, or 'it contains the strongest decongestion available without prescription'. What they should be selling is 'will take the pain away for a long time' or 'is most effective at relieving your nasal symptoms'. When pharmacists start expounding their pharmaceutical knowledge on the active ingredients in a product, it has little positive effect on most customers, in fact it may have a negative effect. The art is to use your pharmaceutical knowledge to structure the conversation at a level that meets the customer's understanding.

All these skills have to be learnt. As well as the pharmacist keeping their pharmaceutical knowledge up to date, it is important that they are skilled in the art of customer communication. It is also important that the staff within the pharmacy are suitably trained. Customers expect the staff within the pharmacy to have specialist knowledge. This could be used to differentiate your service from that of the competition. This has to be taught. The skills required to serve the customer also need to be taught. Well-trained staff are confident and this pays dividends within the business.

References

1. Kotler P. *Marketing Management*, 7th edn. New Jersey: Prentice Hall, 1991.
2. Maslow A. *Motivation and Personality*. New York: Harper & Row, 1954.
3. Drucker P. *Management*. New York: Harper & Row, 1973.
4. Cave S. *Understanding Consumer Behaviour in a Week*. London: Hodder & Stoughton, 2001.
5. Joint Industrial Working Party. *An Evaluation of Social Grade Validity*. London: Market Research Society, 1981.
6. Kotler P. *Marketing Management: Analysis, Planning, Implementation and Control*, 9th edn. New Jersey: Prentice Hall, 1997.

Further reading

Brittney L. *Which? Way to Drive Your Small Business*. London: Consumers' Association, 2001.

Engel J F, Blackwell R D, Miniard P W. *Consumer Behavior*. Chicago: The Drydon Press International Edition, 1990.

Lancaster G, Massingham L, Ashford R. *Essentials of Marketing*, 4th edn. Maidenhead: McGraw Hill Education, 2000.

Business booklets available from Reckitt Benckiser Healthcare (Reckitt Benckiser plc, 103–105 Bath Road, Slough, Berks SL1 3UH, UK): SWOT Analysis, Understanding Your Community, Merchandising, Lessons from the Corporate World, Have I Got a Deal for You, Time Management, Team Working, Selling Skills, Negotiating Skills.

14

Pharmacy design, merchandising and stock control

Kirit Patel

Introduction

Historically, consumers were accustomed to buying a whole range of products, including toiletries, baby products and household goods, from the local pharmacy. Aggressive competition from the supermarkets in the last decade has transformed the shopping patterns of the consumer. First went the basic toiletry requirements such as toothpaste and shampoos, followed by an erosion of baby products and vitamins and finally General Sales List (GSL) medicines, their demise exacerbated by the abandonment of retail price maintenance in 2001. The sales of Pharmacy-Only (P) medicines are also under threat as more supermarkets open in-store pharmacies. Pharmacists have tended to focus on the dispensing side of the business, but with falling dispensing remuneration there is a need to maximise the potential of other sectors and services. Associated with this is a requirement for well-designed premises, good merchandising and efficient stock management.

Design problems

The pharmacy depicted in Figure 14.1 has a poor layout, with far too little space allocated to P medicines, much of it behind the counter. GSL medicines are also poorly merchandised, again with many displayed behind the counter, thus decreasing their visibility. There could be a tendency for the shop to appear untidy, with dump bins and manufacturers' display stands randomly scattered around.

A typical pharmacy often does not have enough visibility given to its aisles. The display gondolas are high and obstruct vision on other shelves around the pharmacy. Handwritten posters in the windows should be replaced by proper promotional signage promoting the pharmacy services. Inadequate lighting, protruding stands, shelves and

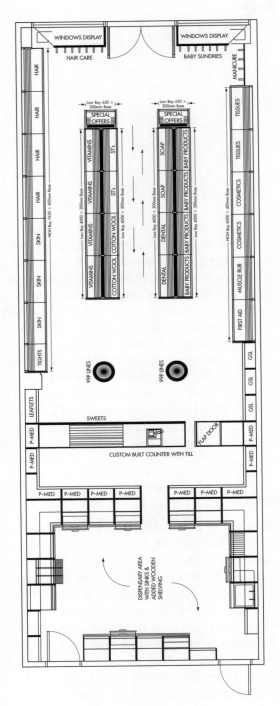

Figure 14.1 Layout 1.

metal pegs can cause health and safety hazards and could also discourage customers from shopping in the pharmacy. Because this layout does not have any provision for a consultation room, the pharmacist/patient interaction is reduced. The layout encourages customers to take the shortest route to the medicine counter and impulse shopping is minimised as a result.

A raised floor behind the counter, and in the dispensary, would be beneficial. Better visibility would increase security. Often in these types of pharmacies, the manufacturers' displays are acquired as an afterthought and hinder rather than enhance sales. Pharmacies such as these do not promote a healthcare image and this could put off customers from shopping within, and thus lead to a loss of prescription business as well as other products. It is essential to retain the focus on healthcare.

Refitting a pharmacy

Shop fitting should be thought of as an investment and one should bear in mind that the return on capital should relate to the perceived increase in sales. It is an expensive exercise and at the outset it would be prudent to evaluate whether the pharmacy is in the correct location. Often as a result of changing shopping patterns for example the opening of a supermarket or car park facility, the current location of a pharmacy may no longer be ideal.

Before a refit the following items should be carefully considered:

- Has the focus of the business changed? Is it the ideal location? Should it be relocated?
- Is it due for a total refit or a facelift? Does the shop front/fascia need to be changed?
- Is the door in the right location to improve customer flow?
- Does it need a new shop front?
- What is the budget? Is it adequate?
- Should you refit the front shop or the dispensary first?
- Do the electrics need total rewiring?
- Is there provision for plumbing in the right area of the proposed dispensary?
- Have you examined the plan of the proposed refit?
- Does the plan create an even flow of customers within the pharmacy?
- Have you discussed the time and period of refit?
- How are you going to dispose of old stands and fittings?
- Does the shop need destocking?

- Is there inventory that can be marked down and sold off?
- Is the inventory appropriate for the purpose and location of the shop? Have local factors been taken into consideration?
- Are there adequate storage boxes for taking goods off the shelves during refit?
- Have you marked out on the plan the areas where various categories will be displayed?
- Is there adequate shelving in the different parts of the pharmacy to cater for the individual categories?
- What will you do with discontinued stock?
- How can the staff be involved in this refit and/or relocation?
- Does the layout encourage customers to shop?
- Is there adequate staffing resources, or does temporary help need to be recruited?

A refit to the existing pharmacy could be best undertaken as follows.

- Examine the door opening in order to ensure even flow of customers in all areas.
- Maximise the display shelving along the side walls.
- Provide for adequate seats in the waiting area near the dispensary.
- Create sufficient storage cupboards on top of the shelves.
- Products prone to impulse shopping should be positioned where there is maximum flow of customers.

It is important to design the new layout in order to:

- maximise customer flow within the store
- improve security
- maintain the health and safety of customers
- improve merchandising and the display of products
- reduce pilferage
- look bright and welcoming.

Space allocation should reflect the breakdown of sales of various categories of products. High-value products need to be positioned on or nearer the counter, where they are clearly visible to staff. It is important to involve staff, as their full co-operation is crucial in the successful refitting of a pharmacy. Any unplanned refit can be stressful and demotivating and could damage the business.

Suggested pharmacy design

An improved pharmacy design is shown in Figure 14.2.

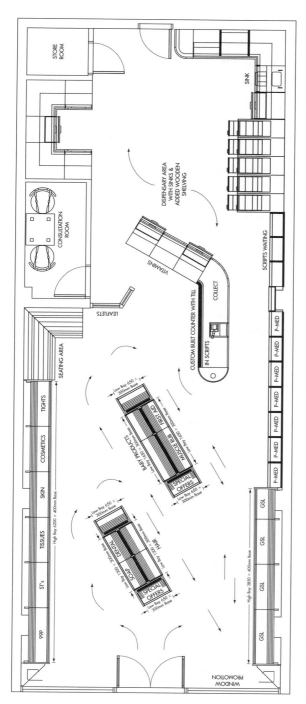

Figure 14.2 Layout 2.

Space allocation

The new design, with a focus on healthcare, allocates more space to GSL and P medicines and vitamins and minerals.

- No less than half the shop area should be allocated to healthcare.
- P medicines on the side would give increased display – floor to ceiling.
- Vitamins are on open display in front of the dispensary.
- The toiletries range would need to be reduced in order to create more space for display of health-related products.

The possibility of relaxation of regulations preventing the display and self-selection of P medicines should be borne in mind and if this were to happen, then the size of the counter should be reduced to a minimum and the open display area of P medicines increased.

There should be ample space for customers to shop freely; they should not be made to feel claustrophobic. The shop space should be open and free and care should be taken that as time goes by this discipline is maintained. Manufacturers' stands are not scattered around on the shop floor or obstructing the windows. A seating area should be provided for patients awaiting prescriptions. The space adjacent to the waiting area is used to display patient information leaflets, encouraging an uptake of health information and related services.

Dispensary and counselling areas

The Royal Pharmaceutical Society of Great Britain (RPSGB) also imposes specifications with regards to layout of dispensary of a new pharmacy including the provision of an adequate wet and dry bench, and provision of private counselling areas. The plan of a new pharmacy has to be approved by the regulatory body and before approval the inspector may decide to visit the premises for verification. The open plan raised dispensary also offers better supervision of the shop and helps reduce pilferage. The dispensary should be fitted in such a manner that it improves ergonomics. The height of the dispensing bench should possibly reflect the heights of the pharmacist and dispensing staff working there. If there are any other obstructions or blind spots, care should be taken to avoid placing expensive stock behind these, as they would be outside the field of vision. This improves not only supervision but also the security of the shop. The consultation area is situated in an area unsuitable for displaying other products.

Counter and till positions

Proper use should be made of the counter in order to improve the display of P medicines further. A delicatessen type of counter can help increase display of P medicines. The majority of sales in most pharmacies take place at the rear of the shop near the medical counter and this is an ideal position for the cash till. If necessary it is better to have two tills near each other, rather than at different ends of the store. By positioning both tills near each other and near the dispensary, one can improve service level at busy times, as there would be more staff available to serve the customers. It is important to take into account the way the door opens in deciding the position of the till and gondolas within the shop, i.e. if the door opens from left to right then position the till and the counter along the right-hand wall and vice versa.

On one end of the counter is a till and the continuation of it is used by the pharmacist.

Display gondolas

The gondolas must not be more than 1 m high to avoid creating blind spots. Such a placement of the gondolas forces customers to walk along most aisles. This improves visibility that could stimulate impulse buying, as customers would visit evenly various areas of the shop. This reduces 'dead' areas within the pharmacy.

Window and fascia

Marketing begins outside the shop. The fascia and windows should be clean and neat. Adequate provision should be made for the window display and consideration given as to whether a canopy is necessary to protect products in the window from glare. The fascia should be well illuminated and visible from a distance. Care should be taken not to put too much information on the fascia. It is important to project a correct image. Space should also be allocated in the window to promote the services offered in the pharmacy, e.g. diagnostic testing, prescription collection and delivery. This information should be changed for fresh material about every 6 weeks.

Fixtures and fittings

A higher quality of finishing near the area selling perfumery and cosmetics would be appropriate in an affluent area compared with shops selling only essential products in a deprived area. Although wooden fittings are more attractive they tend to be expensive. All the display stands are incorporated in the fittings along the side walls. Instead of using some of the manufacturers display units, more space should be allocated along the wall for slat panels and display hooks where these promotional products could be displayed. When one considers the 80/20 rule, 20% of the products account for the majority of the sales. By making judicious use of the side walls, the pharmacy will be able to carry the fast selling ranges. This, coupled with appropriate ordering, will reduce the need to buy extra volume, thus reducing inventory costs. The slat panels should be positioned such that they enhance the sales of that category. More use of these should be made near baby products. Having considered the general layout one needs to allocate linear footage to different categories. Proper space should be allocated for display units to ensure the shop does not look cluttered. One then needs to consider how many shelves there should be on each bay, as not all products are of the same size. It is advisable to have more shelves on the bays selling these product categories – baby foods, hair colorants, soaps, medicines, toothpaste, etc. Depth of the shelves should increase downwards for better visual display. This will help improve merchandising, increase sales and enhance business and also improves working conditions and staff morale. Better motivated staff are more productive. Support-staff training should be such that the total focus is on selling a service of which the product is only a part of the transaction.

Electrics

With regards to the electrical work there should be adequate power outlets in strategic places and the shop should be well lit. One should consider if a complete rewiring is overdue. The ticket edging on the shelves should be wide enough to incorporate Electronic Point of Sale (EPoS) produced pricing labels and be able to clip on to it the point of sales material. In shops located in areas of high crime levels and pilferage, CCTVs may be placed with a video recorder as a deterrent. There should be proper signposting of various categories and advice/consultation points in order to guide customers.

Stock management (see also Chapter 12)

Effective stock management in a well-designed pharmacy is a basic retailing skill and forms a sound basis for effective management. Proper control and management of stock is crucial to:

- achieve improved margin
- prevent a build-up of inventory
- minimise loss of sales
- minimise wastage.

Range of stock

There is no standard inventory applicable to every pharmacy, however the core inventory of fast-selling and popular brands may be similar. In each category of products there are the market leaders that should be stocked. Apart from the core inventory, one needs to adapt the inventory to suit the needs of the local community The demographic profile of the location would give a good indication of the purchasing power and local preferences (see Chapter 13). The size, layout and location of the pharmacy and local demographics of potential customers should determine the product category, range and number of variants kept.

Carlos Criado-Perez, CEO of Safeway and responsible for initiating the supermarket's 'think local' strategy, said, 'Shopping is about stimulation'. Even the multinational supermarkets realise the importance of local environment, and in spite of their size, supermarkets such as Safeway have attempted to adapt to local needs. Safeway was taken over by the Yorkshire-based company William Morrison plc in 2004.

Pharmacy stock can be broken down into the healthcare and the non-healthcare ranges. The healthcare range consists of Prescription-only Medicines (POMs) in the dispensary, the P medicines behind the counter, and GSL medicines on open display, e.g. vitamins and minerals, health preparations such as dressings, plasters, appliances and diagnostic equipment. The non-healthcare range would consist of toiletries, skincare products, cosmetics, perfumery, photographic and baby products and sundry items.

In the health centre pharmacy, due to the constraints of space and the high number of prescriptions, the space for dispensing products would be more extensive, with the balance used up for other medicinal products. An average pharmacy, say about 60 square metres in size, would keep the entire product category but not all brands, variants or sizes. The larger shops, over 120 square metres, would tend to carry an extended brand range. The financial resources available would also affect the quantities of each product in the inventory. SWOT and PEST analysis would also help decide on products (see Chapter 12). Pharmacy owners over a period introduce new lines without necessarily discontinuing others to make space. Inventory range should be regularly reviewed and any lines that are not sold easily discontinued, with new products being introduced as applicable. This is especially important to do when a new pharmacy is acquired. Often decisions to stock a line are made on the buyer's personal preferences and may not reflect the needs of the community.

Quantity of stock

The number of linear metres of shelf space available to display the stock must be considered carefully. Many independent pharmacies carry far too large an inventory. As a result the fast selling lines are lost among the many slow sellers. This not only reduces sales of popular lines, but also ties up financial capital (see Chapter 10). There is ample industry data about the best and the worst sellers of each category and these should form a good guideline. It is important that one offers a complete range of certain products, e.g. hair colours. One cannot simply choose certain variants of popular shades as it would give customers the perception of a poor stock holding. Only by keeping a full range will one be able to expand sales of the particular hair colorant brand.

Stock control

There is a substantial cost involved in holding the inventory. Good stock rotation reduces the cost of holding and minimises wastage of inventory. Reduced stock holding helps improve space allocation and reduces insurance and handling costs. Proper stock control through increased frequency of ordering can help maintain optimum stock levels. In the case of pharmacy the *just in time*, or *one for one* ordering is done electronically. Stock should be priced so as to maximise profits but not at the expense of reducing the stock turn and stocking up slow sellers. Regular checking of expiry dates should be conducted in the dispensary, especially with regards to lines stored in the fridge, as these tend to have short expiry dates.

One can also adopt a manual system to identify slow-selling ethical products. Six different coloured dots representing a quarter of a year may be used on dispensary medicines. Every quarter, a dot is added and this helps identify the actual slow sellers. If all six colours were to appear, it would mean that that single pack was not used up in 18 months. Likewise those products which are fast sellers would not have more than one or two dots.

Purchasing

The practice of obtaining discounts on purchases from wholesalers is highlighted in Chapter 4 and can be a highly significant source of increased profit. However, one of the constraining factors, faced especially by independent contractors, is that they have to commit to purchasing a large quantity of their products from the full line wholesalers in return for financial assistance. This trade-off is important to understand before accepting the guarantee scheme.

Manual or electronic systems will help control the purchasing of products. If using a manual system it is important to record the frequency and quantity ordered, as well as stock on the shelves at the time of order. Modern EPoS systems enable these functions to be carried out automatically. The EPoS system can be configured to order stock on a one-for-one basis, or 'outers' as the sales take place.

Dispensary

In the dispensary the patient medication record (PMR) computers have a software programme to allow stock control, but many pharmacies simply operate on a 1–1 replacement from the wholesalers, not wishing to trust the automated system entirely. The software in both EPOS and PMR can be programmed so that orders automatically go to the preferred supplier. To hold optimum stock the frequency of reordering needs to be increased. In case of the dispensary it is usually on a twice-daily basis from a full-line supplier and daily from short-line suppliers but at a higher discount (see Chapter 4). Most of the generics and parallel imported are generally purchased from shortliners. In the case of the dispensary the optimum stock level can be reached by increasing the frequency of ordering. Often an annual stock turn as high as fifteen may be achieved.

Although nearly 60% of prescriptions dispensed in UK pharmacies are for generics, they make up only 20% of the drug cost. Historically the short-liners have used the competitive pressure to increase their market share. They have been able to do so by stocking a smaller range of popular products and giving fewer deliveries. The parallel imported (PI) products, branded ethical products, made in other European countries at cheaper prices, are imported, repackaged and relabelled in English and sold mainly by the shortline wholesalers at a much lower price. The full-line wholesalers have recently entered the market by setting up their own shortline companies, e.g. OTC Direct, a subsidiary of Unichem and Trident, is a subsidiary of AAH. If using PI products pharmacists should ensure that they have marketing authorisations granted by the UK authorities.

Counter medicines

With counter medicines economies of scale are important. There is a trade-off between buying in bulk at a greater discount and increasing the frequency of ordering to reduce stock holding. The average stock turn is approximately six times a year, equal to a stock turn every 8 weeks. Many independent pharmacies are members of buying groups and thus benefit from reduced level of stock purchases whilst qualifying for higher discounts.

Promotional allowance

Promotional allowance from the manufacturers should be negotiated at the time of purchase and utilised to promote the special offers. It is important to compare prices from many wholesalers as these can vary enormously. This is true for generics and PIs from short-line wholesalers. Although the exercise is time-consuming it is financially rewarding as any discount enhances the bottom line. Full advantage should be taken of seasonal bonus deals offered by manufacturers on a cyclical basis. Some manufacturers tend to negotiate a contract price for a certain period. It is important to take advantage of cyclical promotions and buy sufficient stock until the next promotional period. One should always avoid the temptation to buy up heavily discounted products if they are slower sellers.

The Internet

Current advances in technology have brought business-to-business e-commerce companies, which allow an owner to shop around on the Internet and obtain the best prices. The growth of this form or purchasing has been slow, but is expected to pick up in years to come (see Chapter 15).

Dealing with slow lines

Care should be taken before purchasing seasonal lines, as any unsold lines will eat into the profit. It is unlikely that this would be sold until the next year and then the packing could have changed, making the older stock obsolete and difficult to sell. In the case of toiletries, some whole-salers have devised schemes that offer discounts for split purchases. EPOS systems can also reorder stock when it reaches a minimum level. The system could also identify slow lines. Slower lines are reordered on a one-for-one basis and attract a lower or no discount while good discounts can be obtained for faster moving lines.

In the dispensary, the PMR functions can be used to identify products not dispensed since a particular date and this can be sold to the other pharmacy contractors by advertising for free in pharmacy journals or by use of Business to Business (B2B) stock transfer programme offered by certain e-businesses. The biannual stock takes by outside agencies are also a good indicator of stock turn and pilferage. Stock takers should be briefed to remove any stock with less than 3 months' expiry date. Some manufacturers representatives will exchange this stock for new stock. This not only saves money, but is good practice for clinical governance, i.e. preventing the dispensing of short-dated stock to patients.

Merchandising

The Seven Rights

As mentioned on page 277, the product categories should be placed in a logical order. Merchandising is a retail science developed for self-selection shopping. It is often defined as the Seven Rights:

- displaying the Right product
- in the Right place
- in the Right quantity
- in the Right condition
- in the Right way
- at the Right price
- at the Right Time.

Category management

The seven rights of merchandising are supplemented by market share data and local knowledge. One would expect to find related product categories adjacent to one another, for example, hair sprays and hair colour together and shampoo next to conditioner. Similarly, one would normally seek dental products next to the bath section and sanitary products with other paper products. This is known as **category management** (see Chapter

13). To create visual impact, it is important to merchandise a category in a vertical block. It is also important that whilst standing in one location, an entire product category be visible so it would be easy to spot products. Placing the signpost brands in the middle would draw the shopper to that category. Oil of Olay being a signpost brand would be expected to be placed in the middle of skincare range and similarly Kleenex in the paper products range. Certain products, due to their nature and the size, would need to be kept on the lower shelf, for example products in large glass bottles such as Lucozade. In all it is important to give more space allocation to the best selling products. Categories may be subdivided if necessary.

EPOS tills have an in-built programme that can give shelf allocation based on unit sales and also on value of sales. A good example of this would be acne creams in a separate block from other skincare products for the elderly. Therefore a middle-aged woman walks past and reaches the signposted division, whilst the teenager would not necessarily have to browse through other skincare ranges to locate acne cream of choice. Research has shown that the best selling shelf is the one located 14° below eye level. Fastest selling products or those that generate more revenue due to high unit sales should be placed in this premium position.

Positioning products on the shelf

Vitamins and mineral supplements and GSL medicines should be placed on open display for self-selection and not behind the counter. The larger size packs should be kept on the right-hand side of the aisle as the majority of people are right-handed and tend to pick the product from the right. This may increase the value of the sale by inadvertently encouraging sales of large pack sizes. It is important to create an image that you are offering quality, good range and value for money. There should be no empty gaps between the products which should be arranged from front to back and packs should be brought forward as they are sold to create a good visual display.

Planograms

Planogrammers take data collected from EPOS systems and combine it with their knowledge of the potential customer to create a shelf design that encourages more sales. A planogram is a detailed map that determines where every product in an establishment should be situated. It details not only in what area every product should be placed but also on which shelf every item should be accommodated. Shelf by shelf, aisle by aisle, the planogram assigns selling potential to every item in a store. It is now possible to customise assortments of products to fit the patterns of demand for each individual store, which will increase sales while reducing inventories. Space management also helps to present an eye-catching display and links products that consumers are tempted to buy along with their intended purchase. Planogramming produces a stocking plan such that merchandise fits on the shelves and in the fixtures when it arrives at the store. It helps to increases sales and improve inventory turns. Several wholesalers and manufacturers provide planograms for different categories of products.

Special offers

Any special offers should be well promoted by use of shelf barkers or 'talkers' (generally point of sale display). The use of window posters and other promotional materials increases the sales of the products advertised. These should be changed regularly. Dump bins should be used for promoting special offers rather than 'dumping' slow-selling items. Proper signage directs consumers to relevant categories. Display materials could be obtained from manufacturers and wholesalers. Full use should be made of the EPOS tills to choose the inventory, the number of facings given to each and also to discontinue slow sellers to make space for the introduction of new lines. This free space on the shelf can be used for increasing the facing given to popular selling products. Furthermore by flagging up these products by use of the point of sale material, one creates an appropriate impression of giving good value for money. The supermarkets are extremely good at creating this image, even though their prices may not always be the lowest. In fact up until 2002 all medicines were price maintained and could be sold no cheaper in supermarkets or other larger stores. It is important to make use of all the reporting functions of the EPOS to help select and market the inventory. Full use should be made of manufacturers counter medicines display units. Similarly all medicinal and non-medicinal products advertised on national TV and press should also be promoted. One needs to take advantage of impulse shopping by placing products in a frequently visited location so that sales are maximised.

Further reading

McGoldrick P. *Retail Marketing*, 2nd edn. Maidenhead: McGraw Hill, 2002.
Varley R. *Retail Product Management: Buying and Merchandising*. London: Routledge, 2001.

15

e-Pharmacy – Information Technology and the Internet as a business resource

Lee Kayne and Rebecca Kayne

Introduction

In 2002, the BBC reported that more people than ever are turning to the Internet as a source of health information for themselves and their families[1] and both the quantity and scope of information available is truly astounding. There are websites with information on every imaginable ailment and every conceivable type of therapy. A search for 'aromatherapy' yields in excess of 1.5 million results or 'hits', 'homeopathy' over 1 million and 'gemstone therapy' almost 20 000. There are online doctors who will diagnose your ailments and online pharmacies providing not only health and beauty products, but full prescription services. There is also a wealth of information available for the professional community. It is not only academic communities that have websites these days – virtually every professional body and business has some online presence. As a marketing tool, the Internet is unsurpassed – it allows even the smallest business to cost-effectively reach a global market.

Healthcare and the Internet

Advances in information technology have had direct implications for the delivery of healthcare, both in primary and secondary care. The speed and nature of communications has changed drastically with the invention of email, web conferencing and entirely new mediums for the sharing of data. Electronic transmission of referrals, test results, medical records, appointment bookings, prescriptions and a centralised NHS Net are all at various stages of development within the NHS and pharmacists are involved in trials of electronic prescribing around the country.

Such advances have also had a major influence on the way pharmacies are managed. If we consider the traditional definition of 'pharmacy' as 'the science or profession of dispensing drugs used as medical treatments' or 'a place where the drugs used for treating diseases are dispensed or sold', we notice that the *business* aspect is not evident. Nowadays, a pharmacy also supplies wide-ranging healthcare-related products, advice and services to the public. In his book *Mind Your Own Business*, Dr Terry Maguire states that the keys to a successful business are vision and strategy (details available from http://www.dotpharmacy. com/myob.html). Pharmacy – like any other business – must be willing to adapt its vision and its strategy to changing conditions, whether they be political, social, economic or indeed technological.

The multimedia marketplace of the Internet, the world wide web, has presented a new channel for business. Before the emergence of this new global technology, sales took place mainly from shop premises. Some beauty products, vitamins and health supplements were available from representatives or via mail order but the scope and availability of these services was often limited. On the Internet, anyone and everyone can have a website and can sell to a potentially global customer pool. With only minimal financial outlay and limited technical knowledge, small businesses can set up their own websites and pharmacies can take advantage of this in many ways:

- Using the Internet to advertise their business to a wider catchment area.
- Providing mail order services to a worldwide market.
- Providing information in specialised areas of pharmacy practice.
- Creating and maintaining business-to-business and professional-to-professional connections.
- Sourcing cheaper supplies.
- Providing and gathering professional information such as continuing education resources and conferences.

Whether there is a place for pharmacy on the Internet is no longer in doubt – e-Pharmacy is very much established in several forms. The problems facing this emerging branch of professional activity are qualitative – many legal and ethical issues are yet to be addressed as existing professional regulations and guidelines have not kept pace with the developments of new technologies. Indeed, there is no current UK legislation that deals specifically with the sale of medicines over the Internet.

According to the UK Medicines and Healthcare products Regulatory Agency (MHRA), the new body formed in April 2003 from the merging of the Medicines Control Agency and the Medical Devices Agency, the rules laid out in the Medicines Act 1968 still apply, despite the vast changes in technology. The Royal Pharmaceutical Society of

Great Britain has amended its Code of Ethics to deal with some of the issues presented by the Internet but only has jurisdiction over pharmacies with registered premises in Great Britain (Scotland, England and Wales – pharmacies in Northern Ireland are governed by a separate body). A 'virtual' pharmacy selling prescription medicines to UK residents falls outside their control and it is unclear as to who should be responsible for regulating these sites. A number of accreditation programmes do exist for healthcare and pharmacy-related websites, both in Europe and worldwide, but these are in the early stages of development and are generally voluntary.

Critical issues requiring examination include:

* the policing of 'virtual' pharmacies (specifically with respect to the sale of pharmacy- and prescription-only medicines);
* regulating the marketing and advertising of medicines on the web;
* assessing the quality of advice and healthcare information available on the web and the question of self-regulation, including the relative success or failure of voluntary accreditation programmes.

In this chapter, we will consider the opportunities for pharmacy on the Internet and the current guidelines and regulations.

History of the Internet

To gain a better understanding of what the Internet is, it is interesting to consider its origins in the Cold War. In the 1960s, the US Defense Department felt that, in the event of a conflict telephone exchanges would be targeted, crippling communication systems. A project was initiated to develop an exchange-less system in which electronic messages would automatically seek the best route to their destination on the network. If one route was closed off for any reason, the message would simply find another. The principles of this new system were first fully tested in 1969 by scientists who successfully exchanged data between five sites in different locations, known as 'nodes'. This network grew to 37 nodes by 1972, becoming known as ARPAnet (Advanced Research Project Agency network) and set early precedents for the technology that would eventually become the Internet. During the 1970s and 1980s, this system continued to grow within the scientific and military communities, with personal messages as well as data and information being exchanged – the concept of 'email' was born. This was further developed in the 1980s by the US National Science Foundation who expanded ARPAnet access into the government community and, in order to distinguish new users from existing ones, added the .gov, .mil and .edu suffixes to electronic addresses. The networks grew rapidly with users all over the world each having a unique address identifying them and their user type and it was not long before commercial networks were established and linked to form a truly global community. Individuals with no particular affiliation could now sign up to an Internet Service Provider (ISP) with an individual address and, with the increasing power and decreasing size and costs of home computers, this new communication medium was established.[2]

However, the Internet did not truly begin its metamorphosis from specialised communications system for the government, military and academic communities to global information depository until the early 1990s, with the development of the world wide web (www). This is the name given to the multimedia part of the Internet, which contains documents available for public access through specialised software 'browsers', the most popular of which are Microsoft Explorer for PC and Apple Safari for Mac. Websites offering a range of information and services began to appear, slowly at first but soon exploding into the millions of sites available today.

Communications

The importance of electronic communication via the Internet cannot be underestimated. Email allows for instantaneous messages to friends, colleagues, service providers or suppliers regardless of where they are located. Correspondence and consultation on professional matters has never been easier as experts in the field may easily be contacted. Businesses also benefit from easier contact with non-local suppliers and potential customers.

Using the Internet, other forms of communication are also now easier. The traditional telephone 'conference call' has given way to Internet phones and video conferencing via cameras connected to the Internet known as 'webcams'. Brainstorming sessions can be conducted remotely via the use of 'virtual whiteboard' technology that allows real-time exchange of notes. Message forums and chat rooms allow for real-time conversations across thousands of miles. Even business administration tasks such as banking and book-keeping can be performed remotely.

For the healthcare professions, email has created a communications medium to share data, documents, expertise, specialist information, obtain supplies and discuss new treatments and approaches. Most email systems cannot be guaranteed as secure, so it is not appropriate for the transfer of sensitive and confidential information, but it is nevertheless a most important tool for less sensitive communications.

The NHS and the Internet

The advances in information technology (IT) in recent years have been astonishing and could not have been predicted even 10 years ago. In 1992 the UK's NHSnet, also known as the NHS Intranet, was developed as a dedicated network for the National Health Service with guaranteed service and availability. It provides a similar range of communication and information services to that of the Internet but in a secure and controlled environment more appropriate for the exchange of healthcare information. Originally connecting about 300 different organisations, NHSnet (http://www.nhsia.nhs.uk/nhsnet) now has in excess of 10 000 connections and is the largest Virtual Private Network (VPN) in Europe.

With such unexpected growth, the capacity and speed of data throughput (known as 'bandwidth') is starting to become insufficient. To address these bandwidth issues and to enable new technologies and services a new network, known as N3, is being developed, and was scheduled to be available in 2004. This IT explosion has largely been fuelled by cheaper, faster and more powerful computers and the rapid growth of the Internet with all its advantages for business, professionals and the public.

A number of now everyday tasks were thought fanciful less than a decade ago and even more advanced developments are becoming available every year. The NHS is working proactively to modernise its systems and procedures. A Department of Health report entitled Delivering IT in the NHS, published in June 2002, clearly set out the intended major future developments:[3]

- Connecting all NHS services to a central network.
- Electronic transfer of test results.
- Electronic booking of appointments.
- Electronic healthcare records.

Another key component of the IT programme for the NHS, and perhaps of more interest to pharmacists specifically, is the move away from paper-based dispensing and towards full Electronic Transfer of Prescriptions (ETP). A variety of models have been tested, some completely paperless and some using a combination of paper and electronic prescribing.

In England, a TRANSCRIPT pilot in East Hampshire used direct electronic messaging from the GP to a nominated pharmacy for repeat prescriptions and bar-coded paper prescriptions for acute prescribing.[4] The PHARMACY2U pilot in Leeds, Stockport and London uses direct electronic messaging from the GP to the Pharmacy2u central office for both repeat and acute prescribing and is now moving into a second phase, called E-SCRIPT.[4,5] The FLEXISCRIPT pilot in Peterborough uses a 'relay' or 'pull' approach. The GP sends the prescription electronically to a central server for both repeat and acute prescribing and at the same time issues the patient with a bar-coded paper prescription. A pharmacist participating in the pilot can scan the barcode to initiate download of the prescription from the server. The advantage of this system is that the patient can take the prescription to any pharmacy, whether participating in the pilot or not.[4,6]

By the end of 2002, approximately 20 000 electronic prescriptions had been processed by the three schemes and they are now in discussion with the Department of Health and the Prescription Pricing Authority to develop a common model to be implemented across England.[5]

In Scotland, there is an ETP pilot being carried out in Ayrshire at the time of writing that uses the same approach as FLEXISCRIPT. There is also an extended trial of Electronic Prescribing and Administration (EPA) at the Ayr Hospital. Like the ETP trials, EPA aims to replace the existing paper-based hospital procedures with an electronic system.[7] A repeat dispensing pilot is also being undertaken by Alison Strath, principal pharmaceutical officer at the Scottish Executive Health Department. This pilot involves the issue of up to six 'master' and 'slave' prescriptions, which use the same type of barcodes as the Scottish ETP pilot. The ultimate aim is to bring together supplementary prescribing, repeat dispensing and ETP into a single e-Pharmacy initiative for Scotland.[8]

The Internet as an information resource

The Internet, and especially the world wide web, is the most exhaustive and freely accessible information resource available today. 'Traditional' sources of health information are still available: the family GP, the community pharmacist, national telephone helplines, etc., but with growing pressure on these resources to speed up patient throughput and generate more revenue, it can be difficult for a healthcare professional to spend a significant amount of time with any one patient. When gathering information on the Internet, the patients are limited only by their own time and resources and not by the schedule of a busy professional.

The Internet also allows a patient to be more proactive in the management of their own health. A patient might use the Internet to research treatments for their condition to discuss with their GP or to find support groups and information on treatments and therapies in use in other parts of the world. Others might use online doctors to find answers to a particularly embarrassing problem. In all such cases, of course, one hopes that the Internet is being used in addition to the personal care of GPs and pharmacists, rather than as a sole healthcare provider. Increasingly it is the community pharmacist that is being called upon to consider the wealth of information that a patient may obtain and provide an expert 'filter and focus' service to help the patient understand what might be appropriate for their particular needs.

There is a wealth of professional information designed specifically for members of the public. NHS Direct Online (http://www.nhsdirect. nhs.uk) offers self-help guides and advice on healthy living as well as a searchable database of local resources. You can look up a GP, pharmacy, hospital, dental surgery, walk-in centre or optician anywhere in England by full or partial postcode. There are also similar NHS websites for Scotland, Wales and Northern Ireland. Askyourpharmacist (http://www. askyourpharmacist.co.uk) is the National Pharmaceutical Association's (NPA) website specifically designed for consumers. It contains a searchable pharmacy finder as well as downloadable Acrobat PDF files on a range of subjects relating to women's, men's and children's health. For example, a fact sheet on chickenpox provides information on how the illness is spread, symptoms, recommended treatment and under what circumstances you should contact your GP. A similar service is provided by the independent community pharmacy organisation, Numark (http:// www.numarkpharmacists.co.uk). On an international level, NOAH (New York Online Access to Health), http://www.noah-health.org (not to be confused with the UK National Office of Animal Health which uses the same acronym) offers information, links and resources on more than 50 different topics including arthritis, asthma, cancer, complementary medicine, cosmetic surgery, heart conditions, mental health, pregnancy and childbirth and sleep disorders in both English and Spanish.

Resources specifically aimed at the professional community are also widespread. Health-News (http://www.health-news.co.uk) compiles the latest information on research and clinical trials, reports from the British Medical Association and the Medical Research Council, a guide to health events and television programming and links for a variety of specialties. Pharmweb (http://www.pharmweb.net) is a website developed specifically for the pharmaceutical community. Launched in 1994, it now has approximately 25 000 registered users. The site includes information on job vacancies, conferences, pharmacy education world-wide, mailing lists for drug alerts, a directory of health-related societies, and even discussion forums for matters relating to pharmacy, pharma-ceutical services and health issues. The Association of the British Pharmaceutical Industry (ABPI) (http://www.abpi.org.uk), the Depart-ment of Health (DOH) (http://www.doh.gov.uk), the Medicines and Healthcare products Regulatory Agency (MHRA) (http://www.mhra. gov.uk), and the Royal Pharmaceutical Society of Great Britain (RPSGB) (http://www.rpsgb.org.uk) all have informative websites and across Europe there are websites for the International Conference on Harmon-isation (ICH) (http://www. ich.org), the Veterinary ICH (http://www. vich.eudra.org), and the European Agency for the Evaluation of Medi-cinal Products (EMEA) (http://www.emea.eu.int). The European Direc-torate for the Quality of Medicines (EDQM) have an excellent site (http://www.pheur.org) where an online version of the European Phar-macopoeia, 4th edition, may be browsed.

Professional education

One of the most important professional uses of the Internet is undoubt-edly in education. Distance learning schemes have been in operation for many years, but there is now a trend towards e-Learning – electronic distribution methods can reach a wider audience at costs far lower than those involved in the printing and postal distribution of traditional packages. Within the pharmacy profession, The Centre for Postgradu-ate Pharmacy Education (CPPE) and the equivalent bodies in the rest of the UK (NES, WCPPE, NICPPET) are at the forefront of this new style of education delivery, with eLearning packages available from their websites (see Appendix 1).

Establishing a web presence

The first, and arguably the most important, choice to be made when setting up a new website is the domain name and there are a number of companies who can register the domain name of your choice. This may then be purchased as a package containing space for your website and individual email addresses bearing the new domain name, e.g. dispensary @citypharmacy.co.uk. When most internet service providers (ISPs) will often provide web space free of charge, is a customised domain name really necessary? Web space provided by an ISP will often be accessed using an address such as www.ISPname.co.uk/users/citypharmacy/web/ index.htm, which is obviously not ideal for a company site which should have a distinctive, relevant and memorable address, also known as a Uniform Resource Locater (URL). A domain name such as citypharmacy. co.uk may be purchased relatively inexpensively and fulfils these requirements.

When considering a domain name, there are two important factors.

- Suffix – the most popular (and often most expensive) domain suffix is .com but this may confuse potential site visitors as to the location of the business. A national domain suffix such as .fr, .de, .ca, .co.uk, or uk.com may be preferable for companies based in France, Germany, Canada or the UK respectively.
- Name – this should not only be memorable and representative of the business, but also phonetically straightforward, as the address will often have to be relayed by word of mouth and telephone. Thus, for the example above, a URL of www.citypharmacy.co.uk might be preferable to www.city-pharmacy-anytown.co.uk or www.citpharm.co.uk. If the name required is already taken, try using a slightly different form, e.g. www.thecitypharmacy.co.uk or www.anytowncitypharmacy.uk.com.

Once a domain name has been secured and a hosting package chosen, the information to be contained in the website must be gathered, structured and programmed. Web pages are generally written in HyperText Markup Language (HTML), which contains the text to appear on the page with a number of 'tags' that designate the position, size, style, etc. of that text. These are combined with 'links' to other pages on the same site, external web pages and graphics to build the complete page. As the tags and links of HTML are plain text, web pages can be written in any text editor by an operator with a thorough knowledge of the language and a good reference book. Although this approach gives a good grounding in the basics and is still the method of choice for some website designers, it is time-consuming and most will prefer to use a graphical interface design program. A number of these are available, ranging from the basic Microsoft FrontPage and built-in HTML output tool of Microsoft Word to the advanced Adobe GoLive and Macromedia Dreamweaver.

Professional design companies are also plentiful and, while expensive, will produce a website to any specification using the very latest technologies. In some cases such a service will also manage updates on an ongoing basis.

When a site has been designed, written and tested, it is uploaded onto a server, connected to the Internet and becomes available to the public. A website at this stage is said to be 'live' and, without any further action on the part of the site owners, the keywords contained within the HTML will be remotely indexed by the directories of the Internet – the search engines. This may bring a few casual visitors, but if patients, suppliers, business contacts and customers are to use the website as a point of contact then its existence must be publicised. Company stationery, promotional materials and even dispensing labels might contain the web address.

Online pharmacies

In the early days of the world wide web, there was no such thing as an online pharmacy. Even by the mid-1990s, the number of UK pharmacies with websites was in single figures and a pharmacy providing more than just basic information regarding the business and actually allowing a member of the public to purchase a specific product online was a rarity. By 2000, many businesses had a website and email address – in this technological age, these might be as important to the business as the phone and fax numbers. Most pharmacies now have Internet access and many have their own websites, often provided at minimal or no cost via a professional organisation or supplier.

The range of pharmacy services available on the Internet varies – at one end of the spectrum are pharmacies that use the Internet as an advertising tool. Their home page might provide some basic information about the history of the business, its size, location, contact information and possibly a few photos. For many people the Internet search engine has replaced traditional directories, and so the importance of this online presence is clear. For others, the Internet may be utilised as an additional or, in some cases, the sole revenue stream and online sales of cosmetic products, complementary, P and even POM medicines are increasing.

There are also pharmacies, such as Pharmacy2u (http://www.pharmacy2u.co.uk) and Allcures (http://www.allcures.com), who offer complete online pharmacy services. Private and NHS prescriptions may be dispensed and pharmacy and GSL medicines, vitamins and minerals, personal and healthcare items, baby care, disability and lifestyle equipment are also available 24 hours a day, 7 days a week. Individual direct consultation with a qualified pharmacist via telephone or email is available whenever necessary. Supply is based on the 'warehouse' model – all orders and prescriptions are handled at a central site. This could obviously have serious repercussions for local community pharmacies who rely on prescription fees of less than £1 and OTC sales as major revenue streams of their business. For this reason, the NPA have intimated that a more preferable scheme would be a 'clicks and mortar' model where online sales would be electronically linked to existing pharmacies.

Legitimate sites such as these are run by qualified pharmacists operating from registered pharmacy premises within Scotland, England or Wales and as such fall under the jurisdiction of the RPSGB. In November 1999, when Pharmacy2u launched as the first online pharmacy in the UK they took a calculated risk. They had to prove to the RPSGB that the standards and procedures that apply to all registered pharmacies were still being met and that they were not contravening any ethical or regulatory issues. By working with the RPSGB, both parties have ensured that proper safeguards and controls were in place to ensure the safety of the public (D Lee, Managing Director, Pharmacy2u, personal communication, 2003).

Specialist fields such as complementary medicine are particularly well suited to the Internet for a number of reasons. While most people will have local access to a pharmacy, not all can provide advice on complementary medicines or a full range of these items. The Internet removes the geographical limits and allows healthcare professionals and the public to easily contact those pharmacists who have the required expertise, even if they are thousands of miles away. Within such a specialist sphere, it is possible for a small, family-run business to compete with a large multinational, as a worldwide customer base can be built without a physical presence in many countries. Mirroring the situation in the high street, it is certainly true that, where specialist pharmacy expertise is sought on the Internet, reputation, quality and individual service are becoming increasingly more important than size. The Internet has, at least to some degree, levelled the playing field.

There is another reason why complementary medicine in particular is suited to the Internet – these items generally do not fall under the same guidelines as pharmacy-only and prescription-only medicines. For example, homeopathic medicines are described by the Medicines Act 1968 as 'medicinal products at high dilutions' and most can be supplied by any retailer who already complies with conditions applicable to the sale of GSL medicines.[9] Therefore, the majority of standard remedies do not require a prescription and they need not be sold under the supervision of a pharmacist. Herbal remedies also have exemptions from many of the licensing requirements and controls on retail sales that apply to other types of medicines, although safety concerns and possible interactions mean that patients should be recommended to seek professional advice before purchasing a herbal remedy online. There are currently no restrictions on the sale of aromatherapy products or flower remedies and these are also widely available online.

There are, however, some companies that use the Internet in less legitimate ways. Some sites sell anti-ageing or anti-cellulite creams of dubious quality and even less certain outcomes. Others go so far as to promote and sell 'lifestyle' drugs such as Prozac, Cialis, Viagra and Xenical. They do not require prescriptions, despite the fact that these are POMs in the UK. Often, all they ask is that the purchaser answer an online questionnaire, usually with the 'correct' answers already filled in. They do not always require proof of any personal information such as age, gender, medical history or other medications the patient may be taking. Anyone with a credit card can purchase these medicines without consulting a doctor, pharmacist or other healthcare professional. Not only do these sites often violate UK regulations regarding both the marketing and sale of such medicines, but they may put members of the public at risk of potentially dangerous, even fatal, interactions and adverse reactions. How do they get away with it? In most cases, simply by exploiting loopholes in legislation and falling through the cracks of jurisdiction.

Legal and ethical issues

The 'openness' of the Internet is also what makes it so potentially dangerous. Advice may be sought and products purchased without the limitations of local resources but this also means that those products and services may not fall under the same laws and guidelines that seek to protect consumers within the UK and those offering advice may not be qualified to appropriate standards. An online pharmacy only falls under the jurisdiction of the RPSGB if it operates from registered pharmacy premises with an address in Scotland, England or Wales. Suspicious sites like those mentioned above can attempt to avoid regulation by basing themselves in other countries or by hiding their actual physical location – appearing to be truly 'virtual'. Many such sites will claim to be based in the UK in order to attract consumers but any attempt to discover an address or phone number will be futile. They may have mirror sites in a number of different countries with a physical base in yet another.

The Medicines Act (see also Chapter 6)

In the UK, the legal controls regarding the manufacture and distribution of medicines are set out in the Medicines Act 1968 and Medicines for Human Use Regulations 1994, by which the production, sale and supply of all medicines are controlled through a strict licensing system. The enforcement of the regulations laid out in the Act is the responsibility of the UK Minister for Health in England and the Minister for Health and Community Care in Scotland. In addition, the RPSGB oversees the Register of Pharmacy Premises and currently has inspection and disciplinary powers over all retail pharmacy premises in Scotland, England and Wales. There are other statutes that have an impact on e-commerce in general including the EU Directive on Distance Selling 1997, the Data Protection Act 1998 and the Electronic Communications Act 2000, but the Medicines Act 1968 is still the primary piece of legislation affecting all forms of retail pharmacy.

According to the Act, every medicine publicly available is assigned to one of three legal categories: Prescription-Only Medicine (POM), Pharmacy (P) or General Sales List (GSL). POM and P medicines can only be sold or supplied from registered pharmacy premises by or under the direct supervision of a pharmacist. POMs must be sold or supplied in accordance with a prescription or requisition from a practitioner and, at present, it is legally required for the pharmacist to be in actual physical possession of the requested document, signed by the practitioner. Thus, prescriptions cannot, as yet, be transmitted electronically except as part of one of the pilot studies currently being conducted. Pharmacy medicines may only be sold or supplied from registered pharmacy premises under a pharmacist's supervision. GSL medicines are those which 'can with reasonable safety be sold or supplied otherwise than by or under the supervision of a pharmacist'.[9] They can be sold from a wider range of premises provided those premises can be closed to the public (i.e. they are lockable) and the medicines are pre-packed. There are also pack size restrictions for some GSL products which may be sold through retail outlets other than a pharmacy.[9]

The MHRA has taken the position that these controls apply 'without distinction to medicines sold or supplied through internet transactions and mail order' (A Ryan, Executive Support, MHRA, personal communication, January 2003), so it would appear that the Internet and mail order sale/supply of medicines are acceptable provided the above requirements are met. If the appropriate requirements are not met, licenses will not be granted and disciplinary action can be taken.

However, the 'virtual' nature of the Internet means that many businesses are still able to supply medicines without regard for such licences or controls. If a company supplies POMs to patients in the UK over the Internet without a prescription, but it is not possible to prove that the company is actually based in the UK, policing by the MHRA is not possible.

However, if the MHRA can identify offenders, they can and do prosecute to the extent of the law. The offender in the November 2002 case of Regina v Groombridge received a custodial sentence of 12 months, with 6 months suspended, when found guilty of supplying Viagra without a prescription via the Internet from his UK company. In addition to being imprisoned, Mr Groombridge was banned from being a company director for 7 years and a later review hearing also imposed a £630000 confiscation order and £12500 costs. At the time of writing, this case is subject to appeal.[10]

Websites that offer questionable services to customers in the UK are often based abroad to escape MHRA regulation. A consumer more concerned with ready availability than with the implications for their health can order POMs, including 'lifestyle' drugs and drugs withdrawn or not licensed in the UK, from any number of foreign sites and have them imported. Surprisingly, HM Customs & Excise concede that this is completely legal without a licence or prescription if the drug is not considered a controlled drug under the Misuse of Drugs Act 1971 and is for personal use. The only exceptions to this are drugs banned under any circumstances such as thalidomide[11] (K O'Sullivan, Policy and Law Enforcement, HM Customs & Excise, personal communication, March 2003). One site based in Hong Kong confirmed that their customs declarations do show the true contents of the packages they despatch. Indeed, according to the Medicines Act 1968, 'No product licence is required for the importation of a medicinal product . . . by any person for administration to himself'.[9]

Code of Ethics

For Internet pharmacies such as Pharmacy2u that operate from registered pharmacy premises, the RPSGB has updated their Code of Ethics and Standards[12] and issued a Professional Standards Directorate Fact Sheet (No. 8: Pharmacy and the Internet)[13] to address some of the specific issues raised by the sale of medicines on the Internet. Section 9 of the Code of Ethics and Standards, entitled 'On-line pharmacy services' states:

The public is entitled to expect the same high quality pharmaceutical care irrespective of whether the service is provided on-line or face-to-face on pharmacy premises. At all times pharmacists must act in the best interests of the patient and seek to provide the best possible health care.

Internet pharmacies must comply with all existing professional requirements relating to the sale or supply of medicines, including the Medicines Act. In addition, they must ensure compliance with the following RPSGB guidelines specifically for pharmacy websites:

- The name of the business owner and the pharmacy address must be clearly displayed.
- Security and confidentiality of all patient information must be ensured.
- All product-related information must comply with marketing regulations.
- All product-related information must include relevant contraindications and side-effects.
- All healthcare advice must be of a high professional standard and the pharmacist providing such advice must be identified.
- Where a P or POM is requested, the pharmacist must ensure that sufficient information is available to correctly assess the request.
- Where a P or POM is provided the pharmacist must ensure that the patient receives sufficient information regarding the safe and effective use of the medicine.
- Where P or GSL medicines, vitamins or minerals are purchased, there must be an opportunity to receive counselling and advice.
- Pharmacists must advise patients to seek a face-to-face consultation at a convenient pharmacy if this is in the patient's best interest.
- The pharmacy must keep records regarding the supply of medicines and the identification of the pharmacist for every supply of a P or POM.

The fact sheet also provides information on how to comply with some of the above guidelines. For example, when purchasing a pharmacy medicine online a health screening questionnaire must be completed in order to enable the pharmacist to fully assess the situation. The fact sheet also specifies that pharmacies must be in possession of an original, written prescription in order to supply a POM.[13] This means that in order to purchase a POM online, you must still post your prescription to the pharmacy before the medicine can be dispensed. Websites that allow purchase of POMs without a prescription are in clear violation of this regulation but, in a similar way to the MHRA, policing by the RPSGB is impossible without evidence of operation from registered pharmacy premises in Great Britain. Some foreign online pharmacies offer to procure prescriptions for POMs from a doctor in their own country.

Global perspectives

United States customs regulations are slightly different to those in the UK – drugs approved by the Food and Drug Administration (FDA), including some controlled substances, may be imported into the USA for personal use in limited quantities (generally no more than 90 dose units). While appearing straightforward, these regulations only concern items specifically bearing an FDA licence – the same drug, manufactured under a different name in a different country may be disallowed.[14]

According to their website, the official advice from the FDA to consumers is:

> Don't purchase from foreign websites at this time because generally it will be illegal to import the drugs bought from these sites, the risks are greater, and there is very little the U.S. government can do if you get ripped off.[14]

Over and above these basic regulations, the FDA also has a 'personal use guidance' policy that relates to the importation of unapproved prescription medication under certain circumstances: the medicine must be used to treat a serious medical condition (i.e. cancer or AIDS); it must be used under the care of a US-licensed doctor or as continuation of treatment begun in a foreign country; it must be for personal use and provided in no more than a 3-month supply; there must be no known similar treatment available domestically. This policy is not law but a guideline for FDA officials, and again specifically prohibits the purchase of foreign-made and licensed versions of drugs already available in the USA.[15]

Interestingly, Internet pharmacies within the USA are licensed and regulated by individual state boards of pharmacy and exact laws can vary from state to state. In cases where there is possible criminal activity within a given State, the State Pharmacy Board will act in conjunction with the Drug Enforcement Agency (DEA) to investigate and, if necessary, prosecute offenders. In other cases, the FDA may send 'cease and desist' warnings by email to suspicious sites – about 30% of sites that receive such communications do cease trading.[15] There is much cross-border trade with Canada where prices of prescription drugs are up to 40% cheaper than in the US.

In **Canada,** it is the policy of the Health Products and Food Branch Inspectorate to permit individuals to import a 3-month supply of a given drug for their own personal use, once during each quarter of the year. In the Enforcement Directorate for this policy, the Inspectorate raises concerns over patients ordering prescription drugs directly from foreign suppliers as a means of avoiding the higher costs of the same drugs available from Canadian suppliers. It recognises that this situation can result in a competitive disadvantage to domestic companies who are compliant with local regulations. Therefore, their importation policy is restricted to persons coming from abroad receiving prescription medication only with pharmacy or hospital labelling. A Special Access Program also exists to allow patients with certain conditions to obtain drugs that are new or not available in Canada.[16]

Instead of policies that may be informally applied and occasionally may be exploited, some countries have preferred to deal with the issue of Internet sales of medicines by supplementing, updating and replacing existing laws or introducing new ones. While it was against existing **New Zealand** law for overseas pharmacies to sell prescription medication to NZ residents without evidence of a written prescription, new legislation introduced in 2000 also made it illegal for NZ Internet pharmacies to sell to overseas customers.[17]

In continental **Europe,** the situation is more complicated, with different regulations existing in the various EC Member States. In some cases these even appear to conflict with Article 28 of the EC Treaty guaranteeing the free movement of goods. In December 2002, the European Court of Justice considered a case against a Dutch Internet-based pharmacy that illustrates the problems in this area.[18]

The focus of this hearing concerns the German Pharmaceutical and Medicine Advertising Act, which, in paragraph 43, prohibits the mail order sale of medicines directly to German patients by foreign pharmacies. Paragraph 73 further states that generally, individuals may not import any medicine into Germany by mail, even from other EU Member States. When a Dutch pharmacy began an Internet operation to supply medicines to German patients by mail order, a practice legal in the Netherlands, German authorities attempted to have their actions prevented by court order and the case was ultimately referred to the European Court of Justice in Luxembourg for a ruling on the compatibility of the German regulations with the EC Treaty.[18]

The German case was built around the landmark Keck/Mithouard ruling of 1993, where it was recognised that, in some cases, certain national regulations regarding procedures for sales could restrict the free movement area if they applied equally domestically and abroad. Thus, they argued, the restrictions on sales of pharmaceuticals by mail order were exempt from the EC Treaty on the grounds that they refer only to procedures of sale to and from Germany and not actual products.[18]

However, in rulings since the original in 1993, the 15 judges of the Court of Justice and the Solicitor General attempted to make the so-called 'Keck Formula' legally less ambiguous and repeatedly raised issues of market access. If distribution regulations in a Member State prevent or impede access to imported goods in the favour of domestically produced ones, it could be argued that there was a contravention of the Treaty on grounds of restriction of free movement. This was rejected by the German plaintiffs in the 2002 case as many pharmaceuticals manufactured outside Germany are readily available without restriction via the whole-saler-pharmacy chain and so the regulations did not prevent patient access to these items, only those being supplied outside this chain. Solic-itors acting for the Dutch pharmacy argued that the basis of the EC Treaty is that the freedom of movement for goods should be guaranteed at every level in every market. Thus, the German regulations introduced an obstacle to market access for pharmacies in other Member States to directly supply patients. The final ruling in this case is still pending at the time of writing, but is being eagerly anticipated in all Member States.[18]

Marketing of medicines

The Medicines Act 1968 also sets out the legal guidelines for the market-ing and promotion of medicinal products in the UK. For the most part, however, it is the Association of the British Pharmaceutical Industry (ABPI), the industry's trade association, which oversees these regulations. The ABPI Code of Practice for the Pharmaceutical Industry regulates the advertising of prescription medicines to health professionals and admin-istrative staff and also assesses information about prescription medicines intended to be made available to the general public. Acceptance of the Code is a condition of membership of the ABPI and non-member com-panies may also give formal agreement to abide by the Code. As a result, the Code of Practice is accepted by almost the entire UK pharmaceutical industry. The Prescription Medicines Code of Practice Authority was set up in 1993 to regulate the ABPI Code of Practice independently of the association.[19]

While promotional activity is necessary to keep the healthcare pro-fession informed of products, their uses and their safety, it is the primary aim of the Code to ensure that such activity is carried out in a responsible and ethical manner. The Code encompasses and extends well beyond the legal requirements set out in the Medicines Act. According to the Code:

- POMs and certain P medicines may not be advertised to the public, only to health professionals.
- Information supplied to health professionals must be objective, fair, accurate, and based on up-to-date evidence.
- Information supplied must not be misleading, either directly or by implication.
- Substantiation of information must be provided to any health professional who requests it.

Clause 21 of the Code of Practice specifically covers promotional materials available on the Internet:

- Access to promotional materials provided on the Internet must be limited to health professionals if that material relates to products that may not legally be advertised to the public.
- Such materials will come within the scope of the Code if they are directed to a UK audience, placed there by a UK company or an affiliate of a UK company and make reference to the availability or use of the medicines in the UK.
- Such materials may be advertised in a 'relevant independently produced electronic journal intended for health professionals' even if the journal can be accessed by members of the public.

While the ABPI Code of Practice guidelines may seem straightforward, issues of jurisdiction and enforcement may again become apparent on closer inspection. The ABPI only has authority over those members of the pharmaceutical industry that have agreed to abide by the Code. Those websites openly advertising and selling prescription medicines will therefore fall outside the jurisdiction of the ABPI.

In October 2000, the ABPI published a position paper on Pharmaceuticals and the Internet[20] setting out its aims to proactively increase the public's awareness of the pharmaceutical industry by improvements in the quality and quantity of information available. The ABPI is also working against the availability of substandard, unlicensed and illegal products over the Internet. These two objectives may be linked in that placing fewer restrictions on the information available to the public will serve to educate the public, increase awareness and reduce the level of custom given to dubious websites. The ABPI have suggested that the way forward lies in company self-regulation and external accreditation of websites.

USA and New Zealand allow the direct advertising of prescription drugs to consumers. As a result the content of manufacturers' websites in these countries reflects a promotional rather than informative bias. The New Zealand situation may change as harmonisation proceeds with Australia. Canada, under pressure from cross-border television, is currently considering whether to allow DTCA.

Controlling content on the Internet

Self-regulation

There is much debate about self-regulation of the Internet, but it is far from clear what this term actually means. Some argue that there should be no national or international government-imposed regulation of Internet content and practices whatsoever, while others would prefer that non-government global committees were established to fulfil a regulatory role. Although self-regulation is unlikely to work in practice without some form of legislation to support it, such legislation would have to address issues of privacy, censorship and jurisdiction. Not surprisingly, views on these issues vary from country to country, further complicating any form of global enforcement.

Legal regulation

The private sector approach of the USA conflicts with EU directives on privacy. EU authorities cannot compel US service providers to reveal the identity of website authors even where there is suspicious or even potentially criminal content.[21] In addition, there are US laws that assert jurisdiction over foreign nationals in their own countries – the US Anti-Cybersquatting Consumer Protection Act (ACPA) became law in December 1999 and specifies US ownership of the three most popular top-level domain names: .com, .net and .org, by virtue of the physical location of the international registry in the State of Virginia. Therefore, under the ACPA, Virginian courts have legal authority in all cases where one of these domains is involved, even where all parties concerned are based outside the USA. The first case to be brought under this legislation involved a dispute between Argentine and British companies over the use of the name Harrods in a number of Internet domain names. This case was settled by the US Fourth Circuit Court of Appeals who, in affirming the decision of the Federal District Court, ordered the transfer of 54 domain names to the British company and upheld the right of a US Court to rule in such matters between foreign plaintiffs connected to the US only by the ownership of a domain name.[22]

Even more wide-ranging, the US Patriot Act 2001, which was rushed through Congress in the aftermath of 9/11, allows the US government to claim criminal law jurisdiction over any computer located anywhere in the world if it is used in a manner that affects US commerce or communications.[22]

Despite the difficulties presented by conflicts of national statute, this is an important issue that must be addressed. Regulation of the Internet touches on many different areas aside from healthcare: the protection of children, collection/storage of data with/without user's knowledge, the sale of products from unlicensed sources, and accuracy and reliability of website content. One possible solution that addresses some of these issues is voluntary rating or accreditation schemes. Increasingly, multinational service providers such as AOL and individual websites are adopting recognised rating schemes to let users know the level of 'child friendliness' for a given site.

Website accreditation programmes

A number of national and international schemes exist to assess the content of medical and pharmaceutical web pages. However, all these schemes are currently voluntary and are undertaken by only a small percentage of sites. For such schemes to increase in value there must perhaps be a greater business or legislative incentive for their use. It can also be hoped that the new breed of 'empowered' patient will demand such quality assurances, making it a financial disadvantage not to seek some form of accreditation.

The Pharmaceutical Society of New Zealand (PSNZ) demonstrated a willingness to address these issues in August 2000, developing an Internet Pharmacy Accreditation scheme to officially recognise New Zealand pharmacy sites that meet required professional standards. Accreditation is intended to display to the public that the website is endorsed by the PSNZ (http://www.psnz.org.nz). To apply for accreditation pharmacies must meet the following requirements:

* Compliance with the same ethical, legislative and quality standards of registered pharmacies.
* Compliance with patient confidentiality and privacy rights.
* Compliance with legislation regarding the advertising of medicines.
* Provision of factual and understandable information about medicines.
* Provision of the opportunity for meaningful consultation between patient and pharmacist.

Accreditation can be verified by a hyperlink seal on the pharmacy website – it is a voluntary scheme for which an application must be made. At the time of writing, there are two Internet pharmacies accredited by the scheme. Feedback from the PSNZ would suggest the onerous accreditation procedure, as well as apathy from the public, who do not seem to care that they are purchasing from an un-accredited site, are major hurdles. To battle these, the PSNZ plan to make the benefits of accreditation more desirable by prosecuting those who contravene the legal requirements of advertising and selling of medicines:

> We developed the programme as a carrot to encourage pharmacists to do it correctly at the beginning of internet trading in medicines. It was to be a marketing advantage to show the public they were dealing with a reputable supplier. . . . . . . [Our] plan this year is to put aside the carrot and get out the stick. (E Galloway, Pharmacy Practice and Legislation Manager, Pharmaceutical Society of New Zealand, personal communication, January 2003)

The RPSGB's guidelines for pharmacies on the Internet are similar to the accreditation standards outlined above for the PSNZ scheme.

In the USA, The National Association Boards of Pharmacy (NABP, http://www.napb.net), whose members also include Canadian and Australian regional boards, has a Verified Internet Pharmacy Practice Sites (VIPPS) programme. This programme was developed in 1999 in response to public concern over questionable Internet pharmacy practices. The aim of this programme is once again to highlight to the public those pharmacy websites that meet certain minimum legal and ethical requirements and member sites can be verified by a hyperlink seal. In Canada, the National Association of Pharmacy Regulatory Authorities (NAPRA) has recently developed its own programme modelled on the VIPPS programme (www.napra.org/docs/0/95/158/165.asp).

At the time of writing, there were 13 verified VIPPS sites including national US pharmacy chains such as CVS and Walgreens. Review of accredited sites is ongoing, with one recently suspended. However, if an online search is conducted for any of the 'lifestyle' drugs, it is apparent that these may still be bought freely and without prescription from any number of sources, predominately in the USA. While the VIPPS programme is a step in the right direction, there is clearly a long way to go.

A European Commission working group is currently drafting pan-European guidelines on the quality of health-related websites but at present the HON Code of Conduct is the most widely used European scheme, with nearly 3000 member sites. Not specific to pharmacy, it was developed by the Health on the Net Foundation (http://www.hon.ch), a non-profit organisation based in Switzerland and launched in early 1996 in order to assess the quality of medical advice provided on any health-care-related website. Since its inception, it has been translated into 23 different languages and is used by sites across the USA and Europe, including the UK. The HON code does not rate the accuracy of the information itself but rather ensures that users always know the source and purpose of the information they are reading. Member sites must adhere to the eight governing principles of the code:

- Health advice must only be given by medically qualified professionals unless a clear statement is made to the contrary.
- Information provided is designed to supplement, not replace, the patient/physician relationship.
- Patient confidentiality must be protected.
- Information provided will be supported by clear references to source data.
- Claims regarding specific treatments will be supported by appropriate evidence.
- Website designers and authors will be clearly identified along with contact details.
- Website sponsors will be clearly identified.
- Advertising and marketing material will be clearly differentiated from site content.

The increased availability and use of these schemes is certainly a start in the fight against the illegal and unethical practices so evident on the Internet, even by pharmacists. However, without tighter controls and legislation to enforce those controls, the onus is still on the website visitor to be sceptical and vigilant about their own healthcare.

e-Pharmacy is an integral component of the NHS Plan (see Chapter 12), but it would appear that the relevant legislation is in need of a 'digital' update, possibly together with the creation of new agency to oversee its implementation.

This chapter was almost entirely researched by way of the Internet.

References

1. BBC (2002). *Health websites gaining popularity.* http://news.bbc.co.uk/1/hi/health/2249606.stm (accessed 21 July 2004).
2. Fisher J G. *E-Business for the Small Business,* London, Kogan Page Limited, 2001.
3. *Delivering IT in the NHS – A Summary of the National Programme for IT in the NHS,* London, Department of Health, Information Policy Unit, 11 June 2002. (This report can be ordered from http://www.doh.gov.uk)

4. Prescription Pricing Authority. *Electronic Transmission of Prescriptions (ETP) Pilots*, 2 August 2002 (http://www.ppa.org.uk/news/etp.htm)

5. Anon. *Common model to be sought for electronic prescription transfer. Pharm J* 2003; 270: 218.

6. Buisson J, Gross Z. *Department of Health speeds up ETP assessments as pilots make slow start. Pharm J* 2002; 269: 242–244.

7. Bellingham C. *Modernising pharmacy services: some of the latest developments in Scotland. Pharm J* 2002; 268: 204–205.

8. Anon. *Repeat dispensing will merge with ETP and medicines management. Pharm J* 2003; 270: 200.

9. Appelbe G E, Wingfield J. *Dale and Appelbe's Pharmacy Law and Ethics,* 7th edn. London: Pharmaceutical Press, 2001.

10. *Enforcement of medicines legislation: Prosecutions,* London, MHRA, 12 March 2003 (http://www.mca.gov.uk/ourwork/enforcemedleg/prosecutions.htm).

11. *Taking medicines with you when you go abroad (Notice 4).* London: HM Customs & Excise, July 1998.

12. *Code of Ethics and Standards in Medicines, Ethics and Practice – A Guide for Pharmacists.* London: Pharmaceutical Press, 28 July 2004.

13. *Professional Standards Directorate Fact Sheet: Eight, Pharmacy and the Internet,* London, Royal Pharmaceutical Society of Great Britain, 2 August 2001.

14. *Buying Medicines and Medicinal Products Online,* Rockville, Maryland, U.S. Food and Drug Administration (http://www.fda.gov/oc/buyonline/default.htm).

15. Meadows M. *Imported Drugs Raise Safety Concerns,* FDA Consumer Magazine, 2002, Vol. 36 (http://www.fda.gov/fdac/features/2002/502_import.html).

16. *Importation of Human-Use Drugs for Personal Use Enforcement Directive,* Ottawa, Canada, Health Canada, Health Products and Food Branch, 1 January 1998.

17. Anon. *Net medicine sales restricted,* New Zealand Doctor, 8 November 2000.

18. Anon. *DocMorris Internet Pharmacy appears before the European Court of Justice,* ZeiReport 2003, 12/13: 1–2.

19. *Code of Practice for the Pharmaceutical Industry.* London: Prescription Medicines Code of Practice Authority, 2001.

20. *The ABPI Position Paper on Pharmaceuticals and the Internet.* London: Association of the British Pharmaceutical Industry, 1 October 2000.

21. Anon. *Committee sceptical about Internet self-regulation,* CESInfo 2002; 07/2002: 1.

22. Hines J. *Jurisdiction: Should nations extend their legal reach beyond their borders?,* Reston, Virginia, Internet Society, 4 December 2002 (http://www.isoc.org/pubpolpillar/juris.shtml).

Websites for further information

Pharmacies

Allcures	www.allcures.com
Pharmacy2u	www.pharmacy2u.co.uk

Organisations

American Pharmaceutical Association	www.aphanet.org
Association of the British Pharmaceutical Industry	www.abpi.org.uk
Department of Health	www.doh.gov.uk
European Agency for the Evaluation of Medicinal Products	www.emea.eu.int
European Commission – Pharmaceuticals, Regulatory Framework & Market Authorisations	pharmacos.eudra.org
European Directorate for the Quality of Medicines	www.pheur.org
HM Customs & Excise	www.hmce.gov.uk
International Conference on Harmonisation	www.ich.org
Internet Society	www.isoc.org
Medicines and Healthcare Products Regulatory Agency (formerly the MCA)	www.mhra.gov.uk
National Association of Boards of Pharmacy	www.nabp.net
NHS	www.nhs.uk
NHS Scotland	www.show.scot.nhs.uk
Prescription Pricing Authority	www.ppa.org.uk
Pharmaceutical Society of New Zealand	www.psnz.org.nz
Royal Pharmaceutical Society of Great Britain	www.rpsgb.org.uk
U.S. Drug Enforcement Administration	www.dea.gov
U.S. Food and Drug Administration	www.fda.gov
Veterinary International Conference on Harmonisation	www.vich.eudra.org

Information resources

Ask Your Pharmacist	www.askyourpharmacist.co.uk
Centre for Postgraduate Pharmacy Education (CPPE)	www.cppe.man.ac.uk
Health On The Net Foundation	www.hon.ch
Health-News	www.health-news.co.uk
NHS Direct	www.nhsdirect.nhs.uk
NHS Education for Scotland (NES)	www.nes.scot.nhs.uk/pharmacy
NHS Net	www.nhsia.nhs.uk/nhsnet
NI Centre for Postgraduate Pharmacy Education & Training	www.nicppet.org
NOAH: New York Online Access to Health	www.noah-health.org
Numark	www.numarkpharmacists.co.uk
PharmWeb	www.pharmweb.net
Welsh Centre for Postgraduate Pharmacy Education (WCPPE)	www.cf.ac.uk/phrmy/WCPPE

16

Human resources management in community pharmacy

Kirit Patel, Gerry Gracias and Anne Loh

Introduction

One of the most undervalued resources in any business is its people. The importance of investing in human resource cannot be stressed too highly. These hidden resources carry the goodwill and can help make or break any business. They must be correctly recruited and retained.

Managing human resources

Human resources management is a very broad subject, but the four most relevant areas with respect to community pharmacy are:

- recruitment and retention
- training and development
- performance management
- time management.

Another prominent aspect is clinical governance, which looks at the wide-ranging implications to ensure high-quality services and get the most from the staff. Training and development is now formalised by the Royal Pharmaceutical Society of Great Britain (RPSGB) with mandatory CPD requirement expected soon for validity of pharmacists on its active register.

Long after vendors have passed on the goodwill to a purchaser, it is the staff – 'hidden resources' – that take over, who carry this goodwill in the true sense, although it is often attributed to the premises and profitability of the business. Long-serving staff are often seen as a liability, but they have built up years of knowledge and skills and know most of the customers by name. It is their knowledge that the organisation must tap, manage and transfer to use to its maximum potential.

Any investment in these 'hidden resources' will pay long-term dividends and equally any shortcomings in skills and attitudes will be detrimental to the business. The cycle of knowledge transfer should be continuous within the organisation or else it would mean reinventing the wheel each time. Because we tend to underestimate the value of human resources, we tend not to seek professional advice on human resources management. For any organisation to achieve its objectives, the management need to be clearly aware of the mission and act cohesively and each employee must be a part of the overall strategy. In a community pharmacy, like most small or independent businesses, its people really are the most valuable resource, one that needs to be nurtured and fully developed. Often any advantage that one pharmacy has over another lies as much in its people as in the products or services it offers. So finding and holding onto good people is of major importance, especially at a time of severe manpower shortages of pharmacists and trained pharmacy staff.

In order to achieve any objective, as a football team manager, or head of a mountain climbing expedition, not only the leader but also every single member needs to be clearly aware of the importance of acting cohesively in one direction. Every member has a role to play – be it the pharmacy manager, owner, counter assistant, dispenser, Saturday girl or deliveryman. No company can achieve its goal in the stated time period unless they are empowered to do their job. The key is communication and developing an effective pathway for this must be a priority.

Imagine a mountaineering expedition. The team would consist of a navigator, a radio expert, one handling the food provisions, one or two experts in climbing, a medic, a team leader etc. If one of them gets it wrong then the whole expedition is jeopardised and could even result in the group being trapped half way up the mountain without provisions. Each team member has to be carefully recruited, inducted and trained. This would mean well-defined job descriptions, skills set and training needs have been identified. Collectively the functions enable the team to move up the mountain in a cohesive manner. Every single member of the team knows the mission and the objectives. Similarly in a pharmacy, the pharmacist owner will carry out an appraisal of each member of staff to identify skills needed and the associated training requirements.

Recruitment and retention

Within community pharmacy, especially independents, responsibility for recruitment will often lie with pharmacy owners or managers, with limited experience and training in recruitment and selection. Yet it is in these smaller businesses that getting recruitment right is most crucial.

CASE STUDY 1

Communication within a pharmacy business
In 1997 Day Lewis had 20 shops managed by individual pharmacists. This group did not have an identity except that they were owned and managed by a single person. The owner made all the decisions. Communication between the shops and the owner was minimal. The company had few staff training programmes in place. Consultants brought in specifically to tackle the problems of low morale found that compliance was poor. With average margins on the shop floor, there was room for improvement and growth in business. This family business had been able to achieve a 'family culture' at the individual shops. The programme began with the development of the senior management team. A professional team was needed to take the company forward and look into its future growth. Starting from basic things taken for granted in any company, a mission statement was spelt out. The next stage was to set the objectives and develop a strategy. This was achieved through team building sessions for the senior team, which in turn helped create a group identity. Roles and responsibilities were identified for the senior and middle management. The development of the management team was achieved through communications, monitored meetings, careful planning and management information systems, which have now become an integral part of the company.

After a period of coaching the team began to operate effectively. There were regular meetings at all levels. The backlog of outstanding decisions was worked through methodically and professionally. This led to growth in the company, which has been mainly through acquisitions. With increasing number of retail outlets to manage, the role of area coordinator was identified. It is this crucial level in the organisation structure that forms the link between senior management and staff in the shops. They are also crucial in transferring core skills to the staff in the shops. There are now special meetings where the area coordinators discuss issues amongst themselves and also with the senior management team members.

The mission and objectives statement was revisited at a meeting of the senior management team and area coordinators abroad. They are empowered to take many more decisions and have also developed confidence to cascade skills and responsibilities to the shop staff.

Recruitment is an expensive business in terms of both time and money, and getting it wrong means you end up investing resources repeatedly. Bringing in the wrong people can also cause havoc, by disrupting the balance of a small business and lowering morale. The problem with recruitment is that it is often unplanned, and only becomes an issue when an employee leaves. Then the need to fill the vacancy quickly means that many of the key principles of good recruitment and selection are bypassed.

If recruitment is going to help you achieve your business aims, it needs a planned and long-term approach. You need to identify what types of people and skills your pharmacy needs, and how you can bring them in. Are you looking to take on a professionally focused pharmacist who can develop new pharmacy services for your business? What do you need to do to attract high-calibre candidates to you? Is your pharmacy an attractive and professional environment to work in? And if you are going to focus on developing professional services will you need to recruit a qualified dispensing technician, or a higher standard of pharmacy assistant that you can develop into a dispensing assistant? After getting the right people, it is also about improving your chances of retaining them. Taking care to match people and their skills to a role, and offering opportunities for development, means people tend to be more satisfied and more productive.

Once you have recruited the right person, the quality of their induction will largely determine how quickly they settle in and start contributing effectively to the pharmacy. It will also determine how long they stay with the pharmacy. The first few days and weeks are also crucial in shaping attitudes towards the job and the new employer. Beyond the induction, incentives such as flexible working arrangements, performance-related bonuses, a pleasant working environment, and the social aspects of work have an important role in motivating and retaining staff. The key, however, lies in you being proactive in helping your staff realise their own potential for development. With pharmacists this could be by encouraging and supporting their CPD. For other pharmacy staff, a similar personal development plan should be devised. As pharmacists continue to develop their professional roles, they will require the full support of skilled pharmacy staff. The key principles of recruitment and retention are:

- Develop a planned approach to recruitment, in line with your business objectives.
- Ensure there is a clear reason for each recruitment decision, which is linked to achieving your business objectives.
- Set clear guidelines for the role by writing a job description.
- Organise a positive and effective induction for the new person.
- Manage staff performance using a system of appraisal and personal development plans.

Recruitment within community pharmacy may be for any of the following – pharmacists (permanent or locum), pharmacy managers, pre-registration trainees, dispensing technicians, pharmacy assistants and other pharmacy support staff.

Pharmacist recruitment

In most independently owned community pharmacies the proprietor acts as the sole or main pharmacist, who will carry out all the professional duties plus the retail management role, with support from pharmacy assistants. Locum pharmacists would be employed to cover occasional days off and holidays. As the business expands, there will be a need to recruit pharmacists as managers. Often these roles may be of a predominantly professional nature, leaving much of the business administration to the pharmacy owners.

An increasingly popular trend for newly registered pharmacists has been to work as self-employed locums on short- or long-term placements, in preference to taking on the responsibilities of a permanent pharmacy manager position. The benefits of this type of working have also attracted a large number of experienced pharmacists to move out of traditional pharmacy management roles into more flexible and often more lucrative locum work.

Employers are having to look at ways of attracting and keeping good pharmacists, by offering professionally stimulating roles. This may include collaborative work with doctors and a local primary healthcare team, developing new services such as diagnostic testing, conducting health promotion clinics, and encouraging the pharmacy to be active and fully supportive of local healthcare projects. It will additionally require employers to recruit or develop a higher calibre of pharmacy staff, who are well trained and can also manage much of the pharmacy and business administration.

As a pharmacy owner you will always be looking to maintain business stability in terms of staffing and management. However there may be times when it is necessary to manage the pharmacy with your pharmacy staff and different pharmacist locums. When this happens it is useful to develop a simple locum induction guide to your pharmacy, detailing relevant information such as ordering sources, useful contacts, computer information, etc. It should also include something on what you expect from the locum, and their responsibilities.

Supporting staff recruitment

The changing role of the pharmacist, and the increasing reliance on locums, means that recruiting the right pharmacy staff is now more important than ever. Consumers will often say that they choose their local independent pharmacy over a high street or supermarket pharmacy, based not on convenience, but on the friendly service they receive from the staff. This may be as simple as the staff knowing and greeting them by their name. The reputation of a pharmacy can often be greatly influenced by the quality of the staff, who are essentially the 'face' of that pharmacy. When recruiting, the focus should be on customer service, communication and 'people' skills, plus the ability and interest in developing pharmacy-related skills such as dispensing.

The recruitment process

Even for the smallest independent pharmacy business, it is important to project a professional image to new employees. This begins with the job advertisement, be it for pharmacy staff in a local newspaper or a pharmacy manager in *The Pharmaceutical Journal*. Once a simple advert may have yielded a healthy number of applications, but not now. With the current shortage of skilled people, you will need to sell the merits of your business in order to attract the best candidates and beyond the financial package, think about the other potential benefits available. Compile a job description with clear, justifiable criteria so that both you and the applicant understand what is involved in the job.

It begins with the drawing up of a clear job description, for use first in the recruitment and selection process, and then as a benchmark against which to appraise performance. A job description would include job title, responsible to, main purpose of the job, and main duties and responsibilities. Consideration should be given to the number of hours, whether it could be a job share, or other flexible ways of working. If you are able to offer hours that allow people a healthy work–life balance, it will not only attract more applicants, but it is likely they will be happier in their work and stay with you longer.

Employment legislation, such as working time regulations and anti-discrimination legislation, should be thoroughly known to the employer and interviewer. Candidates should be asked to fill in an application form before interview, which besides showing professionalism is a useful tool in the selection procedure. It ensures that applicants are selected and treated on the basis of their merits and abilities. You will also need to consider a variety of staff benefits such as paid annual leave, sick pay, stakeholder pension schemes and ensure that new employees are provided with a written contract of employment within the first two months of employment.

As a general guideline wages and salaries should represent between 13% and 15% of sales value.

 CASE STUDY 2

Recruiting a supervisor
Our pharmacy is situated in a typical suburban shopping parade, just 200 yards from a large doctor's practice. It is a busy dispensing branch, and the pharmacist, Peter, manages it with the support of a full-time dispenser and two part-time pharmacy assistants, Shilpa and Mary. Shilpa has just notified Peter that she wishes to retire from work in 3 months time, and we need to plan how best to approach this replacement.

Our starting point would be to look at the business aims and objectives. The pharmacy has potential to develop much closer working links with the doctor's practice, by developing new professional services. To do this, Peter will need additional support with the day-to-day branch management and administrative duties.

Peter favours recruiting a full-time pharmacy supervisor, as a replacement for Shilpa. This will be a major investment for the business, so he needs to be clear that these changes will help achieve his business aims. Consideration should also be given to other options, such as promoting and training Mary.

A job description needs to be written setting out clearly the role of the supervisor and their position within the pharmacy. The job description will form the basis against which their performance will be appraised over time. An example would be:

Job title: Pharmacy Supervisor
Responsible to: Pharmacy Manager (Peter)
Overall purpose: To co-ordinate pharmacy activities and procedures
Key result areas: Maintaining high standards of customer service
                        Effective stock control and merchandising
                        Maintaining high standards of pharmacy appearance
                        Ensuring optimal staffing cover
                        Implementing staff training

continued

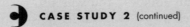

> **CASE STUDY 2** (continued)
>
> Key competencies: Good communication skills
>   Customer service skills
>   Supervisory/people management skills
>   Knowledge of computerised EPOS systems
>
> Peter carries out interviews, and using criteria from the job description selects Brenda from amongst six applicants. References are sought, and a formal job offer and terms of employment are offered. Peter knows that if Brenda settles in properly, and is made to feel part of the team, she will enjoy the responsibilities of her new role as pharmacy supervisor. He arranges to spend time with her on her first day and also pays attention to her settling in the new job. Peter explains how Brenda's first few weeks are planned and answers her questions. He monitors her progress over the following weeks and months, both informally and through appraisals. Together, he and Brenda devise a personal development plan to support her with the additional skills she needs in her new role. This will allow Peter the time to concentrate on developing the professional services of the pharmacy.

Training and development (see also Chapter 17)

After having invested time and money in recruiting the right candidate, a plan for their training and development has to be drawn up. This will not only bring new skills needed to your business, motivate them but also ensure a higher regard for you as an employer.

The NHS Plan has indicated the government's agenda with respect to clinical governance and CPD. Any training and development of dispensing personnel needs to include these professional elements as well as other non-professional elements such as correct sales and marketing. Proper time management can help free up time that can be better utilised to drive forward the strategy plan of the business.

A personal development plan should be drawn up for each member of staff, which begins on their first day with induction training. A planned, step-by-step approach to training is most effective. Within community pharmacy the majority of the training is work-based, through coaching, mentoring and distance learning. It is often impractical for pharmacy staff to attend courses or other training events away from their branch. The National Pharmaceutical Association (NPA) offers a comprehensive range of training courses specially designed for community pharmacy. It also offers a training pathway that can take your staff right through. Courses offered by the NPA for pharmacy staff include the following:

- Getting To Know Your Pharmacy – Induction Training
- Guidelines to Selling Medicines and Giving Advice – Pharmacy Protocol
- Pharmacy Interact – an accredited counter medicines training course
- Skills development programme
- Dispensing Assistant's course
- Dispensing Technician NVQ level 3

There is much discussion about the possible mandatory regulation of pharmacy staff by the Royal Pharmaceutical Society of Great Britain (RPSGB). It has been suggested that all pharmacy staff will be required to be trained to at least NVQ level 2 standard. Many of these recommendations form the core of the clinical governance agenda. Currently any member of staff working in a pharmacy involved in the sale of medicines is required to complete an accredited counter medicines course. It is recommended that all staff complete this as their foundation, and then develop areas such as customer service, supervisory and management skills. There are currently no mandatory training requirements for dispensary staff, although there is much discussion about the registration of dispensing technicians by the RPSGB.

What is essential is that this training be planned, recorded and evaluated and of practical benefit to the individual and the business. It should follow a cyclical process of identifying, planning, recording and evaluating the benefits to identify further training needs.

CPD and education

The RPSGB requires that pharmacists keep up to date with changes in pharmacy practice, the law relating to pharmacy and the knowledge and technology applicable to pharmacy, and must maintain competence and effectiveness as a practitioner. This responsibility is recognised in the RPSGB's Code of Ethics. The Society recommends that pharmacists fulfil this responsibility by adopting the concept of continuing professional development (CPD). This will include regular participation in continuing professional education (CPE) and other activities, e.g. professional audit.

There is an important distinction between CPE and CPD:

- **Continuing Professional Education (CPE)** is a tangible and finite element. If one were to complete a Centre for Pharmacy Postgraduate Education (CPPE) distance learning package and answer the multiple-choice questions, one would have completed some CPE.
- **Continuing Professional Development (CPD)** is not a finite process, it has no end. It is a 'way of working' – a process in which continual assessment, evaluation and development is present. To anyone who has undergone a modern training programme, this process is only an extension. It has four essential steps: review, plan, act and evaluate.

At any point, something may take us back to a previous stage in the process or we may be at several stages at once. It is important to realise however, that all of these stages are visited in the process of CPD and it may simply require that you take an objective look at the process before realising this.

Whilst it is true that we apply CPD in our daily working lives it is important to focus on key areas so that we can produce a portfolio of our CPD. Quite rightly, continuing education may be part of this process, but it is only development if all stages of the process are completed, i.e. that an evaluation and subsequent review of any learning are undertaken and if that learning is put into actual practice. This is an area in which many pharmacists experience great difficulty – accounting for actual time spent on CPD. Whenever a pharmacist is involved in 'evidence based practice', the documentation associated with it is key documentation of CPD. The Case study below shows a case study that demonstrates a CPD process.

CASE STUDY 3

CPD project – medicines management (see also Chapter 18)

Review
A pharmacist is providing pharmaceutical care to a number of nursing and residential homes and is offering advice on medication matters to these homes. Frequently, the subject of medication reviews comes up and the pharmacist decides to approach the local GP surgery with a view to being involved in medicines management with these homes, thus providing a more complete package of care.

→

CASE STUDY 3 (continued)

Plan
Since the National Service Framework for older people states a requirement for regular medication reviews to be undertaken it is likely that any assistance in this area will be welcomed by the GPs.

Writing to the local GPs gives the pharmacist an opportunity to suggest this project and contacting the local Pharmaceutical Advisors for advice on the best way of managing the project, provides an endorsement from the PCT. The PCT may also have useful material, which will save time devising reporting schemes and documentation. It is advisable to undertake some CE on the subject of Medicines Management and CPPE run workshops could be an excellent starting point.

Act
- Meet GPs and Pharmaceutical Advisors for discussion. With this as the basis plan the project.
- Conduct the medication reviews and feedback to GPs.

Evaluate
- Meet GPs and discuss the results and their value to patients, GP and pharmacist.
- Review the project then begin the cycle again by planning the next set of reviews or changes to be made to the project.

In this project, the CPPE workshops will provide certification to demonstrate participation and will have a set number of hours accredited to them. It is important to realise that the whole process is CPD and the total hours spent on all four stages can be counted towards CPD. The time spent planning may be harder to quantify, but a written record of this will help. The time spent in the 'Action' phase is the time, which will accrue most quickly, and documentation of this activity is an essential part of the CPD portfolio. For this project, a copy of each of the medication review forms together with the time spent will provide the bulk of the evidence for CPD.

Pharmacy as a profession is changing rapidly. Training and development will always be an important issue. Employers will need to actively encourage their staff to develop their skills, support them through training, and provide them with working time to focus on these issues.

Providers of CPD and CPE

The RPSGB began introducing its CPD programme for pharmacists in October 2002. By February 2004, more than 20 000 pharmacists had received their CPD pack. The roll-out to all pharmacists resident in Great Britain was planned for completion by the end of 2004 (although this does not extend to retired pharmacists over 60), and the roll-out to overseas pharmacists during 2005. Shortly after this, there will be a mandatory requirement for pharmacists to adopt CPD.

Pharmacists taking part in the programme are sent a CPD pack, produced in collaboration with the CPPE. There has also been collaboration with the Scottish and Welsh centres. The CPD pack includes a guide to all aspects of CPD, entitled *Plan and record*. Although participants can keep paper-based records, they are being encouraged to keep records electronically, using the CPD website. All working members of the Society have been sent a videotape, *Introducing CPD*, also produced with the CPPE.

There are several other organisations providing CPD and CPE apart from RPSGB including the College of Pharmacy Practice, the National Pharmaceutical Association and the Institute of Pharmacy Management. A full list of contact addresses may be found in Appendix 1.

Performance management

This is an area that brings together and draws upon the two previous functions – recruitment and training and development. Your staff being your most valuable business resource they would require your support and encouragement to perform to the best of their ability. This is not only to maximise their contribution to the business but also for their own job satisfaction.

A regular system of **appraisals** should be implemented. This should start with frequent, informal appraisals as part of the induction process, followed by twice-yearly appraisals. These can be used as a way of recognising good performance, offering praise where due, giving staff opportunities to discuss their work with you, and identify training needs. Appraisal need not be complicated or bureaucratic, and can be by asking simple questions on a one to one basis such as:

- What do you enjoy or do well in your job?
- What don't you enjoy, or find difficult?
- What would you like to improve upon?
- What training would help you do your job better?
- How can I, as your manager, support you better in your job?

Appraisals can help identify those staff who want to move above and beyond their current role, and can assist in developing their training plans. They can similarly highlight areas for improvement in other staff. The appraisal system could be an important link to reward systems.

Another effective process in managing performance, both for individuals and for the business, are **team briefings**. Here business objectives are discussed openly between managers and staff. Targets are set at business and individual levels. Such team briefings can be useful communication exercises and result in improvements in business performance, staff morale and team spirit.

Time management

Time lost is time lost forever. Ever-shrinking margins in retail pharmacy have led to a cutback in workforce development in order to compensate. This has often meant working on reduced or semi-skilled staffing levels. The way a lot of pharmacies are managed, the pharmacy owner is forced to work as the captain in the engine room instead of being on the deck. Anything that can be delegated should be done by more junior members of staff. As there are only a limited number of hours per day a lot needs to be established in this time to run a pharmacy efficiently. If the captain were to roll up his sleeves and shove coal in the engine room of the ship, the ship would inevitably drift and lose its bearings. Things are no different in managing a pharmacy. In order to maximise patient care and optimise revenues the pharmacist needs to make full use of the support staff and free up time for himself/herself and only in this manner can objectives be fulfilled.

One needs to encourage and empower support staff such as counter assistants, dispensers and others to take ownership of their actions. With limited financial resources available for training, this should be done prudently and in a time-efficient manner. Having identified through appraisals the requirement of skills or knowledge, any time invested in training would pay ample dividends in the future by saving the owner's time.

The current political debate on supervision and regulation of support staff may well be a blessing in disguise. The pharmacist owner must delegate all routine tasks, that often form a part of running the pharmacy – putting the goods away, checking invoices, dispensing, etc. This means having to trust the employees. This trust can only come from selective recruitment, induction and proper training, and implementation of good standard operating procedures.

Daily time management involves planning out the day and apportioning appropriate time to carry out various functions. These functions vary from day to day; some for example may involve CPE/CPD while others may be spent in training, apart from carrying out other professional activities. It is only by conducting an audit of these daily tasks that one realises the need for input by others – all working in a limited time scale. Often pharmacists tend to take unfinished work home and this impinges on the social life. Many pharmacists undertake compliance workload, such as accounts and bookkeeping, in time meant for social life. It is important to devote adequate time to one's hobbies and family.

All businesses are stressful and pharmacy is no different. Even answering the phone can be disruptive. Pharmacists really need to delegate routine phone answering to others and ensure that calls are filtered. Only those queries not dealt with by others should be passed on to the pharmacist, as continuous disruption breaks concentration and could lead to errors.

Retail pharmacy tends to create an abundance of paper work. It is necessary to manage this correctly. One should avoid retaining and filing papers if the same information is readily available at a later date from other sources. The daily delivery notes and invoices should be filed in a manner that is easy to check against statements received at the end of the month. For example, full-line wholesaler's statements list as many as a hundred invoices on an average for each month. The VAT breakdown is shown on most of the statements. Customs and Excise accept the entry of this statement and VAT breakdown and all invoices may not have to be entered into the purchase ledger. This saves considerable time. Correspondence that can be done by email or fax should be in that manner. One of the common ways of saving time taken up claiming for short delivery on an invoice is by faxing the invoice with the comments to the credit control department of the supplier. This avoids having to replicate the name, address, account number, invoice number etc. on a letter. A copy of the invoice under query should be marked and retained. When correspondence is to be sent to many people at the same time, a group email can be used.

Opening unsolicited junk mail is also a waste of time and one may end up buying something not needed from attractive offers. Every incoming mail should be separated on the basis of need and urgency. It pays to have three files, which one looks at daily, the second weekly and a third one for miscellaneous filing. So there is no need to look at all mail twice. In addition, filing it on the same day after sorting is helpful. The daily file should be looked at every day and all letter or correspondence should be dealt with urgently. The semi-urgent correspondence can be dealt with during the week as time permits, whilst the non-urgent can be looked at every so often.

Similarly it is important to prepare clear agendas for any meetings that you may hold. This agenda will help you keep focused and will prevent time wastage and make meetings more efficient. All meetings should be run on a strictly allocated time basis and a clear action plan must be drawn up for anyone for whom it is intended. It is important not to allow others to hijack the meeting or simply keep repeating their point of view. If a decision can be reached quickly then it is not necessary to prolong the debate. It is crucial to understand how to participate in a meeting – as a delegate, secretary or a chairman. This skill also helps internal communication at staff meetings of the pharmacy. Meetings with pharmaceutical representatives should be handled in a manner that does not waste anyone's time. Before the meeting one should research which products are required based on their average usage and a tentative order can be kept ready.

One should always optimise the shop trading hours and not necessarily extend the hours and open during lunchtime unless absolutely essential. The basis for these decisions can be made from the information available on your EPOS tills and patient medication records. It is important that one justifies that the revenue generated from these offpeak hours is able to pay for the overheads generated. Any time saved at offpeak hours can be utilised to carry out non-dispensing functions and training.

Proper time management enriches our lives and helps to derive satisfaction. Personal visits must be avoided when it is possible to deal with it over the telephone. This is one way of saving travel time. Modern technology provides many powerful tools in order to manage time and commitment, such as electronic diaries and software. Proper ergonomics in planning a dispensary can reduce dispensing time. A recommended exercise is to log all activities done for a period with the time taken in a day and evaluate the time taken for each and identify the manner in which these could be done more effectively. One should learn to put a value to one's own time.

Further reading

Anon. Managing manpower, managing medicines. Report, BPC Glasgow 2001. *Pharm J* 2001; 267: 470–481.

Anon. Recruitment squeeze helps employees. *Pharm J* 2002; 268: 487–492.

Thomas T. Staff development. *Pharm J* 2002, 269: 17–19.

Maguire T. Time management. Part of *Mind Your Own Business*. Booklet provided free from *Chemist & Druggist Online* (details available from http://www.dotpharmacy.com/myob.html).

17

Pharmacy management in secondary care

Andrew Radley

Introduction

A pharmacy manager within the modern NHS ensures that:

- clinical standards are met;
- services are developed to meet patients' needs;
- the corporate change agenda is carried forward.

These broad functions, together with generic questions such as 'What products and services are we providing?' and 'To whom are we providing them?' do not vary greatly from the secondary care sector to community pharmacy; however there are differences in emphasis and interpretation because of the particular environment and specialised needs of patients. These factors are addressed in this chapter.

The hospital environment

The pharmacist's role

Crucial to the pharmacy management function in the hospital sector is an appreciation of what hospital pharmacy is actually all about and who are its customers. However, answering these questions seems to be progressively more complex. At one time, when a patient was admitted to your district general hospital, you could be certain that a hospital pharmacist would provide the pharmacy services during the patient's stay and that after discharge, pharmacy services would be provided by their local community pharmacy contractor. Care would have passed from a secondary care hospital organisation to primary care.

For some secondary care services within the primary care environment, patients may be provided from within a primary care organisation. Changes envisaged across the UK are expected to introduce single organisations managing primary and secondary care services across localities. The emergence of Community Health Partnerships (CHPs) in Scotland will promote this.

The development of intermediate care, in which supportive care is provided for patients outside the traditional hospital environment, is an example of how the health service landscape is changing. Intermediate care may be provided for patients undergoing rehabilitation following an acute hospital care episode or may be to support a community-based patient needing greater input from health workers. Managed service pharmacists often provide professional input into primary care trust facilities and some have taken up the responsibilities of seamless care, as patients move between care environments. Community pharmacists also provide contracted services to hospitals for medicine supply and provide aspects of clinical pharmacy. To complete the description, it is necessary to mention outreach secondary care services to patients' homes and inreach primary care contractor services to hospital beds. Managed service pharmacists now often work in general practices as practice pharmacists, but managed service community pharmacies have not yet developed to the extent seen in general medical and dental services. The simple concepts that divided what a community pharmacy contractor undertakes and what a managed service pharmacist undertakes has blurred.

The pharmacists who manage secondary care pharmacy services have to deploy excellent communication skills. They need to build customer relationships with doctors and nurses, local hospital managers, primary care health and social care services, regional and national teams, as well as lead the pharmacists, technicians and assistant staff that make up their own teams.

The customer

Successful services satisfy customer needs. The corollary of this is that high quality services are ones that completely satisfy the customer. The insights provided by the marketing discipline are an important part of the awareness required to grow services in a hospital environment. In commerce, the business marketing model is one where the processes of selling products and services drive the business (Figure 17.1). The concepts of selling and of profits are not directly applicable to hospital pharmacy practice in the way that they might be in a community pharmacy. However, the marketing concept, in which the hospital pharmacy service gains influence by satisfying the needs of consumers of the service, most

Figure 17.1 Marketing in business.

definitely is. Building relationships and networks and gaining credibility are ways to communicate and market the need for pharmacy services.

Within a successful pharmacy service in secondary care, meeting the needs of customers effectively is recognised by rewards such as further investment in the service by the organisation, the ability to develop professional pharmacy practice in adjacent areas and by the recognition and prestige arising from delivering a valued contribution (see Figure 17.2). Patient and public involvement in the design of service developments is becoming an activity that managers have to utilise successfully. The ethos of designing services in partnership with patients is just emerging as a new way to market and target services.

However a patient focus is insufficient to satisfy all customers within a secondary care environment. There are a wide range of expectations of a hospital pharmacy service. Not only is it necessary to provide efficient and effective patient services through activities such as medicines dispensing, but also it is also necessary to meet the needs of professional groups in the hospital, through services such as clinical pharmacy and medicines information. The Director of Finance will look to see that budgets for staff and consumables are balanced and that targets for Cash-Releasing Efficiency Savings are met. The Trust Board

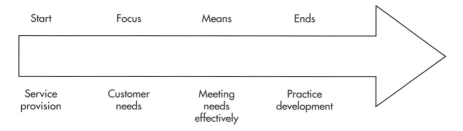

Figure 17.2 Marketing in secondary care.

and external standard setting bodies will want to see that new policies and guidelines are implemented and the demands of clinical governance are met.

Demand management

The concept of demand management is used extensively in the hospital pharmacy setting. Secondary care services have the same problems with managing demand as any other sector, but in some ways have less options to successfully deal with the problem. Secondary care services experience a wide variety of different demand patterns (Table 17.1). Because pharmacy practice often changes and adapts very slowly, the different demand patterns that are seen may often be the result of the requirements of patients and the hospital changing and placing different demands on an established pharmacy service provision.

Although available strategies to manage demand may be fewer in secondary care than in the commercial environment, public managed services are cushioned from the risk of failure that is experienced in the high street. Whereas the successful private business has the option to increase its resources with business expansion, driven by profits and business loans, the managed service can only increase resources through the organisational acceptance of business plans. The current political direction towards primary care led services means that secondary care trusts often reallocate resources from the existing pot, rather than deliver

Table 17.1 Examples of demand patterns in a secondary care environment

Type of demand	Description	Example
Negative demand	The service is avoided	Junior doctors use of formulary management services
No demand	The customers are uninterested	Clinical pharmacy services to orthopaedic theatres
Latent demand	Existing services do not satisfy	Provision of timely discharge prescriptions
Falling demand	Reduced need for the service	Extemporaneous dispensing of creams and ointments
Irregular demand	Demand varies by the hour or day	Dispensing of outpatient prescriptions
Full demand	The service is full to capacity	Aseptic dispensing of TPN
Overfull demand	Demand is higher than capacity	Hospital pharmacy outpatient anticoagulant clinics

new resources into expanding services. The implementation of new technology into hospital services is often slow, partly because the gaining of capital investment is an internal competitive process within the organisation. Implementation of new technology is also slow because of the inertia that is inherent in public sector services.

With a relative inability to grow services according to demand, the pharmacy manager is therefore left with options around improving the efficiency of the current service as a means of coping with increased activity. Common strategies for achieving this include redesign of work systems and skill mix review. The development of pharmacy support staff has gone far further in publicly funded services than in the private sector. It might be argued that the necessities of making better use of the skills available within the cash-limited service have led to developing pharmacy technicians into operational managers and dispensary checking technicians.

Hospital pharmacy services often use strategies such as 'cut-off times' to manage demand, after which a service cannot be used, or mechanisms to prevent direct access to services, such as placing requests for medicines through a ward pharmacist. These barriers to accessing services are practical measures to manage demand, in situations where services are unable to cope with the available activity.

Marketing management

Societal marketing

Hospital pharmacy solely exists within the NHS political context and draws its marketing philosophies from the wider organisation. With previous governments, the internal market allowed for competitive practices, so that successful services could be grown at the expense of others, if health commissioners wished to invest in a particular service. Needless to say, changes of administration bring new philosophies and policies to bear in the NHS.

The societal marketing concept is a relatively new approach to marketing that has gained increased importance with the new administration. The concept holds that the organisation should determine the needs, wants and interests of the target market. This marketing philosophy changes the balance between the perceived interests of an individual customer or group of customers and the overall well-being of society at large. The growth of this approach can be seen to be closely linked to concerns about the environment, resource shortages, global economic awareness and the contribution of life chances to an individual's health outcomes. As part of this change in focus, the NHS is currently seeing the growth in importance of public health practitioners and the widening of the health debate to include education, housing and employment. New organisations that will manage both primary and secondary care organisations should be persuaded to view the pharmacy workforce as a single entity, deployed to achieve the maximum health gain for the population.

This change in direction is a reflection of the rise of social responsibility, as witnessed by the legal actions that have been undertaken against cigarette manufacturers and current litigations against fast food chains. Successful developments in healthcare services now deliver health gain to the population. Successful marketing strategies for new services draw heavily from the conclusions drawn from evidence-based practice and the language of clinical effectiveness.

Marketing myopia – 'We dispense medicines'

A number of different marketing approaches are in existence and influence how a service deals with its customers. The production approach holds out that producing a product efficiently will lead to consumer satisfaction; the product approach is that in which added value is created for the customer through quality improvement; the selling approach is that in which demand for a product needs to be created through selling and promotion; the marketing approach is that success is achieved by meeting customer needs. In the societal marketing approach, a product or service must be seen to have a wider benefit.

Some pharmacists may find that each of the different approaches have a resonance with the way that hospital pharmacies behave in marketing services (Table 17.2). A good example of the 'production approach' might be how pharmacy managers work to increase the output of dispensing services as a way of coping with increasing hospital activity. The Patient Pack initiative has provided opportunities to streamline dispensing processes. An example of the 'product approach' might include how centralised intravenous additive services (CIVAS) work to improve the documentation, labelling and the shelf-life of its intravenous antibiotic reconstitution service.

The 'product approach', in which a producer believes that customer value is derived from a high quality, efficient service, is also the approach associated with 'marketing myopia'. Marketing myopia is a term associated with the belief that the consumer wants an improved

Table 17.2 Approaches to marketing services

Marketing approach	Description of concept	Approach works best	Limitations of approach
PRODUCTION APPROACH	Consumers want cheap products. Managers work to improve efficiency to increase value.	Where demand exceeds supply, e.g. dispensing of discharge prescriptions.	Where product quality becomes more important, e.g. patients require assessment and address of their compliance needs.
PRODUCT APPROACH	Continuous quality improvement of a product or service.	In a closed market, where a sole consumer works jointly with a supplier, e.g. CIVAS and antibiotic reconstitution.	The possibilities provided by innovation are ignored and product development follows a single track. Note: marketing myopia.
SELLING APPROACH	Product promotion is used to publicise the benefits of a product or service.	Where an increase in market share can be gained in a static market, e.g. prescription collection and delivery.	Short-term gains can have longer-term consequences. The costs of improving customer value are borne by the producer.
MARKETING APPROACH	Success is achieved through understanding consumer needs and meeting them.	In a well-defined market in which customer needs are met and success is defined through creating customer satisfaction.	In an emerging market, e.g. services provided to PCTs in which the service standards are not defined.
SOCIETAL MARKETING APPROACH	Services should increase the well-being of society as a whole, e.g. enable health gain.	In situations from which long-term goals are more important than short-term success, e.g. reducing heart disease.	Where the financial climate makes it necessary to achieve short-term gains in order to gain support or balance the books.

product, when in fact what the consumer fundamentally wants is a better way of fulfilling their need, or solving their problem. In pharmacy traditional approaches to service provision do not meet customer needs and continuing to provide pharmacy services in the same way, even if these services are provided more efficiently, is not a beneficial strategy in the long term.[1]

The authors identify three key issues as important to the overall success of development initiatives:

- The critical importance of partnerships within the NHS, within sectors and across primary and secondary care interfaces.
- The need to secure changes in the way that clinical practice is presented to managers and clinicians, so that direct associations between local services and clinical effectiveness are secured.
- The need to take account of local circumstances and views in a flexible way, when determining the pace and priorities of change.

Ensuring success in developing the profession therefore lies in seeing the service contribution as part of a joined up system of health, presenting the benefits of service change in terms of health gain to the population and by meeting local health priorities and needs.

Consumers of pharmacy services will continue to want effective medicines, provided in a safe and efficient manner, but not necessarily by a pharmacist based in a dispensary. Emerging models in hospital services include satellite-dispensing stations that provide medicines as part of the medical admission ward, continuous use of patients' own medicines to smooth admission and discharge processes and local aseptic dispensing for critical care areas. From the viewpoint of a single primary-secondary care organisation, the chronic oral medicines required by the patient on admission to hospital should be carried with the patient from primary care. With truncated acute hospital stays and bed shortages, the pressure to discharge a patient after an acute intervention may mean that a community pharmacist should provide the additional medicines required.

The redesign of hospital pharmacy services is therefore a response to a greater understanding of what consumers want from pharmacy services and in a resource-challenged service, removing elements of practice that do not address consumer needs.

The modern trend of removing restrictive professional practices that do not benefit the public also impinge on pharmacy. However, many professional practices, such as double-checking of prescriptions, increase patient safety although they may slow the preparation of prescriptions. Marketing of new services such as medicines management draw heavily on the emergent risk management culture that is seen in the NHS. Medicines management services can be marketed so that pharmacy is presented as an integral part of the patient care team, responsible for valued contributions that minimise clinical, financial and corporate risk. Increasing customer awareness of the benefits of a system, in protecting them from harm, may change perceptions of value.

Leading reports and strategies published recently reflect the change in ideas of the way the profession believes that pharmacy services should be marketed. The recent Audit Commission report, *A Spoonful of Sugar*[2] establishes the existence of significant problems that patients experience when using medicines, and then uses evidence-based (Table 17.3) and risk management approaches to demonstrate effective methodologies by which these problems can be addressed through pharmacy services. Pharmacy managers may have to develop evidence of the effectiveness of their own services on health outcomes for patients.

The Scottish Pharmacy strategy, *The Right Medicine*,[3] requires actions including that each patient should see a pharmacist during their hospital stay and that each Health Board should have access to pharmaceutical public health advice. The recognition that research has an important place in developing pharmacy services is also recognised as one of the key actions and requires that the profession should harness research in order to deliver benefits to patients. Thus establishing patient benefit through high-quality practice research is highlighted as being an essential part of the successful continued development of pharmacy services.

The hospital pharmacy manager therefore operates in a complex environment in which numerous customers can be identified and many different strategies are employed to satisfy their needs. Current trends in improving the customer value of services include re-engineering centralised pharmacy services to take them upstream, closer to the areas where patient activity is carried out. Key requirements for successful marketing will encompass the agendas of evidence-based practice, clinical effectiveness and risk management. These can be understood in the context of a societal marketing approach. Evidence that your service improves the health of the population or contributes to that health gain may be the most effective marketing strategy for pharmacy yet.

Table 17.3 Analysis of clinical pharmacy services that reduce mortality[3]

Clinical pharmacy service	Number of hospitals	Significance level	Lives saved
Clinical research	108	$P < 0.0001$	21 125
Medicines information	237	$P < 0.043$	10 463
CPR team	282	$P < 0.039$	5047
Admission Medicine History	30	$P < 0.005$	3843

Resource management

Capacity planning

Pharmacists working in manufacturing units or aseptic dispensing laboratories are well acquainted with the concept of capacity planning, in which the physical resources of buildings and equipment together with staff resources are explicitly accounted for when planning activity. Capacity planning ensures that the service can achieve the required output in a sustainable and controlled manner. The concept of capability can be thought of as an extension of capacity planning; the skills and knowledge base required by staff are considered and developed in a way that ensures that the service can deal with the required range of tasks and activities in a sustainable and controlled manner. Thus, pharmacy managers must consider what competencies are required from the staff resource and to what level they are needed, as well as considering the numbers of staff and what they will work with.

Service control

Service provision in the health service is closely controlled, through the accountabilities required by clinical, financial and corporate governance. Governance in this context relates to the quality and robustness of output that is required from services across a broad range of areas. Hospital pharmacy managers must therefore ensure that their staff have appropriate competencies and sufficient staff possess the levels of competency required to meet governance standards. For professional activities such as clinical pharmacy and aseptic dispensing or the leadership activities encompassed by management, this process becomes one of training groups of staff in the competencies required of them now at the present time, or for their later careers.

Clinical guidelines are published by government organisations such as NICE and SIGN. These clinical guidelines set out the responsibilities to patients of providers to enable access to evidence-based care and specific standards of care. In Scotland, the Clinical Standards Board for Scotland (CSBS) produces a range of standards that encompass many aspects of service provision. In this system, individual service providers are audited by peers on the quality of service provided in such areas as cancer care and cardiovascular services; but also staff development and patient focus. Achievement of clinical standards is part of the process of corporate governance, because hospital Chief Executive Officers are responsible for ensuring that all patients receive safe and effective clinical care and treatment based on available evidence. An example of a service log is given in Table 17.4. Many of the standards of performance required from pharmacy services in England for managing medicines are set out in the Controls Assurance document. The achievement of the standards set out in these assessment frameworks requires that pharmacy managers put in place systems, staff training and monitoring, in order to ensure that the desired target is met.

Staff development

Especially in the NHS, highly performing services rely on well-trained motivated staff. Professional and organisational standards require that the pharmacist manager is responsible for the standard of work produced by staff under their control. Hospital Trusts have corporate policies on staff performance and development review, personal development plans, training plans and policies for managing poor performance. Staff management and training are components of everyday work.

The benefits of training and developing of staff are not only that new knowledge and skills are gained and these improve effectiveness and adaptability, but also that staff feel more valued and are more likely to invest the discretionary effort in their work that is necessary for a successful service. Pharmacy managers need to develop the coaching and mentoring skills required to develop the staff that report to them and also ensure that there is the capability to undertake this function elsewhere in their management structure.

The process of developing staff is one of the most satisfying and rewarding activities that a manager can be involved with. The process of engaging with a group of staff or individual staff member and gaining that individual's contributions towards the success of the service is the benefit that should be achieved from this process. A successful performance management system requires the communication of a vision for the service that staff can see as worthwhile. The staff group must be equipped and prepared in terms of their own skills and their knowledge of the performance management process. A successful process will allow staff members to see how achievement of their personal objectives fits into the greater whole and to the success of the department.

Personal development planning (PDP) is a way of engaging with and motivating staff, but also preparing them for future roles. Successful PDP can be used for succession planning either for the benefit of the local service or as a contribution as part of the wider NHS family. In the PDP

Table 17.4 Example from Clinical Standards Board for Scotland Generic Standards – Risk Management

STANDARD 2 – SAFE AND EFFECTIVE CLINICAL CARE
All patients receive safe and effective clinical care and treatment based on available evidence.

Component	Current Actions/Status	Gaps/Deficiencies
2.1 Clinical Guidelines		
2.1.1 Care is delivered in accordance with evidence-based clinical guidelines to produce better outcomes for patients	SIGN Guidelines reviewed for implementation. Compliance with professional standards. RPhSGB Registered Pharmacy. CRAG Framework for Practice	Guidelines not implemented uniformly in all sectors. Business plans to be developed to provide resources.
2.2 Audit		
2.2.1 Departmental audits are carried out to monitor the performance of the pharmaceutical service provided with the aim of improving the service and minimising risks	Twice yearly audit cycle for: Dispensing, Aseptic Dispensing Stores and Distribution, Procurement Drug Information Quality Assurance	Ensure carried out biannually and actions taken as identified
2.2.2 National External Audit Programme using the Aseptic Dispensing Services Audit Schedule	Aseptic dispensaries are included in external audit programme	Ensure identified actions are achieved and reviewed
2.3 CNORIS		
2.3.1 Clinical and non-clinical risk is identified, evaluated and managed in accordance with the requirements of the Clinical Negligence and Other Risks Indemnity Scheme (CNORIS)	Risk control plans are developed and reviewed every three months	Ensure Clinical Governance Committee provides control and monitoring
2.4 Risk environment		
Compliance with health and safety regulations is systematically monitored	Risk assessment and systems monitoring is carried out in identified sectors where moving and handling, chemical risks, display screen hazards are found	Key staff trained in risk assessment qualification by IOSH. Routine assessment of environment

process, individuals reflect on their past and present experiences, identify strengths and weaknesses and use this thinking to target their development needs and to help focus on planning their career. An example of the PDP planning process is shown in the case study below. PDPs are useful tools for identifying training needs and for formulating training plans. This technique can be used successfully with both pharmacist and technician groups. Managers may be able to provide support for this themselves or may have to bring in help from Trust Organisational Development departments. The process of evaluating training needs and completing training plans is an essential part of ensuring the capability of the service.

 CASE STUDY 1

An example of the personal development planning process
The PDP process must answer five questions:

1. Where have I been?
   - What is my background?
   - What have been my previous experiences?
   - What have I learnt from them?

2. Where am I now?
   - What skills and qualities do I possess?
   - What are my strengths and weaknesses?

3. Where do I want to get to?
   - What kind of person do I want to be?
   - What skills and qualities do I need to develop, and to what level?

4. How do I get there?
   - What experiences do I require to learn what I need to learn?
   - What learning programmes do I need?
   - What experiments do I need to try?
   - What kind of help do I need, and from whom?
   - What is the overall timescale?
   - What are the key stages/steps along the way?

5. How will I know when I have arrived?
   - How will I evaluate my learning?
   - What measures do I need to assess my progress and myself?
   - What feedback do I need and from whom?

In terms of individual development, a lot of current focus is on continuing professional development (CPD). Whilst CPD is an individual pharmacist's responsibility, managers cannot avoid providing support and opportunities for their staff to plan how they will achieve their needs for professional development. Indeed altering staff perspectives, so that opportunities for continuing education are viewed in the context of planned development needs, means that expenditure on training becomes a planned part of achieving service goals. Tying in CPD with PDP has advantages in the managed service, because the individuals then make use of their training efforts to contribute towards agreed organisational targets.

Skill mix

Increasingly with the shortage in availability of all staff grades within hospital pharmacy, pharmacists are being seen as clinicians whose skills are needed to provide care directly to patients. Alongside this thinking comes the realisation that technical staff can successfully undertake many of the tasks that were traditionally performed by pharmacists. There are very few roles that need to be undertaken strictly by a pharmacist. The *Pharmaceutical Journal* carries advertisements for technician dispensary managers and national courses exist to accredit dispensary checking technicians. The development of the practice of the clinical pharmacist into areas previously undertaken by medical staff such as prescribing, means that many of the ward pharmacy roles are being handed to clinical technicians; pharmacy technicians working within a ward environment.

Developing staff to take on new roles requires the pharmacy manager to work on two fronts – preparing the skills of pharmacy support staff to perform different tasks competently and safely and also creating the attitudes and orientation of pharmacists and technicians who may be challenged by the change agenda. Thus, as the change agenda progresses, ward top-up, which may at one time have been an activity undertaken by technical staff, becomes part of an assistant's work, with technicians undertaking supply of dispensed non-ward stock items. Ensuring sufficient capability to make this change means that managers must have a clear idea of the competencies required for staff to undertake the identified roles and have a means of training and assessing staff who they plan to do the work. Ensuring the competence of staff is a risk management issue.

Vocational training schemes

Vocational training schemes for pharmacists are designed to provide staged development, so that a staff resource with the required capability is ensured within the NHS family. The first UK scheme was the Scottish Hospital Pharmacists Vocational Training Scheme, a good example of how cooperation within the service can produce a worthwhile end result (Figure 17.3).

This scheme takes preregistration pharmacists (Stage 1) and provides structured experience in hospital pharmacy (Stage II). The trainee pharmacist is assessed through provision of evidence of their achievement of six performance criteria, recorded in a training portfolio. On successful completion of Stage II training, pharmacists have evidence that they are competent to practice in hospital pharmacy and managers employing these staff are assured that candidates at interview, possess the competencies necessary for their service. A joint agreement with the

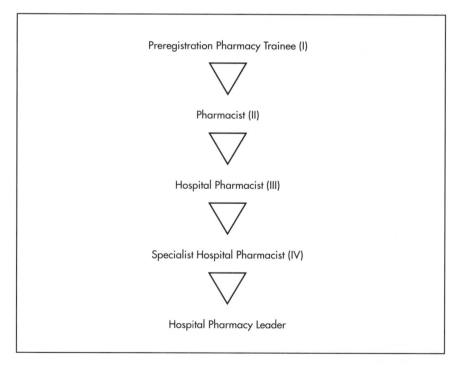

Figure 17.3 Scottish vocational training scheme staged development process.

College of Pharmacy Practice recognises this achievement with membership of the College. Stage III training is provided for hospital pharmacists and allows them to develop the competencies required by Specialist Hospital Pharmacists. Stage IV is designed to train Hospital Pharmacy Leaders. The competencies set out for Stage IV require the candidate to demonstrate a wide range of abilities in a strategic thinking, planning and service evaluation. Similar schemes are also required to support the development of services provided by primary care pharmacy staff and pharmacy technical staff.

Measuring performance

Much is made of the pharmacist's scientific training and it may be this that makes an evidence-based and logical style of management a natural choice. The traditional 'Plan, Do, Review' management model is therefore one with which pharmacists can identify with well. The review part of this model requires that the performance of the service be measured in an objective, quantifiable way. For the pharmacy manager, the prospect of using performance measures to direct and motivate staff, as well as create a greater understanding of their service, is very attractive.

Performance measurement can create concerns from groups of staff with previously bad experiences, or who fear that the process is designed to show incompetence, or those who see it as a method of top-down management control. Rather than using performance measurement as part of an accountancy-based tool of scientific management, it should be used as a method of taking services forward and managing change.

Performance indicators

Performance measures should be forward-looking and based on achieving the structural changes in performance that will enable key organisational objectives to be achieved. Given that poorly designed measures and poorly implemented processes are counter-productive, it is important to plan and enact the management process with care. The process of developing effective measures is much more important than what the measures are themselves and creating a process that stakeholders buy into is a better achievement than ensuring the measures themselves are precisely right. Performance measurement used expertly, is capable of changing the culture of the group providing the service, through what has been called organisational learning.[4]

The core management process for this has been modelled by Meekings.[5] This model addresses the need to take account of organisational objectives, the needs of customers for service and the needs of staff groups to have ownership of the system of performance measurement (Figure 17.4). The model makes it clear that design of performance indicators ('Visible Feedback Indicators') are not sufficient in themselves as a framework for performance measurement and to achieve service improvement, but how they are used and the value placed on them by staff is of key importance.

The elements of designing a framework for performance measurement resemble a generic process for a standard change management programme:

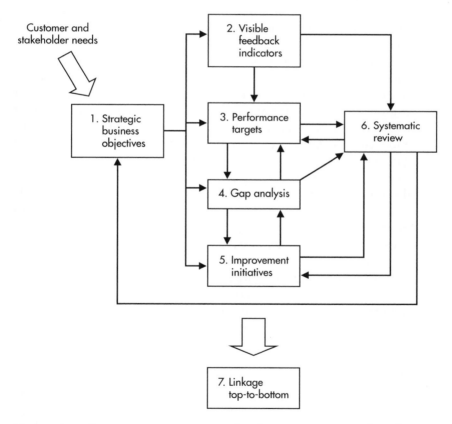

Figure 17.4 Core management process for designing a system of performance measurement.

- Ensuring that the organisation's strategic objective is understood and that senior managers support the work that is to be undertaken to achieve its implementation. The area for performance improvement should be one that improves customer service, so that staff in all sectors can appreciate the value of undertaking the work.
- Communicating the way that the work will be undertaken. Effective communication is time-consuming and requires repeated delivery through different mediums to ensure that the message is received successfully. Effective communication is the best tool to ensure that resistance from stakeholders is avoided. Resistance may come from many different areas, including senior managers, line managers and members of staff.
- Making sure that leaders from different levels in the organisation support the work and appreciate that the motivation for implementing a performance framework is to create service improvement.
- Making sure that the implementation is a positive learning experience for those involved. Creating a climate where staff learn and reflect on what they undertake and achieve is an important part of empowering them and gaining the input of discretionary effort that marks out successful departments. Accepting that failures do occur and that this should not stop more attempts to be successful and gain experience in the process is part of this.
- Making sure that the performance measures are used to improve the service through utilising ideas that emerge from the people doing the performance measurement. Giving staff the power to improve the service through innovating around a strategically chosen performance measure is a very powerful method of changing the service.
- Making sure that groups undertaking the work receive recognition for success. The recognition could be in the form of publicity within the organisation or publication of work or attendance at courses or conferences that deal with the area in a wider sense.

Different approaches in hospital pharmacy

Sectors of the pharmacy remit such as medicine procurement and storage and distribution have been easy targets for imposition of top-down reviews of performance by government. For example, Audit Scotland has recently published an audit of supplies organisations in NHS Scotland.[6] The service has a responsibility to ensure best practice and deliver on the changes required. Making the change process a positive experience for staff is a challenge. Pharmacy managers can utilise elements from official publications in order to gain a start towards measuring performance and implementing the changes required. The publication of performance indicators on procurement (see Case study below) and a timetable for implementation have to be taken up by local managers and put in context for staff, if any value is to be achieved from the resource invested in designing the report.

The strategic messages contained in the report are standard ones for supplies organisations, in that centrally negotiated contracts achieve better value for money; procurement is often undertaken by staff who are not involved in the organisation's purchasing function; technology is implemented slowly and the benefits to the NHS are not realised; procurement performance is not systematically measured. The gap between the strategic messages and the stated performance indicators is wide and the report does little to assist managers with creating the joined up processes that will enable service improvement and organisational learning to be achieved. These types of indicators do not fulfil Meeking's criteria for use of performance indicators to achieve strategic change and leave the local manager with a lot to do.

Clinical pharmacy activities are more difficult to measure than the processes involved in procurement, storage and distribution. Clinical

 CASE STUDY 2

Procurement performance indicators[6]

- Local level indicators
- Financial
- Total operational costs
- Total value of inventory holding
- Average value per purchase order
- Cost per transaction
- Inventory
- Number of product lines held in stock
- Number of days stocks held
- Percentage of stock inactive
- Value of write-offs

pharmacy is about patient assessment and cognitive and communication processes. These features make it less amenable to managerial control or indeed of imposed top-down assessments of performance. However, the pharmacy manager has a greater need to monitor and improve the performance of this aspect of pharmacy practice. Not only is the most expensive part of staff resource in place in this sector, but also an effective clinical pharmacy service makes an obvious contribution to improving the health of patients and also acts as a marketing tool for pharmacy in general.

Clinical pharmacy services are often managed using flat structures, rather than more traditional hierarchical structures. Flat structures require that systems of control be put in place using more sophisticated tools than those used to control hierarchical structures. Useful tools may include group objective setting, team briefing, joint team development events and walk-about management.

Critical points in the patient admission process, where clinical pharmacists can influence patient outcomes, are at admission and discharge. Healthcare evidence has shown that these points are places where pharmacists can improve patient outcomes. In terms of the successful management of clinical pharmacy services, a framework of performance measurement, using performance indicators to demonstrate how well pharmacists interact with patients at admission and discharge, is a key management strategy. The standard way to involve clinical staff in performance measurement is to create an audit cycle using performance indicators (visible feedback indicators) around their interaction with patients at these points, as the standard for audit.

Patient-centred performance indicators around the patient journey include the following:

- Each patient should have an accurate admission drug history.
- Each patient should have continuity of medicine supply.
- Each patient should have their medicine-related problems assessed and care issues addressed.
- Each patient should have an accurate and timely discharge process.

The further steps to creating a framework for performance measurement are to empower staff to innovate and learn around these processes and supporting those staff managerially with resource allocation and targeted professional development. From the Meekings model, such an approach would be utilised to deliver a change in the staff's perception of priorities and of their investment in achieving service improvement.

The cost of measurement

With a medicine manufacturing production line, a sample of the finished product might be taken and assayed to make sure that its characteristics match those required in the product specification. The size of the sample that needs to be assessed can be reduced if all the processes that led to the production of the medicine are guaranteed to have been completed accurately. Confidence in the suitability of the completed product increases if the processes that were used to produce it are controlled.

In a hospital pharmacy service, destructive testing of an end product is not undertaken routinely. Rather, the processes that are used to dispense aseptic products or discharge prescriptions are set out in standard operating procedures. Audit activities are undertaken to test that the product or service are fit for the purpose intended. The safety of operating systems in pharmacy has received close attention through review of dispensing errors, problems with aseptic dispensing environments and of systems to prepare and administer chemotherapy. The cost to an organisation of failing systems is real and justifies investment in quality assurance procedures.

Many pharmacy services seek external validation that corroborates that their operating systems are well maintained and that staff are able to use them accurately. Thus accreditation systems such as the Kings Fund Organisational Audit and ISO 9000 have had widespread attention from pharmacy managers. External accreditation systems give organisations an assurance that a methodical process for creating and reviewing systems is in place.

The need to measure performance and to create confidence that the organisation is not exposed to excess risk is one at the forefront in the modern NHS. Hospital pharmacists need to be aware of the complexity of what they do and of its effects on patients and the wider environment. Managing safely in this context means making sure that staff are trained and systems are fit for purpose.

References

1. Cousins D H, Luscombe D K. A new model for hospital pharmacy practice. *Pharm J* 1996; 256: 347–351.
2. Audit Commission. *A Spoonful of Sugar – Medicines Management in NHS Hospitals*. London: Audit Commission, 2001.
3. Scottish Executive. *The Right Medicine: A Strategy for Pharmaceutical Care in Scotland*. Edinburgh: HMSO, 2002.

4.   Likierman A. Performance indicators: 20 early lessons from managerial use. *Public Money & Management* 1993; 13(4): 15–22.
5.   Meekings A. Unlocking the potential of performance measurement: a practical implementation guide. *Public Money & Management* 1995; 15(4): 5–12.
6.   Audit Commission for Scotland. *In Good Supply*. Edinburgh: Audit Commission for Scotland, 2002.
7.   Radley A S, Millar B W, Hamley J. Development of patient-centred performance indicators to guide the delivery of pharmaceutical care in a district general hospital. *Pharmacy World & Science* 2001; 23(3): 111–115.

Further reading

National Pharmacy Management Seminar – Crystallising the Vision (held in London in April 2004) (available from http://www.pharman.co.uk/cms/view. php/3209.html).
Association of Scottish Chief Pharmacists (ASCP). Improving Pharmaceutical Care and the Patient Journey: Redesign of Medicines Management Across the Primary/Secondary/Tertiary Care Interface, March 2001 (available from http://www.show.scot.nhs.uk/astcp/; accessed 9 August 2004).

18

Medicines management

Richard Seal

Introduction

In this chapter we see how management skills are involved in the provision of a clinical service that is the basis of the expanded role central to the NHS Contract for community pharmacy. Medicines management is shaping up to be the most important service in community pharmacy and in time will surely become the critical factor in determining how much of the material in the preceding chapters is applied, for example layout of the sales and dispensing areas, staffing and continuing professional development (CPD).

What is medicines management?

The concept of medicines management is not new. From a historical perspective, individuals have been making their own decisions about using substances with alleged therapeutic properties for centuries. However, as medical practice has advanced, medicines have become more potent and complex to use. Their potential to both help and harm has increased; particularly since the middle of the last century. Managing medicines has become vitally important for both patients and practitioners alike.

However, the term medicines management has come to mean different things to different people. A good example is the debate about the relationship between medicines management and pharmaceutical care.[1]

In Scotland (and other countries too, especially New Zealand and Denmark), the concept of pharmaceutical care is considered to be more encompassing than medicines management alone and forms a major part of pharmaceutical strategy in these countries.

To some extent, a precise definition is perhaps less important than an appreciation of the sort of activities that could come under the broad heading of medicines management. However, there are a number of key elements that run through many of the definitions that have been proposed. Prerequisites for good medicines management practice include:

- Involving patients as partners in decisions made about their care.
- Identifying and addressing the patient's pharmaceutical care needs.
- Helping them to get the most from the medicines they use, thereby maintaining or increasing their quality or duration of life.
- Avoiding ill health caused by inappropriate or inadequate therapy.
- Improving access to efficient and cost-effective medicines for those that would benefit from them.
- Reducing waste and inefficiency in the way that drugs are procured, supplied or used.
- Making better use of the skills of professionals, particularly pharmacists, working together as part of a multidisciplinary approach to medicines usage.

Hence medicines management is concerned with the design, implementation and delivery of accessible, appropriate and cost-effective care for patients based on their needs. It should help prevent, identify and resolve problems that could interfere with the goals of drug treatment or improved health outcomes. Medicines management also includes all aspects of the therapeutic use of medicines from organisation to individual patient level. Good medicines management should also lead to better use of professional time and save resources.

The need for medicines management

A variety of clinical practitioners, with specialist knowledge and skills, make significant decisions about which medicines to use for patients, the circumstances under which to use them and the likely outcomes of any intervention. It might even be argued that they have assumed the role of 'medicines managers', sometimes at the expense of the involvement of the patients under their care. In fact, the prescribing of medication is now the most common therapeutic intervention made within the NHS in the UK. Around 550 million prescription items are issued by GPs each year, with hospitals contributing an additional 200 million or more.[2]

There is compelling evidence that medicines are not used as well as they could be and this provides a strong argument for better medicines management. For example, between 5% and 17% of all hospital admissions in people over 65 years old are estimated to result from problems with medicines.[3] Adverse events related to medicines cost the NHS about £500 million a year in additional bed-days.[4] Up to half of all patients with chronic conditions do not use their medicines in a way that is fully effective.[3] This statement is backed up by a recent small-scale study in older people recently discharged from hospital, which found that nearly a third said that they needed more help to take their medicines as intended and up to 40% were taking a medicine that could be safely stopped without affecting their care (Sati Urbi, Medication Review Project Pharmacist, Huntingdonshire Primary Care Trust, personal communication, March 2003).

In an average population of about 100 000 people, it has been estimated that up to 22 people each year will suffer acute congestive heart failure as a result of taking non-steroidal anti-inflammatory drugs that they have been prescribed.[5] These are potent medicines that are often prescribed for pain relief where a simple analgesic would be just as effective.

In contrast, there are people who would benefit from certain medicines, for example drugs to reduce excessive cholesterol levels, but who do not receive them.[6]

Nor is it just the medicines themselves or the way that they are used that cause problems. Sometimes aspects of the whole system create difficulties, for example the repeat dispensing processes used in general practice. These have evolved to deal with the need for patients to have long-term medications re-prescribed without the need to see a doctor on every occasion. In fact, up to three-quarters of all prescriptions in general practice are issued in this way.[7] It has been recognised that the operation and maintenance of repeat prescribing systems is less than perfect.[8] As an example, the wastage due to inequivalence in prescription quantities has been estimated to account for between 6% and 10% of total prescribing costs in family health services.[9]

This is not to underestimate the cost in terms of staff time and other resources too. On average a general practitioner prescribes between 250 and 350 prescription items every week[10] and they spend up to two hours a week just authorising repeat prescriptions.

Clearly better medicines management is likely to have an impact wherever medicines are involved and used.

Medicines management and the pharmacist

Medicines management in its broadest sense is a diverse, multifaceted and complex issue. Clearly, there is a substantial need to better understand and begin to address some of the difficult issues that poor medicines management raises. It is also apparent that no one profession in isolation can accept primary responsibility for all aspects of medicines management.

However, there is a growing awareness and acknowledgement that pharmacists can and should have a greater role in how medicines are used and how medicines management can be improved. There is a worldwide trend to use pharmacists' knowledge and skills in new and innovative ways. For example, in the USA, Spain, New Zealand and Australia, some pharmacists already receive remuneration from insurance companies, health maintenance or government organisations for medicines management activities.

In the UK, the development of medicines management and pharmaceutical care (a term preferred in Scotland) has been boosted by a number of governmental policy documents and initiatives.[11,12] For example, in September 2001, the Department of Health in England announced the investment of up to £30 million over 3 years to support the implementation of *Pharmacy in the Future. Implementing the NHS Plan*.[11] This included the funding of two major new initiatives for developing the concept of medicines management and the involvement of pharmacists. As well as the statement that all primary care organisations should provide convenient access to a range of appropriate medicines management services by 2004.

In addition, a significant restructuring of the NHS, which involves the devolution of responsibility for decision-making and supporting funds to a more local level, has opened up a wide range of new opportunities for pharmacists interested in providing medicines management services.

The advent of robotic dispensing technology, repeat dispensing pathfinder schemes, the move towards electronic transfer of prescriptions, commissioning of local pharmaceutical services schemes and supplementary prescribing by pharmacists all have the potential to improve medicines management. Although it is likely to be some years before some of these services are fully implemented, pharmacists need to be ready to respond to them in a positive way. For some, this may mean working in perhaps new and quite different ways than previously.

Getting started in medicines management

For some people, the idea of getting involved in medicines management is a daunting prospect. This is understandable given the broad scope of the subject, but such concerns should be tempered by the realisation that practising pharmacists already provide medicines management services to a greater or lesser degree.

Jenkins and Ghalamkari[13] propose a helpful, stratified approach to developing medicines management services that recognises concerns about engaging in new work and extending roles. Their medicines management matrix provides a conceptual framework for developing services incrementally and includes recognition for activities already undertaken. Although it uses examples with a community pharmacy focus, their approach can be applied to other sectors of pharmacy practice too.

A similar philosophy underpins the national collaborative medicines management services programme, hosted by the National Prescribing Centre (NPC) in Liverpool (http://www.npc.co.uk/mms). This uses a proven improvement methodology, the 'collaborative approach', to bring about rapid, small-scale but incremental changes in services. This is achieved by encouraging the sharing and adoption of existing good practice by people working together towards a common goal. It involves learning from others and testing out ideas for change. What works well elsewhere may not fit in with your own way of working or your own local situation. However, this approach has been proven time and again to lead to sustainable improvements in services.

The Medicines Partnership Centre was established with the aim of putting the concept of concordance into practice. It co-authored a guide to medication review,[14] a key component of better patient care, with the collaborative medicines management programme. Its website (http://www.medicines-partnership.org/medication-review) also contains a range of tools for developing medication review services.

Clearly, those contemplating providing more advanced medicines management services may need to acquire new knowledge or develop new skills or refresh existing ones. Happily, there are a range of opportunities and approaches available. Many of the existing academic institutions offer courses tailored specifically towards medicines management from both a clinical and non-clinical perspective. The Centre for Pharmacy Postgraduate Education (CPPE) in England and equivalent organisations elsewhere have well-developed programmes for supporting pharmacists interested in medicines management. The National Prescribing Centre provides a range of educational materials, activities and events that focus on medicines management. National pharmacy bodies such as the Pharmaceutical Services Negotiating Committee, the National Pharmaceutical Association and the Guild of Healthcare Pharmacists can also offer support.

In 2001, the College of Pharmacy Practice (CPP) established the Faculty of Prescribing and Medicines Management. Its remit is to provide a professional forum, continual professional development, education and training and further support for pharmacists engaged in, or with an interest in medicines management. It has already described a set of competencies for pharmacists working in this specialist area of practice.[15]

Medicines management in practice

Prerequisites for good medicines management have already been established but it is perhaps less clear how they can be translated into practice.

A more specific approach to underpin all medicines management activities will help practitioners focus on the connection between theory and practice and clarify responsibilities for any interventions.

- Ensure that medicines are appropriately indicated, as safe as possible, effective for the given indication, able to be taken as intended and cost-effective.
- Enable and empower the patient to be involved as a partner in decisions made about their treatment.
- Identify, resolve and prevent any problems that might interfere with first two responsibilities.
- Make sure that the goals of therapy are met and the best possible outcomes realised.

This approach can be adopted at all levels of medicines management, applied by any practitioner involved in medicines management and in all environments in which medicines are used.

Hospital pharmacy

Medicines are a central component of care and medicines management in NHS hospitals is well established. The Audit Commission report[4] provides a precise definition:

> Medicines management in hospitals encompasses the entire way that medicines are selected, procured, delivered, prescribed, administered and reviewed to optimise the contribution that medicines make to producing informed and desired outcomes of patient care.

Examples of medicines management activities in hospitals include:

- Drug utilisation review and formulary development.
- Pharmacist-led medication review services.
- 'One-stop' dispensing schemes.
- Pre-admission and discharge planning medication counselling.

- Robotic dispensing systems.
- Pharmacist input to clinical ward rounds.
- Medication error recording and reporting.
- Directorate-based pharmacy teams.
- Promoting self-administration of medicines by patient.
- Development and implementation of patient group directions.

Community pharmacy

Community pharmacists already play an important role in medicines management in the community. They have the advantage that they are easily accessible, often have extensive knowledge of patients and their medicines and can tailor services to a patient's particular needs. The advent of new initiatives such as supplementary prescribing, repeat dispensing and the electronic transfer of prescriptions will open up a whole range of exciting new possibilities for medicines management.

Examples of medicines management activities provided by community pharmacies include:

- medication review
- minor ailment schemes
- medication monitoring
- waste medicines schemes
- prescription intervention schemes
- public health information
- extended services to care homes
- repeat dispensing
- prescribing advice to GPs
- enhanced prescription collection and delivery services
- monitored dosage systems.

Primary care pharmacy

Although a relatively new sector of practice, pharmacists working in GP surgeries and primary care organisations are rapidly establishing their value to others in the primary care team. The range of medicines management services provided in primary care is developing quickly. A recent workforce census suggested that approximately 6% of pharmacists work in primary care.[16]

Examples of medicines management activities provided by primary care pharmacists include:

- medication review clinics
- prescribing advice
- analysis of prescribing data
- commissioning of pharmaceutical care
- policy development and implementation
- therapy management services (e.g. anticoagulant clinics)
- dose synchronisation and optimisation in GP surgeries
- medicines information helplines
- therapeutic substitution.

Medicines management involving other professionals

Medicines management is not the sole remit of any one profession and there are many examples of medicines management services that do not directly involve pharmacists. Given the scope of medicines management this is not surprising. From the perspective of the patient or carer, improved access to medicines management is likely to be welcomed as long as the person involved is competent to perform the required activity and works within these limits.

Examples of medicines management activities provided by other professions include:

- clinical medication review by general practitioners
- compliance checking by nurses as part of chronic disease management clinics
- use of non-prescription medicines in residential accommodation for older people
- identification of medication problems by social care professionals as part of the single assessment process
- medication counselling by pharmacy technicians.

Summary

The development of pharmacy as a profession is heavily focused upon medicines management. There is a strong political and professional imperative to make better use of the knowledge and skills of the pharmacy workforce and medicines management is the vehicle that could be used to deliver it. Pharmacists are well placed to provide high-quality medicines management services in all sectors of practice.

However, to excel there needs to be strong professional leadership coupled with a clear demonstration that modernisation of the profession has embraced both the concepts and practice of medicine management.

New services must be based on the needs of patients and their carers, as a 'one size fits all' approach is unlikely to be appropriate except at the most basic level. Practitioners of medicines management will need to ensure that they apply the principles of good clinical governance to their work and strive to acquire new knowledge and skills where these are currently deficient.

However, medicines management offers pharmacists tremendous opportunities for both personal and professional fulfilment, as well as improving care for patients. It is our duty to make sure that such opportunities are embraced and made part of 'the way we do things now'.

References

1. Simpson D. What is medicines management and what is pharmaceutical care? *Pharm J* 2001; 266: 150.
2. *Prescription Cost Analysis: England 2001*. London: Department of Health, 2002 (http://www.publications.doh.gov.uk/stats/pca2001.htm).
3. *Medicines and Older People. Implementing Medicines-related Aspects of the NSF for Older People*. London: Department of Health, 2001 (http://www.doh.gov.uk/asset/Root/04/06/72/47/04067247.pdf).
4. *A Spoonful of Sugar – Medicines Management in NHS Hospitals*. London: Audit Commission, 2001.
5. Bandolier (2000). More on NSAID adverse effects (http://www.jr2.ox.ac.uk/bandolier/band79/b79–6.html; accessed 27 July 2004).
6. Department of Health. *National Service Framework for Coronary Heart Disease London*, 2000 (http://www.doh.gov.uk/asset/Root/04/07/71/58/04077158.pdf).
7. Harris C M, Dajdar R. The scale of repeat prescribing. *Br J Gen Pract* 1996; 46: 649–653.
8. Zermansky A. Who controls repeats? *Br J Gen Pract* 1996; 46: 643–647.
9. Davidson R. An analysis of the quality and costs of repeat prescriptions. *Pharm J* 1998; 260: 458–460.
10. Anon. *GP prescribing support: a resource document and guide for the new NHS*. Liverpool: National Prescribing Centre, 1998 (http://www.npc.co.uk/annualreports/1997–98/dissemination03.htm).
11. *Pharmacy in the Future. Implementing the NHS Plan*. London: Department of Health, 2000 (http://www.doh.gov.uk/asset/Root/04/06/82/04/04068204.pdf).
12. The Scottish Executive. *The Right Medicine: A Strategy for Pharmaceutical Care in Scotland*. Edinburgh: The Scottish Executive, 2002 (available from http:// www.scotland.gov.uk/library3/health/pcis-00.asp).
13. Jenkins D, Ghalamkari H. *A pragmatic way forward. Pharm J* 2001; 266: 281.
14. Task Force on Medicines Partnership and the Collaborative Medicines Management Services Programme. *Room for Review. A Guide to Medication*

Review: the Agenda for Patients, Practitioners and Managers. London, 2002 (http://www.medicines-partnership.org/medication-review).

15. Competency Framework (http://www.medicines-partnership.org/medication-review/room-for-review/downloads).

16. Anon. Pharmacy workforce census. Overview of main census findings. *Pharm J* 2003; 270: 314–315.

Further reading

Bellingham C. Establishing pharmacy's future standards. Medicines management 'not about rocket science'. Report of AAH Pharmaceuticals and Vantage Convention, Las Vegas 2001. *Pharm J* 2001; 266: 728.

Fitzpatrick R W, Mucklow J C, Fillingham D. A comprehensive system for managing medicines in secondary care. *Pharm J* 2001; 266: 585–588.

Managing Medicines website, a resource centre for medicines management and pharmaceutical care (http://www.managingmedicines.com).

Tweedie A, Rutter P, Jones I. Independent pharmacy contractors' views on the new medicines management service. *Pharm J* 2004; 273: 121–123.

Further information may also be obtained from the College of Pharmacy Practice Faculty of Prescribing and Medicines Management (http://www.collpharm.org.uk/fpmmain.html).

In July 2004 the Welsh Executive of the RPSGB produced a paper entitled 'Pharmacy Involvement in Medicines Management across Wales'. (Available from http://www.rpsgb.org.uk/wales/pdfs/devrep.pdf).

Appendix 1

Pharmaceutical organisations involved in business practice

The following organisations have important input to community pharmacy.

The Royal Pharmaceutical Society of Great Britain (http://www.rpsgb.org.uk/)

The Royal Pharmaceutical Society of Great Britain (RPSGB) is a regulatory as well as a professional body for pharmacists in all aspects of practice. It has a statutory duty to maintain the register of pharmacists and pharmacy premises. As well as fulfilling its statutory roles in public health, the RPSGB operates widely to promote the development of the science and practice of pharmacy. It is governed by a Council, which meets six times every year to discuss key issues affecting pharmacy and to decide on policies and practice. The Society is the most important and influential body in the pharmacy world. It is strategically located in Lambeth High Street, London, near Richmond House, which houses the Department of Health (DoH) and is in the vicinity of Westminster. Some research projects of the Society are funded by the DoH. It has over 250 employees. The Society is now aiming to develop a common code of ethics for all pharmacy staff.

RPSGB branches and regions

The Society's 130 branches provide a local focus for professional and educational matters, with regular meetings on a wide range of scientific and current affairs topics. There are also 11 regions in England, which act as a link between the branches and the Society's Council, and co-ordinate larger-scale public relations activities. The Society also has an office in Cardiff to oversee Welsh affairs.

The Royal Pharmaceutical Society Scottish Department (http://www.rpsgb.org.uk/scotland/)

The Royal Pharmaceutical Society's Scottish Department operates from the Society's House in York Place in Edinburgh, and looks after the professional needs of Scottish pharmacists. The department was established in 1851 and gained statutory recognition as an integral part of the Society in the supplemental royal charter granted in December 1953. The department can provide advice on a range of topics, including pharmacy law and ethics and the law as it applies in Scotland. The Royal Pharmaceutical Society in Scotland (RPSiS) is particularly active in lobbying on behalf of the profession in Scotland at the Scottish Parliament.

The Pharmaceutical Society of Northern Ireland

The Pharmaceutical Society of Northern Ireland (RPSNI) is a regulatory and a professional body for pharmacists registered in Northern Ireland. It has similar statutory roles to the RPSGB and is similarly responsible for driving standards and ensuring continual professional development among the pharmacists in Northern Ireland as well as being responsible for the registration of pharmacy premises. The Ulster Chemists Association in Belfast is a trade organisation for pharmacies in Northern Ireland (http://www.kellysearch.com/company-82590647.html).

The Pharmaceutical Services Negotiating Committee (http://www.psnc.org.uk/)

The Pharmaceutical Services Negotiating Committee (PSNC) has 25 members on its main committee: 15 members elected on a regional basis; five members from the Board of the National Pharmaceutical Association; four members from the Company Chemists Association and a representative from the Co-operative Pharmacy Technical Panel. The Secretary and Registrar of the RPSGB also attends the PSNC meetings. The PSNC is empowered by the government to negotiate remuneration for all contractors in England and Wales. It is recognised by the Secretary of State for Health as representative of community pharmacy on NHS matters. Its main objective is to secure the best possible remuneration, terms and conditions for NHS pharmacy contractors in England and Wales. Much of the PSNC's work involves discussions and negotiations with the National Health Service Executive (NHSE). The constitution of the PSNC is currently being examined to see how it can best reflect the current pharmacy demographics.

The PSNC also operate the National Prescription Research Centre (NPRC) based in London. A percentage of all prescriptions sent to the Prescription Pricing Authority (PPA) are checked and errors in pricing are corrected. Each year, after negotiations with the PSNC, the Department of Health allocates a lump sum of money, called the Global Sum, which is the budget to pay community pharmacy contractors for providing the NHS pharmaceutical service in the ensuing financial year.

The Scottish Pharmaceutical General Council (http://www.42queenstreet.org.uk/)

The Scottish Pharmaceutical General Council (SPGC) represents the interests of pharmacy contractors in negotiations with the Scottish Executive. The Council negotiates with the Scottish Executive on behalf of Scottish community pharmacists the terms and conditions for the provision of National Health pharmaceutical services. There are 42 members of the General Council, elected by the various Area Pharmacy Contractors Committees across Scotland. In addition, representatives of the Company Chemists' Association and of the Co-operative Chemists are members. The SPGC also invites to its meetings, as observers, representatives from RPSiS, the Scottish Pharmaceutical Federation and the Northern Ireland Contractors' Committee. The General Council meets twice or three times a year. The Standing Committee, consisting of 13 members elected by the SPGC plus two Company Chemists' nominees, is the executive committee of the SPGC, and meets monthly.

Community Pharmacy Wales (http://www.psnc.org.uk/index.php?type=cpwpage&pid=32&k=10)

The PSNC has a long history of supporting Welsh pharmacy contractors under the auspices of the PSNC's Welsh Committee, the 'Welsh Central Pharmaceutical Committee'. Following devolution and the formation of the National Assembly for Wales, the Welsh Committee has been called on more to liaise with the Assembly and negotiate on behalf of Welsh contractors.

In November 2001, the Welsh Central Pharmaceutical Committee changed its name to Community Pharmacy Wales (CPW) to reflect more clearly the Committee's role.

In December 2002, pharmacy contractors in Wales voted unanimously for a single representative committee, Community Pharmacy Wales (CPW), supported by three regional committees based in the new NHS Regions of North Wales, Mid & West Wales and South & East

Wales. CPW outlined the proposed new structure to pharmacy contractors at a meeting in Llandrindod Wells in October 2003 followed by a postal ballot of all pharmacy contractors in Wales.

The Welsh Assembly has now endorsed this new structure and has formally recognised Community Pharmacy Wales as the statutory contractor committee.

The National Pharmaceutical Association (http://www.npa.co.uk/)

The National Pharmaceutical Association (NPA) is the national body of community pharmacy owners; it has a sister organisation in Scotland (see below). It was formed in 1921 to champion the interests of pharmacy owners and to promote, improve and protect an essential service to the public. NPA represents 5000 members owning 11 000 pharmacies. Large national multiples, apart from Boots, are members of the NPA. The regional multiples (5–150) like Cohen, Day Lewis, MacFarlane and Peak are also members of the NPA. Pharmacy Mutual, an insurance company owned by the NPA, provides insurance of premises, stock, fixtures and vehicles, as well as selling indemnity insurance to self-employed locum pharmacists. Another company, the Chemist Defence Association (CDA) provides indemnity insurance for all its members at a highly competitive rate. The legal department of the NPA helps members handle indemnity claims. As a trade organisation the NPA offers a number of services including training, insurance, banking and business advice. The Education and Training Department of NPA provides a number of training courses for dispensary staff. Often dubbed 'the voice of community pharmacy', the NPA is called one of the strongest and most successful trade associations in the world and is the envy of other retail groups. The NPA is run by a Board of Management, whose 21 members are elected on a regional basis for a three-year term of office, and give generously of their energy and time to the affairs of the association. The Board focuses on the NPA's key mission: to ensure the members prosper commercially and professionally; to promote, represent and protect the members' interests at all times and to deliver effective support services and advice of the highest quality to meet the members' present and future needs.

The Scottish Pharmaceutical Federation

The Scottish Pharmaceutical Federation (SPF) represents all pharmacy contractors in Scotland. It has a representation on the board of management of the National Pharmaceutical Association, but retains its own independence. The SPF enjoys a strong lobbying power at the Scottish Assembly.

Company Chemist Association Ltd

The Company Chemist Association Ltd (CCA) is the recognised body of UK multiple pharmacy and member companies are responsible for the running of over 4250 pharmacies. The CCA is comprised of Boots, Lloyds Pharmacy, Moss Pharmacy, Safeway Stores, Superdrug, Tesco, Sainsbury's, Rowlands and Asda. It was founded under the Companies Act in 1898 as 'The Drug Companies Association Limited'. Boots was one of its original members. The board of the CCA delegated the majority of its powers to a representative Council who were charged with delivering the main objective – supporting and protecting the character, status and interests of companies who carry on the business of chemists and druggists.

Despite having a relatively low profile, the CCA has actively championed the position of corporate pharmacy on many issues. Today the CCA is extensively consulted on pharmaceutical issues by the government and professional bodies. Its influence is felt at both national and local level. The CCA is represented on the PSNC, LPCs and the RPSGB's Community Pharmacy Group and is a partner in the Community Practice Consortium Group. The expertise, experience and commitment to pharmacy of the member companies are widely respected. This is a reflection of the importance placed by the companies on working together for the future vitality and viability of the pharmacy industry.

The Association of Independent Multiple Pharmacies

The Association of Independent Multiple Pharmacies (AIMp) has been formed as its members have similar businesses and thus similar interests. The regional multiples form about 15% of all pharmacies. Each member has regional strength. The primary aim of the AIMp is to help support the RPSGB, PSNC and NPA in securing a sound future for pharmacists using the strength of these businesses. This is often by way of providing information on pharmacies that would substantiate the case for negotiations towards the new contract. Apart from these the association offers a platform to address common problems peculiar to such businesses. It offers a ready network to discuss relevant issues for pharmacy owners. The members include companies such as Cohens, Day Lewis, Peak Pharmacy, Paydens and Weldricks.

The NHS Confederation

The NHS Confederation is the voice of NHS management and is the only membership body for all NHS organisations. Their members include over 95% of NHS trusts, PCTs and health authorities in England; local health boards and trusts in Wales; health boards and trusts in Scotland; and health and social services trusts and boards in Northern Ireland.

They add value to the NHS by bringing people together to generate fresh thinking – the different parts of the NHS, executives and non-executives, NHS partners and government. The confederation interacts well with the government at both local and ministerial level.

Bodies providing CPE and CPD

The **College of Pharmacy Practice (CPP)** (http://www.collpharm.org.uk/) is an independent organisation of pharmacists, from all branches of the profession, whose objectives are to provide post-registration training and continuing professional development (CPD) and to promote the highest professional standards to benefit patients and healthcare provision. Since its birth in 1981, the College has established an enviable record for its innovative approaches to CPD, assessment and accreditation. The College's mission statement is 'To promote professional and personal development, through education, examination, practice and research, benefiting patients and healthcare provision'. The College also has two faculties serving special interests, including prescribing and medicines management and paediatric pharmacy (http://www.collpharm. org.uk/facultymenu.htm). It also has a branch in Scotland (CPPiS).

The **Centre for Pharmacy Postgraduate Education (CPPE)** http://www. cppe.man.ac.uk/ is the organisation situated in the University of Manchester that provides continuing education and CPD opportunities for all the community pharmacists in England. The Centre was established in 1991 by the NHS Executive and it is funded directly by the Department of Health. It provides a wealth of training courses.

The **NHS Education Board for Scotland (NES)** (http://www.scppe.strath. ac.uk/home.html) was established in Glasgow as a Special Health Board on 1 April 2002. It was set up to oversee professional development for all health professionals working in the NHS and has taken over the function of the Scottish Centre for Post Qualification Pharmaceutical Education (SCPPE). The Pharmacy Directorate of NES provides an education and training programme, which includes face-to-face courses, distance learning, video conferencing, open learning opportunities and specially commissioned courses for hospital and community pharmacists working within the NHS in Scotland.

The **Welsh Centre for Post-Graduate Pharmaceutical Education (WCPPE)** (http://www.cardiff.ac.uk/phrmy/WCPPE) is a discrete unit within the Welsh School of Pharmacy, Cardiff University. It provides an inclusive CPD service, which is available to all pharmacists and their support staff in Wales.

WCPPE has the broadest remit of all UK centres, allowing them to offer comprehensive educational opportunities and resources. This resource is funded almost exclusively through successive budgets provided by the Welsh Assembly.

The **Northern Ireland Centre for Postgraduate Pharmaceutical Education and Training (NICPPET)** (http://www.nicppet.org/index.asp) provides CPD to pharmacists and other healthcare professions in Northern Ireland.

The **Institute of Pharmacy Management (IPM)** (http://www.pharmweb.net/pwmirror/pw9/ipmi/about.html) aims to promote and inspire education, research and excellence in pharmacy management across all branches of the profession for the benefit of its members. Incorporated in 1964 under the Companies Act, the Institute is essentially an educational body which is non-profit-making and which issues no shares. The Institute caters for all branches of pharmacy: community, hospital, academia, the pharmaceutical industry and wholesale distribution. It is international in its membership, with around 10% of its members living in some 25 countries outside the UK. Institute members are encouraged to develop their management skills as a part of CPD. By way of support the Institute offers CPD and CPE through regular conferences, seminars and courses. The Institute has a Membership and Fellowship by portfolio programme.

Index

Page numbers in *italic* refer to figures or tables.

AAH, 58, *59*, 101–102
accidents
    causes, 123–125
    prevention, 126
accountability, professional, 6
accountants, 83, 97, 180
accounting, 180–183
    conventions, 181–182
    equation, 181, 188
    principles, 180–181
    process, 181
    reducing costs, 241
    standards, 182–183
Accounting Standards Board (ASB), 182–183
Accounting Standards Committee (ASC),
        182, 183
accounts, 185–190
    analysis, 190–193
    publishing, 190
accreditation schemes
    hospital pharmacy services, 347
    online pharmacies, 305–307
acid test ratio, 190–191
ACORN technique, 250
acquiring a pharmacy, 85–104
    assessing risks, 87–97
    calculating cost of business, 98–101
    checklist, *89*
    financing aspects, 101–104
    identifying a target, 87–88
    on leasehold premises, 91–96
    as a limited company, 96–97
    location issues, 88–90
    NHS contract, 90, 96
    obtaining tax relief, 83–84
    structural alterations, 104
    survey of premises, 90–91
adaptive zone, employee discretion model,
        201, 202, 203
added value, 199–200, *200*
adverse incidents *see* accidents
advertising, 260, 261–262
    Internet, 294

job, 316
    legal and ethical aspects, 302–303
advice
    healthcare and lifestyle, 235
    legal aspects of supplying, 115, 119–120
    online pharmacies, 299
age groups, customer, 254
ageing, population, 25
alarms, burglar, 94, 170–171
Allcures, 294
Alliance UniChem, 58, *59*
analgesics, substitutes, 31
Anti-Cybersquatting Consumer Protection
        Act (ACPA), 304
anxious zone, employee discretion model,
        201, 202
apothecary, 108
appraisals, staff, 322–323
approachability, 11
arbitration, insurance disputes, 162
architecture, 35
ARPAnet, 287–288
Articles of Association, 108
'Ask your Pharmacist' campaign, 262, 291
assets, 181
    current, 188, *189*, 191
    fixed, 188, *189*
    intangible, 188
    net, 181
    tangible, 188
Association of Independent Multiple
        Pharmacies (AIMp), 363–364
Association of the British Pharmaceutical
        Industry (ABPI), 292, 302–303
assurance, 198
audit
    financial, 83, 183
    performance *see* performance measurement
Audit Commission report, 335, 354
availability, pharmacist, 11

baby products, 276
balance sheet, 185, 187–188, *189*

bank
  loans, 101–102, 191
  overdrafts, 191
banking, Internet, 195
benefits, external, 39
'Big Mac' index, 52–53
blight notice, 94
book-keepers, 180
Boots the Chemist, 57, *57, 59*, 363
bottlenecks, 206, 213
brand(s)
  advertising, 260, 261–262
  family (umbrella), 260–261
  importance, 260–261
  leaders, 259
  range, 262
branded medicines, 60
  price controls, 61
  umbrella, 260–261
briefings, team, 323
'brown-bag review,' 234
budgeting, 193–195
  flexible, 193
Building a Safer NHS for Patients
    (Department of Health), 143
burglary and theft
  insurance, 168
  insurance claims, 172
  prevention measures, 94, 170–171
business plan, marketing strategy, 247
business rates, 91
business structures, 76–79, *78*
Business to Business (B2B) stock transfer, 281
buying *see* purchasing

Canada, online pharmacies, 301, 306
capability, 336
capacity, service *see* service capacity
capital, 181
  account, 188, *189*
  employed, return on (ROCE), 191–192
  formation (investment), 44, 51–52
  initial operating, 101
capital gains tax, 77
care pathways, 145
caring, being, 11–12
carousels, 214
cash flow statement, *194*, 194–195
cash till position, 275
catchment area, geographical, 249
category captain, 259
category management, 259–261, 281–282
Celesio (formerly GEHE), 58
centralised intravenous additive services
    (CIVAS), 332
Centre for Postgraduate Pharmacy Education
    (CPPE), 292, 322, 353, 364

chains, retail pharmacy
  large, 8, 56, *57*
  small, 66
  trends, 55, 56, *57*
change management, 151–152, 343–344
  approaches in hospital pharmacy,
    344–346
chase strategy, 210
checking procedures, 150
chemist, in company or business names,
    108
Chemist Defence Association (CDA), 175,
    362
cheques, 195, 239
civil commotion, insurance cover, 161
'claimant count,' unemployment, 51
clients *see* customers
clinical governance, 127–128, 218, 311, 336
clinical guidelines, 144, 336
clinical risk management, 142–146
  government influence, 143
  professional viewpoint, 143–146
clinical standards, 336–337, *338*
Clinical Standards Board for Scotland
    (CSBS), 336, *338*
clothing, protective, 137
Code of Ethics and Standards (RPSGB),
    114, 298–299, 319
Code of Practice for the Pharmaceutical
    Industry (ABPI), 302–303
coincident index, 46–48, *47*
College of Pharmacy Practice (CPP),
    353–354, 364
command social/economic systems, 23
common law, 115
communication
  in change management, 344
  with clients, 12–13, 263–265
  Internet, 288–289
  non-verbal, 263
  within pharmacy business, 313
  with staff, 13
community (retail) pharmacy
  acquisition *see* acquiring a pharmacy
  business structure, 76–79, *78*
  buying from wholesalers, 74–76,
    279–280
  chains *see* chains, retail pharmacy
  competitive risks, 73, 85–87
  consumer law, 115–122
  design, merchandising and stock control,
    269–283
  entry of wholesalers into, 55, 58–59
  financial management, 179–196
  geographical catchment area, 249
  goods and services sold, 66–67
  human resources management, 311–325

independent proprietor-run *see*
    independent proprietor-run
    pharmacies
  insurance, 155–175
  legal aspects, 105–114
  managed service, 328
  margins, 68–69, *70, 71*
  marketing, 243–267
  medicines management, 349, 355
  NHS remuneration, 71–74
  organisations involved, 359–365
  ownership patterns, 66
  ownership types, 76, 105–109
  premises *see* premises
  product mix, 69–70
  profit management, 225–241
  refitting, 271–272
  risk management, 123–153
  running the business, 65–84
  service delivery, 197–223
  structural changes, 55–56, *57*
  taxation *see* tax
Community Pharmacy Wales, 361–362
companies (corporate bodies), 106–109
  Articles of Association, 108
  directors, 108–109
  Memorandum of Association, 107–108
  names, 108
  private limited *see* limited companies
  private unlimited, 107
  public limited, 107
  see also chains, retail pharmacy
Companies Act 1985 (and amendments),
    83, 106
Company Chemist Association Ltd (CCA),
    363
competence, professional, 6
  public expectations, 9–10
competition
  dealing with, 252–253
  determinants of supply and, 26–27
  lack of, 32–33
  between products, 246–247
  risks of retail pharmacy, 73, 85–87
competitive advantage, 35–37
competitiveness, national indicators, 53
complementary medicines, 31, 295–296
complements, 31
  cross price elasticity, 32
  demand and price, 25
compliant zone, employee discretion model,
    201, 202
computer errors, 149
Conference Board, 46
conferencing, web, 288
configuration, service activities, 205–206
conflicts of interest, 18

consequential loss insurance, 164, 174
conspicuous consumption products, 26
Consumer Association, 9
consumer law, 115–122
Consumer Prices Index (CPI), 49
consumers *see* customers
containers allowance, 72
continuing professional development (CPD),
    311, 319–322
  case study, 320–321
  hospital sector, 340
  providers, 322, 364–365
  risk management aspects, 147–148
continuing professional education (CPE),
    319–322
  online delivery, 292
  providers, 322, 364–365
continuity of staffing, 16–17
contract(s), 116
  breach of, 119
  consumer, 116–117
  law, 115, 116
  relating to services, 117, 118–119
  terms, 116–117
contribution (insurance principle), 162
Control of Substances Hazardous to Health
    (CoSSH) Regulations 1994,
    140–141
controlled drugs, 113
  cupboard, 110
  disposal of unwanted, 112
Controlled Waste Regulations 1992, 111
copayment, 61
'coping' strategy, 211–212
corporate bodies *see* companies
corporate governance, 127, 336–337
corporation tax, 82
costs
  buyer switching, 37
  external, 39
  financing, 103–104, 186, *187*, 241
  premises, 240
  purchases, 186, *187*
  purchasing a business, 98–101
  start-up, 101
counselling
  area, *273*, 274
  services, 234
counter medicines *see* over-the-counter
    (OTC) medicines
counter positions, 275
counter sales
  enhancing, 238
  margins, 69, 70
  seasonality, 67
  staff training, 319
  suppliers of goods, 56, 75–76

court action, against insurers, 174
CPD *see* continuing professional
   development
CPE *see* continuing professional education
CPPE *see* Centre for Postgraduate Pharmacy
   Education
cross price elasticity, 32
cultural beliefs, 18
current ratio, 190–191
customers (clients; consumers; patients),
   197, 247–249
   change in tastes, 25
   characteristics, 249
   communication with, 12–13, 263–265
   competitors, 252–253
   contract law issues, 116–117
   dealing with disappointed/angry, 217–218
   expectations
      product choice, 246–247
      of professionals, 9–17
      service quality, 198–199
   factors affecting purchasing decisions,
      253–266
   geographical catchment area, 249
   handing out medicines to, 150
   hospital pharmacy, 328–330, 346
   imperfect information, 39
   improving interaction with, 235, *241*
   income, 25, 26, 253–254
   information from Internet, 13, 290
   legal issues, 115–122
   loyalty, 33, 251–252
   non-judgemental attitude, 18
   payments by, 72
   primary importance, 243, 245
   relationship management, 235
   retaining existing/attracting new, 251–252
   rights and protection, 115, 120
   switching costs, 37
   types, 250–251
   uncertainty, 37, 39
   understanding your, 247–253
   views of profession, 8–9, *9*
   see also marketing
Customs and Excise *see* HM Customs and
   Excise
cyclical turning points, 47–48

decision trees, customer, *256, 257*
decision-making, financial, 184–185
delegation, 323
demand, 24–26
   curves, 24, *25*
      perverse, 26, *26*
   derived, 24
   determinants, 24–25
   elasticity *see* elasticity of demand

law of, 24
   sensitivity to price changes, 30
demand management
   community pharmacy, 210, 211
   hospital pharmacy, *330*, 330–331
demographic change, 25
demographic profile, customer, 250–251
density forecasts, 43
Department of Health (DOH), 143, 292
depreciation, 186
design, pharmacy, *259*, 269–276
   dispensary and counselling areas, 274
   problems, 269–271, *270*
   refitting, 271–272
   space allocation, 274
   suggestions, 272–276, *273*
development, staff *see* training and
   development
dilapidation, premises, 93, 240
directors, company, 108–109
disclosure, by pharmacy vendors, 93–94, 97
discounts, wholesale supplies, 75–76
discretion, employee, *201*, 201–203
dispensary
   area, layout, *270*, 271, *273*, 274
   environment, 148
   purchasing stock, 279–280
   quality matrix, 216, *217*
dispensing
   bottlenecks, 213, 214
   checking procedures, 150
   computer errors, 149
   by doctors, 86
   fees, 72
   improving profit margins, 238
   increasing revenue, 234
   marketing aspects, 258
   pressure of work, 148
   product selection, 149–150
   profitability, 68–69
   reading errors, 148–149
   risk management, 151
   risks, 147–151
dispensing assistants, 235
dispensing technicians, 235, 319, 340
display gondolas, 269, 275
display units/stands, 269, 271, 275–276, 283
distinctive capabilities, 35
distribution, 22
dividends, 77, 193
doctors, dispensing, 86
'doing it right first time,' 125–128, 152
Domino's Pizza, 36–37
door locks/security, 94, 170
drawings, 181, 188
drug rehabilitation centre, 69
drug tariff, 73, 238

drugstores, 66
dual effect principle, 181
due diligence, 96–97
dump bins, 269, 283
duty of care, 119, 133

earnings per share, 193
earnings yield, 193
economics, 21–54
    macro scale, 22–23, 40–53
    micro scale, 22, 23–39
    PEST analysis, 231
education
    continuing professional *see* continuing
        professional education
    medicines management, 353–354
    see also training and development
elasticity of demand
    income, 32
    price, 29–32
eLearning, 292
electrical equipment, 138, *139*
electricity
    costs, 240
    design issues, 276
    supply, safety, 138
Electricity at Work Act 1990, 138
electronic point of sale (EPoS) systems, 276,
        282–283
    category management, 260, 282
    stock management, 279, 281
Electronic Prescribing and Administration
        (EPA), 290
electronic transfer of prescriptions (ETP),
        56, 235, 258, 289–290
email, 288–289
    communication with customers, 235, *241*
    history of development, 287–288
empathy, 198
employee discretion model, *201*, 201–203
employees *see* staff
employers
    legal requirements, 110–111, 133
    liability insurance, 141, 165–166
    PAYE taxation, 81–82
employment
    legislation, 110–111
    measures, national, 50–51
e-Pharmacy, 285–309
equilibrium, market, *28*, 28–29, *29*
equipment
    electrical, 138, *139*
    protective, 137
    risk assessment, 137
    valuation, 100
ergonomics, *325*
E-SCRIPT, 290

ethical issues, Internet, 296–307
ethical medicines *see* Prescription-Only
        Medicines
ETP *see* electronic transfer of prescriptions
euro currency debate, 40
Europe
    e-Pharmacy regulation, 301–302, 304
    parallel trading of pharmaceuticals, 60
    prices and inflation, 48–49, *49*
    pricing of pharmaceuticals, *59*
    website accreditation schemes, 306–307
European Agency for the Evaluation of
        Medicinal Products (EMEA), 292
European Directorate for the Quality of
        Medicines (EDQM), 292
European Foundation for Quality
        Management (EFQM) Excellence
        Model, 218, *219*
evidence based practice, 320
exclusions, insurance policy, 160–161
expectations, market, 25, 27
expenditure, 186, *187*
    reducing, 239–241
Expenditure and Food Survey (EFS), 50
expensive prescriptions allowance, 72
expiry dates, checking, 278
explosion risks, insurance, 163, 165
externalities, 39

family brands, 260–261
Family Health Services Authority (FHSA), 73
family life cycle, *254*
fan chart, 43, *43*
fascia, pharmacy, 275
financial governance, 336
financial management, 179–196
    accounting, 180–183
    analysis of accounts, 190–193
    elements, 179–180
    planning and control, 193–196
    recording and reporting financial data,
        183–190
    risk management aspects, 126–127,
        141–142
financial ratio analysis, 190–193
Financial Reporting Council (FRC), 182
Financial Reporting Review Panel (FRRP),
        182
Financial Reporting Standards (FRSs), 182
financial reports, 185–190
financing, 101–104
    costs, 103–104, 186, *187*, 241
    sources, 101–103
fire
    certificates, 138
    insurance, 163–164
    risk control measures, 170

Fire Precautions (Workplace) (Amendment)
  Regulations 1999, 138
firms *see* partnerships
first aid provisions, 137
fitness for purpose, 118
fittings *see* fixtures and fittings
fixtures and fittings
  leasehold premises, 93, 94
  merchandising aspects, 275–276
  valuation, 100
FLEXISCRIPT, 290
Food and Drug Administration (FDA), 300
foot and mouth epidemic, 2001, 229–230
forecast
  density, 43
  interval, 43
  point, 43
forecasting
  in decision-making, 185
  macroeconomic, 42–45, *43*
free rider problem, 38
frustrated zone, employee discretion model,
  201, 202, 203
Funds Flow Statement, 186

gas supply, 240
gearing ratio (GR), 192
GEHE (now Celesio), 58
general practice surgeries
  assisting, 235
  location near to, 88–89
  relocation risks, 89–90
general practitioners (GPs), prescribing
  habits, 87
General Sales List (GSL) medicines, 60,
  112–113, 277
  competition for sales, 86
  Internet sales, 297, 299
  list changes, 227
  merchandising, 269, 274, 282
general sales tax (GST), 79
generic medicines, 60
  improving margins, 237
  price controls, 61
  purchasing, 279
  substitution of equivalent, 61
geodemographic technique, 250
Germany, ePharmacy regulation, 301–302
Giffen products, 26
gondolas, display, 269, 275
goods
  configuration, 205–206
  fitness for purpose, 118
  legal aspects of sale, 115, 116, 117–118
  limiting liability, 120

location within pharmacy, 259–261
quality of, 118
see also product(s); stock
goodwill, *65*, 98–99, 188
  factors affecting, 92
  tax relief, 84
  valuation, 98–99
governance, 336
  see also clinical governance; corporate
    governance
government
  clinical risk management and, 143
  intervention, case for, 37–39
  macroeconomic management, 40, 43–44
government policies, 85–86, 227–228
  creating market power, 34
  PEST analysis, 231
Great Depression,1930s, 44
Great Eastern, SS, 146
Greece, ancient, 3–4
Green, Gerry, 101
gross domestic product (GDP), 48
gross profit (GP), 186, *187*, 191
growth
  monetary, 50
  rates, national, 48
GSL medicines *see* General Sales List (GSL)
    medicines
guidelines, clinical, 144, 336
guilds, craftsmen's, 4

hair colourants, 278
Harmonised Index of Consumer Prices
    (HICP), 49, *49*, 50
hazard, 134
Health & Safety at Work Act 1974, 133
health and safety, 111, 132–141
  basic risk assessment, 134–136, *135*
  policy, 132, 133
  risk assessment of related issues,
    136–141
Health and Safety (First Aid) Regulations
    1981, 137
Health and Safety (Display Screen
    Equipment) Regulations 1992, 137
Health Boards, 71
Health on the New Foundation (HON)
    Code of Conduct, 306–307
healthcare
  advice, 235
  Internet and, 285–287
  stock range, 277
Health-News, 291–292
heating, 240
HELP mnemonic, 151

herbal remedies, 296
history, pharmacy, 3–4, 5–6
HM Customs and Excise
  ePharmacy and, 298
  VAT regulation, 80, 81, 97
homeopathic medicines, 295
hosiery items, 237
hospital pharmacy, 327–348
  customers, 328–330
  demand management, 330–331
  emerging service models, 334
  environment, 327–330
  marketing management, 331–335
  medicines management, 334–335,
    354–355
  performance measurement, 342–347
  pharmaceutical supplies, 56–57
  pharmacist's role, 327–328
  resource management, 336–342
hours, opening, 17, 239, 325
HTML (HyperText Markup Language), 293
human resources management, 311–325
  see also staff

identification problem, 29
ignorance, consumer, 39
immobility of factors, 38–39
importing
  drugs from online pharmacies, 298,
    300–302
  parallel see parallel importing
income
  consumer, 25, 26, 253–254
  distribution, 25
  elasticity of demand, 32
  increasing, 234–246
  national, indicators, 48
  statement see profit and loss account
income tax, 82
  PAYE deductions, 81–82
incorporated businesses see companies
indemnity, 162–163
independent proprietor-run pharmacies, 8, 66
  acquisition see acquiring a pharmacy
  benefits of new contract, 74
  business structures, 76–79, 78
  ownership categories, 76, 105–109
  threats to viability, 55–56, 73, 85–87
  see also sole traders
inflation
  forecasts, 43, 43
  headline rate, 48
  indexes and indicators, 48–50
  underlying rate (RPIX), 48
information leaflets, 274

information resources
  Internet role, 290–292
  useful websites, 308–309
information technology (IT), 285–309
  see also Internet
injections, 87
Inland Revenue, 82, 83, 97
innovation, 35
insolvency (acid test) ratio, 190–191
Institute of Arbitrators, 174
Institute of Pharmacy Management (IPMI),
    365
insurance, 155–175
  claims
    complaints, 173–174
    condition, 162
    making, 171–173
    previous history, 158–159
  further information, 175
  hard and soft markets, 156
  history, previous, 159
  importance, 157–158
  leasehold premises, 94–95
  nature, function and benefits, 155–156
  policy
    conditions, 161–163
    exclusions, 160–161
    structure, 160–163
    types, 163–168, 174–175
  pricing and rates, 157
  process, 158–160
  proposal, 158
  as risk management tool, 141–142,
    169–171
  see also specific types of insurance
Insurance Ombudsman, 174
insurers, specialist, 159
interest rates, 50
  base, 45
  business loans, 102
intermediate care, 328
International Accounting Standards Board
    (IASB), 183
International Conference on Harmonisation
    (ICH), 292
International Labour Office (ILO), 51
International Monetary Fund, 50
international trade, 51
Internet, 285–309
  banking, 195
  communications via, 288–289
  competitive threat, 86–87
  controlling content, 304–307
  dubious uses, 296
  establishing a web presence, 292–294

Internet (*continued*)
  healthcare and, 285–287
  history, 287–288
  as information source, 13, 290–292
  legal and ethical aspects, 286–287,
      296–307
  legal regulation, 304–305
  NHS and, 289–290
  pharmacies *see* online pharmacies
  professional education, 292
  self-regulation, 304
  service delivery problems, 203
  stock purchasing, 280
  see also websites
Internet Service Providers (ISPs), 292–293
inventory *see* stock
investment strategy, 14
investors' return, 193
invoices, 324

job description, 316, 317–318

Keynes, John Maynard, 44

Labour Force Survey, 51
labour market, 44
Landlord and Tenants Act, 94, 95, 96
lateral thinking, capability, 13
Law of One Price, 53
layout, pharmacy *see* design, pharmacy
leading index, 46–48, 47
leapfrogging, 89
learned societies, 4
lease
  anti-competitive clauses, 93
  assignment, 91–92, 93
  break clauses, 92
  landlord covenants, 95
  negotiation, 92–96
  personal guarantees, 92
  renewals, 95
  rent reviews, 95–96
leasehold premises, 91–96
legal aspects, 105–114
  employment of staff, 110–111
  Internet, 286–287, 296–307
  lease negotiation, 92–96
  NHS Contract acquisition, 90
  pharmacy ownership, 105–109
  registration of pharmacy premises,
      109–110
  transactions with consumers, 115–122
  working conditions, 111–112
legislation, 115, 126
level capacity strategy, 210
leverage ratio, 192

liability(ies)
  current, 188, *189*, 191
  financial, 181
  insurance, 141, 165–167
    claims, 172, 173
  legal, 119–120
  long-term, 188, *189*
  risk control, 171
  third party, 171
  vicarious, 133
liaison, interprofessional, 16
LIBOR, 50
life cycle, family, 254
lifestyle advice, 235
lifting, 137
lightning, insurance cover, 163
limited companies, 76–79, 78
  financial records and reports, 184, 190
  purchase, 96–97
  taxation, 83
  see also companies
Limited Partnerships Act 1907, 106
liquidity, 191
  ratios, 190–191
listening, 16
Lloyds Pharmacy, 56, 57, 57
loans, bank, 101–102, 191
local council
  blight notice claims, 94
  business rates, 91
  planning department, 90
location
  goods and services within pharmacy,
      259–261
  premises, 88–90
    insurance aspects, 160, 161, 165
    market power and, 34
locked out workers, insurance cover, 161
locum pharmacists, 239, 315
London Interbank Bid/Offer Rate (LIBOR),
      50
loss adjuster, 172–173
loss assessor, 172, 173
losses, 181
loyalty, customer, 33, 251–252
luxury goods, seasonal sales, 67

macroeconomic indexes and indicators,
      45–53
  based on intended/actual behaviour,
      52–53
  categories, 46
  competitiveness, 53
  leading indicators, 45–52
macroeconomics, 22–23, 40–53
  business manager and, 41–42

forecasting, 42–45, *43*
Virtual Economy Model, 45
mail, incoming, 324
mail order pharmacy, 87, 297–298
managed service community pharmacy, 328
management effectiveness, 192–193
Management of Health and Safety at Work
      Regulations 1999, 134–136
Manual Handling Operations Regulations
      1992, 137
manufacturers
  direct supply by, 56–57, 75
  displays, 271, 274, 283
  promotional allowance, 280
  surveys of, 52
margins
  improving, 237–238
  retail pharmacy, 68–69, *70*, *71*
market(s), 24–27
  definition, 24
  demand, supply and price, 24–27
  equilibrium, *28*, 28–29, *29*
  failure, 37–39
  systems, 23
market power, 32–34
  achieving and sustaining, 34
  determinants, 32–34
  vs competitive advantage, 35
market research, 248–249
marketing, 243–267
  approaches, 332–333, *333*
  concept, 244–247
  definition, 244
  factors affecting purchasing decisions,
      253–266
  hospital sector, 328–329, *329*, 331–335
  marketing approach, 332, *333*
  mix, 247
  myopia, 332–335
  product approach, 332–333, *333*
  production approach, 332, *333*
  regulation, e-commerce aspects, 302–303
  selling approach, 332, *333*
  societal, 331–332
  societal marketing approach, 332, *333*
  strategy, 247
  understanding the customer, 247–253
mark-up rates *see* margins
Maslow's hierarchy of needs, 244, *245*
Medical Finance Ltd, 102
medicines
  added value, 199–200
  adverse effects, 350–351
  bagging and handing out, 150
  categories, 60
  dispensing *see* dispensing

distribution, 56–59
  information, resource mapping, 204, *204*,
      205
  parallel importing *see* parallel importing
  pricing, 59–63
  returned by patients, 111–112
  review, 234
  sale or supply, 112–113
  selection errors, 149–150
  see also specific categories of medicines
Medicines Act 1968, 108, 109
  ePharmacy controls, 297–298
  marketing of medicines, 302–303
Medicines and Healthcare products
      Regulatory Agency (MHRA),
      286–287, 292, 297–298
medicines management, 349–358
  case study, 320–321
  collaborative approach, 353
  concept, 349–350
  getting started, 352–354
  hospital pharmacy, 334–335, 354–355
  involving other professionals, 356
  pharmacist's role, 351–352
  in practice, 354–356
  rationale, 350–351
  revenue benefits, 234
Medicines Partnership Centre, 353
meetings, 325
Memorandum of Association, 107–108
merchandising, 259, 281–283
  category management, 281–282
  pharmacy layout aspects, 269–276
  planograms, 282–283
  positioning products on shelf, 282
  seven rights, 281
  special offers, 283
microeconomics, 22, 23–39
mineral supplements, 274, 282, 299
mission statement, 232–233
Misuse of Drugs Act 1971, 110
money stock, 50
moral beliefs, 18
moral hazard, 61
Moss Pharmacy, 56, 57, 58
motivation
  provision by pharmacist, 13–15
  staff, 203

names
  company, 108
  products with similar-sounding, 149
  website domain, 292–293
National Consumer Council (NCC), 8–9, *9*
National Health Service *see* NHS
national insurance (NI), 77

National Patient Safety Agency (NPSA), 143
National Pharmaceutical Association (NPA), 362
  'Ask your Pharmacist' campaign, 262, 291
  financial services, 70, 74, 75, 103
  health and safety advice, 133
  on online pharmacies, 295
  professional indemnity insurance, 175
  training courses, 319
National Prescribing Centre (NPC), Liverpool, 353
National Prescription Research Centre (NPRC), 361
natural resources, ownership, 34
needs
  in marketing terms, 244–247
  Maslow's hierarchy, 244, *245*
negligence
  law of, 115, 119
  limiting liability, 120
  vicarious liability, 133
New Zealand
  ePharmacy regulation, 301
  website accreditation scheme, 305–306
NHS
  business, profitability, 68–69, 70, *70*
  Internet systems, 289–290
NHS Confederation, 364
NHS Contracts (for Pharmacies), 65
  acquisition, 88, 90
  legal aspects, 112–114
  new proposals, 74
  OFT report, 56, 73, 85–86
  transfer, 96
NHS Direct Online, 291
NHS Education Board for Scotland (NES), 364
NHS Plan, 227–228, 307, 318
  SWOT analysis, 228–229
NHS remuneration, 71–74
  advances against, 102
  current position, 71–73
  difficulties, 56, 73
  future developments, 73–74
  improving profit margins, 237–238
NHSnet (NHS Intranet), 289
NOAH (New York Online Access to Health), 291
non-judgemental attitude, 18
Northern Ireland, 360
Northern Ireland Centre for Postgraduate Pharmaceutical Education and Training (NICPPET), 365
NPA *see* National Pharmaceutical Association

Nucare, 55
Numark, 55, 291
nursing and residential homes, 69, 73

objectives, setting, 232–233
observant, being, 15
The OECD in Figures, 52
Office for National Statistics (ONS), 48, 51
Office of Fair Trading (OFT), 2003 report, 56, 73, 85–86
one-stop healthcare centres, 56, 87, 206
online pharmacies, 287, 294–296
  accreditation schemes, 305–307
  global perspectives, 300–302
  legal and ethical issues, 297–307
  questionable sites, 296, 298
opening hours, 17, 239, 325
opportunity cost, 185
An Organisation with a Memory (Department of Health), 143
organisations, pharmaceutical, 359–365
OTC Direct, 279
OTC medicines *see* over-the-counter (OTC) medicines
out-of-town retail parks, 56, 66
output, national, indicators, 48
overdrafts, 191
overheads *see* expenditure
over-the-counter (OTC) medicines, 60
  distribution, 56, 57
  enhancing sales, 238
  pricing, 63
  purchasing, 280
  resale price maintenance, 55, 63
  see also General Sales List (GSL) medicines; Pharmacy-only medicines
own-brand products, 238
oxygen supplies, 87

P *see* Pharmacy-only medicines (P)
packaging, medicine, 149–150
panic buttons, 171
paperwork *see* records
parallel importing (PI), 60, 69, 237, 279–280
partners, sleeping, 106
Partnership Act 1890, 105
partnerships (firms), 76–77, 78, 105–106
patient medication record (PMR), 149, 150, 279, 281
Patient Pack initiative, 332
patients *see* customers
Patriot Act 2001 (USA), 304
pay as you earn (PAYE) taxation, 81–82
pensions, 77, 78
performance management, 322–325, 337

performance measurement, 342–347, *343*
 approaches in hospital pharmacy,
  344–346
 cost, 347
 indicators, 342–344
 small organisations, 220–221
personal development planning (PDP), 318,
 337–339
Personal Protective Equipment at Work
 Regulations 1992, 137
PEST analysis, 225, 231–232
pharmaceutical care, 349, 352
 see also medicines management
Pharmaceutical Price Regulation Scheme
 (PPRS), 61
Pharmaceutical Services Negotiating
 Committee (PNGC), 74, 360–361
Pharmaceutical Society, 5
Pharmaceutical Society of New Zealand
 (PSNZ), 305–306
Pharmaceutical Society of Northern Ireland
 (RPSNI), 66, 360
pharmaceuticals *see* medicines
pharmacists
 additional roles, 235
 clinical risk management, 143–146
 continuity of staffing, 17
 CPD *see* continuing professional
  development
 locum, 239, 315
 medicines management role, 351–352
 pharmacy ownership, 76–79, 105–109
 professional dilemmas, 18
 qualified status, 66
 recruitment, 315
 requirement to be on premises, 66
 retention of good, 314
 secondary care sector, 327–328
 services offered, 67
 superintendent, 97, 107, 109–110
 time management, 323–325
 vocational training schemes, *341*,
  341–342
Pharmacists' Professional Indemnity Limited
 (PPI), 175
pharmacy
 definition, 285–286
 eLearning trends, 292
 history, 3–4, 5–6
 online *see* online pharmacies
 retail *see* community (retail) pharmacy
 wholesalers *see* wholesalers
Pharmacy Act 1852, 5
Pharmacy and Poisons Act 1933, 5–6
pharmacy manager, 337, 340
Pharmacy Mutual, 362

Pharmacy Partners, 102
pharmacy sector, 55–64
 distribution, 56–59
 entry system control, 56
 pricing of pharmaceuticals, 59–63
 structural change, 55–56, *57*
Pharmacy2u, 294, 295
PHARMACY2U pilot, 290
Pharmacy-only medicines (P), 60, 112, 277
 Internet sales, 297, 299
 list changes, 227
 merchandising, 269, 274, 275
 Which? report, 9
Pharmweb, 291
Phoenix Healthcare Distribution, 58, *59*,
 101–102
photographic developing/printing service,
 239
pilferage, 239
planning
 financial, 193–196
 personal development (PDP), 318,
  337–339
 in profit management, 232–233
 tax, 196
planning department, local council, 90
planning permission, 104
planograms, 282–283
point forecast, 43
poisons, sale or supply, 113–114
POMs *see* Prescription-Only Medicines
posters, window, 269, 283
power, market *see* market power
PPD9 form, 71
premises, 65–66
 acquisition, 90–96
 blight notice claims, 94
 business rates, 91
 consumer expectations, 11–12
 costs, 240
 dilapidation, 93, 240
 insurance, 94–95, 163–165
 leasehold, 91–96
 location *see under* location
 maintenance and repair, 91, 93, 240
 registration, 66, 96, 109–110
 risk assessment, 136
 safety, 96
 structural alterations, 104
 survey, 90–91, 158
 vacant, 91
 valuation, 91
pre-registration trainees, payments for, 72
prescription(s)
 charges, 61–62, 68
 collection and delivery, 234, 258

prescription(s) (*continued*)
  electronic transfer *see* electronic transfer
    of prescriptions
  expensive, allowance, 73
  forms, checking/endorsement, 237
  habits of GPs, 87
  health, 113
  legal aspects, 113
  NHS, 68–69
  price elasticity of demand, 62
  private, 69
  reading, 148–149
  reminder service, 234
  repeat, 149, 351
  repeatable, 113
Prescription Pricing Bureau, 71
Prescription-Only Medicines (POMs)
    (ethical medicines), 60, 277
  distribution, 56–57
  Internet sales, 296, 297–298, 299–300
  legal aspects of sale/supply, 113
  list changes, 73–74, 227
  pricing, 60–62
  purchasing, 279–280
  suppliers, 74–76
price
  controls, 56, 60–63
  demand and, 24–26, *25*
  determination, 28–32
  elasticity (of demand), 29–32
    cross, 32
    prescriptions, 62
  equilibrium or market clearing, 28
  importance to customers, 254–255
  indicators and indexes, 48–50
  makers and takers, 32
  supply and, 26–27
price earnings ratio, 193
pricing
  insurance premiums, 157
  pharmaceuticals, 59–63
Primary Care Centres, 87, 89–90
primary care pharmacy, 86
  medicines management, 355–356
Primary Care Trusts (PCTs), 327–328
private medical insurance (PMI), 31
process flow, service *see* service process
    (flow)
producers, objectives of, 27
product(s)
  category management, 259–261, 281–282
  competition between, 246–247
  differentiation, 33
  features on offer, 257–258
  location within pharmacy, 259–261
  merchandising and layout, 259
  mix, and margins, 70, 70–71

  position on shelf, 282
  price *see* price
  public, 38
  selection errors, 149–150
  see also goods; medicines; stock
production, 22
  prices of factors of, 27
  substitutes, 26–27
profession
  definitions, 4–5
  development of pharmacy, 3–4
  nature of, 4–6
professional allowance, 72
professional indemnity insurance, 141–142,
    175
professionalism, 3–20
  business and, 7–8
  client views, 8–9, *9*
  consumer-led expectations, 9–17
  dilemmas, 18
profit(s), 181
  gross, 186, *187*, 191
  margins *see* margins
  net, 186, *187*
profit and loss account, 185, 186, *187*
profit management, 225–241
  analytical stage, 225–232
  managing stage, 233–241
  planning stage, 232–233
profit on cost (POC), 192
profit on return (POR), 192
profitability
  in business valuation, 99–100
  dispensing prescriptions, 68–69
  product mix and, 69–70, *70*
  ratios, 191–192
  target levels, 61
promotion, 261–266
  legal and ethical aspects, 302–303
  special offers, 283
promotional allowance, 280
proposal, insurance, 158
proprietor's funds, 181
protocols, 144–145
Provision and Use of Work Equipment
    Regulations 1998, 137
public liability insurance, 141, 166–167
public products, 38
purchasing
  decisions, customer, factors affecting,
    253–266
  ease of, 255
  a pharmacy *see* acquiring a pharmacy
  stock, 279–281
  from wholesalers, 74–76, 279–280
purchasing power parity (PPP)
    hypothesis, 53

quality
    matrix, 216, *217*
    product, price and, 255
    risk management and, 128, 151–152
    of service, 216–218
        customer expectations, 9–17,
            198–199
        customer purchasing decisions and,
            256, 256–257, *257*
        recovery from poor, 217–218
quality management model, 218, *219*
questions, open and closed, 264–265

radioactive contamination, insurance, 161
rateable value, 91
RATER mnemonic, 198
recession, economic, 46–48
records
    financial, 83, 183–190
    management, 324
    online pharmacies, 299
    PAYE, 82
    prescription-only medicines, 113
    transfer to purchaser, 97
    VAT, 80
recruitment, 312–318
    case study, 317–318
    pharmacist, 315
    process, 316–317
    supporting staff, 316
refitting, pharmacy, 271–272
registration
    pharmacists, 5–6
    pharmacy premises, 66, 96, 109–110
reliability, 198
religious beliefs, 18
rent, 92
    at lease renewal, 95
    reviews, 95–96
repairs, leasehold premises, 91, 93, 240
repeat prescriptions, 149, 351
repeatable prescriptions, 113
reputation, 35, 37
resale price maintenance (RPM), 63
    abolition (2001), 33, 59, 63
research, 335
residential and nursing homes, 69, 73
resource(s)
    asymmetry, 35–36
    'hidden,' 311–312
    management, hospital sector, 336–342
    natural, ownership, 34
    stock of, 35
resource audit matrix, 204, *205*
resource mapping, 203–204, *204*
resource-based theory, 35–36
responsiveness, 198

retail pharmacy *see* community (retail)
        pharmacy
Retail Prices Index (RPI), 48, 50
    excluding mortgage interest (RPIX), 48, 49
return on capital employed (ROCE),
        191–192
revenue, increasing, 234–246
The Right Medicine (Scottish Executive), 335
riot, insurance cover, 160, 161
risk
    definitions, 128, 134
    dispensing, 147–151
    in pharmacy setting, 125–126
risk appetite, 130
risk assessment, 128, 131
    basic health and safety, 134–136, *135*
    form, *135*
    related health and safety issues, 136–141
risk control, 169–171
risk estimation, 128, 129–130
risk evaluation, 128, *130*, 130–131
risk management, 123–153
    clinical, 142–146
    dispensing, 147–151
    doing it right first time, 125–128, 152
    health and safety issues, 132–141
    insurance aspects, 141–142, 169–171
    learning from the past, 123–125
    managing, 132, *132*
    philosophy, 131, 132
    processes involved, 128–131
risk map, *131*
risk profile, 130, 131, *131*
role
    ambiguity, 201
    conflict, 201
Roskill Report to the Monopolies
        Commission (1970), 10
rota service payments, 72
Royal Pharmaceutical Society of Great
        Britain (RPSGB), 292, 359
    branches and regions, 359
    Code of Ethics and Standards, 114,
        298–299, 319
    company name approval, 108
    ePharmacy regulation, 286–287, 295,
        296, 297, 298–300
    history, 5–6, 8
    registration of pharmacy premises, 66,
        96, 109–110
    Scottish Department, 360
    staff training and development, 311, 319,
        322
RPSGB *see* Royal Pharmaceutical Society of
        Great Britain
rural areas, profitability of NHS dispensing,
        68–69

safes, 170
safety
    policy, 132, 133
    premises, 96
    see also health and safety
salaries, 239–240, 317
sale(s)
    adding profit, 238
    goods or services, legal aspects, 115–122
    medicines, 112–113
    poisons, 113–114
    promotion, 261–266
    records, 184
    reporting, 186, *187*
    see also counter sales
Sale of Goods Act 1979, 117–118
sales to fixed assets ratio, 193
scarcity, 21–22
Scotland
    electronic transfer of prescriptions (ETP),
        290
    pharmaceutical care, 349
    RPSGB, 360
Scottish Centre for Post Qualification
        Pharmaceutical Education
        (SCPPE), 364
Scottish Pharmaceutical Federation (SPF),
        362
Scottish Pharmaceutical General Council
        (SPGC), 74, 361
seasonal variations, pharmacy sales, 67
seating area, 274
secondary care sector, 327–348
    see also hospital pharmacy
security
    pharmacy layout aspects, 271, 274
    precautions, 94, 170–171, 276
selection errors, product, 149–150
self-discipline, 15–16
self-regulation, Internet, 304
selling
    linked, 265
    skills, 263–265
service(s)
    enhancing, 235
    features on offer, 257–258
    location within pharmacy, 259–261
    price *see* price
    quality *see under* quality
    recovery from poor, 217–218
    retail pharmacies, 67
    SHIP characteristics, 198–199
service capacity, 209–213
    case studies, 211, 213, 214
    leakage, 215

management, 214–215, *215*
managing bottlenecks, 213
planning, hospital sector, 336
strategies, 210–212
service delivery, 7, 197–223
    added value, 199–200, *200*
    analysis, 203–209
    capacity considerations, 209–214
    case scenario, 221
    contract law, 117, 118–119, 120
    control, hospital sector, 336–337
    converting demand to output, 214–215
    customer expectations, 198–199
    legal aspects, 115
    measurement *see* performance
        measurement
    negligence law, 120
    overhauling, 208–209
    points to remember, 221
    quality aspects, 216–218
    staff roles, 200–203
    waste, 219
service demand, 214
service organisation, 197–198
service output, 198, 214
service process (flow), 197–198
    enhancing, 206
    walk-through, 206–207
service resource, 214
service transaction analysis (STA), 207, 208
sex discrimination, 112
shelves
    layout, 276
    planograms, 282–283
    position of products, 282
    special offers, 283
shoplifting, 239
skill mix, 340–341
Small Business Service (SBS), 102–103
Small Firms Loan Guarantee Scheme,
        102–103
Smith, Adam, 37
social class groups, 250
social factors, PEST analysis, 232
societal marketing, 331–332
societies, learned, 4
sole traders, 76–77, *78*, 105
    see also independent proprietor-run
        pharmacies
sonic bang, insurance cover, 160
special offers, 283
special perils insurance, 164–165
Special Waste Regulations 1996, 112
A Spoonful of Sugar (Audit Commission
        report), 335, 354

staff, 311–325
    additional roles, 235
    applying discretion, *201*, 201–203
    appraisals, 322–323
    communication with, 13
    configuration, 205
    consumer expectations, 12
    continuity, 17
    employment legislation, 110–111
    health and safety *see* health and safety
    hospital sector, 337–342
    insurance, 142
    new, business case for, 215
    PAYE deductions, 81–82
    performance management, 322–325, 337
    recruitment and retention, 312–318
    roles in service delivery, 200–203
    service capacity levels and, 209–210
    skill mix, 340–341
    training and development *see* training and
        development
    uniforms, 12
    wage costs, 239–240, 317
    working conditions, 111–112
    working under pressure, 148
stamp duty, 101
standard operating procedures (SOPs), 120,
        144, 145, 148
standards, clinical, 336–337, *338*
Statements of Standard Accounting Practice
        (SSAPs), 182
Statutory Sick Pay (SSP), 111
stock
    burglary/theft risk, 168
    control, 239, 241, 278
    expiry dates, 278
    explosion risk/insurance, 165
    fire risk/insurance, 164
    keeping adequate, 234
    management, 276–281
    purchasing, 279–281
    quantity, 278
    range, 66–67, 277–278
    slow lines, 280–281
    valuation, 100
    see also goods; product(s)
stock market indexes, 52
stock to cost of sales ratio, 193
stock turn ratio, 192–193
stocktaking, 195, 241, 281
store choice, reasons for, 256, *256*
strategic planning, 233
strategies
    business, 35–36
    profit maximising, 233

structural survey, premises, 90–91
subrogation, 161
substitutes, 31
    cross price elasticity, 32
    demand, 25
    generic equivalents, 61
    price elasticity and, 31
    production, 26–27
superintendent pharmacist, 97, 107,
        109–110
supermarkets, 34, 63, 66, 86
    acquiring a nearby pharmacy, 90
    merchandising, 277, 283
supervisor, pharmacy, 317–318
suppliers *see* wholesalers
supply
    curves, 27, 27
    determinants, 26–27
    market, 24, 26–27
surgeries, GP *see* general practice surgeries
survey, premises, 90–91, 158
surveyor, chartered, 90–91, 92, 94, 95–96
SWOT analysis, 225, 226–230, 253
    case studies, 227–230
    components, 226–227

tangibles, 198
tastes, consumer, 25
tax, 79–84
    business structure aspects, 76–77, 78
    payments, 195, 196
    planning, 196
    relief, obtaining, 84
    see also specific taxes
team briefings, 323
technicians, pharmacy, 235, 319, 340
technology
    new, 27
    PEST analysis, 232
telephone
    answering, 148, 324
    costs, 240
theft *see* burglary and theft
till position, 275
time lags, 38–39
time management, 323–325
Titanic disaster (1912), 124–125, 146–147
Toft Report, 143
toiletries, 269, 274, 276
trade, international, 51
trading groups, voluntary, 55
traditional societies/economies, 23
training and development, 266, 311,
        318–322
    hospital sector, 337–340

training and development (*continued*)
    vocational training schemes, *341*,
        341–342
    see also continuing professional
        development; education
TRANSCRIPT, 290
turnover, 99–100

Ulster Chemists Association, 360
umbrella branding, 260–261
uncertainty, buyer, 37, 39
Understanding your Community
        (Reckitt Benckiser booklet), 248
underwriting
    cycle, 156
    factors, 159–160
unemployment, 44
    definition, 50–51
    national measures, 50–51
UniChem, 58, 101–102
uniforms, staff, 12
United States (USA)
    ePharmacy regulation, 300, 304
    Verified Internet Pharmacy Practice Sites
        (VIPPS) programme, 306
urban areas, profitability of NHS
        dispensing, 68–69
utilities, reducing costs, 240
Utmost Good Faith principle, 158

vaccines, 87
valuation
    business, 98–100
    for insurance purposes, 94
    premises, 91
value added tax (VAT), 79–81, 102
    charging, 80
    history, 79
    payments/refunds, 80, 195
    rates, 80
    rationale, 79–80
    records, 80
value for money, 254–255
Verified Internet Pharmacy Practice Sites
        (VIPPS) programme, 306
Veterinary International Conference on
        Harmonisation (ICH), 292
veterinary pharmacy, foot and mouth crisis,
        229–230
Viagra, Internet sales, 296, 298
violence, risk assessment, 136
Virtual Economy Model, 45

virtual pharmacies *see* online pharmacies
vision statements, 257
visual display units (VDUs), 137
vitamins, 274, 282, 299
vocational training schemes, *341*, 341–342

wages, 239–240, 317
walk-through, 206–207
Wal-Mart, 252–253
wants, in marketing terms, 244–247
war risks, insurance, 160
warranties, by vendors, 96–97
waste
    controlled, disposal, 111–112
    in service delivery context, 219
    special, 112
Water Resources Act 1991, 111, 112
water supply, 240
web conferencing, 288
websites, 286, 288
    accreditation programmes, 305–307
    as advertising tools, 294
    domain names, 292–293
    questionable, 296, 298
    setting up new, 292–294
    useful, 308–309
    see also online pharmacies
Welsh Central Pharmaceutical Committee,
        361
Welsh Centre for Post-Graduate
        Pharmaceutical Education
        (WPPE), 365
Which? (magazine), 9
wholesalers, 56–59
    buying from, 74–76, 279–280
    diversification into retailing, 55, 58–59
    full-line and short-line, 57–58
    loan guarantee schemes, 101–102
    market share, 58, 59
    shopping around, 237
windows, 275
    posters, 269, 283
workforce, 51
working
    conditions, 111–112
    environment, 148
    under pressure, 148
World Development Indicators, 52
World Trade Organization (WTO), 51
world wide web, 286, 288
    see also websites
Worshipful Society of Apothecaries, 108